Social Work Educ
and the Grand Ch

The Grand Challenges for Social Work (GCSW) provides an agenda for society, and for the social work profession. The 13 GCSW have been codified by the American Academy of Social Work and Social Welfare and are emerging as a significant underpinning in the education of undergraduate and graduate social work students throughout the USA. This volume serves as a guide as to how this can best be achieved in alignment with the 2022 Educational Policy and Accreditation Standards (EPAS) from the Council of Social Work Education.

Divided into four parts:

- Individual and Family Well-Being;
- Stronger Social Fabric;
- A Just Society;
- The Grand Challenges in the Field.

Each chapter introduces a Grand Challenge, situates it within the curricula, and provides teaching practices in one of the targeted domains as well as learning objectives, class exercises, and discussions. By showing how to facilitate class discussion, manage difficult conversations, and address diversity, equity, and inclusion as part of teaching the topic, this book will be of interest to all faculty teaching at both undergraduate and graduate levels. It should be noted that there are additional supplementary chapters beyond the 13 GCSW that provide further context for the reader.

R. Paul Maiden (PhD), Professor Emeritus (teaching) at the University of Southern California Suzanne Dworak-Peck School of Social Work. Prior to his retirement from USC, he was Vice Dean, and subsequently, Executive Vice Dean of Academic Affairs and Professor

(2007–17). From 2017–21 he taught in the school's online MSW and DSW. His research and scholarship are focused on occupational social work, including workplace behavioral health, workplace violence, trauma management, managing organizational change, and executive leadership.

Dr. Maiden has extensive international experience and has twice been the recipient of Senior Fulbright Scholar awards to Russia and South Africa. He is also the recipient of the 2017 Lifetime Achievement Award, given by the Employee Assistance Professionals Association and the 2015 Outstanding Leadership in the Profession, given by the Employee Assistance Society of North America. Email: rmaiden@usc.edu.

Eugenia L. Weiss (PhD, PsyD) is a bilingual-bicultural licensed clinical social worker and licensed psychologist. She is Associate Professor and MSW Director at the School of Social Work at the University of Nevada, Reno. She was previously Clinical Professor at the University of Southern California (USC), Suzanne Dworak-Peck School of Social Work. Weiss served in the roles of Academic Center Director for the school's San Diego and Orange County Academic Centers, and as Senior Associate Dean of faculty affairs. She was a recipient of the Hutto Patterson Foundation Award for Distinguished Social Work Faculty.

She is the author and co-author of multiple peer-reviewed journal publications and book chapters and has co-authored/co-edited books on social work practice; military veterans; Latinx executive leadership; diversity, equity, and inclusion; and women's issues. Weiss served as a board member of the Council of Social Work Education (CSWE) – Council on the Role and Status of Women in Social Work Education, as Feminist Scholarship Track Co-Chair, and currently serves on CSWE's Council on Leadership Development. Email: eugeniaw@unr.edu.

Social Work Education and the Grand Challenges

Approaches to Curricula and Field Education

Edited by R. Paul Maiden and Eugenia L. Weiss

LONDON AND NEW YORK

Cover image: © Getty Images

First published 2023
by Routledge
4 Park Square, Milton Park, Abingdon, Oxon OX14 4RN

and by Routledge
605 Third Avenue, New York, NY 10158

Routledge is an imprint of the Taylor & Francis Group, an informa business

British Library Cataloguing-in-Publication Data
A catalogue record for this book is available from the British Library

ISBN: 978-1-032-31075-6 (hbk)
ISBN: 978-1-032-31144-9 (pbk)
ISBN: 978-1-003-30826-3 (ebk)

DOI: 10.4324/9781003308263

Typeset in Sabon
by Apex CoVantage, LLC

Contents

Figures

Tables

Contributors

Juan Carlos Araque, PhD, has over 20 years of experience working in the fields of leadership and management, program evaluation, equity and diversity, education, and positive youth development. Dr. Araque is currently Associate Professor (teaching) and teaches leadership, research, and policy graduate courses at the University of Southern California. Dr. Araque has published numerous peer-reviewed studies and has presented extensively at academic and professional conferences.

David W. Babbs, DSW, recently joined the new hybrid DALT/NCAHV Advanced Fellowship in August of 2020. Dr. Babbs holds a DSW from the Suzanne Dworak-Peck School of Social Work at the University of Southern California. During his time in the DSW program, he socially architected the Victory 21 Veterans Village project, which was approved by industry experts and is nearly implementation ready.

Robin Benton is an anti-racist activist, community organizer, and human rights educator. He presently works as Chairman of the Racial Equity Committee for his neighborhood association. He also sits on the US Human Rights Cities Alliance Steering Committee. Committed to grassroots organizing, he led organizing efforts to establish the Black Lives Matter movement in Asheville, NC. Mr. Benton developed virtual organizing strategies and tactics as Social Media Manager of Anti-Racism Media with a two million reach a month before being removed from Facebook in 2019.

Sandra Bernabei, MSW, is Past President of the National Association of Social Workers–New York City Chapter (NASW-NYCC). She is a metro area community organizer and private practitioner. Sandy is a founding member of the Antiracist Alliance, an anti-racist organizing collective of New York City area human service practitioners. ARA is building a movement to undo structural racism in our lifetime and to bring an analysis of structural racism to thousands in the NYC area.

Candida Brooks-Harrison, MSW, is a nationally recognized consultant, speaker, and clinician, and holds degrees in social work and education. She is the principal at the Village Enrichment Associates, which provides organizational consultation, professional development, reflective process and supervision, and direct services across Race, Diversity, and Intersectionality (RDI)™. Ms. Brooks-Harrison is dedicated to transformative changes within systems that increase efficacy and reduce hurt and trauma within diverse and/or oppressed communities. Part of this systems change includes developing workforce diversity and leadership, and implementing equitable policies, procedures, and practices.

Wendy Cholico, DSW, has over 20 years of experience working in the fields of education, positive youth development, health and human services, equity and diversity, and leadership. Dr. Cholico is currently a leader at the Los Angeles Unified School District and ensures students and families receive equitable access to resources and preventative services, in order to reach their full potential. Dr. Cholico has an extensive background in working with diverse populations in various capacities, and shares her expertise in county and state agencies, multi-disciplinary teams, and research projects.

Elise Marie Collins, MA, is a researcher and writer on topics including older adults' innovative housing solutions, health disparities, creating an environment of respect and belonging, and yoga as a form of exercise and a lifestyle practice to increase the health span for all ages. Her latest books are *Super Ager: You Can Look Younger, Have More Energy, A Better Memory and Live a Long and Healthy Life* and the second edition of *Chakra Tonics, Essential Elixirs for the Mind, Body, and Spirit*. She also hosts "How to Super Age," a podcast on the New Cleveland Radio network.

Tory Cox, EdD, is Assistant CalSWEC Project Coordinator for the California State University, Long Beach School of Social Work, and manages the CalSWEC child welfare grant's budget. Dr. Cox teaches school social work and field education, and oversees the school's distance education program. His research interests are in organizational change, distance learning, field education, and the specialization of school social work, for which he won the 2022

SSWAA National Book Award as lead editor for *The Art of Becoming Indispensable: What School Social Workers Need to Know in Their First Three Years*.

Elena Delavega, PhD, is Professor of Social Work and MSW Program Director at the University of Memphis, where she teaches Social Welfare Policy and Poverty. Consistent with the values and goals of the profession of social work, her research aims to enhance human well-being and opportunity. Her research consists of three broad areas, grounded in the promotion of social justice: 1) understanding poverty, 2) social and economic exclusion, and 3) promoting social and economic development. She is the author of the 2018 Memphis *Poverty Report: Memphis Since MLK*. She is also the recipient of the 2019 University of Memphis Excellence for Engaged Scholarship award.

Annalisa Enrile, PhD, is Professor (teaching) at the USC Suzanne Dworak-Peck School of Social Work, turning classrooms into brave spaces to train the next generation of changemakers. She traces her roots back to the Philippines, where she became a human rights defender and anti-trafficking warrior. She continues to work on both sides of the Pacific and across other oceans fighting to end modern-day slavery.

Michael B. Fileta, PhD, is the Coordinator of Research and Evaluation and Administrative Faculty member at the University of Nevada Reno School of Social Work. Fileta has worked as an evaluator for federally funded early childhood education programs, served as a consultant for many education-based non-profit organizations, and spent many years utilizing assessment, evaluation, and research to guide his work as a scholar/practitioner within a higher education setting.

Kari L. Fletcher, PhD, is Professor at the School of Social Work in the Morrison Family College of Health at the University of St. Thomas in St. Paul, Minnesota. Dr. Fletcher's experience working with military/veteran-connected populations across age cohorts within direct practice contexts spans more than two decades. In addition, most of her scholarship and research focuses on support systems for military/veteran-connected populations including clinical practice, higher education, and outside of military/veteran-supported settings more broadly.

Mary E. Fortson-Harwell, PhD, is a licensed clinical social worker specializing in military and medical social work, with work in institutions such as the University of California Los Angeles, the University of Colorado–Colorado Springs, and Emory University Hospital in Atlanta. Dr. Fortson-Harwell holds board certification through the American Board of Clinical Social Work. She currently practices at Deliberate.ai and serves as a Behavioral Health Officer in the Army National Guard.

Mike Gent, DSW, is Deputy City Manager for the City of Surprise, Arizona. As a member of the city's executive leadership team, he helps guide the city's commitment to strengthening the capacity, for all residents, to engage in productive relationships that enhance well-being and promote community. Through his work with individuals and neighborhoods, as well as academically, he has been drawn to the need to advance social connection as a public health priority.

Bianca Harper, DSW, is Clinical Associate Professor at the Arizona State University School of Social Work and directs the Arizona Child and Adolescent Survivor Initiative (ACASI) within the ASU Family Violence Center. Bianca has taught social work practice with children, youth, and families and advanced clinical practice courses. As a licensed clinical social worker, she has worked with children, adolescents, and families affected by relational trauma. Bianca has direct practice experience in psychotherapy, child forensic interviewing, family advocacy, crisis counseling, and school social work.

Robert Anthony Hernandez, DSW, has a strong knowledge base in working with vulnerable youth populations and the impact community trauma has on healthy youth development. He aims to educate and engage in practice-driven research to address critical areas of society that continue to hinder communities from flourishing. His areas of interest include adolescent social issues, adolescent gang intervention, strength-based/resiliency and youth empowerment models of practice. In particular, Dr. Hernandez's work examines risk and protective factors within communities that are associated with vulnerable youth populations residing in trauma-exposed communities. He has focused on advancing marginalized populations through a range of practice approaches addressing violence-related trauma through violence reduction, prevention, and intervention strategies.

Melissa Hirschi, PhD, is Assistant Professor at the School of Social Work at the University of Memphis. Her research focuses on the intersection of first responders and individuals living with mental illness, including their role as frontline mental health workers. She is also interested in better understanding power, including the role of power in racism, oppression, and stigma. In addition, she does work with individuals living with HIV and children with special health-care needs, focusing on improving access, health outcomes, and social justice for these individuals.

Suh Chen Hsiao, DPPD, is Clinical Associate Professor (field) and Associate Director for Field Education at USC's Suzanne Dworak-Peck School of Social Work. Currently, she is Principal Investigator for the HRSA Scholarship for Disadvantaged Students: Primary Care Project focusing on enhancing the education of master of social work students from disadvantaged backgrounds who are committed to seek employment in medically underserved communities. Her research interests are with integrated health/behavioral health topics related to cancer, substance abuse, immigrant health, trauma and interdisciplinary and interprofessional education.

Harry Hunter, PhD, is Associate Professor (teaching) at the University of Southern California's Suzanne Dworak-Peck School of Social Work. He holds a doctoral degree in industrial/organizational psychology, a master's degree in social work, and a master's degree in business administration. As a clinical associate professor, Dr. Hunter develops course curricula and teaches in the school's MSW and DSW programs. Dr. Hunter's clinical expertise, leadership, and work experiences are reflected in the fields of addiction rehabilitation, mental health treatment, employee assistance programming, and community development.

Jane James, JD, is a social worker and lawyer who has also worked in the Public Health arena, where her work and innovative thinking led to the development of community health programs that provided health education about communicable diseases and prevention in schools, communities, and health-care institutions in St. Lucia, BWI. She has been Assistant Professor (teaching) at the University of Southern California, Suzanne Dworak-Peck School of Social Work since 2011. While at USC, she has developed curricula and taught graduate classes at the MSW and doctoral levels. Dr. James's research interests are varied, but currently focused on advocacy towards promoting inclusive social work curricula.

Joyce James, PhD (Hon.), has worked in the social work profession for over 40 years. For the past 25 years she has been leading and supporting multiple systems and institutions across the county in efforts to create an anti-racism institutional culture that reduces and ultimately eliminates racial inequities and improves outcomes for all populations. Dr. James previously led Texas Child Protective Services and the State Office of Minority Health. She is President and CEO of Joyce James Consulting.

Bryan Jebo, MNLM, has over 25 years of experience working with youth development programs in Los Angeles County. He earned his master's degree in Nonprofit Leadership and Management from Arizona State University. Mr. Jebo has worked with the Boys and Girls Clubs of the Los Angeles Harbor for the past 22 years and has been the Chief Operating Officer for the last four of those years where he has helped provide youth from underserved communities with programs such as academic support including aligning high school youth with pathways to colleges and careers, athletics, fine arts, music, digital media, dance, character development, and leadership opportunities. Mr. Jebo oversees 20 club site locations, approximately 200 staff, and over 6,000 registered members.

Deepa Karmakar, MSW, is a University of Southern California, Suzanne Dworak-Peck School of Social Work graduate. She is current Program Coordinator at Visionary Youth, LA that focuses on healthy youth development from a trauma-informed approach. Her work experiences have focused on skill development, rehabilitation, addressing treatment needs, and successful reintegration of justice-involved youth into the community.

Steven Kim, MSW, is Co-Founder and Executive Director of Project Kinship where he serves individuals impacted by gangs and incarceration, with the aim to successfully reintegrate them back into our communities. His commitment to healing cycles of incarceration, gang membership, and community violence stems from over 20 years of working with traumatized and abandoned youth throughout Orange County. He is an adjunct faculty member at the University of Southern California, Suzanne Dworak-Peck School of Social Work, lecturing on best practices that focus on adolescent gang prevention and intervention strategies.

Jennifer Lewis, PhD, is Fulbright Scholar, Associate Professor (teaching), and experienced social worker with a passion toward interdisciplinary care and education. She develops and provides leadership to courses in both the MSW and DSW programs in Los Angeles and the Virtual Academic Center at the University of Southern California. As a USC Center for Excellence in Teaching Fellow, her scholarly interests include working with individuals with complex co-occurring disorders such as trauma and addiction. She serves in leadership roles the University as Curriculum Co-Director in the Institute for Addiction Sciences at USC. Prior to serving in academia, Lewis worked in integrated health and mental health settings at the University of California San Diego Health.

Andreja Lukic, PhD (ABD), is currently Assistant Professor of social work at Texas A&M University–Central Texas and adjunct faculty at the Tulane University School of Social Work and Fordham University School of Social Work. He has a master of social work from the University of South Carolina and is currently a social welfare doctoral candidate at Florida International University. Mr. Lukic's research focuses primarily on incarcerated veterans and factors contributing to their incarceration, such as PTSD, substance use disorders, and domestic violence. Andreja has a strong background and training in understanding the various contextual factors and dynamics surrounding incarceration, recidivism rates, veterans, PTSD and older adults, and his research aims to incorporate these various aspects into the design of interventions and programs.

Ron Manderscheid, PhD, serves as Adjunct Professor at the Suzanne Dworak-Peck School of Social Work, University of Southern California, and the Bloomberg School of Public Health, Johns Hopkins University. Until recently, he was President/CEO of the National Association of County Behavioral Health and Developmental Disability Directors and National Association for Rural Mental Health. Concurrently, he serves on the boards of the American Academy of Social Work and Social Welfare, the National Grand Challenge for Social Work Initiative, the Danya Institute, and the NASMHPD Research Institute.

Lauren Marlotte, PsyD, is the Director of Learning and Development for the Division of Population Behavioral Health, the Nathanson Family Resilience Center, and the Prevention Center of Excellence within the UCLA Jane and Terry Semel Institute for Neuroscience and Human Behavior. She is also an attending supervisor at UCLA's Stress, Trauma, and Resilience Clinic and the UCLA-VA Veteran Family Wellbeing Center. Dr. Marlotte currently oversees the content of the Wellbeing for LA Learning Center, a Learning Management System to support trauma- and resilience-informed practices throughout Los Angeles County's workforce.

Onaje Muid, DSW, is Co-Chair of the Health Commission, National Coalition of Blacks for Reparations in America. He is also an alternate for the United Nations Non-Governmental Organization Representative, International Human Rights Association of American Minorities (IHRAAM). Dr. Muid's research interests focus on historical trauma and public health, reparations, social work, and decolonizing social innovation.

L. Debbie Murad, MSW, is Lecturer with USC Suzanne Dworak-Peck School of Social Work, whose courses include domestic abuse and clinical practice courses. Ms. Murad is in private practice, and a clinical consultant for social service agencies in the Los Angeles area. Her expertise includes the intersectionality of intimate partner violence, trauma, and co-occurring substance abuse and mental health issues. Ms. Murad has a 20+ year history in the domestic violence movement. Her professional experience includes managing domestic abuse programs, addiction treatment, and developing and implementing unique services.

Murali Nair, PhD, is Adjunct Professor of Social Enterprise Administration, School of Social Work, Columbia University. In his last positions, he was Clinical Professor of Social Change and Innovation at the University of Southern California, Suzanne Dworak-Peck School of Social Work, and Professor Director at Cleveland State University School of Social Work. His cross-national field studies among the Healthy Centenarians are documented in multiple articles and mini documentaries at www.muralinair.com.

Cathy Newman Thomas, PhD, is Associate Professor of Special Education in the Department of Curriculum and Instruction at Texas State University. Her work focuses on technology in teacher education and for professional development, including study of video and mixed/virtual reality to improve teacher knowledge and skills.

Michael G. Rank, PhD, is Associate Professor (teaching) at the University of Southern California, Suzanne Dworak Peck School of Social Work, Virtual Academic Center. He is a decorated Vietnam veteran, having served honorably as an infantryman in the U.S. Army (196th Infantry; Americal Division). His research interests include the Grand Challenges of social work, virtual education, doctoral education, academic leadership and reaccreditation, military social work, veterans' issues, post-traumatic stress disorder, traumatic stress, bioterrorism, and compassion fatigue. His publications include articles on academic leadership and accreditation, doctoral education, virtual education, post-traumatic stress disorder, compassion fatigue, bioterrorism, traumatic stress, critical incident stress debriefing, fatherhood, and resistance to change.

Kimberly Richards, EdD, Core Trainer/Interim Executive Director for the People's Institute for Survival and Beyond. As a graduate of Clark College in education and theater, Kimberley received her master's degree in education from Westminster College, and completed her doctorate in education in 1995 from the University of Pittsburgh as a Lilly Endowment Fellow. She has studied theater arts and education in London, England, and fabric arts in Gambia, West Africa. Dr. Richards is particularly interested in what the concept of race has done to dehumanize all people of every race and what we can do to undo that dehumanization. This includes working in reflective practice, assessment, documentation, and evaluation from a humanistic and anti-racist approach.

Amelia Roeschlein, DSW, is a consultant at National Council for Mental Wellbeing. She is also Clinical Fellow and Clinical Supervisor, American Association for Marriage, and Family Therapists, and is a member of the British Council of Psychoanalysis. Her research interests focus on innovation and creating large-scale social change through transdisciplinary training of health practitioners, trauma-informed, resiliency-oriented, and equity-focused organizational change practices.

Sara L. Schwartz, PhD, is Associate Professor (teaching) at the University of Southern California, Suzanne Dworak-Peck School of Social Work, educating students in the MSW and DSW programs. Dr. Schwartz's current research focuses on community building in virtual social work education, documenting the stories of communities disproportionally impacted by HIV/AIDS and examining the experiences of individuals 50 years and older aging with hemophilia. In addition to her work in academia, she applies her social science research skills to her roles on the Board of the National AIDS Memorial and as Vice President of Research and Evaluation for Kramer, Blum and Associates in San Francisco. In this capacity, Dr. Schwartz works with philanthropic organizations to guide grant making and evaluate outcomes.

Katherine Chism Selber, PhD, is Professor in the School of Social Work at Texas State University. She was appointed the Texas State University System Research Fellow from 2017–18. Dr. Selber was awarded the statewide Texas Veterans Commission Patriot

Award in 2015 and numerous campus awards for her work with veterans. She co-founded the Texas State Veteran Advisory Council in 2008 that still develops and evaluates the campus award-winning model to serve student veterans.

Melissa Indera Singh, EdD, is Associate Professor (teaching) at the University of Southern California Suzanne, Dworak-Peck School of Social Work, where she teaches in the MSW and DSW programs. She joined USC in 2013 as an adjunct faculty member and in 2014 became a Clinical Assistant Professor in the Department of Social Change and Innovation. In 2016, a program that she co-led won the Award for Innovative Teaching in Social Work Education from SAGE/CSWE for Educating Social Work Students for Macro Practice. In 2017, Dr. Singh was awarded the Hutto Patterson Distinguished Faculty Award for excellence in teaching; service to the university, the school, and the community; and accessibility to students. Currently, she is Co-Investigator on a $3.25M HRSA grant to assist educationally and economically disadvantaged and historically underrepresented students and a $2M HRSA Behavioral Health Workforce Education and Training grant.

Kelly Smith, DSW, is Founder and Director of the Institute for Social Work and Ecological Justice. Additionally, she is Lecturer at Columbia's School of Social Work and Adjunct Professor at Adelphi University. Dr. Smith earned her doctorate in social work from the University of Southern California.

Kenneth Scott Smith, PhD, is Associate Professor and Director of the XReality lab at Texas State University School of Social Work. He manages an interdisciplinary team of computer scientists, psychologists, engineers, and graphic designers and has spent the last seven years perfecting virtual reality design methodology used to develop and evaluate the impact of technology on human performance. Dr. Smith and his team have developed multimedia trainings using 360 video, smartphone applications for WIC mothers, and virtual environments to treat addiction and social anxiety in veterans. Moreover, his team has been recognized as one of the first labs to develop virtual and augmented reality training for AMBUS first responders (20 bed ambulances used by first responders in disaster situations) to address situational awareness while responding to hurricanes, mass casualty incidents, and active shooter scenarios.

Renée Smith-Maddox, PhD, is Professor (teaching) at the University of Southern California, Suzanne Dworak-Peck School of Social

Work. She is an anti-trafficking advocate, equity strategist, and champion for social and gender justice. As a social work educator, she trains social impact designers, develops curriculum for graduate level courses, and uses design thinking as a process for complex problem-solving. Dr. Smith-Maddox has built a formidable career helping organizations and those that are driven to advancing equity, diversity, and inclusion.

Darla Spence Coffey, PhD, assumed the duties of CSWE President on July 2, 2012. Prior to her appointment as president, she served as Professor of Social Work, Associate Provost, and Dean of Graduate Studies at West Chester University. Coffey has an extensive background in social work practice in the areas of mental health, substance abuse, and domestic violence, and is a nationally recognized author and speaker on these topics. After years of working with and researching the effects of domestic violence on children, Coffey developed a curriculum, *Parenting After Violence*, and trained cohorts of social workers in the child welfare system in Philadelphia, PA in its implementation.

Ruth Supranovich, EdD, is Associate Professor (field), and Director of Field Education at USC's Suzanne Dworak-Peck School of Social Work. In this role she leads a large team of faculty and staff who manage field practicum experiences for students completing the Master of Social Work (MSW) program attending both the on-campus and online MSW programs. Annually, over 1,000 MSW students attending the school complete a minimum of 1,000 hours of internship at health and social service organizations in Los Angeles and across the US under the supervision of MSW graduate social workers working in the community. Prior to joining academia, Dr. Supranovich was a case manager, clinician, supervisor, manager, and executive leader both in non-profit and government agencies. Her primary practice focus has been around children, youth, and families.

Todd Vanidestine, PhD, is Assistant Professor at West Chester University, Department of Graduate Social Work. His research interests include racial and ethnic health inequities, critical race theory, community organizations and organizing, critical discourse analysis, and emphasizing socially just education and practice. He integrates his research and practice experiences by facilitating a community-learning environment within the classroom. Within these spaces, students are supported and encouraged to combine their critical insights from lived experiences with course content to build collective power and strategically challenge social injustices.

Amy Ward, DSW, is Social Work Program Director and Assistant Professor at East Central University in Ada, Oklahoma. She earned her bachelor of social work from East Central University, her master of social work from the University of Oklahoma, and her doctor of social work from the University of Southern California. She is a licensed clinical social worker and holds a trauma certification and has specialized in this area while working with traumatized children and families in the child welfare system. Before entering academia, Dr. Ward worked as a frontline social worker in a tribal community in child protective services, specializing in the Indian Child Welfare Act, and serving families as an advocate in tribal and state courts.

Colonel (U.S. Army RET) Jeffrey S. Yarvis, PhD, is Senior Professor of Practice for the Tulane University School of Social Work. He is a 35-year veteran leader in executive medicine, clinician, lifelong educator, and military social work scholar in the field of psychological trauma. A transformational leader, Dr. Yarvis has built, restored, and grown large medical organizations and optimized their performance using high reliability principles. His dissertation, titled "Subthreshold PTSD in Canadian Peacekeepers with Different Levels of Traumatic Stress," served as springboard into hundreds of international and national peer-reviewed conference presentations and over one hundred publications on the deleterious effects of posttraumatic stress disorder (PTSD) and the reintegration of America's returning warriors to their families and to campus.

Foreword

In 2015, along with several others, I heeded the call of the committee comprised of members of the American Academy for Social Work and Social Welfare to propose a Grand Challenge to solve some of the world's most vexing and wicked social problems facing the world at the time. In my case, the Grand Challenge I proposed was one of creating social responses to changes in the natural environment that were themselves the consequences of social activities. Our task was not merely to identify the problem, however; it was to offer a solution to the problem with the perhaps overly ambitious goal of doing so in ten years. Since that time, each of the 13 Grand Challenges has enjoyed varying degrees of success. Each Grand Challenge has experienced changes in goals as societies themselves have changed. Many of the original leads and co-leads of these Grand Challenges have passed the torch to a new generation of social work leaders, each with new perspectives and new ideas of how to solve these problems.

Key to each of these Grand Challenges was the creation of a pipeline of future generations of social workers with the same passion and commitment to solving these wicked problems by utilizing the tools of social work science and collaborating with others representing different professions, disciplines, and occupations. In this respect, while the problems addressed by each Grand Challenge may differ, the means to solving them were very similar. However, pursuit of these Grand Challenges was expected to require a transformation of social work education. As part of this transformation, the social work science supporting the Grand Challenges was envisioned as being transdisciplinary, translational, and team based.

The themes of transdisciplinary, translational, and team-based social work education pervade this outstanding collection of chapters prepared by a group of social work scholars, practitioners, and policymakers, each of whom stands at the forefront of a new approach to social work education. This book represents the first volume to date that has placed the educational enterprise of social work front and center of each of the Grand Challenges.

Much of the content embedded in each of the Grand Challenges is hardly new to the field of social work. Even my own Grand Challenge to Create Social Responses to a Changing Environment is founded on principles of environmental and social justice that have existed since the days of Jane Addams and Hull House, long before climate change became one of the most significant social problems facing the planet. However, as illustrated throughout this volume, what is novel about the Grand Challenges from the perspective of social work education is the approach taken to solve these problems. For instance, rather than ensure that students have some familiarity of statistical methods they may never employ in day-to-day practice, several of the chapters provide illustrations of how these and other methods may be applied to solve specific problems introduced in the form of case studies. Whether the focus is homelessness, social isolation, extreme poverty, or interpersonal violence, these case studies provide opportunities to bring to life not just the problem in human terms, but a systematic approach to solving the problem through the exercise of leadership by social workers on the one hand and the willingness to adopt ideas and solutions from leaders in other fields on the other hand. In this instance, the Grand Challenges constitute a model of as well as a model for transdisciplinary action that moves beyond working in an interdisciplinary fashion to a mutual exchange of knowledge, attitudes, and behaviors. The synergy behind such an exchange in the classroom creates a response to these wicked social problems that is greater than the sum of the whole individual responses.

Just as social work education must be transformed to advance the principles and practice of transdisciplinarity, it must also advance the translational nature of social work. Moving from research to practice involves efforts to design and develop programs, practices, and policies that are grounded in scientific evidence, personal experience, and client preference. It requires developing solutions that are evidence-based but are used routinely and in a manner that adheres to the principles underlying their design and development. This requires teaching students to understand the process of moving from demonstrations of efficacy to real-world effectiveness to practical implementation and sustainability of new programs, practices, and policies. While the use of case studies borrows on teaching practices that have long been utilized in social work education, the Grand Challenges provide incentives and opportunities for new techniques such as the use of simulation labs to train undergraduates described in Chapter 15 of this volume. It also provides incentives and opportunities for social work students to apply the information acquired in the classroom to their practice in field placements as described in Chapter 16.

The third element of the transformation of social work education is providing instruction in how to operate in solving problems as a team. Perhaps the best illustration of the challenges involved in teamwork is found in the Close the Health Gap Grand Challenge described in Chapter 3. Teamwork involves a division of labor and a degree of trust in the willingness and capacity of other team members to complete their assigned tasks, but also a willingness to assume additional burdens as required in the event one or more team members are unable to perform their tasks. Working together as a team requires a sensitivity to the strengths and weaknesses of each of its members. As with the translation of research to practice, acquiring this sensitivity occurs in both the classroom and in the field.

The Grand Challenge to Eliminate Racism (Chapter 10) offers another illustration of how the Grand Challenges could transform social work education. As the authors note, although the intention of the Organizing Committee was to ensure that a focus on racism be part of each Grand Challenge, that strategy was made obsolete by recent events demanding a more explicit focus that was not diluted by virtue of not being a Grand Challenge of its own. In one respect, the focus on eliminating racism extends far beyond social work education; hence, it provides an opportunity to contribute to a much broader dialogue and approach to solving this particular "wicked problem." However, the specific examples of antiracism teaching practices included in Chapter 10 have relevance to every Grand Challenge, demonstrating how the activities in solving one wicked social problem are linked to similar efforts to solve all social problems.

The importance of inserting an antiracism perspective in each Grand Challenge also calls into question the extent to which the other Grand Challenges relate to one another. Although tacitly acknowledged in the Second Edition of *Grand Challenges for Social Work and Society*, the extent to which the Grand Challenges are independent or interdependent is not entirely clear. An illustration of this conundrum is the last chapter of the book. Food insecurity is an issue that could fall under the Grand Challenge of building financial capability for all, achieving equal opportunity and justice, and reducing extreme economic inequality. The COVID pandemic could be addressed by creating social responses to a changing environment, eradicating social isolation, or closing the health gap. No one Grand Challenge can solve the major social problems facing the world today. Social work education should promote the collaboration of researchers, practitioners, and policymakers in solving interrelated problems.

If we view social work education the same way we view social work science as being transdisciplinary, translational, and team-based, what unifies all three of these elements is their reliance on social interaction and collaboration. Whether this occurs in the classroom or in the field, students must be given instruction through didactic exercises and practical experience in using their own social skills to solve the wicked problems caused by the disrupted or dysfunctional social relations of others. The key to integrating the Social Work Grand Challenges will require that attention be paid to the social interactions between students and teachers, between social work practitioners and their clients, and between social work students and practitioners and other students and professionals dedicated to a common cause. This volume represents an important step in paying attention to such interactions.

Larry Palinkas
Lawrence A. Palinkas, PhD
Albert G. and Frances Lomas Feldman Professor
of Social Policy and Health
Fellow, American Academy of Social Welfare
and Social Work
Co-Lead, Social Work Grand Challenge to Create
Social Responses to a Changing Environment
Suzanne Dworak-Peck School of Social Work
University of Southern California

Preface

So, What Is It That Professional Social Workers Actually Do? The 13 Grand Challenges!

I (Paul) began my career in social services well before I became a professional social worker. I started when I became a volunteer when I was a junior in high school, in the 'Big Buddies' program at the MH/MR Center for Greater West Texas in San Angelo, Texas. The 'Big Buddies' program was modeled after Big Brothers/Big Sisters but focused on youth with intellectual and developmental disabilities and behavioral disorders. A few years later, while a freshman in college, I became the director of the program. While working at this agency, I had the good fortune of having an MSW supervisor, who nudged me towards graduate school upon completion of my bachelor's degree. I was admitted to the University of Tennessee at Knoxville and started my journey to become a professional social worker. While taking my first-year practice courses I had an 'awakening' experience.

Before I began work on my MSSW, I had seven years of volunteer and employment experience and an undergraduate degree in psychology. I had no doubt in my mind that I was 'doing good.' However, my professional 'awakening' occurred in the foundation year of my social work practice courses, when I realized that while I was intent on 'doing good,' I had no professional grounding on which to base my work. I began to learn and understand social work theories and concepts and applications in practice. I realized then that almost all the work I had been doing prior to graduate school had been absent theories and concepts and I had been practicing without these important underpinnings. Once I understood this, I knew that I was well on my way to becoming a professional social worker.

After I received my MSSW, I often became frustrated by what I perceived as an 'image problem' for social workers and a lack of understanding of what social workers do in their work. I can't even begin to count how many times I have heard "Oh, you're a social worker!" Followed by "So what do you do?" These explanations and questions came from community members, friends, and family alike.

I have enjoyed a long and satisfying career as a professional social worker having had the opportunity to complete both a master's and a doctoral degree in social work. And my professional social work career has included practice and consulting in numerous settings including alcoholism and substance abuse treatment; home adoptions studies; employee assistance and work/family life; managed behavioral health care; organizational change and strategic planning; executive leadership; social administration; international social work in Southern Africa, China, and Russia; and three academic appointments at the University of Illinois, Jane Addams College of Social Work, the University of Central Florida, School of Social Work, and most recently the University of Southern California, Suzanne Dvorak-Peck School of Social Work, proudly a long and highly satisfying professional social work career.

Before I ended my second term as Executive Vice Dean at the USC Suzanne Dworak-Peck School of Social Work, I led the development and launching of the school's online Doctor of Social Work (DSW) program.

Our faculty work group had numerous meetings around the curriculum focus. At the time there were a few other schools of social work that had either launched a new DSW or would do so in the next few years. Our faculty work group's challenge was to develop a doctoral degree that focused on the 'scholar/practitioner' and was substantially different from the other DSWs, and of course, would be an attractive option. And then the Grand Challenges for Social Work Initiative (GCSWI) was introduced to our profession in 2016 by the American Academy of Social Work and Social Welfare (AASWSW). The Grand Challenges became the primary focus of our DSW. The Grand Challenges were identified by social work educators, policymakers, practitioners, and researchers (across disciplines) to address society's toughest to solve social problems utilizing scientific approaches. I was so taken by them, and the courses that we developed, that I decided to move into a full-time teaching position in the DSW. The first DSW course I taught was Strategic Innovations for the Grand Challenges. And students are expected to develop an innovative approach to solving one of the 13 Grand Challenges in their DSW capstone project.

I was so excited by what our DSW students could accomplish, but I also concluded the Grand Challenges content should be infused across all levels of social work education. Thus, the seed of an idea for this book has now been bought to fruition.

Moving fast forward, my colleague and co-editor (Eugenia), has joined me in this editing journey and we have organized the book around the 13 Grand Challenges (which were originally the 12 Grand Challenges). AASWSW has more recently (Barth et al., 2022), incorporated the Grand Challenge to Eliminate Racism which is addressed in this book. Our conceptualization for this book would be as a teaching and curricular guide for faculty to use in the application of the Grand Challenges in social work curricula at both undergraduate and graduate levels. Additionally, this volume is intended to serve as a handbook of how this can be best achieved in alignment with the newest Educational Policy and Accreditation Standards (EPAS) from the Council of Social Work Education (CSWE, 2022).

Each chapter is generally structured to introduce a Grand Challenge and situate it within the foundation year curricular domains, such as Human Behavior and the Social Environment (HBSE), Social Work Policy and/or Practice courses. Teaching practices are presented in at least one of the curricular domains along with student learning objectives. We have asked our contributing authors to set the stage in terms of how to prepare students for learning and classroom engagement with the GCSW topic (mostly for in-person teaching) and to describe the highlights of some example lecture material to be provided to the students. The authors also describe how an instructor can best facilitate class discussions around the Grand Challenge and/or provide classroom exercises. Addressing diversity, equity, and inclusion are also part of the teaching topics for each chapter as well as how to manage difficult classroom conversations. Lastly, the chapters offer tips on evaluating student learning and provide any supplementary teaching materials or areas for future teaching/curricular considerations.

The Appendices contain the identified EPAS for each of the Grand Challenge chapters so that instructors can embed these into their syllabi as applicable. The reader will also find four chapters that are not directly related to the Grand Challenges but offer insights into various areas for teaching and curricular guidance. For example, Chapter 1 provides the research on the use of the Grand Challenges in social work education, and we would argue, the rationale for this book. The use of simulation labs for undergraduate education (Chapter 15) provides an innovative way to teach Grand Challenges in the field. The general application of Grand Challenges in field education (Chapter 16) offers the reader a field perspective as our signature pedagogy. Lastly, Chapter 17, on evaluation capacity building for organizations during the closures associated with COVID-19, provides concepts associated with program accountability that can be applied across the Grand Challenges.

We hope that you enjoy this book and glean important insights into how you can successfully incorporate the Grand Challenges into your classroom or in field education. We also look forward to any feedback that you can provide us on how the integration of Grand Challenges into your teaching or curricula has worked well and what challenges you might have encountered if any.

R. Paul Maiden

References

Barth, R. P., Messing, J. T., Shanks, T. R., & Williams, J. H. (Eds.). (2022). *Grand challenges for social work and society: Milestones achieved and opportunities ahead* (2nd ed.). Oxford University Press.

Council on Social Work Education (CSWE). (2022). *Educational policy and accreditation standards*. Author. www.cswe.org/accreditation/standards/2022-epas/

Fong, R., Lubben, J., & Barth, R. P. (2018). *Grand challenges for social work and society*. Oxford University Press.

Acknowledgments

We would like to thank Claire Jarvis, Senior Editor at Routledge (Taylor & Francis Group) for believing in our project from the beginning of the proposal phase. Sully Evans, Editorial Assistant at Taylor & Francis, for his guidance throughout the editing process. The external book proposal reviewers took the time to provide us with substantive feedback on ways to improve the project. A special thank you to Dr. Larry Palinkas, who wrote our foreword and was one of the original lead authors of *Create Social Responses to a Changing Environment* (GC #7). And to our contributing authors who poured their hard work, knowledge, and expertise into each of the chapters. The creation of the chapters was not easy during the height of the COVID-19 pandemic, and we are grateful for everyone coming together to help us finish this project.

A special thank you to our spouses and family members who supported us throughout the development of this book.

R. Paul Maiden and Eugenia L. Weiss

1 Integration of the 12 Grand Challenges Into Social Work Curricula

Michael G. Rank, Ron Manderscheid and Darla Spence Coffey

Introduction

Led by the American Academy of Social Work and Social Welfare (AASWSW), the Grand Challenges for Social Work and Society (hereafter GCSW) is an innovative initiative to leverage social progress powered by science. It is a call to action for important collaborations to tackle our nation's toughest social problems. Although the Grand Challenges of Social Work had to various extents been taught in schools of social work, a new fresh approach to solving these problems and issues is needed. The purpose of this study was to investigate the integration of the 12 GCSW into social work curricula at all levels to inform subsequent actions of the GCEC. The 12 GCSW represent a dynamic social agenda, focused on improving individual, family, and community health, well-being, and equity to strengthen the social fabric and help create a more just society (see http://aaswsw.org/grand-challenges-initiative/).

(Editor note: research described in this chapter was conducted before AASWSW adopted the 13th Grand Challenge of *Eliminate Racism*.)

Chapter Overview

This chapter includes a brief historical perspective about the development of the 12 GCSW, a brief overview of the 12 GCSW, a deeper description of each GCSW, and an Appendix at the conclusion of the chapter with charts displaying the results of the survey. The focus of the chapter, a GCSW survey of social work schools and departments, is explained, followed by presentation of the survey findings.

DOI: 10.4324/9781003308263-1

Historical Context

The GCSW initiative emerged as an innovative agenda of AASWSW. The initiative (Lubben et al., 2018a, p. 1) was created to:

- Promote scientific innovation in social work;
- Engage the social work profession in strengthening the ties among social work organizations;
- Foster transdisciplinary research;
- Expand the student pipeline into the social work profession; and
- Create greater acknowledgment of social work science within the discipline and by other, related disciplines.

Dean Eddie Uehara at the University of Washington School of Social Work is credited with the initial GCSW idea. She has built upon the work of John Brekke (2012) who identified a science of social work (Lubben et al., 2018a). The GCSW was informed by the National Academy of Engineering 14 Grand Challenges of Engineering (www.engineeringchallenges.org). AASWSW embraced these ideas and examined other Grand Challenges initiatives of the William and Melinda Gates Foundation, the National Institute of Mental Health (NIMH), and Grand Challenges Canada (Lubben et al., 2018a). The AASWSW Grand Challenge Executive Committee introduced the GCSW initiative in 2013. After three years of planning and research, the GCSW initiative was finalized 2016. In a bold move, the USC Suzanne Dworak-Peck School of Social Work created an executive DSW informed specifically by the 12 GCSW in 2016.

The Learning and Education Subcommittee of the Grand Challenges Executive Committee

A Learning and Education Subcommittee of the Grand Challenges Executive Committee (GCEC) originally was formed to promote the GCSW as a foundational activity in social work training programs at the bachelor, master, and doctorate levels. Members of the Subcommittee were selected from the GCEC and the senior leadership of the social work field.

In the summer of 2018 the Subcommittee designed and conducted a brief survey of deans and directors of CSWE training programs. The purpose was to investigate the integration of the 12 GCSW into social work curricula at all levels by providing data to inform subsequent actions of the Subcommittee such as webinars, technical assistance efforts, and publications.

Three GCSW Clusters

The 12 GSCW are divided into three separate and distinct clusters although there is obvious interaction and overlap between them all. The three clusters are health, well-being, and equity. The Health Cluster includes: Ensure healthy development for all youth; Advance long and productive lives; Close the health gap; and Stop family violence. The Well-Being Cluster includes: End homelessness; Eradicate social isolation; Harness technology for the social good; and Create social responses to a changing environment. The Equity Cluster includes: Promote smart decarceration; Build financial capability for all; Achieve equal opportunity and justice; and Reduce extreme economic inequality.

Literature Review

Descriptions of the 12 GCSW

Ensure Healthy Development for All Youth (by Unleashing the Power of Prevention)

Behavioral health issues are preventable in youth with early intervention (Hawkins et al., 2015). Behavioral health problems surpass communicable diseases as the country's most pressing concerns for the health and well-being of youth (Jenson & Hawkins, 2018, p. 32).

This Grand Challenge proposes seven action steps (Jenson & Hawkins, 2018): 1) Develop and increase public awareness; 2) Ensure 10% of public funds earmarked for youth are spent on prevention; 3) Implement assessment and tools to assist communities in prevention efforts; 4) Develop criteria for preventive interventions that are cost beneficial; 5) Cultivate states' infrastructures to support preventive interventions; 6) Supervise and proliferate access to effective preventive interventions; 7) Educate and train a workforce to specifically create preventive interventions.

The Coalition for the Promotion of Behavioral Health (CPBH), founded in 2014, has taken on the task of ensuring the progress and implementation of the seven action steps. An added imperative is the need for innovative transorganizational collaborations and approaches from all sectors of society, especially the for the benefit sector.

Close the Health Gap

According to the literature, individualized and behavioral interventions are not sufficient to eradicate health inequities. Rather, health professions collaborate to deliver transdisciplinary approaches in the study of social determinates and health inequities. There are ten initial priority areas for Closing the health gap clustered into three domains (Spence et al., 2018): Population Health Through Community and Setting-Based Approaches; Strengthening Health Care Systems: Better Health Across America; and Reducing and Preventing Alcohol Misuse and Its Consequences. "Specifically, social work has an unyielding focus on lifting the health of a nation by lifting the health of the most disenfranchised and marginalized populations" (Spence et al., 2018, p. 36).

The first four areas address a community approach: 1) Focus on settings to improve the conditions of daily life; 2) Advance community empowerment for sustainable health; 3) Generate research on social determinants of health inequities; and, 4) Stimulate multisectoral advocacy to promote health equity policies.

The second domain involves three areas of focus: 5) Cultivate innovation in primary care; 6) Promote full access to health care; and 7) Foster development of an interprofessional health workforce. The third domain offers the final three areas: 8) Develop research and scholarship in alcohol misuse and its consequences; 9) Develop interdisciplinary, multisectoral, and sustainable collaborations; and 10) Develop the workforce in social work to address alcohol misuse.

Health determinants also are referred to as the social determinates of health (Spence et al., 2018). These include the economic and social conditions defined by one's community and living environment. Racial and ethnic minorities endure an unbalance and significant burden from oppressive conditions. Health equity is the goal; to assure an absence of systemic inequities in health care and outcomes.

Stop Family Violence (Now Reworded to Build Healthy Relationships)

(Focus on Child Maltreatment [CM] and Intimate Partner Violence [IPV].) Stopping family violence is accomplished effectively through interventions that respond to both CM and IPV in coordinated ways that build upon their common denominators (Barth & Macy, 2018). The common risk factors of low income, unemployment, poverty as well as many other related interconnections need to be conscientiously addressed with strategic innovative interventions; some examples include cross-sector involvement, coordination of vital records, research-driven interventions, targeting new parents, therapy/family work, early screening, assessment, brief interventions, and using technology.

There are many existing federal, state, local, and foundation initiatives to reduce family violence including CM and IPV. Partnering with the Centers for Disease Control (CDC) in a "connect-the-dots" approach will influence an integrated collaboration with the goal of avoiding duplication of services but more importantly to gain knowledge from successful efforts (Barth & Macy, 2018).

Advance Long and Productive Lives

The world's population is changing. Lower birth rates and increasing life expectancies are creating older populations. *Productive aging* (Butler, 1983) must become our societal goal. Older adults are becoming productive past traditional retirement age as health education and economic security have improved (Morrow-Howell et al., 2018). The challenge is to optimize productive engagement for industrious older adults through innovative and gainful employment, caregiving, and volunteering opportunities. Also, of critical importance is to "shift public discourse" from a problem narrative to a productive narrative and to see older adults as assets and not deficiencies and to end discrimination and bias.

Morrow-Howell et al. suggest: 1) Improving work environments and employment policies so older adults can work longer; 2) Restructuring educational curricula to include knowledge and skills across the life span; 3) Creating more diverse opportunities to engage the older adult talent pool; 4) Improving and supporting caregiving to facilitate positive outcomes and reduce negative ones (like stress and compromised health).

Potential outcomes for the productive engagement of older adults are organized into four domains (Morrow-Howell et al., 2018): individual, family, organization, community, and society. Individual outcomes include enhanced physical and mental health; self-efficacy, purpose in life and economic well-being. Family outcomes include engaged grandparents and caregivers, the transfer of incomes and assets from older to younger generations, and heathier, happier, and productive older relatives. For organizations and communities, the potential outcomes are experienced, loyal, and dependable workers and volunteers, generational diversity, and mentors for younger workers. For society the outcomes are less reliance on public pensions and savings, more intergenerational exchange, and less demand for long-term care and possible postponement of disability.

Eradicate Social Isolation

"Social isolation is a potent killer" (Lubben et al., 2018b). The World Health Organization declared social isolation as a major health risk factor in 1979. Social isolation is especially deadly for youth as school shootings, youth violence, psychological distress, and loneliness are especially characteristic of the socially isolated. Social isolation among older adults leads to poor social and health outcomes as well as increased likelihood of elder mistreatment. The challenge of eradicating social isolation will require innovative interdisciplinary and cross-sector collaboration.

End Homelessness

"Whether affecting young or old homelessness is a 'grand challenge' for which solutions are available" (Padgett & Henwood, 2018). Despite concerted efforts to reduce homelessness, millions live in slums, substandard dwellings, and public spaces. Burgeoned by systemic causes such as a shrinking supply of affordable housing, employment opportunities and livable wages, poor social and health care programs and "blame the victim" attitudes through factors such as mental illness, addiction, and family violence, homelessness remains an intractable problem difficult to solve. Political will is a significant obstacle. Homelessness intersects with most other Grand Challenges in direct and indirect ways. Homelessness is simultaneously misunderstood and overgeneralized. Innovative solutions must develop from the interaction of local initiatives with national collaboration.

Create Social Responses to a Changing Environment

According to the United Nations (2015) the world's population will increasingly be at risk from climate-related disasters and environmental challenge (sea level rise, extreme weather, overpopulation, etc.). Social work professionals must respond to and confront the unique challenges that environmental policies and practices are presenting (Kemp et al., 2018). Kemp and Palinkas (2015) proposed a multi-tier approach to include mitigation, adaptation, and treatment. *Mitigation* includes actions to limit potentially negative or disastrous environmental effects; *adaption* refers to preventive actions to build capacity in preparation for environmental crises; and *treatment* includes actions to alleviate the impact of health and mental health sequelae. Priority action areas are in disaster risk reduction, with environmentally displaced populations, and community adaptation and resilience to environmental change.

Harness Technology for Social Good

Information and communication technology (ICT) has transformed our lives and creates new opportunities to enhance responsiveness for the social good. Social work and other helping professions have been slow to embrace technology largely due to the face-to-face nature of these professions (Berzin & Coulton, 2018). However, reaching a wide range of diverse participants as well as geographically isolated and dispersed populations, those economically challenged, and those technologically challenged is relatively easy. These populations have been excluded because of their lack of proximity, transportation, or for other random reasons of inaccessibility. Today and into the future, opportunities for connection through social media mobile technology, wearable technology, sensors, robotics, artificial intelligence, gaming, geospatial technology, bug data, and data analytics are robust (Berzin & Coulton, 2018).

Social work and human services educational programs are integrating the use of technology for the social good into their curricula. From online bachelors programs to doctoral programs, the integration of technology for the social good is necessary pedagogy to attract new technologically savvy students. In many ways the new I-generation of students are driving the pedagogical shift.

Promote Smart Decarceration

The United States has been immersed in an era of decarceration (Epperson et al., 2018). The negative effects and social injustice of mass incarceration have taken their toll on the social, economic, and cultural fabric of the US society. On any given day, nearly 1.5 million individuals reside in state or federal prisons, and more than 728,000 are confined in a local jail; in addition, approximately 13 million people cycle in and out of American prisons and jails each year (Minton & Zeng, 2015; Pew Center on the States, 2008; Subramanian et al., 2015).

Smart decarceration is effective, sustainable, and socially just with three simultaneous outcomes (Epperson et al., 2018): 1) Decreasing incarcerated populations in jails and prisons; 2) Remedying the social, racial, and economic disparities in the criminal justice system; and 3) Ensuring public safety and well-being.

Reduce Extreme Economic Inequality (REEI)

The gap between the rich and poor continues to increase across all demographics. The gaps in both wealth and income are especially acute by race, ethnicity, and gender (Henly et al., 2018). Since 2005, the US is one of the least likeliest countries in the Organization for Economic Co-operation and Development (OECD) to assist families out of poverty through governmental policies and/or programs (Smeeding, 2005).

The issues surrounding REEI include: inequality in employment and income, unemployment and underemployment, working conditions and benefits, home ownership, financial accounts, tax credits, and universal child allowance. Also included are public employment programs, place-based wages, workplace benefits, child care and early education supports, and policies for lifelong inclusive asset building. According to Henly et al. (2018), widespread economic change needs concerted political, economic, and policy initiatives to spearhead the change required.

Build Financial Capability for All

Financial capability and asset building (FCAB) for all individuals and families, but especially for low and moderate income (LMI) families as well as other economically marginalized populations, is indeed a Grand Challenge (Sherraden et al., 2015). Two disturbing trends in the United States are fueling the continuing rise in financial instability and insecurity (Huang et al., 2018). More individuals and families are experiencing deleterious effects of income and wealth inequality, and the financial sector is changing rapidly contributing to financial vulnerability. Complex financial skills and knowledge largely unavailable to middle-class and LMI families, as well as predatory practices, obstruct participation in financial growth.

Many potential initiatives include lowering service fees, using new accessible financial technologies, motivating desirable financial behaviors, facilitating program participation, integrating financial and social services, creating new policies and financial institutions, promoting lifelong asset building with universal and progressive child development accounts, eliminating asset limits for public assistance programs, creating FCAB opportunities in public sectors, and enhancing FCAB education for all (Huang et al., 2018).

Achieve Equal Opportunity and Justice (AEOJ)

Systemic denial of equal access to health care and education, as well as to opportunities for participation in an upwardly mobile economy, are unjust and marginalize sectors of our population (Calvo et al., 2018). The unequal distribution of wealth between the *haves* and *have-nots* has widened significantly especially in the last 30 years (Heatcote et al., 2010, as cited in Fong et al., 2018). AEOJ is insidiously entwined with the other 12 Grand Challenges.

A special focus of AEOJ is to assist new generations, especially African American and Latin (and Latinx includes the wide variety of gender identities within the Latin populations) youth. The challenge is to build a society reflective of equal opportunity and social justice (Calvo et al., 2018). Changing behaviors will not ameliorate oppressive conditions; rather systemic approaches like universalization of health care access, elimination of zero tolerance policies in schools, and stigma elimination practices are required. Additionally, other approaches include removing barriers to housing and employment, promoting a livable wage, reducing gentrification, and investing in those previously incarcerated.

GCSW Survey Methodology

After considerable analysis and deliberation by the GSEC to what would actually be considered valuable to inform the AASWSW, the final GCSW Survey included 11 questions and was estimated (by field test) to take less than five minutes to complete. The 11 questions were:

1. What degrees do you offer?
2. What is the total enrollment of your program(s)?
3. Do you integrate knowledge about the AASWSW 12 Grand Challenges into your curricula/coursework/program(s)?
4. If yes, please check in what program.
5. If yes, please check which Grand Challenge is integrated.
6. If yes, please indicate where in the curriculum the Grand Challenges are addressed.

7. Are you currently funded to incorporate any Grand Challenge into your current curriculum?
8. What would be helpful for you to include in your planning to integrate the Grand Challenges into your curricula?
9. Please add any additional comments you wish to include.
10. Please provide the name and address of your school.
11. If you are interested in participating further with this initiative, please include your name and email address and we will contact you.

Survey Monkey was employed to solicit data from all 493 Council on Social Work Education (CSWE) accredited programs of social work in the United States (BSW, MSW, MSS, PhD, and DSW). There were 107 responses or a 21.7% response rate.

Findings

Question one asked what degrees are offered by the responding institutions. The results indicated that BSW degrees (81.9%) were most reported; MSW/MSS degrees (71.4%) were next with PhD degrees (33.3%) and DSW degrees (4.7%) following and finally other degrees (5.7%). (See Figure 1.1 in Appendix 1A.)

Question two requested the total student enrollment of the respondents. Programs with less than 250 (45.8%) were the most represented followed by 250–500 (23.4%), 500–750 (15.9%), and more than 750 (14.9%). (See Figure 1.2 in Appendix 1A.)

Question three inquired if knowledge about the AASWSW 12 Grand Challenges is integrated into their curricula, coursework, or programs. Fifty percent of the responding institutions stated that knowledge about the GCSWs was integrated into their coursework; almost 42% indicated they did not integrate the Grand Challenges and nine programs didn't know. (See Figure 1.3 in Appendix 1A.)

Question four queried if the answer in question three was affirmative, in what program was the Grand Challenge content integrated. Of the programs integrating GCSWs, 81% were MSW/MSS programs, 62.1% BSW, 29.3% PhD, and one responded other. (See Figure 1.4 in Appendix 1A.)

Question five requested if the answer from question three was affirmative, check the GCSWs most integrated into their curricula. Their responses were as follows: Achieve Equal Opportunity and Justice (78.33%); Close the Health Gap (70%); Reduce Extreme Inequality 68.33%); Ensure Healthy Development for All Youth (66.67%);

Stop Family Violence (65%); End Homelessness (65%); Create Social Responses to a Changing Environment (60%); Advance Long and Productive Lives (58.33%); Promote Smart Decarceration (46.67%); Eradicate Social Isolation (41.67%); Build Financial Capability for All (41.67%); and, Harness Technology for Social Good (41.67%). (See Figure 1.5 in Appendix 1A.) Question six asked where in their curriculum the GCSWs are addressed. Their responses were: Foundation (68.33%); Practice (63.33%); Policy (61.67%); Diversity and Social Justice (60%); Specialized Practice (55%); Field (51.67%); Research (50%); Theory (45%); Ethics (25%); and Other (8.33%). (See Figure 1.6 in Appendix 1A.)

Question seven asked if there is current funding to incorporate GCSW into their curricula. Only three programs (2.8%) reported being currently funded to incorporate any GCSWs into their curriculum, although eight programs (7.5%) were currently seeking funding. Ninety-seven programs (90%) reported receiving no funding and nine programs were not seeking funding. (See Figure 1.7 in Appendix 1A.)

Question eight asked what would be helpful in planning to integrate GCSW into their curricula. Ninety-seven programs (90%) requested assistance for integrating GCSW content into their curricula. Of this total, 71% were seeking webinars and conferences; 61% would like technical assistance and support for curriculum design; 38% requested technical consultation and support; and 16% asked for other forms of assistance. (See Figure 1.8 in Appendix 1A.)

Question nine requested additional comments. An *a posteriori* method of data analysis (Jahoda et al., 1951) was employed to review the qualitative comments. In the *a posteriori* method, significant ideas and themes are identified systematically. Categories are derived by induction from the content and then used to classify the content. Twenty-eight respondents (26.1%) chose to make a statement in question nine. The statements were categorized into three domains: positive (7%), questioning (21%), and negative (7%). The positive responses contained statements that were supportive of the GCSWs and their integration into curricula; the questioning statements requested more information, more research, and were generally undecided about the integration of the GCSW into curricula; the negative statements were "not convinced of relevance" and "did not see a place or the time for the content in an already packed curriculum".

Question eleven asked if respondents wanted to participate further with the 12 GCSW initiatives; 57% indicated interest and provided their contact information.

Discussion

The response rate to the survey was only 21.7%. The responses from the preponderance of deans and directors answering the survey demonstrate most are clear about the Grand Challenges and require further training as to how to implement them into their respective curricula.

Of great importance, the results of this survey indicate that 90% of the responding social work training programs want more education, training, and assistance on the GCSW. Respondent organizations felt this assistance should be delivered in the forms of webinars and conferences, technical assistance, support for curriculum design, and technical consultation and support.

In the survey, BSW programs were the most represented (81.9%) and programs of less than 250 comprised 45.8% of the respondents. Fifty percent stated knowledge of the Grand Challenges were integrated into their curriculum; 81.7% reported this content is most likely integrated into the masters curriculum. The Grand Challenge most represented in curricula is Achieve Equal Opportunity and Justice (78.3%). A foundation course is where Grand Challenges content is most likely to be integrated (68.3%). Only three programs (2.8%) reported being currently funded to incorporate any GCSWs into their curriculum.

The leadership organizations in the field of social work must make a concerted effort to offer assistance to the programs requesting the aid, both in kind and financial. Additionally, it is recommended that more research regarding each GCSW be funded to include doctoral dissertations and capstone projects.

The 12 Grand Challenges of Social Work and Social Welfare are ambitious and place the profession at the forefront of solving society's most intractable and wicked problems. Schools of social work and the professions' organizational leadership must support the work of the broader profession by educating a workforce prepared to intervene and tackle these challenges.

References

Barth, R. P., & Macy, R. M. (2018). Stop family violence. In R. Fong, J. E. Lubben, & R. P. Barth (Eds.), *Grand challenges for social work and society* (pp. 56–80). Oxford University Press.

Berzin, S. C., & Coulton, C. (2018). Harness technology for the social good. In R. Fong, J. E. Lubben, & R. P. Barth (Eds.), *Grand challenges for social work and society* (pp. 161–180). Oxford University Press.

Brekke, J. (2012). Shaping a science of social work. *Research on Social Work Practice*, *22*(5), 455–464.

Butler, R. N. (1983). An overview of research on aging and the status of gerontology today. *The Milbank Memorial Fund Quarterly, 61*(3), 351–361. https://doi.org/10.2307/3349862

Calvo, R., Teasley, M., Goldbach, J., McRoy, R., & Padilla, Y. C. (2018). Achieve equal opportunity for all. In R. Fong, J. E. Lubben, & R. P. Barth (Eds.), *Grand challenges for social work and society* (pp. 248–264). Oxford University Press.

Epperson, M. W., Pettus-Davvus, C., Grier, A., & Sawh, L. (2018). Promote smart decarceration. In R. Fong, J. E. Lubben, & R. P. Barth (Eds.), *Grand challenges for social work and society* (pp. 181–203). Oxford University Press.

Fong, R., Lubben, E., & Barth, R. P. (Eds.). (2018). *Grand challenges for social work and society*. Oxford University Press.

Hawkins, J. D., Jenson, J. M., Catalano, R. F., Fraser, M. W., Botvin, G. J., Shapiro, V., Bender, K. A. . . . Stone, S. (2015). Unleashing the power of prevention. *Grand Challenges for Social Work Initiative*. Working Paper No. 10. American Academy of Social Work & Social Welfare. https://grandchallengesforsocialwork.org/wp-content/uploads/2013/10/Unleashing-the-Power-of-Prevention-formatted-4.29.15.pdf

Henly, J., Jones, R., Lein, L., Shanks, T., Sherraden, M., & Tillotson, A. (2018). Reduce extreme economic inequality. In R. Fong, J. E. Lubben, & R. P. Barth (Eds.), *Grand challenges for social work and society* (pp. 204–226). Oxford University Press.

Huang, J., Sherraden, M. S., Despard, M. R., Rothwell, D., Friedline, T., Doran, J., & Zurlo, K. A. (2018). Build financial capacity for all. In R. Fong, J. E. Lubben, & R. P. Barth (Eds.), *Grand challenges for social work and society* (pp. 227–247). Oxford University Press.

Jahoda, M., Deutsch, M., & Cook, S. W. (1951). *Research methods in social relations. With special reference to prejudice. Part two: Selected techniques*. Dryden Press.

Jenson, J. M., & Hawkins, J. D. (2018). Ensure healthy development for all youth. In R. Fong, J. E. Lubben, & R. P. Barth (Eds.), *Grand challenges for social work and society* (pp. 18–35). Oxford University Press.

Kemp, S. P., & Palinkas, L. A. (2015). Strengthening the response to human impacts of environmental change. *Grand Challenges for Social Work Initiative*. Working Paper No. 5. American Academy for Social Work and Social Welfare. http://volweb.utk.edu/~envchange/wp-content/uploads/2018/03/Strengthening-the-Social-Response-to-the-Human-Impacts-of-Environmental-Change.pdf

Kemp, S. P., Palinkas, L. A., & Mason L. R. (2018). Create social responses to a changing environment. In R. Fong, J. E. Lubben, & R. P. Barth (Eds.), *Grand challenges for social work and society* (pp. 140–160). Oxford University Press.

Lubben, J. E., Barth, R. P., Fong, R., Flynn, M. L., Sherraden, M., & Uehara, E. (2018a). Grand challenges for social work and society. In R. Fong, J. E. Lubben, & R. P. Barth (Eds.), *Grand challenges for social work and society* (pp. 1–17). Oxford University Press

Lubben, J. E., Tracy, E. M., Crewe, S. E., Sabbath, E. L., Gironda, M., Johnson, C., Kong, J., Munson, M. R., & Brown, S. (2018b). Eradicate social isolation. In R. Fong, J. E. Lubben, & R. P. Barth (Eds.), *Grand challenges for social work and society* (pp. 103–123). Oxford University Press.

Minton, T. D., & Zeng, Z. (2015). *Jail inmates at midyear 2014*. Bureau of Justice Statistics.

Morrow-Howell, N., Gonzales, J. B., Matz-Costa, C., & Putnam, M. (2018). Advance long and productive lives. In R. Fong, J. E. Lubben, & R. P. Barth (Eds.), *Grand challenges for social work and society* (pp. 81–102). Oxford University Press.

Padgett, D. K., & Henwood, B. (2018). End homelessness. In R. Fong, J. E. Lubben, & R. P. Barth (Eds.), *Grand challenges for social work and society* (pp. 124–139). Oxford University Press.

Pew Center on the States. (2008). *One in 100: Behind bars in America, 2008*. The Pew Center on the States: Public Safety Performance Project.

Sherraden, M. S., Huang, J., Frey, J. J., Birkenmaier, J., Callahan, C., Clancy, M. M., & Sherraden, M. (2015). Financial capability and asset building for all. *Social Work Grand Challenges Initiative*. Working Paper No. 13. American Academy for Social Work and Social Welfare. https://grandchallengesforsocialwork.org/wp-content/uploads/2016/01/WP13-with-cover.pdf

Smeeding, T. M. (2005). Public policy economic inequality and poverty: The United States in comparative perspective. *Social Science Quarterly*, *86*(1), 955–983.

Spence, M. S., Walters, K. L., Allen, H. L., Andrews, C. M., Begun, A., Browne, T., Clapp, D., DiNitto, D., Maramaldi, P., Wheeler, D. P., Zebrack, B., & Uehhara, E. (2018). Close the health gap. In R. Fong, J. E. Lubben, & R. P. Barth (Eds.), *Grand challenges for social work and society* (pp. 36–55). Oxford University Press.

Subramanian, R., Delaney, R., Roberts, S., Fishman, N., & McGarry, P. (2015). *Incarceration's front door: Vera Institute of Justice*. http://www.vera.org/sites/default/files/resources/downloads/incarcerations-front-door report_02.pdf

United Nations (2015). *Global sustainable development report, 2015*. https://www.un.org/en/development/desa/publications/global-sustainable-development-report-2015-edition.html

Appendix 1A

Questions One Through Question Eight Charts

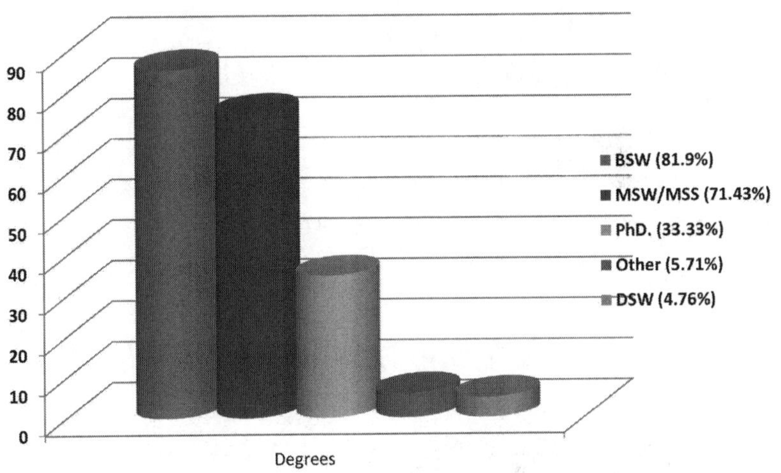

Figure 1.1 Question one: What degrees do you offer?

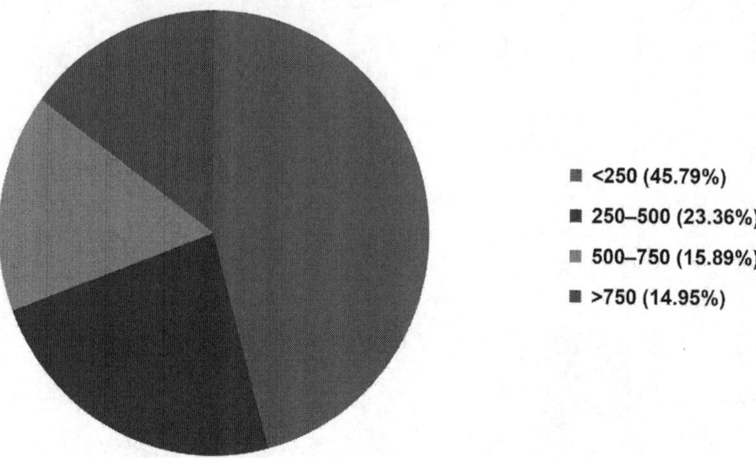

Figure 1.2 Question two: What is the total student enrollment of your programs?

Integrate Grand Challenges

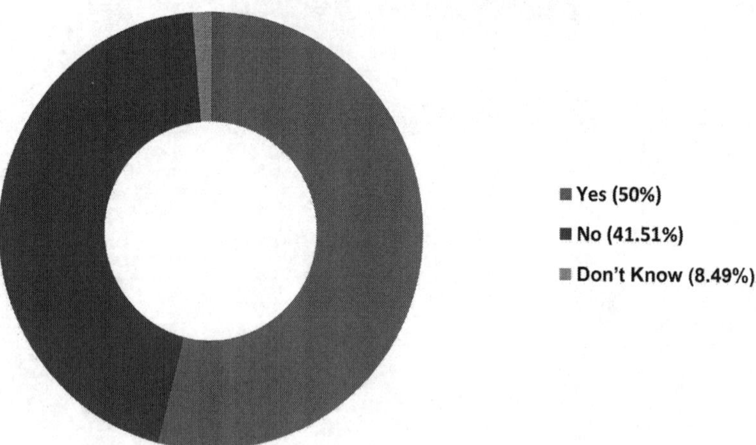

Figure 1.3 Question three: Do you integrate knowledge about the AASWSW 12 Grand Challenges into your curricula/coursework/program(s)?

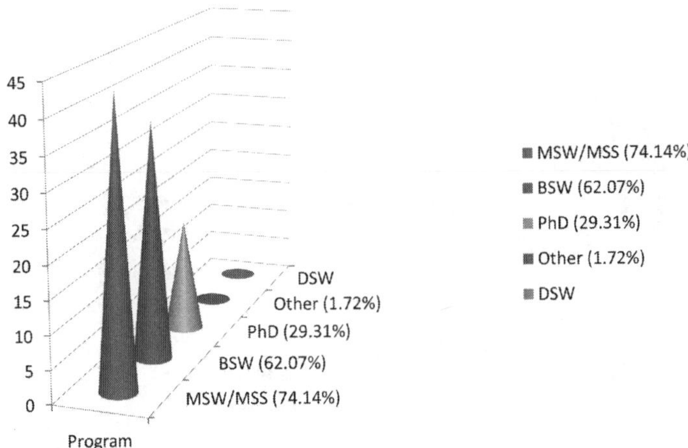

Figure 1.4 Question four: If YES, in which program? (Check all that apply)

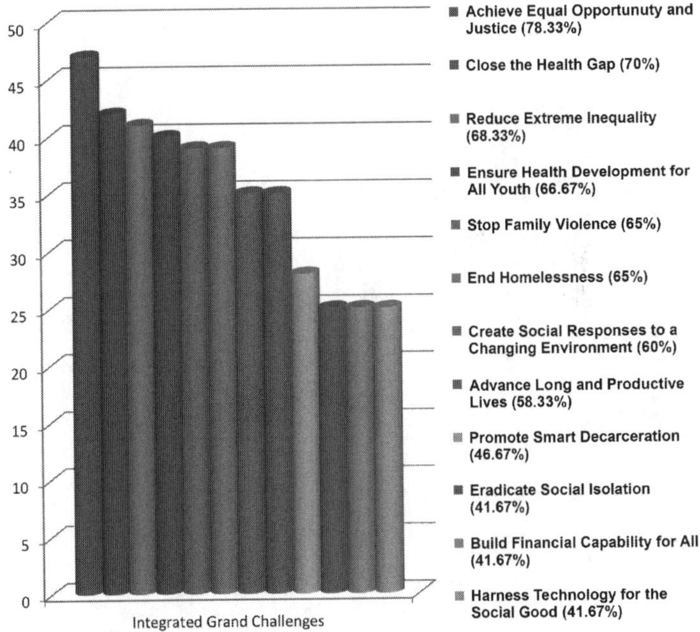

Figure 1.5 Question five: If YES, please check which Grand Challenge is integrated

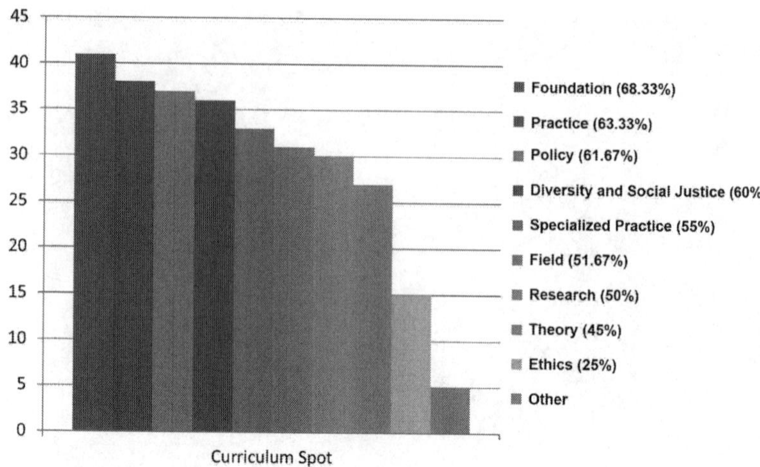

Figure 1.6 Question six: If YES, please indicate where in the curriculum the Grand Challenges are addressed

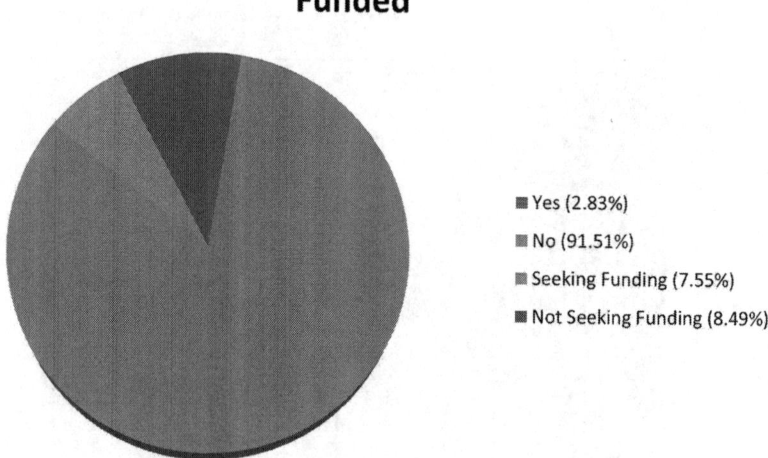

Figure 1.7 Question seven: Are you currently funded to incorporate any Grand Challenges into your curriculum?

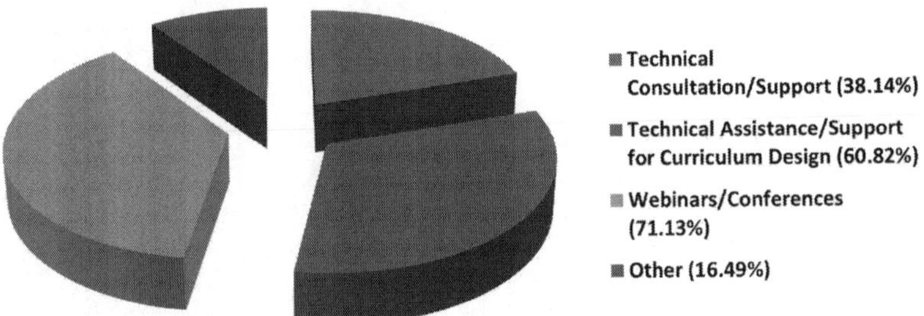

Figure 1.8 Question eight: What would be helpful for you to include in your planning to integrate the Grand Challenge into your curricula?

Part One

Individual and Family Well-Being

2 Ensuring the Healthy Development of All Youth

Juan Carlos Araque and Wendy Cholico

Introduction

Behavioral health problems in youth surpass the incidence of communicable diseases in the US, and the evidence notes that these behavioral health issues can be preventable (Hawkins et al., 2015). Scaling up of evidence-informed prevention and intervention programs to local and state systems is the key to reducing the prevalence of behavioral health problems in youth. This chapter provides an understanding of human behavior, policy, and practice contexts for social work students to develop core knowledge of child and youth behavioral health problems, interventions, and outcomes within the social environment. The curriculum in this chapter covers in-depth material in several human behavior and social environment domains of knowledge and theories (e.g., neurobiology, psychodynamic, behaviorism/social cognitive, and family/social networks). Values and ethical standards of social work, the profession's person-in-environment, and biopsychosocial frameworks are critically examined with special considerations on equity, diversity, and inclusion to understand how social workers can become effective change agents in micro, mezzo, and macro contexts in serving the mental health needs of children and adolescents.

A discussion of the utilization of scientific evidence (through evidence-based practices) applied in real-life settings will be introduced and developed through case scenarios as examples of reducing the incidences of behavioral health problems and the associated racial and economic disparities (see Appendix 2A). The cases illustrate how interdisciplinary cross-sector collaboration (Mattessich & Rausch, 2014) can be utilized to provide interventions that reduce risk and increase community and state capacity for prevention and intervention efforts in juvenile justice settings. An examination into youth developmental assets and cultural considerations in practices and policies

DOI: 10.4324/9781003308263-3

that tend to be biased, and stereotype children, youth, and families of color will be outlined along with policy and practice recommendations to advance the prevention of behavioral problems in youth through sustainable infrastructures towards the healthy development of youth (Scales et al., 2000).

Ensure the Healthy Development of All Youth Grand Challenge

Adverse childhood and adolescence experiences have taken a heavy toll over a lifetime that can result in significant impacts on economic independence, morbidity, and mortality (Larkin et al., 2014). A large body of scientific evidence over the past 30 years shows that behavioral health problems can be prevented (Hawkins et al., 2015). The original overall goal of this Grand Challenge was

> to reduce the incidence and prevalence of behavioral health problems in the population of young people from birth to age 24 by 20% from current levels and reduce racial and socioeconomic disparities in behavioral health problems by 20 percent through the widespread implementation of tested and effective preventive interventions.
>
> (Fong et al., 2017, p. 2)

The Grand Challenge to Ensure Healthy Development for All Youth responds to the observation that behavioral health problems in childhood and adolescence often have lifelong repercussions on physical, emotional, and financial well-being. Led by the Coalition for the Promotion of Behavioral Health (CPBH), this interdisciplinary group includes more than 150 researchers, educators, and practitioners. They have been working under the following seven action steps to reduce prevalence, incidents, and inequities to behavioral health problems: increase public awareness; increase public funding of prevention programs; implement community-assessment and capacity building tools; establish and implement criteria for preventive interventions; increase infrastructure for preventive interventions; develop data systems; and create workforce development strategies (Hawkins et al., 2015). These action steps are focused to accomplish the following objectives (Uehara et al., 2014, p. 213):

- Develop and increase public awareness of the advances and cost savings of effective preventive interventions that promote healthy behaviors for all.

- Ensure that 10% of all public funds spent on young people support effective prevention programs and policies.
- Implement community-assessment and capacity-building tools that guide communities to systematically assess and prioritize risk and protective factors and select and implement evidence-based preventive interventions that target prioritized factors.
- Establish and implement criteria for preventive interventions that are effective, sustainable, equity-enhancing, and cost-beneficial.
- Increase infrastructure to support the high-quality implementation of preventive interventions. Monitor and increase access of children, youth, and young adults to effective preventive interventions.
- Create workforce development strategies to prepare practitioners in health and human service professions for new roles in behavioral health promotion and preventive interventions.

Mainly, this Grand Challenge has led sustainable efforts in research, education, and policy. The research has been spearheaded by the Social Development Research Group at the University of Washington School of Social Work with the goal of evaluating elementary-school interventions that helped children form healthy attachments to family and school. Educational materials have been created and disseminated, including textbooks, workshop modules, and webinars. Policy changes in primary prevention have taken place in several states, including Colorado, Utah, Massachusetts, and Delaware (Barth et al., 2022).

The Social Work Curriculum

The social work curriculum focuses on four key areas: human behavior, policy, practice, and field practicum. Foundation and specialization materials have been developed on the complex nature and scope of child and youth behavior and the social environment. A deeper understanding of behavior theories and applying evidence-based policies and practices assist social workers in becoming effective change agents in micro, mezzo, and macro contexts (Howard et al., 2003). The goal is for social work students to better understand human interactions in a social environment. First, students are presented with a vast array of theories and evidence-based policies and practices that explain behavior and describe development milestones. Then, the curriculum presents substantial information on human diversity, equity, and inclusion with a variety of groups, including age, class, color, culture, disability, political affiliation, sexual orientation, gender identity, tribal sovereignty status, and immigration rights. This content is coupled with theories and practices that identify child and adolescent behavior with neurobiological, psychological, and cultural factors. Simultaneously, the social work curriculum is always attempting to present material on strategies that promote individual, social, and economic justice. Finally, the overall goal of the social work curriculum is to present material that supports the attainment and maintenance of mental health and well-being of children and youth.

Human Behavior

A sound theoretical foundation is needed for students to develop core knowledge of child and youth behavior within their social environments. During their course work, social work students are often exposed to over 20 different children and youth human behavior theories (Greene, 2017; Hutchison, 2017) (see Appendix 2B). In essence, the curriculum covers in-depth material in four major domains of knowledge: neurobiology, psychodynamics, behaviorism/social cognition, and family/social networks. First, it is critical that social work students learn key areas of the brain, including specific neural structures, genes, and neurotransmitter systems, and their function within social cognition. We know the importance of healthy brain development, especially during the first five years of life, which helps us understand how cortical regions in the temporal lobe contribute to perceiving socially relevant stimuli and how functions of the amygdala participate in motivation, emotion, and cognition (Adolphs, 2001). The research application emphasizes the need to apply neuroscience to prevention and intervention in multiple settings. The goal is to better inform clients about the effects and impact of toxic stress, trauma, early adversity, and adverse child and adolescent brain development (Perry, 2007). Social work students learn to collaborate with medical, child welfare, and juvenile justice professionals with the goal of sharing trauma and resilience-informed support systems (Applegate & Shapiro, 2005).

Another traditional branch of knowledge is drawn from psychodynamic theory and practice. Psychodynamic theories are interested in answering behavior exchanges within the context of the self, family, peers, and other social groups (Guntrip, 2018). The basic concept is that developmental processes occur throughout the life span of individuals. It begins by addressing the importance of early experiences in human development, including continuities and discontinuities in temperament, motivational systems, and how these affect regulations, sense of self, and attachment (Deal, 2007; Schore & Schore, 2008).

Psychodynamic theories also try to better understand adult behavior, focusing on developmental processes in ourselves and those around us (Colarusso & Nemiroff, 2013). These theoretical approaches are coupled with behaviorism/social cognitive and family/network theories, which study human behavior and interactions in groups, including family, schools, organizations, and communities (Bandura, 2005). Within this paradigm, social learning theory is paramount, as we seek to best understand child and adolescent learning, socialization, and child-adult relationships (Hamilton et al., 2020).

A cornerstone element in social work curricula is focused on developing value-driven health professionals who embrace a strong ethical framework in the workplace (Reamer & Reamer, 2018). Based on the National Association of Social Workers, there are six key social work ethical principles: service, social justice, dignity and worth of the person, importance of human relationships, integrity, and competence (Reamer, 2013). These ethical principles are first learned in the classroom, and then they are practiced in the field. As students work with children, adolescents, and their families, they have the opportunity to put into practice these ethical principles regularly. Social work is a highly value-driven profession, whereby respect for individuals and their self-determination is keen. Social work professionals first assess human behavior from the person-in-environment and biopsychosocial frameworks, then they provide the best interventions available with the goal of improving child and youth well-being and functionality within social environments (Horne, 2018).

Policy

A major success in preventing child maltreatment and advancing causes for children and youth in social settings is due to past and current policies at the local, state, and national levels. Policy social work education is based on three pillars: learning historical policy achievements, understanding current pivotal strategies to improve government and institutional support, and engaging in advocacy. Historically, our society has gone from allowing child labor to considering children and youth vulnerable populations, establishing basic protections for children and families (Featherstone & Gupta, 2018). The war on poverty and anti-racial movements of the 1960s and 1970s established comprehensive social reforms to protect children and youth, including an institutionalized child welfare system, free and more equal K-12 education, free children's health insurance, and a more just juvenile justice system (Flynn, 2021).

The current policies dealing with children and youth initiatives are vast and ongoing. These policies are predominantly fueled by the need to establish a strong child welfare policy, and local and state government agencies. One key goal is for potential governmental and non-governmental partners to work towards the reduction of child maltreatment, abuse, and neglect (Glaser, 2000). Parents, caregivers, educators, and other adults receive constant education regarding brain development and trauma exposure in the first five years of life and policies protect children from adults committing child abuse (DePrince et al., 2009). Additionally, policies to support both youths aging out of the foster system and coming out of probation/incarceration continue to evolve. For example, laws increasing the government's support and benefits for emancipated young adults from 21 to 25 years old have made enormous health and mental health improvements to this vulnerable population (Fernandes-Alcantara, 2012).

Due to the increase in mental health problems and suicidal ideation among youth nationwide, new policies are now also focusing on the mental health well-being of our children and youth (Scheffler & Adams, 2005). These mental health issues were accelerated due to the pandemic. COVID-19 has had a detrimental effect on most young people, especially those who are trapped in generational poverty, marginalized youth, the youth of color, and those associated with child welfare and juvenile justice systems (Gabriel et al., 2021). Local and state agencies are currently establishing new policies and protocols in the school systems and communities to support children and youth who have been the most impacted (Ragavan et al., 2020).

These policy efforts can only be successful and signed into law by effectively advocating for services, rights, social justice, and equal protection for children, youth, and families (Flynn, 2021). The first step to becoming a strong advocate is to demonstrate knowledge of the values, purpose, and roles the social work profession practices within the contexts of policy systems and program administration at multiple levels of government (local, state, and national). This requires an understanding of how social workers should intervene and engage in micro, mezzo, and macro advocacy in each of these areas. A successful policy framework, according to Jansson (2015), should include learning the following applications of policy tasks and skills: analyzing problems, deciding right from wrong, navigating advocacy systems, building agendas, writing proposals, enacting, implementing, and evaluating policy. In a democratic society, the use of developing and using power becomes critical to advancing social reform (Heidemann et al., 2011).

Practice

The cornerstone of social work education is founded on practice courses both in the classroom and field placements (or internships). The main goals of practice courses are to 1) increase awareness of individual needs and diverse populations (gender, race, sexual orientation, social class, religion, and vulnerable and other oppressed groups) and to 2) practice effective interventions and services with appropriate supervision. Evidence-based practice (EBP) is the chief framework, which includes the integration of three key elements: best available evidence, clinical expertise, and patient values and circumstances (McNeece & Thyer, 2004). The EBP framework provides social work practitioners with a specific script when interacting with clients by utilizing the following five steps: ask relevant questions, search for evidence, critically appraise the material, implement the intervention/service, and evaluate regularly (Manuel, 2009).

Social work practice focuses on highlighting the importance of the role of theory, empirical research, and evidence-based interventions to support children and youth in different settings. First, the collaboration between health and human service providers sustains healthy development for youth (Mattessich & Rausch, 2014). Social determinants of health and community needs are highly influenced by cross-sector efforts that focus on initiatives that promote community health improvement in collaboration with inter-organizations including those in the health, social, education, juvenile justice, and even financial institutions (Fenstermacher, 2010). Awareness of psychosocial and emotional aspects of health and illness promotes development for children and youth and is a critical role of social work practice. Significantly, social workers are responsible and dedicated to influencing psychosocial factors initiated and triggered by mental health or physical illness in collaboration with health providers (Rosenberg, 2009).

Additionally, social work practice combines classroom learning with field practicum. The primary goal is for social work students to apply the principles of evidence-based practice and clinical case studies when working directly with clients. Students must demonstrate knowledge of major social work practice concepts to support the treatment process: engagement, assessment, planning and contracting implementation, and termination/evaluation (Raines & Cox, 2021). Thus, they learn commonly applied models of practice and experiential activities to practice clinical skills with children, youth, and families (Specht & Vickery, 2021).

Learning how to work with vulnerable and minority populations takes passion, time, and commitment. Most prevention efforts in social work practice with children and youth occur in school settings. School social workers have a key role in promoting and supporting the academic achievement of children and youth. Services provided include individual counseling, group counseling with students and families, home visits, collaborative work with communities and organizations, and engagement in advocacy, policy, and research. School social workers intervene in teams alongside school personnel that include administrators, teachers, guidance counselors, psychologists, nurses, probation officers, and others. Often, school social workers work across multi-systems that may include health care, mental health services, and justice systems (Hopson et al., 2015). Those living in poverty experience extreme adversity, including child abuse, neglect, and trauma throughout childhood, contributing to inequities in mental health, economic, social, and physical well-being throughout adulthood. Although African American and Hispanic youth are less likely to engage in mental health services than their Caucasian counterparts (Bains et al., 2014), when school-based health centers are available, youth are more likely to receive mental health services and appropriate treatments (Allen-Meares et al., 2013).

Teaching Practices and Learning Objectives

Social work courses are created to carry on specific core competencies, which are aligned with the 2022 Social Work Educational Policy and Accreditation Standards (EPAS, CSWE, 2022) (see Appendix 2C).

Each course syllabi includes four to five objectives, focusing on developing critical thinking and problem-solving skills. Primary course learning objectives include: 1) learn typical and development milestones of children from infancy through adolescence and understand the impact of cultural and environmental factors that influence that development; 2) understand risk and protective factors throughout development with a particular focus on how adverse childhood experiences can impact development; 3) apply evidence-based practice skills on conducting ecological and needs assessments, and monitoring progress of children and youth; and 4) examine strategies for engagement with children and families from infancy through adolescence in a culturally and developmentally appropriate way and provide general principles of intervention with children and adolescents.

Setting the Context and Preparing Students for Learning and Engagement

Typically, students receive course instruction weekly or twice per week, and they spend 15–20 hours in field placement. Instructors provide multiple types of classroom activities, including among others, didactic lectures, required reading discussions, case studies, guest lectures, and facilitation of meaningful interactions. Tips for active class participation include setting the stage (listening respectfully, assessing readiness to discuss issue(s), recognizing the diversity of students, setting a framework and objective for the discussion, providing a common base for understanding, being an active facilitator, fostering civility, dealing with tense or emotional moments, summarizing, and reflecting discussions). Evaluating content knowledge and application is essential to ensure students' comprehension. Learning assessment takes different formats, including the use of grading rubrics, quality of discussion and class participation, written and oral assignments, quizzes and exams, capstone projects, and reflections (Carpenter, 2011).

Most of the social work learning is contextual, focusing on the translation of theory into practice. Students are expected to learn not only from the course content but also from each other and their clients. It is important to have a diverse group of individuals, who share their own life experiences and points of view during class discussions. These meaningful class discussions should be framed within developmental assets and cultural proficiency lenses. The developmental assets framework articulates the building blocks that young people need to thrive, including supports, opportunities, relationships, and strengths (Roehlkepartain & Blyth, 2019).

Addressing Diversity, Equity, and Inclusion

Cultural proficiency and cultural humility encourage students to understand clients and communities from multiple cultural dimensions, including age, race/ethnicity, nationality, income, culture, gender, and/or sexual orientation (Lindsey et al., 2018). It is essential students learn about implicit and explicit biases, and discuss awareness and management of biases, transference and countertransference, prejudice and stereotyping children, youth, and families of color (Sukhera & Watling, 2018). The goal is twofold, 1) to break barriers when implementing services, such as cultural/economic blocks to utilization, cultural marginalization, language differences, stigma, confusion, anger, and fear of professionals; and 2) to create new best practice models in prevention and intervention.

Diversity

Traditionally, diversity was limited to legally protected categories like race or gender, but over the years this has evolved. Today, diversity experts are increasingly considering a wider range of factors from age and sexual preference to disabilities, abilities, gender expression, nationality, color, relationship status, religion/spirituality, and socio-economic status (Sue et al., 2016). It is essential to enhance cultural competence by raising students' awareness of their own values, assumptions, and biases, as well as their relationships and styles of interaction and communication with people from cultures different than their own. Competence is considered in dimensions of values, knowledge, skills, and cognitive and affective processes (Finney & Fitzgerald, 2020). The profession of social work celebrates the diversity that characterizes and shapes the human experience and the formation of both individual and group identity for all.

Equity

Regardless of cultural background and life experiences, every person has fundamental human rights, such as freedom, safety, honor, and recognition of worth, privacy, an adequate standard of living, health care, and education (Finney & Fitzgerald, 2020). More than ever, social workers are needed to provide leadership dispelling harmful biases and stereotypes, exposing and rectifying unfair practices and policies, eliminating unjust disproportionalities and disparities, and eradicating systemic oppression and social injustice (Lindsey et al., 2018). It is important for students to recognize the importance of expanding opportunities and continued efforts to achieve justice and equality for children, youth, and families they serve.

Inclusion

As students prepare to serve youth and families as professional social workers, it is key that they aim to enhance their intercultural competence, particularly their ability to engage in diversity and difference in practice, and to advance human rights and social, economic, and environmental justice. Ideally, students are encouraged to examine cultural groups that exist and ways they have been oppressed with social injustices and exclusion from decision making (Sukhera & Watling, 2018). Additionally, students should be provided with frameworks and strategies that can be applied to varied populations, issues, and contexts and highlight cultural groups and issues that are particularly salient or relevant to social work practice today (Sue et al., 2016).

The learning process is strengthened and promotes diversity, equity, and inclusion as students invest time directly with clients. This invaluable experience allows social workers to learn firsthand about interventions, system delivery, and client support. Field placement helps increase the understanding of the rationale, processes, and challenges of evidenced-based practice and skills. Students utilize relevant and practical empirically supported assessments and interventions to children, youth, and families in conditions or situations facing children/youth and their caregivers. They learn the application of positive behavior interventions in schools, youth centers, and juvenile justice facilities (Poulin et al., 2018). Appropriate supervision is critical and required, as social work students receive feedback that is specific, timely, and based on observations of cases, behaviors, and actions (Kourgiantakis et al., 2019).

Conclusion

Children and adolescents are our future. Institutions must understand how to welcome and engage with diverse populations. How we work with the next generation has significant implications for social work practice in the 21st century. Health and human service practitioners are leaders who are in a position to apply innovative skills with their clients, organizations, and communities (Araque & Weiss, 2018). They must continue learning new theories and practices to best support the development of children and youth. Human behavior can best be explained through theory, research, and observation. Once we better comprehend child and adolescent behavior, then we can establish evidence-based practices and policies to best support them.

References

Adolphs, R. (2001). The neurobiology of social cognition. *Current Opinion in Neurobiology*, *11*(2), 231–239. https://doi.org/10.1016/S0959-4388(00)00202-6

Allen-Meares, P., Montgomery, K. L., & Kim, J. S. (2013). School-based social work interventions: A cross-national systematic review. *Social Work*, *58*(3), 253–262. https://doi.org/10.1093/sw/swt022

Applegate, J. S., & Shapiro, J. R. (2005). *Neurobiology for clinical social work: Theory and practice*. W. W. Norton & Company.

Araque, J. C., & Weiss, E. L. (2018). *Leadership with impact: Preparing health and human service practitioners in the age of innovation and diversity*. Oxford University Press.

Bains, R. M., Franzen, C. W., & White-Frese', J. (2014). Engaging African American and Latino adolescent males through school-based health centers. *The Journal of School Nursing*, *30*(6), 411–419. https://doi.org/10.1177/1059840514521241

Bandura, A. (2005). The evolution of social cognitive theory. *Great Minds in Management*, 9–35.

Barth, R. P., Messing, J. T., Shanks, T. R., & Williams, J. H. (Eds.). (2022). *Grand challenges for social work and society*. Oxford University Press.

Carpenter, J. (2011). Evaluating social work education: A review of outcomes, measures, research designs and practicalities. *Social Work Education*, *30*(2), 122–140. https://doi.org/10.1080/02615479.2011.540375

Colarusso, C. A., & Nemiroff, R. A. (2013). *Adult development: A new dimension in psychodynamic theory and practice*. Springer Science & Business Media.

CSWE. (2022). *2022 educational policy and accreditation standards*. www.cswe.org/accreditation/standards/2022-epas/

Deal, K. H. (2007). Psychodynamic theory. *Advances in Social Work*, *8*(1), 184–195. https://doi.org/10.18060/140

DePrince, A. P., Weinzierl, K. M., & Combs, M. D. (2009). Executive function performance and trauma exposure in a community sample of children. *Child Abuse & Neglect*, *33*(6), 353–361. https://doi.org/10.1016/j.chiabu.2008.08.002

Featherstone, B., & Gupta, A. (2018). *Protecting children: A social model*. Policy Press.

Fenstermacher, J. L. (2010). Social work in a pediatric hospital: Managing a medically complex patient. In T. Kerson, J. McCoyd, & Associates (Eds.), *Social work in health settings: Practice in context* (3rd ed., pp. 108–118). Routledge.

Fernandes-Alcantara, A. L. (2012, October). *Youth transitioning from foster care: Background and federal programs*. Library of Congress, Congressional Research Service.

Finney, K., & Fitzgerald, T. (2020). *The reality of diversity, gender, and skin color: From living room to classroom* (1st ed.). Cognella Publishing.

Flynn, S. (2021). Learning from the literature on social work and social care with children: The utility of a Jansson framework of policy-practice. *Child Care in Practice*, 27(3), 281–294. https://doi.org/10.1080/13575279.2019.1628007

Fong, R., Lubben, J., & Barth, R. P. (Eds.). (2017). *Grand challenges for social work and society*. Oxford University Press.

Gabriel, M. G., Brown, A., León, M., & Outley, C. (2021). Power and social control of youth during the COVID-19 pandemic. *Leisure Sciences*, *43*(1–2), 240–246. https://doi.org/10.1080/01490400.2020.1774008

Glaser, D. (2000). Child abuse and neglect and the brain – a review. *The Journal of Child Psychology and Psychiatry and Allied Disciplines*, *41*(1), 97–116. https://doi.org/10.1017/S0021963099004990

Greene, R. R. (2017). *Human behavior theory and social work practice*. Routledge.

Guntrip, H. Y. (2018). *Personality structure and human interaction: The developing synthesis of psychodynamic theory*. Routledge.

Hamilton, K., van Dongen, A., & Hagger, M. S. (2020). An extended theory of planned behavior for parent-for-child health behaviors: A meta-analysis. *Health Psychology*, *39*(10), 863. https://doi.org/10.1037/hea0000940

Hawkins, J. D., Jenson, J. M., Catalano, R., Fraser, M. W., Botvin, G. J., Shapiro, V., Hendricks, C., Beardslee, W., Brent, D., Leslie, L. K., Rotherham-Borus, M. J., Shea, P., Shih, A., Anthony, E., Haggerty, K. P., Bender, K., Gorman-Smith, D., & Stone, S. (2015). Unleashing the power of prevention. *NAM Perspectives*. Discussion Paper, National Academy of Medicine, Washington, DC. https://doi.org/10.31478/201506c

Heidemann, G., Fertig, R., Jansson, B., & Kim, H. (2011). Practicing policy, pursuing change, and promoting social justice: A policy instructional approach. *Journal of Social Work Education*, 47(1), 37–52. https://doi.org/10.5175/JSWE.2010.2010.200800118

Hopson, L. M., Franklin, C., & Harris, M. B. (2015). Social work in schools. In *Social work practice in health, mental health and communities: A meta-framework for micro, mezzo, macro and global action*. Sage.

Horne, M. (2018). *Values in social work*. Routledge.

Howard, M. O., McMillen, C. J., & Pollio, D. E. (2003). Teaching evidence-based practice: Toward a new paradigm for social work education. *Research on Social Work Practice*, *13*(2), 234–259. https://doi.org/10.1177/1049731502250404

Hutchison, E. (2017). Families. *Essentials of human behavior theory: Integrating person, environment, and life course* (2nd ed., pp. 191–222). Sage Publications.

Jansson, B. S. (2015). *Social welfare policy and advocacy: Advancing social justice through 8 policy sectors*. Sage Publications.

Kourgiantakis, T., Sewell, K. M., & Bogo, M. (2019). The importance of feedback in preparing social work students for field education. *Clinical Social Work Journal*, 47(1), 124–133. https://doi.org/10.1007/s10615-018-0671-8

Larkin, H., Felitti, V. J., & Anda, R. F. (2014). Social work and adverse childhood experiences research: Implications for practice and health policy. *Social Work in Public Health*, *29*, 1–16. https://doi.org/10.1080/19371918.2011.619433

Lindsey, R. B., Nuri-Robins, K., Terrell, R. D., & Lindsey, D. B. (2018). *Cultural proficiency: A manual for school leaders*. Corwin Press.

Manuel, J. I., Mullen, E. J., Fang, L., Bellamy, J. L., & Bledsoe, S. E. (2009). Preparing social work practitioners to use evidence-based practice: A comparison of experiences from an implementation project. *Research on Social Work Practice*, *19*(5), 613–627. https://doi.org/10.1177/1049731509335547

Mattessich, P. W., & Rausch, E. J. (2014). Cross-sector collaboration to improve community health: A view of the current landscape. *Health Affairs*, *33*(11), 1968–1974. https://doi.org/10.1377/hlthaff.2014.0645

McNeece, C. A., & Thyer, B. A. (2004). Evidence-based practice and social work. *Journal of Evidence-Based Social Work*, *1*(1), 7–25. https://doi.org/10.1300/J394v01n01_02

Perry, B. D. (2007). *Stress, trauma and post-traumatic stress disorders in children*. The Child Trauma Academy. https://naturalstatecounselingcenters.com/wp-content/uploads/2020/04/PTSD_Intro_Perry_1.pdf

Poulin, J., Matis, S., & Witt, H. (2018). *The social work field placement: A competency-based approach*. Springer Publishing Company.

Ragavan, M. I., Culyba, A. J., Muhammad, F. L., & Miller, E. (2020). Supporting adolescents and young adults exposed to or experiencing violence during the COVID-19 pandemic. *Journal of Adolescent Health*, *67*(1), 18–20. https://doi.org/10.1016/j.jadohealth.2020.04.011

Raines, J. C., & Cox, T. (2021). The process of ethical decision making in school social work. In M. G. Leitch & C. J. Rushton (Eds.), *School social work: Practice, policy, and research* (pp. 81–93). Oxford University Press.

Reamer, F. G. (2013). The NASW code of ethics. In *Encyclopedia of social work*. https://doi.org/10.1093/acrefore/9780199975839.013.134

Reamer, F. G., Blyth, D., & Reamer, F. G. (2018). Social work values and ethics. In *Social work values and ethics*. Columbia University Press.

Roehlkepartain, E. C., & Blyth, D. A. (2019). Developmental assets. *The Encyclopedia of Child and Adolescent Development*, 1–13. https://doi.org/10.1002/9781119171492.wecad341

Rosenberg, J. (2009). Social work in health care. In *Working in social work* (pp. 89–106). Routledge.

Scales, P. C., Benson, P. L., & Leffert, N. A. (2000). Contribution of developmental assets to the prediction of thriving among adolescents. *Applied Developmental Science*, *4*(1), 27–46. https://doi.org/10.1207/S1532480XADS0401_3

Scheffler, R. M., & Adams, N. (2005). Millionaires and mental health: Proposition 63 in California: What it is, and why it passed. *Health Affairs*, *24*(Suppl1), W5–W5. https://doi.org/10.1377/hlthaff.w5.212

Schore, J., & Schore, A. (2008). Modern attachment theory: The central role of affect regulation in development and treatment. *Clinical Social Work Journal*, *36*(9), 9–20. https://doi.org/10.1007/s10615-007-0111-7

Specht, H., & Vickery, A. (Eds.). (2021). *Integrating social work methods*. Routledge.

Sue, D. W., Rasheed, M. N., & Rasheed, J. M. (2016). *Multicultural social work practice*. John Wiley & Sons, Inc.

Sukhera, J., & Watling, C. (2018). A framework for integrating implicit bias recognition into health professions education. *Academic Medicine*, *93*(1), 35–40. https://doi.org/10.1097/ACM.0000000000001819

Uehara, E. S., Barth, R. P., Olson, S., Catalano, R. F., Hawkins, J. D., Kemp, S., & Sherraden, M. (2014). Identifying and tackling grand challenges for social work (Grand Challenges for Social work Initiative, Working Paper No. 3). American Academy of Social Work and Social Welfare. https://grandchallengesforsocialwork.org/wp-content/uploads/2015/04/FINAL-Identifying-and-Tackling-GCSW-4–2–2015-formatted-final.pdf

Appendix 2A

EPAS Addressed in Grand Challenge #1

Ensuring the Healthy Development of All Youth

Competency 5: Engage in Policy Practice. Social workers understand that human rights and social justice, as well as social welfare and services, are mediated by policy and its implementation at the federal, state, and local levels. Social workers understand the history and current structures of social policies and services, the role of policy in service delivery, and the role of practice in policy development.

Competency 6: Engage With Individuals, Families, Groups, Organizations, and Communities. Social workers understand that engagement is an ongoing component of the dynamic and interactive process of social work practice with, and on behalf of, diverse individuals, families, groups, organizations, and communities. Social workers value the importance of human relationships. Social workers understand theories of human behavior and the social environment, and critically evaluate and apply this knowledge to facilitate engagement with clients and constituencies, including individuals, families, groups, organizations, and communities.

Competency 8: Intervene With Individuals, Families, Groups, Organizations, and Communities. Social workers understand that intervention is an ongoing component of the dynamic and interactive process of social work practice with, and on behalf of, diverse individuals, families, groups, organizations, and communities. Social workers are knowledgeable about evidence-informed interventions to achieve the goals of clients and constituencies, including individuals, families, groups, organizations, and communities. Social workers understand theories of human behavior and the social environment, and critically evaluate and apply this knowledge to effectively intervene with clients and constituencies.

Competency 9: Evaluate Practice With Individuals, Families, Groups, Organizations, and Communities. Social workers understand that evaluation is an ongoing component of the dynamic and interactive process of social work practice with and on behalf of diverse children and youth, families, groups, organizations, and communities. Evaluation of processes, outcomes, and practice helps social workers to identify, assess, and monitor service delivery effectiveness and measure outcomes that promote healthy youth development. Social workers understand culturally responsive methods and policies guided by human behavior theories and conceptual frameworks that evaluate outcomes and findings to improve practice effectiveness with individuals, families, groups, organizations, and communities that shape healthy development of all youth.

Appendix 2B
Case Studies

Case Study Objectives

- Students will apply theoretical perspectives to case studies giving special attention to the influence of diversity characterized by (but not limited to) age, gender, class, race, ethnicity, and culture;
- Students will identify theories, policies, and practices that may guide understanding of clients in relation to human behavior and empirical knowledge to case studies;
- Students will develop important linkages between theory, practice, policy, and research, specifically in evaluating biopsychosocial factors that impinge on human behavior and the functioning across micro, mezzo, and macro contexts.

Case Study 1

Chris is a 16-year-old who has been referred to you from his high school academic counselor. He has been chronically absent from school, which is not typical of him prior to COVID-19 academic school year. Prior to the COVID-19 school shutdown he had a great relationship with his academic counselor, good attendance and grades. After schools reopened Chris's academic counselor, teachers, and classmates noted that he was often absent and disengaged from school.

Several of his classmates teased him for always wearing a hoodie, and he finally said, "Screw this" and walked out of class.

His teacher sent him to the guidance counselor. Upon discussion, Chris said he had been chronically absent because he and his mom are homeless. Chris showed the counselor that he had a stained white t-shirt under his hoodie and was embarrassed to take off his hoodie. He stated that last week he did not have access to a washer and dryer and shared that he has an upcoming court hearing with his probation officer.

Chris is an only child. His mother is raising him as a single mother while his father is in prison. He has a good relationship with his mother despite the various hardships. He and his mother currently live in his mother's old SUV truck. His father was a former prominent gang member. His mother lost her job and home during COVID-19 and they lived with his grandma for a short period. A consultation with his mother confirms that they are homeless and that she is worried that Chris has been hanging around the wrong crowd. The mother stated that she has witnessed gang members trying to recruit him. She is worried that her financial situation makes her son an easy target.

Chris also discloses that he has been approached to join a gang by his childhood friends and he has been thinking a lot about dropping out of school over the past year. During COVID-19 and financial hardships, his childhood friends helped him with getting access to money, food, and clothing. He is aware that they are gang members but feels a strong brotherhood connection with them and trusts that they will keep him safe from danger and hunger. His mother works two jobs and is often away at work. His mother does not approve of his relationship with his childhood friends, but Chris is thankful for them helping him. Growing up he wanted to be the first member of his family to hold a high school diploma and become a plumber. Chris wants to be a plumber because he likes to work with machinery and make a decent salary.

Chris has been spending most of his time over the past few weeks anxious and trying to decide. He is not interested in joining because he does not want to end up like his father, but his primary support, particularly in regard to his mother's financial situation, is his childhood friends. His father has been in jail throughout most of his childhood, and Chris really misses him.

1. What are the risk and protective factors Chris exhibits in this case?
2. Using the Family Hierarchy Model, discuss how you guide him through this crisis? How might you expect Chris to feel/think?
3. What support systems can be put in place to support Chris and prevent the escalation of isolation?

These guiding questions allow the instructor an opportunity to frame the discussion with students. A 30-minute session will allow an opportunity to explore domains that provide a core set of lenses through which students may analyze how people develop and function across a spectrum of micro to macro social systems (e.g., individual, family, social group/network, organizational/institutional, community, cultural, and temporal), and how these systems promote or impede health, well-being, and resiliency.

Case Study 2

Cindy is a 16-year-old who has been referred to you by her math teacher after being absent for two consecutive weeks. She has been chronically absent from school, which is not typical of her. Prior to the COVID-19 school shutdown her attendance and grades were in good standing. After schools reopened Cindy's teachers and classmates noted that she was often absent and not engaged.

Cindy is the middle child and has two sisters. Her parents are undocumented immigrants from El Salvador and work long hours in low-skills jobs. Cindy reports that she is four months pregnant and is contemplating dropping out of school. Her parents and boyfriend are supportive of her pregnancy but are pressuring her to drop out of school to contribute to the household. A consultation with her parents confirms that they believe that she needs to withdraw from school to support her baby and the household. Unfortunately, money is tight, her mother lost her job, and her father works two part-time jobs. Cindy has also shared that recently her mother appears depressed and is easily irritated, making it hard to communicate with her mother.

She does not want anyone on campus to find out she is pregnant. She is embarrassed of her situation because Cindy believes that people will judge her. Cindy stated that her mother was a teen mom too and admires her for putting family first. By dropping out of school Cindy feels it will help her family be more financially stable. Cindy's boyfriend also supports her decision to withdraw from school so she can take care of their baby.

Her older sister dropped out of high school and is currently a store manager at a local market store. Cindy says her sister has promised to hire her part-time after giving birth so she can contribute to household expenses. Prior to getting pregnant Cindy's dream was to be the first member in her family to graduate high school and attend college. She wanted to graduate college and be an entrepreneur.

Cindy has been spending most of his time over the past few weeks crying and trying to find an answer to her situation. She is struggling with her dreams of continuing her academic career, current financial situation, and pregnancy. Cindy feels overwhelmed and hopeless with her financial and pregnancy situation that she thinks of giving up on school and started preparing herself to have her baby.

1. What support systems can be put in place to support Cindy and prevent the escalation of isolation?
2. What other mental health resources and government benefits can this family access?
3. What prenatal and other health care can be accessed by Cindy?

These guiding questions allow the instructor an opportunity to frame the discussion with students. A 30-minute session will allow an opportunity to explore domains that provide a core set of lenses through which students may analyze how people develop and function across a spectrum of micro to macro social systems (e.g., individual, family, social group/network, organizational/institutional, community, cultural, and temporal), and how these systems promote or impede health, well-being, and resiliency.

Appendix 2C
Theories

Theories help social workers understand complex human behaviors, person-in-environment, social environments, and provide a biopsychosocial perspective that serves as a lens to better address children and youth mental health issues and guide the design interventions. Social workers may draw from theories and perspectives to better understand what may drive and motivate people throughout various stages of life. Human behavior theories help health and human service practitioners understand behaviors, analyze cases, comprehend clients, develop interventions, assess interventions, and identify solutions.

Table 2.1 Significant Theories in Child and Adolescent Development

Theory	*Description*	*Tenets*	*Author*
Attachment Theory	Attachment Theory provides a framework to understand the psychological and biological aspects of human behavior, stress processes, and regulation. Developmental and psychotherapeutic change may also be attributed to Bowlby's emphasis on the integration of psychological and biological models to understand human behavior.	• Secure; • Avoidant, Dismissing; • Ambivalent/Resistant, Preoccupied.	John Bowlby
Behavioral Theory	Behavioral Theory seeks to explain human behavior by analyzing the person-in-environment perspective and how antecedents and consequences present in the individual's environment impact the learned associations acquired through previous experiences. The theory connects behavior and how a person will repeat an action without realizing they have been conditioned to do so.	• Respondent conditioning; • Operant conditioning; • Stimulus response.	B. F. Skinner and Ivan Pavlov

Biopsychosocial Assessment Theory	Human development and the social environment may be understood through the application of a biopsychosocial assessment and provides a framework for social workers to develop clinical assessments and interventions. Utilizing the biopsychosocial framework model urges social workers to become aware of the application and inclusive use of three complexities: biological, psychological, and social.	• Bio (physiological pathology); • Psycho (thoughts, emotions, and behaviors such as psychological distress, fear/avoidance beliefs, current coping methods and attribution); • Social (socio-economical, socio-environmental, and cultural factors such as work issues, family circumstances, and benefits/economics).	George Engel
Cognitive Behavior Theory	Cognitive Behavior Theory is the basis for Cognitive Behavioral Therapy (CBT) which is an evidenced-based approach that focuses on the idea that if an individual can change the way they think, they can change the way they feel. CBT highlights the role of the client and therapist to work together to identify and reframe negative thought processes and goals by replacing them with positive and healthier ways of thinking about these things.	• Requires engaged and positive client-therapist relationship; • Highlights collaboration and active participation; • Emphasizes goal-oriented and is problem-focused.	Aaron Beck, Albert Ellis, Donald Meichenbaum
Emotional Intelligence Theory	The Emotional Intelligence Theory focuses on the ability to monitor one's own and other's emotions, and to discriminate among them. This theory also depicts the importance of using the information to guide one's thinking and actions.	• Self-awareness; • Self-management; • Social awareness; • Social skills.	Daniel Goleman, William James, Carl Lange

(Continued)

Table 2.1 (Continued)

Theory	*Description*	*Tenets*	*Author*
Maslow's Hierarchy of Needs	Maslow stated that people are motivated to achieve certain needs and that some needs take precedence over others. This hierarchy suggests that individuals are motivated to fulfill basic needs before moving on to other, more advanced needs.	• Physiological needs (water, food, shelter); • Security and safety needs (financial security, health/wellness, safety); • Social needs (friendships, family relationships, community/social groups); • Esteem needs (respect and appreciation of others, accomplishment, personal worth); • Self-actualization needs (self-aware, personal growth, achieve full potential).	Abraham Maslow
Resilience Theory	In social work, resilience may be understood as one's ability to do better than expected in the face of adversity. Adversity rarely takes form in an isolated incident and may also arise from chronic conditions and stressors.	• Promotes competence and improving health; • Helps individuals overcome adversity and navigate life stressors; • Boosts the ability to grow and survive.	Norman Garmezy

Psychodynamic Theory	Freud believed human behavior could be explained by forms outside of a person's awareness that explain why they behave a certain way. This theory uses a "global" approach and focuses on deep rooted drives, needs, and desires – a person's emotions versus a person's behaviors – and highlights three parts to personality: the id, ego, and superego.	• Unconscious motivations such as social pressure, biology, and psychology can affect behavior; • Experience shapes personality, which can, in return, affect an individual's response to that experience; • Past experiences affect the present.	Sigmund Freud
Psychosocial Development Theory	Eight-stage life cycle theory that assumes the environment forms self-awareness, adjustment, human development, and identity. This theory suggests that ego identity is achieved by facing goals and challenges throughout the eight stages of development, during the life cycle.	Eight stages of psychosocial development: • *Trust vs. Mistrust* – birth–18 months; • *Autonomy vs. Shame and Doubt* –18 months–3 years; • *Initiative vs. Guilt* – ages 3 years–5 years; • *Industry vs. Inferiority* – ages 5 years–12 years; • *Identity vs. Role Confusion* – ages 12 years–18 years; • *Intimacy vs. Isolation* – ages 18 years–40 years; • *Generativity vs. Stagnation* – ages 40 years–65 years.	Erik Erickson

(*Continued*)

Table 2.1 (Continued)

Theory	*Description*	*Tenets*	*Author*
Social Learning Theory (Social Cognitive Theory)	Individuals learn social behaviors through observation and imitation of others. Social Learning Theory utilizes a social context lens that highlights that people learn from observing each other.	• People learn through observations; • Rewards/punishments have indirect effects on behavior and learning; • Mediational processes influence behavior; • Learning does not always lead to change.	Albert Bandura
Adverse Childhood Experiences	An Adverse Childhood Experience (ACE) is a negative or traumatic event that occurs before a person reaches 18 years of age. As the number of ACEs increase, the risk for emotional and behavioral disorders also increases.	• Abuse (emotional, physical, or sexual); • Neglect, either physical or emotional; • Domestic violence; • Substance abuse by a member of the household; • Divorce or separation of parents/caregivers; • Mental illness of a member of the household; • Having a member of the household go to prison.	The Centers for Disease Control and Prevention (CDC)

Developmental Assets Framework	The framework of Developmental Assets is a theory-based model linking features of ecologies and context (external assets) with personal skills, capacities, and values (internal assets), guided by the hypothesis that external and internal assets are dynamically interconnected.	• Internal assets focus on social–emotional strengths, values, and commitments, such as positive identity and values, social competencies, and commitment to learning; • External assets center on the relationships and opportunities that youth need in their families, schools, and communities, such as support, empowerment, boundaries and expectations, and constructive use of time.	Peter Benson, Peter Scales, Search Institute
Life Course Theory	Life Course Theory (LCT) offers social work practitioners an innovative approach to address complex factors that foster healthy development of youth and promote a thriving productive society. LCT explores factors such as biological to environmental and individual to community as an attempt to analyze patterns that shape overall health and well-being, encouraging health equity and social and economic justice.	• Time and place; • Life span development; • Timing; • Agency; • Linked lives.	Karl Mannheim

(*Continued*)

Table 2.1 (Continued)

Theory	*Description*	*Tenets*	*Author*
Risk and Protective Factors Theory	Risk and protective factors are the outlooks of an individual or group and the environment and life experiences that make it more likely (risk factors) or less likely (protective factors) that people will develop a problem or achieve an outcome. Risk factors are characteristics at the biological, physical, family, community, or cultural level associated with a higher likelihood of negative outcomes. Protective factors are characteristics associated with a lower likelihood of negative outcomes and may be seen as positive countering events.	• Protective and risk factors may be internal to the individual child/youth or may be qualities of their contexts such as family, school, and community; • Protective factors include positive attitudes, conflict resolution skills, good health, positive self-esteem, success at school, and strong social support; • Risk factors include substance abuse, poverty, homelessness, anti-social behavior, presence of neighborhood crime, low self-esteem, negative attitude, academic problems, lack of parental supervision, undiagnosed mental health problems.	David Hawkins, Richard Catalano

Critical Race Theory	The Critical Race Theory (CRT) serves as a multicultural approach to serving clients. Social work educators and students should utilize the CRT to promote a multicultural approach to disrupt social, racial, health, and economic disparities in the United States. Individuals are encouraged to practice self-awareness and be mindful of personal and cultural views, biases, and their own perspective.	• Critique of liberalism; • Storytelling and "naming one's own reality"; • Standpoint epistemology; • Revisionist interpretations of American civil rights law and progress; • Intersectionality; • Essentialism vs. anti-essentialism; • Structural determinism, and race, sex, class, and their intersections; • Cultural nationalism/ separatism; • Legal institutions, critical pedagogy, and minorities in the bar.	Derrick Albert Bell Jr., Richard Delgado, Kimberle Crenshaw

(*Continued*)

Table 2.1 (Continued)

Theory	*Description*	*Tenets*	*Author*
Ecological Systems Theory	Ecological systems provide a conceptual framework that explains the functions of various systems on increasing understanding of complex experiences to create intentional multi-system interventions and promote behavioral health for children and youth. Overall, it provides opportunities to increase cross collaboration among individuals, systems, and policies to improve outcomes for youth and encourages social work professionals to utilize a dual lens focused on person and environment.	• *Microsystem:* family, school, religious institutions, neighborhood, and peers; • *Mesosystem*: interconnections between the microsystems; • *Exosystem:* links between social settings; • *Macrosystem:* geographic location, socio-economic status, poverty, and ethnicity; • *Chronosystem:* pattern of environmental events and transitions over the life course.	Urie Bronfenbrenner
Family Systems Theory	Family Systems Theory focuses on the family as an emotional unit. Family development and behavior are analyzed, interlocking patterns of a relationship system the family exhibits.	• Family members are intensely emotionally connected; • Each family member plays a significant role and must follow certain rules; • Each family member's behavior impacts the other members; • Behavioral patterns can lead to balance or dysfunction of the system.	Murray Bowen

Rational Choice Theory	Rational Choice Theory lies in the belief that individuals are in control of their personal decisions; rational considerations are made upon weighing the costs/benefits.	• Individual preferences; • Beliefs; • Constraints.	Adam Smith
Social Exchange Theory	People make decisions by consciously and unconsciously measuring the costs and benefits of an action, seeking the maximized reward.	• Humans tend to seek out rewards and avoid punishments; • A person begins an interaction to gain maximum profit with minimal cost – the individual is driven by "what's in it for me?"; • Individuals tend to calculate the profit and cost before engaging. Finally, the theory assumes that people know that this "payoff" will vary from person to person, as well as with the same person over time.	George Homans
Systems Theory	Systems Theory utilizes a dual lens focused on person and environment. It is an interdisciplinary study of systems, and the key concept is that the whole is greater than the sum of its parts.	• A complex system is made of many smaller systems; when these smaller systems interact, a complex system is produced.	Ludwig von Bertalanffy

3 Close the Health Gap

Jennifer Lewis, Ron Manderscheid and Amelia Roeschlein

Introduction and Background of Grand Challenge

For almost four decades, attention has focused on the development and implementation of national policy around integrated care. More recently, these efforts became codified in national policy with the passage of the Patient Protection and Affordable Care Act (ACA) in 2010 (Manderscheid & Kathol, 2014). Now, more than a decade later, it seems clear that integrated care has taken root throughout the United States and that it will become the preferred care arrangement going forward. Thus, integrated care will be an important vehicle for addressing the Grand Challenges for Social Work focused on disparities in both health and well-being. In view of the current unprecedented times of a global pandemic and major social unrest, health inequity of Black and Indigenous people of color, it seems clear that social workers can and will play a major role.

Field efforts to implement integrated care have taught several important lessons (Manderscheid & Kathol, 2014). Among them is the observation that behavioral healthcare currently does not have a work force that is well prepared to function in an integrated care environment. Frequently, behavioral health providers lack training in working on a team and in care integration functions essential for an effective integrated care program. Both are skills that are part of social work education.

Transdisciplinary medicine and training are one of the AASWSW recommendations for treating those with mental health, substance use, and corresponding addictive illness (Fong et al., 2018). Integrated care facilitates the achievement of goals that cannot be reached when individual professionals act on their own. Transdisciplinary education and collaborative practice competencies (IPEC, 2016) were designed to promote the development of team-based healthcare identities. A key

DOI: 10.4324/9781003308263-4

component of these identities is development of individual and team-based competencies to work collaboratively with all other health professions. The goal of these competencies is to support the quadruple aim of increasing the quality of patient care, improving population health, reducing costs, and increasing staff satisfaction and healthy work environments (Berwick et al., 2008; Hales et al., 2017).

Today, behavioral healthcare is in crisis. COVID-19 has doubled the prevalence of behavioral health conditions in the United States from 20 to 40% of adults (Reinert et al., 2021). At the same time, the capacity of the behavioral healthcare system has not increased – the size of the workforce remains essentially the same. The net effect is that only about one-quarter of those with behavioral health conditions are being reached with care today, compared with about one half prior to the COVID-19 pandemic. All these constraints portend continuing and growing health disparities due to differences in behavioral health status, access to behavioral healthcare, and varied health outcomes as a result of behavioral healthcare received. As has been known for some time, these disparities exist across racial and ethnic lines, gender and sexual identity, and income.

Social Determinants of Health

Research has shown that only a small proportion of health is determined by healthcare: Only 10–20% of variations in health and mortality are related to healthcare quality and access, and 50% of variations in health and mortality are related to Social Determinants of Health (SDOH) (Braveman & Gottlieb, 2014). Improvement in overall health metrics depends – at least in part – on attention to factors upstream from the clinical encounter. Further motivated by the shift towards value-based payments that incentivize prevention and improved health and healthcare outcomes. The healthcare sector must play a role in mitigating adverse SDOH to achieve more equitable health outcomes.

Transdisciplinary Training

To provide effective care, transdisciplinary or multidisciplinary training of the processionals who provide care is a critical component. Like integrated care itself, this framework is linked to tenets implemented in the ACA in 2010, the importance of public health metrics, and the Institute for Healthcare Improvement's Quadruple Aims described earlier (Hales et al., 2017; IPEC, 2016).

Transdisciplinary domain competencies, applied in conjunction with behavioral health knowledge and skills, prepare all health professions' trainees to collaborate effectively within the changing healthcare environment and service delivery systems focused on enhancing individual, family, and population health. A central feature of transdisciplinary training is that each team member is exposed to foundations of health, chronic illness management, addictive illness, and mental health training (Little, 2010). On a continuum of healthcare teams, the transdisciplinary team works together for a common purpose, as they make different, complementary contributions to client-focused care (Hunt et al., 2016). Borrill and Haynes (2000) found that teams with greater occupational diversity reported higher overall effectiveness. The innovations introduced by these teams were more radical and had significantly more impact both on the organization and on client care. When students and trainees from "different fields work and train side by side, there is hope that they may practice differently, consult each other more often, and perceive each other in a less hierarchical fashion" (Beck, 2005, p. 218). Results from several studies show that healthcare may be more effective in certain professional groups (Waltmann et al., 2012). By learning the principles of transdisciplinary care during their training, social workers will learn how to use a team to provide comprehensive care for their patients, while addressing environmental and social determinants of health, no matter what the patient's motivation level is towards health outcomes (Nandiwada & Dang-Vu, 2010).

Closing the Health Gap in Social Work Curricula

The Institute of Medicine (IOM) has observed that current educational models in healthcare fail to bring together students from diverse disciplines, so they can learn each other's strengths, weaknesses and potential contributions (IOM, 2001). Currently, there is a large gap between research and healthcare education practice; joint approaches between addiction, physical health, and psychiatric providers barely exist (Davis et al., 2015) despite calls for scientific innovations that require multidisciplinary collaboration in education such as National Science Foundation. These problems are compounded by the limitations of some disciplines (Davis et al., 2015), limited understanding of the roles and expertise of other professionals (IOM, 2001), increased requirements for accountability and documentation (Hughes et al., 2016), and complex diagnoses and treatment methods (Schlesinger, 2004).

Less than 30% of schools have any formal transdisciplinary experiences in their residencies or practicums (Nandiwada & Dang-Vu, 2010). Although scattered transdisciplinary training programs exist, they operate almost exclusively within professional schools, and have yet to be systematically integrated into formal educational curricula at either the undergraduate or graduate levels. This lack of systematic education in transdisciplinary science reinforces what has been referred to as the "siloed" nature of research and hinders the transfer of knowledge across disciplines (Gehlert, 2016). Courses on integrated healthcare have been encouraged by the Council on Social Work Education (CSWE). Launched in 2012, the Social Work and Integrated Care Project was a partnership initiative that infused integrated behavioral health and primary care into master's level social work education. The initiative began as a collaborative project between CSWE and the National Association of Deans and Directors of Schools of Social Work and has continued with leadership from the National Council for Mental Wellbeing. Since the initiative was launched, more than 30 schools of social work have agreed to offer a course in integrated care that introduces social work students to the direct practice of integrated behavioral health in primary care. Students develop skills in engagement, assessment, intervention planning and implementation, and practice evaluation. Additionally, integrated health policy courses focus on the role of the "social policy practitioner" in assisting individuals in the maintenance or attainment of optimal health and mental health, social and economic justice, and recovery and wellness. Not unlike healthcare, however, the education of our students is often most often conducted in a siloed manner without transdisciplinary faculty in the social work classroom or social work faculty teaching in other graduate or medical school programs, contributing to or reinforcing attention to the systemic barriers that hold the wicked problem of the health gap in place. A social work program and related courses which promote transdisciplinary collaboration and provide the skills necessary for intervention on the micro practice domains, mezzo organizational level and macro policy and advocacy levels are required to prepare social work students to participate and lead healthcare and social change.

Re-envisioned Transdisciplinary Education in Social Work

As is the case with all intractable social problems, it is beholden on social work educators and administrators to consider how siloed education reinforces the problem. Creating opportunities for dual enrollment of students from other professions such as nursing, public health, medicine, pharmacy, and addiction *and* incorporating faculty from other professions would greatly enhance the educational discourse within the classroom and foster depth of knowledge from the beginning of the educational journey rather than having to unlearn intra-professional behaviors.

Teaching Practices in the Targeted Domains

Social work competence is the ability to integrate and apply social work knowledge, values, and skills to practice situations in a purposeful, intentional, and professional manner to promote human and community well-being (CSWE, 2022). Holistically, the overall objective related to integrative health is for students to have the requisite skills to synthesize the theoretical and methodologic approaches of different disciplines to be better prepared to address the complexities of health and mental health problems. Learning outcomes may include how to navigate within and between disciplines.

Competencies and Student Learning Outcomes

Under the guidance of the World Health Organization, the Health Professions Accreditors Collaborative, and the National Center for Interprofessional Practice and Education, endorsed by Counsel on Social Work Education, have released *Guidance on Developing Quality Interprofessional Education for the Health Professions* (World Health Organization, 2010). The guidance includes:

- Competency 1, Values/Ethics for Interprofessional Practice: Work with individuals of other professions to maintain a climate of mutual respect and shared values.
- Competency 2, Roles/Responsibilities: Use the knowledge of one's own role and those of other professions to appropriately assess and address the healthcare needs of patients and to promote and advance the health of populations.
- Competency 3, Interprofessional Communication: Communicate with patients, families, communities, and professionals in health and other fields in a responsive and responsible manner that supports a team approach to the promotion and maintenance of health and the prevention and treatment of disease.
- Competency 4, Teams, and Teamwork: Apply relationship-building values and principles of team dynamics to perform effectively in

different team roles to plan, deliver, and evaluate patient/population-centered care and population health programs and policies that are safe, timely, efficient, effective, and equitable.

Learning outcomes for transdisciplinary training in social work should relate to CSWE 2022 competencies (i.e., Educational Policy and Accreditation Standards, EPAS). Please see Appendix 3A for updated 2022 EPAS (CSWE, 2022).

Positioned within practice courses, student Learning Objectives include increasing students' competence in selection of evidence-informed interventions based on biopsychosocial perspectives, deepening understanding of individuals' and families' culture ethnicity, gender, sexual orientation, and other salient factors, as well as advancing students' ability to apply practice interventions that have been supported by research by demonstrating effective practice in integrated care settings, including an examination of the strengths and limitations of the interventions in working with diverse groups. These approaches cannot be effectively taught without also integrating the mezzo organizational and macro societal systemic issues impacting care. Courses which provide space for integration of these multi-systemic concepts should be identified as the gold standard of social work education.

Teaching Practices

To achieve support students' mastery of interprofessional competencies, learning activities are optimized when they are integrated into the existing curriculum, spanning the entire length of the program (i.e., from classroom-based to practicum).

STUDENT ENGAGEMENT

For students of one profession to learn about and from another, students having the opportunity to engage and build meaningful relationships in the context of shared work is critical to the success of student preparedness. Principles of adult learning, engagement for understanding perspectives and exchange of information, are important features for facilitating quality programs. Examples of learning activities include problem-based learned and case collaboration. Transdisciplinary education is perhaps best accomplished through didactic and experiential teaching methods (Gehlert, 2016). Learning activities can take place outside the formal classroom or clinical setting to achieve program goals. Examples include service-learning activities, student-run clinics, and student participation in interprofessional seminars and conferences. The University of California, San Diego, for example, provides transdisciplinary student training in three community clinics for vulnerable patients. These community experiences afford trainees the opportunity to practice their classroom learning in real-world healthcare settings. As part of their training program, trainees participate in a daily "learning circle" in which everyone reflects on what they learned in the clinic that day.

COURSE CONTENT AND MATERIALS

Independent learning, online or traditional (e.g., reading assignments), have been proposed as a mechanism to acquire knowledge about other health professions and interprofessional collaborative practice. Examples include watching videos detailing roles/responsibilities of other professions or completing readings which address the complex, often co-occurring biopsychosocial needs of the clients. Addressing medication adherence and retention in care can be addressed by collaborative (between providers) prioritization of patient needs, something that often falls on the patient currently negatively impacting outcomes.

Technology can be a valuable tool for expanding the program capacity through the use of case scenarios, vignettes, or experiential simulation laboratories to create real-world examples of patient problems. If COVID-19 has highlighted anything about our current delivery system, it is that asking people to come to a clinic or a hospital is not always the best approach. Education that supports creative opportunities for transdisciplinary care delivered at home, virtually, will better prepare students to address a post-COVID world where health disparities thrive in under-resourced communities.

COURSE FACILITATION

To ensure that students' professional identities are shaped via simultaneous exposure to experiences that promote interprofessional socialization and extracurricular, clinical learning activities, students may be exposed to transdisciplinary faculty experiences. The emergence of a dual identity, as a member of a distinct profession and as a member of an interprofessional team, allows graduates to contribute their unique professional expertise to team-based care. This may be difficult for universities who have cost structures that de-incentivize cross-disciplinary collaboration and must be negotiated to meet the emerging demands of the scientific and healthcare environment. There is opportunity for social work to redefine its own professional identity as transdisciplinary and join faculty in other departments such as Public Health, Medicine, Nursing and Pharmacy.

ADDRESSING POWER, DIVERSITY, EQUITY, AND INCLUSION

Interprofessional education can be an antidote to longstanding interprofessional conflict and power struggles often fraught with underlying implicit biases. Communication and conflict resolution skills toward the joint goal of providing patient-centered care that are often promoted in IPE (Paradis & Whitehead, 2015) fall short in addressing societal inequity around race and gender, impacting collaboration. Sample activities (IPE Collaborative, 2016) include:

- Develop complex case scenarios that represent different identities and the health or educational disparities that individuals with these identities have experienced. As we review these cases, we need to be explicit in highlighting the effects of discrimination and inequity on decision-making and outcomes of care delivery.
- Examine the power and privilege of different professional roles – and how these roles impact the formation of IPE teams and communication with one another, and the individuals served by those teams.
- Identify ethical issues facing IPE teams when interacting with different cultural groups around decision-making and implementation of assessment and treatment options. Always ensure that the patient/family perspective is brought into focus, paying special attention to issues that provide insight into their values.
- Describe instances of racism in healthcare and in our own discipline. Be honest and forthright in considering these perspectives, and allow learners to offer personal, programmatic, or systemic solutions that could impact change.
- Provide examples of IPE teams successfully and unsuccessfully demonstrating dignity, respect, and inclusion in their interprofessional practice – and offer multiple opportunities to identify those behaviors that led to equitable outcomes.
- Role-play attitudes and practices that contribute to disparities in service delivery. Develop simulation.

EVALUATION OF LEARNING

Learner assessment serves various purposes, including providing feedback to individual students and teams to promote their own learning and improvement; determining levels of competency to meet requirements for grading or certification; and providing aggregate data for interprofessional education evaluation and scholarly research. Robust learner assessment would combine a variety of self-reported, instructor-observed, and objective measures. Such assessment would also provide qualitative feedback as well as comparative performance data to learners. The field of measurement in Interprofessional Education is growing. There are many good instruments with evidence of validity that program leaders and faculty can choose from in designing their assessment strategy. Examples include those reviewed by Thannhauser et al. (2010), such as, the Readiness for Interprofessional Learning Scale (Mattick et al., 2009), and the Interdisciplinary Education Perception Scale (Luecht et al., 1990).

Conclusion and Areas for Further Teaching/Curricular Considerations

A transdisciplinary training model has direct implications to treatment and can be used as an innovative treatment paradigm. Shown to have efficacy in other fields (e.g., engineering), the transdisciplinary training model may be particularly useful to improve health outcomes and well-being among highly traumatized individuals living with co-occurring mental, physical, and addictive health issues. The syndemic nature of these conditions requires a more comprehensive treatment approach that can address the complexity of multiple diseases. In other words, just as illnesses are not separate, seeing providers separately and teaching students separately may not provide the therapeutic effect for patients with complex conditions.

Preliminary data (Reinert et al., 2021) from the impact of the COVID-19 pandemic is showing us that integrated health organizations (those that provide physical and behavioral health services such as Certified Community Behavioral Health Clinics) appear to have managed the rapid transition to the virtual space more successfully. The practices that had clear integrated behavioral health pathways already established, including screening protocols and care pathways in place, tended to transition to telehealth services more easily. Integrated providers of behavioral health services (either in primary care or in an established, ongoing referral and care coordination process with outside primary care providers) are reporting that they were able to maintain these protocols, even when moving to telehealth. The stronger the partnerships are in team-based care services between physical health and behavioral health providers/staff, the more likely they are able to continue to serve and track clients. This includes flagging clients who are worsening in their conditions and utilizing behavioral health staff in new ways, such as protocols or scripted safety screening and "caring contacts." The caring contact approach is when staff check in with clients to see how they are doing, as well as address care gaps and/or encourage people to make appointments with their primary care provider for chronic diseases. By working as a team with primary care, mental health providers can collaborate to address distress behaviors due to COVID-19.

Organizational and policy-driven systems (such as expanded telehealth) that were previously resistant to change discovered they could be flexible and more agile than ever before. Agencies that utilized a transdisciplinary approach found themselves in the unique situation where they were able to design workflows and client care strategies that they previously believed were not possible.

As we plan, we must recognize that COVID-19 forced agencies to address the conflicting and competing needs of clients, staff, best practices, and fiscal stewardship. Educational institutions and schools of social work must now do the same. Along with the tens of thousands of deaths in the United States from the virus, COVID-19 overlays the growing epidemic of deaths of despair threatening to make an already significant problem even worse (Brookings, 2017). A preventable surge of avoidable deaths from drugs, alcohol, and suicide is ahead of us if the country does not begin to invest in solutions that can help heal the nation's isolation, pain, and suffering (Well Being Trust, 2020).

Team-based care and training, especially primary and behavioral healthcare, has historically been fragmented. The result has been that individuals have had to work harder to get the care they need, and often that care is not delivered in a timely or evidence-based fashion. By taking stock of the current crisis, predicting potential loss of life and creatively deploying local community solutions, it may be possible to prevent the impending surge of avoidable deaths from drugs, alcohol, and suicide. This is an opportunity to move towards solutions that bring behavioral health education to the next generation of social workers, into the center of all our discussions on COVID-19 response and recovery (Well Being Trust, 2020).

References

Beck, E. (2005). The UCSD student-run free health clinic project: Transdisciplinary health professional education. *Journal of Health Care for the Poor and Underserved*, *16*(2), 207–219.

Berwick, D. M., Nolan, T. W., & Whittington, J. (2008). The triple aim: Care, health, and cost. *Health Affairs*, *27*(3), 759–769. doi:10.1377/hlthaff.27.3.759.

Borrill, C., & Haynes, C. (2000). Managers' lives. Stressed to kill. *The Health Service Journal*, *110*(5691), 24–25.

Braveman P., & Gottlieb, L. (2014, January–February). The social determinants of health: It's time to consider the causes of the causes. *Public Health Reports*, *129*(Suppl 2), 19–31. doi: 10.1177/00333549141291S206. PMID: 24385661; PMCID: PMC3863696.

Brookings Papers on Economic Activity. (2017). www.brookings.edu/bpea-articles/mortality-and-morbidity-in-the-21st-century/

CSWE. (2022). *2022 Educational policy and accreditation standards*. www.cswe.org/accreditation/standards/2022-epas/

Davis, T. S., Guada, J., Reno, R., Peck, A., Evans, S., Sigal, L. M., & Swenson, S. (2015). Integrated and culturally relevant care: A model to prepare social workers for primary care behavioral health practice. *Social Work in Health Care*, *54*(10), 909.

Fong, R., Lubben, J. E., & Barth, R. P. (2018). *Grand challenges for social work and society*. Oxford University Press.

Gehlert, S. (2016). Social work and science. *Research on Social Work Practice*, *26*(2), 219–224. https://doi.org/10.1177/1049731515570138

Hales, T. W., Nochajski, T. H., Green, S. A., Hitzel, H. K., & Woike-Ganga, E. (2017). An association between implementing trauma-informed care and staff satisfaction. *Advances in Social Work*, *18*(1), 300–312.

Hughes, A. M., et al. (2016). Saving lives: A meta- analysis of team training in healthcare. *Journal of Applied Psychology © 2016 American Psychological Association*, *101*.

Hunt, C. M., Spence, M., & McBride, A. (2016). The role of boundary spanners in delivering collaborative care: A process evaluation. *BMC Family Practice*, 17, 6. doi:10.1186/s12875-016-0501-4

Interprofessional Education Collaborative. (2016). *Core competencies for interprofessional collaborative practice: 2016 update*. www.ipecollaborative.org/ipec-core-competencies

Institute of Medicine (IOM). (2001). *Crossing the quality chasm: A new health system for the 21st century*. National Academy Press.

Little, V. (2010). Transdisciplinary care: Opportunities and challenges for behavioral health providers. *Journal of Health Care for the Poor and Underserved*, *21*(4), 1103–1107.

Luecht, R. M., Madsen, M. K., Taugher, M. P., & Petterson, B. J. (1990). Assessing professional perceptions: Design and validation of an interdisciplinary education perception scale. *Journal of Allied Health*, *19*(2), 181–191.

Manderscheid, R. W., & Kathol, R. (2014). Fostering sustainable, integrated medical and behavioral health services in medical settings. *Annals of Internal Medicine*, *160*(1), 61–65.

Mattick, K., Bligh, J., Bluteau, P., & Jackson, A. (2009). Readiness for interprofessional learning scale. *Interprofessional Education Making it Happen*, *125*, 142.

Nandiwada, D., & Dang-Vu, C. (2010). Transdisciplinary health care education: Training team players. *Journal of Health Care for the Poor and Underserved*, *21*, 26–34.

Paradis, E., & Whitehead, C. R. (2015). Louder than words: Power and conflict in interprofessional education articles, 1954–2013. *Medical Education*, *49*(4), 399–407.

Reinert, M., Fritze, D., & Nguyen, T. (2021, October). *The state of mental health in America 2022*. https://mhanational.org/sites/default/files/2022%20State%20of%20Mental%20Health%20in%20America.pdf

Schlesinger, M. (2004). Editor's note: On government's role in the crossing of chasms. *Journal of Health Politics, Policy and Law*, *29*(1), 1–10. Duke University Press.

Thannhauser, J., Russell-Mayhew, S., & Scott, C. (2010, July). Measures of interprofessional education and collaboration. *Journal of Interprofessional Care*, *24*(4), 336–349. doi:10.3109/13561820903442903. PMID: 20540613.

Waltmann, E., et al. (2012, August). Comparative effectiveness of collaborative chronic care models for mental health conditions across primary, specialty, and behavioral health care settings: Systematic review and meta-analysis. *American Journal of Psychiatry*, *169*(8), 790–804.

Well Being Trust. (2020). https://wellbeingtrust.org/areas-of-focus/policy-and-advocacy/reports/projected-deaths-of-despair-during-covid-19/

World Health Organization. (2010). *Framework for action on interprofessional education and collaborative practice*. http://apps.who.int/iris/bitstream/10665/70185/1/WHO_HRH_HPN_10.3_eng.pdf?ua=1

Appendix 3A

EPAS Addressed in Grand Challenge #2

Close the Health Gap

Competency 1: Demonstrate Ethical and Professional Behavior. Social workers understand the value base of the profession, as well as the role of other professionals when engaged in interprofessional practice. By engaging in interprofessional education and practice, social workers model and apply the National Association of Social Workers Code of Ethic, impacting racial and economic and environmental justice, and health disparities. Further, the implicit curriculum is supported through transdisciplinary education which allows faculty to function as appropriate role models for student learning and socialization into the discipline and profession.

Competency 2: Advance Human Rights and Social, Racial Economic, and Environmental Justice. Social workers are knowledgeable about the global and intersecting and ongoing injustices throughout history that result in oppression and racism, including the social worker's role and response. Interprofessional education attends to the social determinants of health by training social workers to attend to the abuse of power and privilege, advocate for health as a human right, and engage in practices that promote human rights.

Competency 4: Engage in Practice-Informed Research and Research-Informed Practice. Social workers understand that evidence that informs practice derives from multidisciplinary sources and multiple ways of knowing. They also understand the processes for translating anti-racist and inclusive research findings into effective practice and policy. To eliminate the health gap, it is paramount that health disparities are addressed through integrative and transdisciplinary practice, and evaluation.

Competency 5: Engage in Policy Practice. Social Workers recognize that healthcare policy, its formulation, analysis, implementation, and evaluation within the practice settings affect the delivery or a, access to health and social services. Transdisciplinary education and training support critical thinking to analyze, formulate, and advocate for policies that advance human rights and eliminate health disparities.

4 Build Healthy Relationships to End Violence

Bianca Harper and L. Debbie Murad

Introduction

The primary goal of *Build Healthy Relationships to End Violence*, one of the 13 Grand Challenges for Social Work, is to strengthen healthy relationships through universal, targeted interventions that interrupt and ultimately prevent interpersonal violence (American Academy of Social Work and Social Welfare [ASWSW], 2020). Interpersonal violence refers to any violent act by a person(s) against another person(s). Interpersonal violence results in or has a high likelihood of resulting in physical injury, psychological harm, developmental challenges, or death (World Health Organization [WHO], n.d.). Interpersonal violence takes many forms, including, but not limited to, child maltreatment, intimate partner violence, family violence, gender-based violence, physical assault, sexual assault, elder abuse, community violence, and homicide. While interpersonal violence encompasses many types of violence and extends beyond the family unit, this chapter focuses on two specific types of interpersonal violence – child maltreatment and intimate partner violence. This chapter provides an overview of child maltreatment and intimate partner violence, best practices to promote healing and improved relational health, and curricular recommendations to support student knowledge and skill acquisition.

Child Maltreatment

Child maltreatment is a pervasive public health issue that affects families around the world. Child maltreatment is defined as abuse and neglect that occurs before 18 years of age (WHO, n.d.). Types of child maltreatment include physical abuse, emotional abuse, sexual abuse, neglect, and exploitation. Parents are the most common perpetrators of child maltreatment. In 2016, 78% of child maltreatment

DOI: 10.4324/9781003308263-5

perpetrators were parents (Child Trends, 2019). After parents, other trusted adults in the child's life are most likely to engage in child maltreatment. Due to the perpetrator usually being a trusted adult in the child's life, the impact of child maltreatment is complex and multifaceted. Experiences of child maltreatment result in harm across developmental domains and family systems.

Prevalence and Current Trends

A national longitudinal study examining child maltreatment from 2009–2017 found that physical abuse and sexual abuse decreased over the last decade, while neglect has remained relatively stable (Child Trends, 2019). According to the World Health Organization (WHO), two out of three children, under the age of 4, have experienced physical abuse and/or psychological abuse and one in five girls and one in 13 boys have experienced sexual abuse. These global statistics highlight the pervasiveness of child maltreatment internationally (WHO, n.d.). Nationally, approximately 700,000 children experience maltreatment annually (National Children's Alliance, 2019). In the United States, younger children, from birth to 3, experience child maltreatment at three times the rate of adolescents (Child Trends, 2019) and one in four girls and one in seven boys will experience sexual abuse as a child or adolescent (National Child Traumatic Stress Network [NCTSN], n.d.). It is important to consider that prevalence rates are based on reported cases made to child welfare organizations. Therefore, prevalence rates are not representative of the many child maltreatment survivors who do not report and/or who do not come to the attention of child welfare. Additionally, current trends are reflective of substantiated and indicated child maltreatment cases, meaning that only those that met the child welfare criteria for child maltreatment or those where child maltreatment was suspected, are included in national data samples (Child Trends, 2019).

Intimate Partner Violence

Intimate partner violence (IPV) is a pattern of assaultive and coercive behaviors that take place in an intimate relationship. It can include physical, sexual, emotional, and psychological abuse and stalking behavior. It is a pattern of control perpetrated by one partner towards the other. The pattern is systematically intimidating, manipulative, frightening, and harmful (Centers for Disease Control [CDC], n.d.). It develops gradually and intensifies over time. Threats become more dangerous and eventually even life threatening. Over time, the victim, also referred to here as the survivor, becomes trapped by the experience (Peterson, 2020). Leaving such relationships becomes dangerous, often even more dangerous than staying. It may feel impossible to leave. There is the physical fear of trying to leave the relationship, but also the financial fear of being left without resources, as the perpetrator may have total financial as well as emotional control (VAWA Report to Congress, 2018). It is important to understand the types of abuse so that the pattern can be recognized. All types of abusive relationships can cause pain, fear, and even physical harm. However, it is the emotional abuse, which is always present, which amplifies the more severe outcomes such as PTSD which can occur even in the absence of physical abuse (National Coalition Against Domestic Violence [NCADV], 2015).

Prevalence and Current Trends

To understand the extent of the problem, ten million men and women are abused by an intimate partner in the US per year, three-quarters of whom are women ([NCADV, 2020). One in four women and one in nine men experience severe intimate partner physical violence, intimate partner sexual violence, and/or intimate partner stalking with impacts such as injury, fearfulness, post-traumatic stress disorder, use of victim services, contraction of sexually transmitted diseases, etc.

Intimate partner violence can occur in any dating relationship, marriages, among teenagers, same-sex couples – male and female, and can continue into later years (elderly couples). Approximately ten million people are affected by intimate partner violence yearly (Huecker & Smock, 2020). Intimate partner violence is gender based in that it effects more women than men.

> According to the CDC, 1 in 4 women and 1 in 7 men will experience physical violence by their intimate partner at some point during their lifetimes, and 1 in 3 women and nearly 1 in 6 men experience some form of sexual violence.
>
> (Huecker & Smock, 2020, para. 23)

The rates of IPV within LGBT relationships matches the rates of heterosexual relationships at 25%. Men-on-men abuse is more common than female to male. Transgender people experience the highest rates and are more than two times as likely to experience IPV.

Developmental Impact

Neurobiological

Over the past two decades, numerous studies have examined the biological response to acute and chronic stress and the correlation between complex trauma (e.g. child maltreatment and intimate partner violence) and negative health outcomes (childtrauma.org). Complex trauma survivors have difficulty experiencing and modulating affective states. This affect dysregulation can make it incredibly difficult to tolerate and cope with emotional distress.

Psychosocial

Child maltreatment and intimate partner violence survivors face a myriad of complex relational stressors that can have lasting effects on their ability to develop and sustain healthy relationships. Due to the betrayal of trust and the violated relation connection associated with child maltreatment and intimate partner violence, survivors often struggle with feelings of ambivalence towards the perpetrator. For example, a maltreated child may be fearful but protective of the perpetrator. Children have difficulty understanding why someone who is supposed to protect them and keep them safe is hurting them.

These complex attachment dilemmas lead to immense difficulty for child maltreatment and intimate partner violence survivors to feel emotionally and physically safe, and to develop and utilize adaptive coping skills. For interpersonal violence survivors, social connections are lost or severed, creating more dependence on the abuser. Survivors with limited social support struggle with coping and are less likely to engage in services to foster healing (Peterson, 2020). Additionally, survivors are less likely to possess self-efficacy and engage in help-seeking behavior (Huecker & Smock, 2020; NCTSN, n.d.), increasing vulnerability for mental health struggles, sustained isolation, and polyvictimization (NCTSN, n.d.; Peterson, 2020).

Intersecting Stressors/Adversity/Trauma

Child maltreatment and intimate partner violence survivors often live in home environments where multiple and chronic stressors (e.g. financial concerns, housing instability, health issues, substance use, family violence) exist. Additionally, survivors may live in communities where violence is common and community support is limited. These factors increase the likelihood of survivors engaging in maladaptive coping and risk-taking behavior, thereby increasing their vulnerability to experience ongoing adversity and traumatic stress (NCTSN, n.d.; Substance Abuse and Mental Health Services Administration [SAMHSA], 2014).

Health Impact

The relationship between adverse childhood experiences (e.g. child maltreatment and intimate partner violence) and physical health is well documented (Felitti et al., 1998), as is the connection between psychological and somatic symptoms associated with experiencing a traumatic event (National Child Traumatic Stress Network [NCTSN], n.d.; SAMHSA, 2014). Intimate partner violence survivors report a range of negative physical health outcomes that are both acute and chronic in nature. Approximately 35% of female survivors and 11% of male survivors (typically from male partners) will experience physical injuries (e.g. broken bones, internal injuries, and traumatic brain injuries) (Huecker & Smock, 2020; Zieman et al., 2017).

Policy

Numerous policies and programs exist to support child maltreatment and intimate partner violence prevention and intervention. The Victims of Crime Act (VOCA) is a federal fund that is distributed to states to fund victim services including child maltreatment and intimate partner violence programs (Office for Victims of Crime [OVC], n.d.). The Child Abuse Prevention and Treatment Act (CAPTA) provides federal funds to support states in preventing, identifying, and reporting child maltreatment as well as focusing on child maltreatment protective factors (Child Welfare Information Gateway, n.d.). The Children's Bureau is an office of ACYF that supports programs, research, and monitoring systems that prevent child maltreatment while ensuring that child maltreatment survivors receive treatment and support (Children's Bureau, n.d.).

The Violence Against Women Act (VAWA) is the first federal legislation acknowledging intimate partner violence and sexual assault as a crime and provides specific protections for victims of intimate partner violence, particularly undocumented immigrants. VAWA includes the U-Visa and T-Visa. The U-Visa provides a visa opportunity for undocumented victims of crime. The 2013 reauthorization provided for greater protections funding for services for Native American and LGBTQ survivors (National Network to End Domestic Violence [NNEDV], 2017).

The Family Violence Prevention and Services Act (FVPSA), first enacted in 1984, is the first federal legislation to provide funding for traditional intimate partner violence services including shelters, 24-hour crisis lines, and programs for communities throughout the United States (NNEDV, 2017).

Restraining Orders

All states have a protection order allowance for intimate partner violence survivors and their children. They include protections against stalking, harassment, text messaging, etc. The degree of protections varies by state (VAWnet.org, 2015).

Prevention

Child maltreatment and intimate partner violence are best addressed through both universal and targeted services. Prevention services provide education, as well as outreach for identification purposes. A coordinated system of care that encompasses healthcare, law enforcement/legal services, social services, and the educational system is necessary. A multifaceted and strategic approach is needed to identify families at risk for child maltreatment/intimate partner violence and to provide the family with meaningful support that promotes healthy relationships and family safety. Universal home visiting nursing programs have been shown to be effective with prevention and early detection and intervention. These programs are designed to provide short term home nursing care to pre- and post-partum women and their families. In the United States, such programs are targeted to economically disadvantaged communities but in other countries (throughout Europe, including Denmark and Great Britain), such services are universal and very effective (Health Services and Resources Administration [HRSA], 2017). They are administered by the federal government through HRSA.

Patterns of abuse are learned, providing an avenue for prevention. Family relational norms that contribute to the likelihood of child maltreatment and/or intimate partner violence occurring must be addressed. Perpetrators grow up in households of intimate partner violence 80% of the time. These patterns are observable at a young age when children turn to bullying, animal abuse, perpetuating conflict in the service of a maladaptive attempt to feel a sense of control where they have no control (Basile et al., 2007).

Teachers and other school staff are in an optimal position to prevent, identify, and assist students experiencing child maltreatment and/or exposure to intimate partner violence because of their frequent contact with students. School-based child maltreatment prevention programs are comprised of psychoeducation programs to help school personnel recognize, detect, identify, and report child maltreatment as well as prevention programs aimed to educate students about body safety and child maltreatment (Child Welfare Information Gateway, n.d.). Social-emotional learning curriculum in schools is another avenue for prevention of intimate partner violence. Other preventative options with promising results include teaching youth about safe and healthy relationships, providing social-emotional learning programs for young people and providing healthy relationship programs for young couples.

A wraparound approach involving interdisciplinary team members (i.e. healthcare providers, child welfare, schools, mental health, law enforcement, courts, etc.) is necessary so risk factors can be monitored and addressed, and protective factors can be identified and built upon. Finally, child maltreatment and intimate partner violence prevention efforts must challenge stigma that reinforces silence. Through community psychoeducation, children and families are educated and encouraged to come forward if they or someone they know have experienced child maltreatment or intimate partner violence.

Intervention

Due to the nuanced and complex experiences of child maltreatment survivors and intimate partner violence survivors, interventions must be carried out by trained professionals and within the context of trauma-informed care. Trauma-informed care (TIC) is an intentional way of providing services that *realizes* the impact of trauma, *recognizes* the symptoms of trauma, *responds* by integrating trauma knowledge and *resists* re-traumatization (SAMHSA, 2014). Organizations that intentionally and consistently utilize trauma-informed practices are more likely to experience improved client engagement due to creating an environment that is conducive to clients feeling safe, valued, and heard, thereby increasing the likelihood for healing to occur for individuals, families, and communities.

Many services exist to promote healing for survivors of child maltreatment. In mental health settings, trauma-focused interventions are utilized with the child and non-offending caregiver. These evidence-based approaches help child maltreatment survivors establish safety plans, process trauma memories, identify trauma triggers, and develop coping skills (NCTSN.org). Trauma-focused mental health services may also include peer psychoeducation and/or support groups for survivors and psychoeducation and/or support groups for non-offending caregivers.

Additionally, numerous school-based prevention programs (e.g. Play It Safe! Speak Up Be Safe, Stop It Now) exist that focus on educating students, families, and staff about child maltreatment (Child Welfare Information Gateway, n.d.). When families are brought to the attention of child welfare organizations, services focus on enhancing family safety. Parents are referred to services (e.g. parenting classes, mental health services, substance abuse treatment, employment, and housing support) that increase their likelihood of being able to parent effectively and provide physical and emotional safety to their child(ren), therefore decreasing the risk of child maltreatment.

Varied intervention services exist to address intimate partner violence. There are residential and non-residential counseling services, 24-hour emergency hotlines, legal services and family justice centers and batterer's programming. The traditional, and still typical, program model for intimate partner violence includes emergency and transitional shelters, outpatient counseling and case management and legal services that include advocacy and direct legal representation. Effective mental health interventions include trauma-informed, evidence-based practices such as Cognitive Behavioral Therapy (CBT), Cognitive Processing Therapy (CPT), Trauma Recovery and Empowerment Model (TREM), and Seeking Safety (National Center on Domestic Violence, Trauma and Mental Health, n.d.; Conduent, n.d.a, n.d.b, n.d.c).

Healthcare professionals, often nurses, are usually the first professionals to encounter intimate partner violence; 50% of female survivors seeking emergency room services report a history of abuse (Huecker & Smock, 2020). Healthcare professionals can provide an opportunity for early screening and detection, brief education, and warm referrals.

In addition to interventions for survivors of intimate partner violence, treatment programs exist for intimate partner violence perpetrators. The standard treatment for perpetrators (also "batterers") includes a 52-week group program, referred to as Batterers Intervention Programs or BIPs (Voith et al., 2020). Most attend because of some sort of legal mandate, and a minute percentage do so voluntarily. The BIPs provide education to support cognitive and behavioral change among perpetrators to reduce and eliminate the violence and controlling behaviors towards survivors (Voith et al., 2020).

Challenges

Family Adversity

Intergenerational trauma plays a significant role in family dynamics as parents tend to parent the ways in which they were parented. For example, if a parent grew up in a home where child maltreatment and/or family violence was normalized, they are more likely to model these behaviors with their own children. Similarly, children learn how to treat intimate partners based on the relational norms that were modeled within their family system. While these relational norms can be changed, children who grow up in homes where they were maltreated and/or witnessed intimate partner violence are more likely to experience intimate partner violence in their relationships with intimate partners (Carlson et al., 2019). Children are more likely to experience child maltreatment when there is intimate partner violence and/or parental substance use (Victor et al., 2018).

Limited Help-Seeking Behavior

The dynamics of child maltreatment and intimate partner violence promote silence as victims may be told to keep it a secret and/or be threatened by the abuser or other family members if they were to disclose the abuse. Additionally, the survivor may experience feelings of guilt and shame associated with the maltreatment that contributes to the secrecy of the abuse. These issues are difficult to detect and address if the victim suffers in silence and is not able to seek support and if concerns are not identified by stakeholders (e.g. school personnel, healthcare providers, childcare staff, community service providers, family members, etc.).

Inadequate Trauma Knowledge and Training

Stakeholders who do not possess a working knowledge of relational trauma may be unable to appropriately identify and support survivors of child maltreatment and intimate partner violence. When trauma knowledge is absent, stakeholders do not recognize trauma symptoms or trauma triggers and understand how trauma symptoms may manifest through behavior. Without this critical knowledge, stakeholders may have an inaccurate understanding of why a survivor is acting out and respond inappropriately, further exacerbating the problem.

Victim Blaming

Victims blame themselves. Perpetrators blame victims. Family often blames victims, and the courts and legal systems often blame victims by its actions. It must be understood that perpetrating abuse or experiencing it at the hands of others is not a "pathology" in that the rates are too high for that. Rather it needs to be seen as patterns of behavior that are imbedded in our society.

Intersectionality

Survivors from disenfranchised communities have greater burdens to bare. Survivors of color are subjected to implicit and explicit racism. Families of color are less likely to report crimes, disclose abuse, and engage in community-based services (Saykeo & Lawrence, 2018). Previous negative experiences with systems (e.g. law enforcement, courts, child welfare) create doubt and hesitancy to seeking support. Intimate partner violence survivors who identify as LGBTQ are less likely to seek services than heterosexual survivors (Vasquez & Houston-Kolnik, 2019). Undocumented families are less likely to report child maltreatment and/or intimate partner violence, due to fear of deportation repercussions (Sabina et al., 2015). Poverty traps those survivors already living life at the poverty line, as escaping intimate partner violence often leads to homelessness.

Opportunity to Lead Interprofessional Efforts

Due to a multifaceted skillset, social workers are uniquely positioned to foster and facilitate efforts to work within and across service sectors. By utilizing a social work lens (e.g. strengths- based perspective, ecological framework) and practice skills (e.g. empathy, validation, attunement, cross-sector collaborative skills), social workers are able to develop rapport, model relationship building, and promote trust, all of which are critical to developing and sustaining interdisciplinary partnerships.

Social workers are prepared to take on the leadership of improving interdisciplinary team responses to child maltreatment/intimate partner violence through more comprehensive training, screening, brief intervention, and service referral. Social workers are trained in interprofessional skills and can be a bridge to better service delivery across service sectors.

Social workers can also enhance awareness, prevention and intervention activities by joining the many coalitions available at the local, state, and national level. States, cities, and counties have coalitions and networks where child maltreatment/intimate partner violence advocates, legal service providers, health and mental healthcare workers, child welfare workers and first responders such as law enforcement and firefighters come together to address a coordinated response to child maltreatment/intimate partner violence within and across the various systems, to inform and promote child maltreatment/intimate partner violence-related policies and practices. These coalitions provide training to community members and agencies, network on behalf of survivors, and change systems to better address the structural inequalities that perpetuate interpersonal violence.

Teaching Strategies for One Domain: Practice

Objective: Promoting Safety and Self-Efficacy

While instructors can utilize a variety of teaching strategies to effectively teach practice skills, a multimodal approach is helpful to meet both the diverse learning styles of students and enhance student understanding of complex issues associated with child maltreatment and intimate partner violence. Teaching strategies may include incorporating case vignettes, role plays, videos, and guest lectures from survivors. While this is certainly not an exhaustive list, these strategies promote opportunities for experiential learning and skill application which is meaningful for students as it assists them in bridging the gap between course content and practice.

Learning Objectives

1. Students will be able to contextualize their understanding of child maltreatment and intimate partner violence.
2. Students will develop practice skills to effectively support survivors of child maltreatment and intimate partner violence.
3. Students will apply practice skills to address multifaceted interpersonal violence issues.
4. Students will develop skills that can be utilized within and across service sectors and lead the way to address and ultimately prevent child maltreatment and intimate partner violence.

Setting the Context

Prior to introducing the topic of interpersonal violence, it is imperative that the instructor lets students know that child maltreatment and intimate partner violence will be discussed in the course and the potential impact (e.g. emotional distress) the content could have on the student. Additionally, guidance regarding how the instructor will manage the content and support students who struggle with the topics of child maltreatment/intimate partner violence should be clearly articulated. This information should be shared at the beginning of the course, both in the syllabus and verbally, and in the week leading up to child maltreatment/intimate partner violence being discussed. The purpose of this is twofold. It provides students with the opportunity to cognitively and emotionally prepare for the content and voice questions and/or concerns about the upcoming content. Secondly, it allows the instructor to assess the readiness of students to delve into child maltreatment and intimate partner violence content and any identified concerns can be discussed prior to the content being discussed in class. Zosky (2013) found that social work students fared better in courses addressing trauma-related content when the instructor prepared them (verbally and in writing) that heavy and potentially triggering content was going to be discussed in the course.

Managing Difficult Class Discussions

Instructors must thoughtfully prepare for teaching child maltreatment/intimate partner violence content as it often involves difficult classroom conversations that students will have varied thoughts and feelings about based on personal and professional experiences rooted in cultural and systemic values. The range of student responses will have an impact on the overall group dynamic, requiring the instructor to be equipped to manage both the discussion of child maltreatment/intimate partner violence content and student reactions to the content. Some potential challenges associated with teaching this content is one being triggered due to their own history of trauma, individual or collective bias that may surface, and assumptions/stereotypes that perpetuate stigma associated with intimate partner violence. Additionally, these challenges may also be experienced by the instructor, adding to the difficulty of delivering intimate partner violence content while simultaneously recognizing and supporting student needs.

Amidst these challenges is the opportunity for teachable moments. For example, through processing/debriefing, the instructor can model how to manage difficult content and support individuals and groups who are experiencing a range of emotions. The instructor can also model vulnerability and how to utilize social work skills (e.g. empathy, validation, and normalization) in real time. Furthermore, the instructor can facilitate a self-reflection exercise that can further promote processing and enhance self-awareness.

Evaluation of Learning

Child maltreatment/intimate partner violence knowledge can be assessed using targeted benchmarks (i.e. written assignments, class presentations, case analysis, experiential learning exercises) that require students to apply best practices and demonstrate skill acquisition. Additionally, please see the CSWE (2022) competencies (i.e., Educational Policy and Accreditation Standards, EPAS) that could be considered in this context (Appendix 4A).

Course Material for One Class: Safety Planning

Safety planning is essential when working with child maltreatment/intimate partner violence survivors and is implemented throughout the course of the social worker-client relationship. Central to their experiences is the absence of psychological and physical safety. As a result, survivors often struggle with emotional distress, coping difficulties, and informed decision-making. Safety planning provides survivors with specific steps they can take to enhance psychological and physical safety, which promotes emotional stabilization, the capacity to utilize adaptive coping skills, and increased likelihood of engaging in help-seeking behavior. Survivors are encouraged to identify and build upon their strengths and plan for a safe future.

The social work skills needed to competently assist child maltreatment/intimate partner violence survivors with safety planning are multifaceted. Students will need to apply core social work skills to promote engagement (e.g., empathy, validation, and normalization of the client experience) to develop positive rapport. Additionally, students need to be able to utilize their social work lens that includes a strength-based, ecological, and client-centered approach that demonstrates to the client that safety planning is a collaborative process led by the client.

Social Justice Perspective

As students learn about the safety planning process and engage in experiential learning opportunities, it is critical that the issues (e.g.

stigma, structural inequalities, cultural bias, developmental impact, relational dynamics, contextual nuances) discussed in the first section of this chapter inform their approach to safety planning and understanding the client's experience.

While safety planning is critical for survivors of child maltreatment and intimate partner violence, the process of safety planning with a child maltreatment survivor versus an intimate partner violence survivor is distinctly different. When safety planning with a child maltreatment survivor, the objectives of the safety plan include identifying who the safe adults are in their life, how to seek support from those adults when needed, and steps for psychological stabilization when they experience a child maltreatment trigger. The safety plan is developed collaboratively between the survivor, a non-offending caregiver, and a service provider and revisited as needed to ensure the plan aligns with the survivor's wishes, strengths, and needs. The safety plan is consistently utilized in trauma treatment to promote psychological stabilization which is necessary for healing. The goals of safety planning with intimate partner violence survivors are to prevent further injuries, and to help the survivor to feel that they are active and engaged in the process, rather than immobilized by it. Effective safety planning is flexible, as plans vary with situations and could quickly change. The material shared for this class session will focus on safety planning with survivors of intimate partner violence.

After learning the definitions of intimate partner violence and the different types of abuse, students can begin practicing simple screening tool exercises with short vignettes. The purpose is to develop some comfort in asking the questions. They may feel the questions are intrusive and offensive and avoid asking the difficult questions. Intimate partner violence is often considered a private family matter and this belief can be triggered in clinicians. If they are hesitant in their screening, then survivors will not be forthcoming.

The initial step in supporting intimate partner violence survivors is to assess and promote safety. There are several screening tools that help with this. The Hurt, Insult, Threaten, and Scream (HITS) is a brief physical and psychological abuse screening tool that is effective for use with women and men (Sherin et al., 1998). The Woman Abuse Screening Tool (WAST) (Brown et al., 1996) is another commonly used and reliable screening tool. The tool has seven questions and is considered inobtrusive, as it begins by exposing "tensions" in the relationships and then moves on to abusive patterns. If survivors are unaware that their relationship is abusive, this provides a gentle lead into that knowledge.

Screening is important as survivors are often reluctant to disclose their abuse. When asked direct questions, however, they are more likely to report it. It is important that the clinician firsts build rapport and a sense of safety within the help setting. It is also important for the clinician to have a level of comfort with the subject matter. The clinician will also need to normalize the routine nature of the screening questions, due to high rates of intimate partner violence. Then, with direct questioning, the survivor is more likely to disclose their situation. Upon completing the screening, the danger assessment must be applied to understand the level of danger facing the survivor. The danger assessment is a tool that determines the level of danger and potential lethality of the abuser. Once that is complete, a safety plan can be developed (Peterson, 2020).

Highlights of Lecture Material for One Class – Safety Planning: An Ongoing Intervention

After completing the intimate partner violence screening and danger assessment, the clinician will then work with the survivor on a safety plan. They will help the survivor understand their level of danger in the relationship and assess what in their life contributes to safety. For example, in a physically violent and potentially lethal relationship, the clinician will explore who supports the survivor's well-being. Then, if an explosive episode appears to be transpiring, the survivor may plan a temporary escape to a friend or family member's house until it passes. They may have an emergency kit readily available that they can grab and go. They may have money stashed to help with emergency housing, if needed. This can be planned in detail and written down and put in a safe place. There are many useful templates for these safety plans, also available in multiple languages. The National Coalition to End Intimate Partner Violence (NCADV, n.d.) provides a template and also provides a useful safety plan for family, friends, and co-workers.

Most safety plans involve a long-term process of assessing healthy coping skills, supportive individuals, and improving upon financial self-sufficiency and access to resources. The clinician will first explore who are the people providing support and validation. They will be encouraged to spend more time with those individuals. This will break the isolation and expand their safety net. The clinician will assess coping skills and encourage the increased use of safe, healthy coping skills. Survivors struggling financially will be supported to increase their access to resources by a number of means. They may enter or re-enter the workforce and generate a source of income. They may be encouraged to seek more training or skills that support higher earning. They may be provided referrals to public assistance or other resources for housing or legal services. There will be an initial safety plan which will be adjusted throughout the relationship with the survivor.

Conclusion

This chapter provides an overview of two types of interpersonal violence, child maltreatment and intimate partner violence, and delves into the complexity of these issues at the micro, mezzo, and macro levels. Interpersonal violence can have a traumatic effect on the life span development of survivors, families, and communities. To effectively address interpersonal violence, a focus must be on developing healthy relationships, improving physical and mental health, and addressing oppressive inequalities that affect overall well-being. With specialized curriculum development that emphasizes experiential learning, social work students are well positioned to utilize their skills to develop and facilitate targeted assessments and evidence-based interventions, foster and lead interdisciplinary collaborations, and advocate for policy development/reform that meets the nuanced needs of interpersonal violence survivors.

References

American Academy of Social Work and Social Welfare (ASWSW). (2020). *Grand challenges of social work*. https://grandchallengesforsocialwork.org/build-healthy-relationships/

Basile, K. C., Hertz, M. F., Back, S. E. (2007). *Intimate partner violence and sexual violence victimization assessment instruments for use in healthcare settings: Version 1*. Centers for Disease Control and Prevention, National Center for Injury Prevention and Control.

Brown, J., Lent, B., Brett-MacLean, P., Sas, G., & Pederson, L. (1996). Development of the woman abuse screening tool for use in family practice. *Family Medicine*, *28*, 422–428.

Carlson, J., Voith, L., Brown, J. C., & Holmes, M. (2019). Viewing children's exposure to intimate partner violence through a developmental, social-ecological, and survivor lens: The current state of the field, challenges, and future directions. *Violence Against Women*, *25*(1), 6–28.

Child Trends. (2019). www.childtrends.org/indicators/child-maltreatment

Child Welfare Information Gateway. (n.d.). www.childwelfare.gov/

Children's Bureau. (n.d.). www.acf.hhs.gov/cb

Conduent. (n.d.a). *Promising practices: Trauma recovery and empowerment model (TREM)*. https://cdc.thehcn.net/promisepractice/index/view?pid=864

Conduent. (n.d.b). *Promising practices: Seeking safety*. https://cdc.thehcn.net/promisepractice/index/view?pid=864

Conduent. (n.d.c). *Trauma-focused cognitive behavioral therapy*. https://cdc.thehcn.net/promisepractice/index/view?pid=864

CSWE. (2022). *2022 Educational policy and accreditation standards*. www.cswe.org/accreditation/standards/2022-epas/

Felitti, V. J., Anda, R. F., Nordenberg, D., Williamson, D. F., Spitz, A. M., Edwards, V., & Marks, J. S. (1998). Relationship of childhood abuse and household dysfunction to many of the leading causes of death in adults: The adverse childhood experiences (ACE) Study. *American Journal of Preventive Medicine*, *14*(4), 245–258.

Health Services and Resources Administration (HRSA), Maternal and Child Health Branch. (2017). *Home visiting state fact sheets*. https://mchb.hrsa.gov/Maternal-child-health-initiatives/home-visiting/home-visiting-program-state-fact-sheets

Huecker, M. R., & Smock, W. (2020, October 15). *Domestic violence*. StatPearls Publishing. NIH. www.ncbi.nlm.nih.gov/books/NBK499891/

National Center on Domestic Violence, Trauma and Mental Health. (n.d.). *NCDVTMH online repository of trauma-focused interventions for survivors of intimate partner violence*. www.nationalcenterdvtraumamh.org/publications-products/ncdvtmh-online-repository-of-trauma-focused-interventions-for-survivors-of-intimate-partner-violence/

National Child and Adolescent Traumatic Stress Network. (n.d.). *Complex trauma*. www.nctsn.org/what-is-child-trauma/trauma-types/complex-trauma

National Children's Alliance. (2019). *National statistics on child abuse*. www.nationalchildrensalliance.org/media-room/national-statistics-on-child-abuse/

National Coalition Against Domestic Violence. (2015). *Facts about domestic violence and psychological abuse*. https://assets.speakcdn.com/assets/2497/domestic_violence_and_psychological_abuse_ncadv.pdf

National Coalition Against Domestic Violence. (2020). *Domestic violence*. https://assets.speakcdn.com/assets/2497/domestic_violence-2020080709350855.pdf?1596811079991

National Network to End Domestic Violence. (2017). *FVPSA funding*. https://nnedv.org/content/family-violence-prevention-services-act/

Office for Victims of Crime. (n.d.). https://ovc.ojp.gov/

Peterson, C. (2020). *Interpersonal aggression: Complexities and intimate partner abuse*. Wheatmark Publications.

Sabina, C., Cuevas, C. A., & Zadnik, E. (2015). Intimate partner violence among Latino women: Rates and cultural correlates. *Journal of Family Violence*, 35–47.

Saykeo, S. P., & Lawrence, E. (2018). Factors that affect help-seeking: Examining racial differences between Whites, Asians, and African Americans. *Modern Psychological Studies*, *24*(1), Article 8. https://scholar.utc.edu/mps/vol24/iss1/8

Sherin, K. M., Sinacore, J. M., Li, X. Q., Zitter, R. E., & Shakil, A. (1998). HITS: A short domestic violence screening tool for use in a family practice setting. *Family Medicine*, *30*(7), 508–512.

Substance Abuse and Mental Health Services Administration. (2014). *Trauma-informed care in behavioral health services. Treatment improvement protocol (TIP) Series 57. HHS Publication No. (SMA) 13–4801*. Substance Abuse and Mental Health Services Administration.

Vasquez, A. L., & Houston-Kolnik, J. (2019). *Victimization and help-seeking experiences of LGBTQ+ individuals*. Illinois Criminal Justice Information Authority. https://bit.ly/37VidXT

VAWnet.org. (2015). Overview of restraining orders. *WomensLaw.org*. https://vawnet.org/sc/overview-protection-orders

Victor, B. G., Grogan-Kaylor, A., Ryan, J. P., Perron, B. E., & Gilbert, T. T. (2018). Domestic violence, parental substance misuse and the decision to substantiate child maltreatment. *Child Abuse & Neglect*, *79*, 31–41. https://doi.org/10.1016/j.chiabu.2018.01.030

Voith, L. A., Logan-Greene, P., Strodthoff, T., & Bender, A. E. (2020). A paradigm shift in batterer intervention programming: A need to address unresolved trauma. *Trauma Violence Abuse*, *21*(4), 691–705. doi:10.1177/1524838018791268

World Health Organization. (n.d.). *Child maltreatment*. www.who.int/

Zieman, G., Bridwell, A., & Cárdenas, J. F. (2017, February 15). Traumatic brain injury in domestic violence victims: A retrospective study at the barrow neurological institute. *Journal of Neurotrauma*, *34*(4), 876–880.

Zosky, D. L. (2013). Wounded healers: Graduate students with histories of trauma in a family violence course. *Journal of Teaching in Social Work*, *33*(3), 239–250.

Appendix 4A

EPAS Addressed in Grand Challenge #3

Build Healthy Relationships to End Violence

Competency 1: Demonstrate Ethical and Professional Behavior. Social workers understand the values and ethical standards of the profession. Social workers are expected and taught to apply these standards to their interventions addressing intimate partner violence and child maltreatment. To effectively serve this population, social workers must value the safety and humanity of the population.

Competency 2: Advance Human Rights and Social, Racial, Economic, and Environmental Justice. IPV is considered a human right, social/racial/economic justice issue and this is expressed throughout the chapter. To provide effective interventions, social workers are grounded in the philosophy of advancing such rights. A core practice includes advocating for human rights.

Competency 3: Engage Anti-Racism, Diversity, Equity, and Inclusion (ADEI) in Practice. Social workers are taught that injustice based upon race and diversity permeates IPV. To be effective with any IPV client requires a subtle understanding of ADEI in practice. For instance, a survivor of abuse may never consider leaving a partner based on cultural values. It is incumbent upon a social worker to safety plan accordingly, and with compassion and understanding.

Competency 4: Engage in Practice-Informed Research and Research-Informed Practice. Social workers are taught the research and practice recommendations that supports the need for specific training on IPV and child maltreatment as well as effective interventions. For example, it would be unsafe and potentially lethal to attempt any couples' work with couples engaged in domestic abuse. This is clearly indicated by the research and practice.

Competency 5: Engage in Policy Practice. Social workers understand the role of social policies in shaping current practices with IPV. Social workers are encouraged to contribute to research that informs policies and to apply critical thinking to advocate for policies that advocate human rights that enhance protections for survivors of abuse.

Competency 6: Engage With Individuals, Families, Groups, Organizations, and Communities. Social workers are encouraged to utilize this competency comprehensively including having knowledge of the person-in-environment, using empathy, reflection, and interpersonal skills to engage in culturally responsive practices with survivors of IPV and child maltreatment.

Competency 7: Assess Individuals, Families, Groups, Organizations, and Communities. Social workers are encouraged to complete comprehensive assessments for health, mental health, and level of intimate partner violence and child maltreatment.

Competency 8: Intervene With Individuals, Families, Groups, Organizations, and Communities. Social workers are encouraged to engage and provide tested interventions to individuals and groups. Interventions provided to families are done with caution and typically involve the IPV/child maltreatment survivor, non-offending caregiver, and other family members as appropriate.

Competency 9: Evaluate Practice With Individuals, Families, Groups, Organizations, and Communities. Evaluation of practice helps social workers to assess whether their work with survivors of IPV and child maltreatment is effective. Several tools are utilized to measure safety, which can be re-evaluated at regular intervals.

5 Advancing Long and Productive Lives

Murali Nair and Elise Marie Collins

Introduction

Globally, people are living longer than ever before as the proportion of older people in the world rises and continues to rise in the coming decades. To quantify, there were 703 million people over age 65 worldwide in 2019, and this number is projected to double by 2050 to roughly 1.5 billion (United Nations, 2019). In the United States, specifically, the number of adults over 65 is projected to grow to over 20% of the total national population by 2050, while in 1900, when the field of Social Work was just beginning, the number of adults over 65 in the US was 3.1 million and just 4% of the country's total population.

The Grand Challenge of Advancing Long and Productive Lives aspires to ensure that older adults age actively and productively, remaining healthy and engaged in their communities. This Grand Challenge also creates the historic imperative that all people in society age well – not just the privileged and wealthy. Older adults in the 21st century face many and varied challenges. A view of this time of life as merely one of physical decline obscures the opportunities and magnificence that are also a part of growing older. Although greater chronological age has correlated with declining health (Lowsky et al., 2014), the rate at which people age and remain healthy or less healthy can vary greatly (National Institute on Aging, 2022). A large percentage of adults over 65 are healthy and active with many remaining so well into their 80s, 90s, and beyond. It is a smaller percentage of older adults, in fact, who face chronic illnesses and disabilities and need some form of caregiving or assistance. Aging is not equitable, and an individual's social environment is the greatest predictor of longevity and health span. Addressing health-span and life span inequities are focal challenges in Advancing Long and Productive Lives. For example, "The

DOI: 10.4324/9781003308263-6

concept of 'productive aging' puts forward the fundamental view that the capacity of older adults must be better developed and utilized in activities that make economic contributions to society" (Gonzales et al., 2015). When older adults provide tangible goods and services, both paid and unpaid, there is a positive impact on the economy and on the well-being of these older adults.

Older Adults – Social Work Opportunities

Working with older adults around the world presents a tremendous opportunity for social workers and other older adults who interact with them. Advancing Long and Productive Lives emphasizes that the growing number of older adults will create new opportunities and reshape what it means to grow old both in the United States and around the world.

Supporting the older population to experience a productive and healthy "Elderhood," a word adopted by geriatrician and *New York Times* bestselling author of the book *Elderhood, Redefining Aging, Transforming Medicine, and Reimagining Life* (Aronson, 2021), will offer social workers new jobs. However, as inequities based on socio-economic status, gender, sexual preference, and race create cumulative disadvantages throughout the life course, older people are not aging equally (Dannefer, 2003). Social workers are in a unique position to support equity within the aging population to catalyze the Grand Challenge of Advancing Long and Productive Lives.

One groundbreaking longitudinal study showed that people with a positive attitude about aging lived, on average, 7.5 years longer than those with a negative self-perception of aging (Carney & Nash, 2020; Levy et al., 2002). Ageism against older adults has been called the last socially acceptable "ism" and is a "prejudice against your feared future self" (Nelson, 2005, p. 207). Risky and unhealthy behavior is associated with negative internalized views of age. One study showed that older adults in Ireland who had higher measures of negative perceptions of aging had a greater tendency to drink and smoke excessively (Villiers-Tuthill et al., 2016). Gerontological social workers need to embrace a positive view of aging to support older clients who may be experiencing ageism in social environments that harbor implicit and explicit bias. Helping older adults navigate the workplace, healthcare environments, and volunteer opportunities that may not be welcoming or designed to be "age-friendly" will be a part of future social work. Showing empathy and encouraging positive perceptions of aging will also be important for social workers who work with older adults.

Corporations have not yet grasped the potential of an aging workforce. Most companies don't have enough programs to support older workers or to plans create intergenerational cohesion in the workplace. Businesses and the government will have to think of how to support employees' smooth transition to a 21st-century retirement, one that could last multiple decades. On the other hand, while some will choose to retire, many older workers continue in their jobs well past traditional retirement, and they may need support in making their jobs work for them. Very few large and small companies are thinking ahead and creating innovative programs for multiple generations in the workplace. Midlife career changes and layoffs are common and new policies and programs that counsel older workers in choosing a new career paths or finding suitable jobs will be needed.

Grand Challenge in the Curricula

All Grand Challenges support Advancing Long and Productive Lives because our earlier life experiences, circumstances, and challenges greatly affect our later life (Elder, 1998). Adopting a Life Course perspective to productive aging recognizes that cumulative disadvantages must be better addressed earlier in life to lessen inequality in old age (Gonzales et al., 2015). For this reason, the Grand Challenge of Supporting Healthy Families supports productive aging. The Grand Challenge of Eliminating Racism supports the Grand Challenge of Advancing Long and Productive Lives because racism on a macro, mezzo, and micro level adversely affects well-being, productivity, income, and wealth status and leads to far greater economic insecurity for older adults of color (Dumez & Debrew, 2011). Additionally, please see the CSWE (2022) competencies (i.e., Educational Policy and Accreditation Standards, EPAS) in Appendix 5A to see how this Grand Challenge can be applied in the curricula.

Human Behavior in the Social Environment – Life Course Perspective

We age and pass through various stages of life such as childhood, adolescence, adulthood, and old age, yet much of what we perceive about these stages is socially constructed. It's important to be aware of our own internal biases and judgments about all stages of life and especially aging when working with older adults. Age grading or age gradation is a phrase that describes social organization based on age. Cultural norms for age gradation may vary such as when one "should" get married, have children, or complete one's education. Age grading varies across cultures and because we are living much longer, many of these social norms no longer make sense. Examining one's own ideas about social norms of aging and age gradation will be important to social workers that interact with all generations in the 21st century. When we hear the phrase "old age," many things may come to mind. And we may also underestimate the capabilities of someone who is younger or that we view as less experienced. Social workers who work with individuals of all generations will need to consider many factors that influence each person, including putting aside any socially constructed ideas about age and age gradation.

Aging is a complex process that begins at birth and induces physical and mental changes throughout the life course. How a person ages depends on many factors: their social environment, personality, lifestyle, and genetics, as well as their own attitudes about aging. As we get "older" all our life experiences, historical events, and social environments have shaped who we have become. Understanding the effects of personal, interpersonal, and societal factors on aging, including the mechanisms through which these factors exert their effects, is important to consider along with the biology of aging. Most people understand behavioral and psychological factors that affect aging such as how much we exercise, and whether we smoke or drink. Yet there are other health behaviors, cognitive experiences and social practices that are less well known and understood. For example, greater levels of education positively affect health and life expectancy. Environment has a powerful impact on the aging process, often impacting behavior, health, and longevity in ways that researchers are continuing to uncover. For example, living in an area that has high levels of air pollution will affect your health and longevity. Additionally, living alone in an area that is geographically isolated from other people will also affect your mental, physical health as well as your longevity. Humans age in a social environment and a physical environment that both directly and indirectly affects their physiology.

Biological aging is a complex process involving multiple physiological pathways, some of which include diminishing rates of autophagy, cellular senescence, changes in DNA methylation, mitochondrial decline, increased inflammation, and alterations in hormonal states. The slow accumulation of cellular, molecular, and genetic damage that causes aging occurs at different rates for everyone. Accelerated aging can be measured in midlife (Elliot et al., 2021). For others, the momentum of aging seems to continue, but at a much slower pace. For this reason, scientists coined the term "biological age" which describes how people age at varying rates. Research shows that even though there are great variations in how individuals age over time (Elliot et al., 2021), creating an accurate measurement of biological age will require substantial research (Ferrucci et al., 2020). For now estimating one's biological age is not an exact science. The good news is that a person can change their biological age for the better by improving the circumstances that influence the aging process, such as lifestyle, social environment, or even one's attitude towards aging.

Chronological age is the number of years a person has lived according to their date of birth. In addition to chronological and biological age, individuals have a subjective age that describes the age one feels. A person may describe their subjective age in terms of numbers, "I am 57 years old, but I don't feel a day over 30," or "Today I feel like a teenager." Aging, along with life, means change – physical, psychological, relational, social, environmental, situational, behavioral, spiritual, and intellectual. These biological and psychological changes happen at different rates for everyone. Changes brought on by aging require that individuals psychologically adjust to these changes and that those around us also adjust to the changes of aging through the life course. A person's subjective age may vary from day to day or over time. Subjective age emphasizes how one feels in the moment in reference to their "age" and the physical, psychological, and emotional aging process.

Several psychosocial theories of gerontology help us to understand how the aging process affects social groups and how the social environment shapes who we become in old age, as well as how the social environment affects the biological and psychological aging process. The most widely accepted theory of aging is the Life Course perspective because it best captures the complexity of life and how everything before culminates in who we are today. The Life Course Theory tells us a story about aging and about a person's life. Imagine going to a memorial of a person who has lived to be 90 years of age, but whom you do not know well. At the memorial you will learn much about this individual's "life course" through the stories you will hear, by photos or videos that may be shared, and through conversations with those attending the memorial. You will learn about the person's early life or youth, their adulthood, as well as the person's experiences in old age. You will learn what was important to the individual and perhaps hear of some difficulties that they experienced. You may learn about the places where they lived and how different historical events impacted their life. You may discover whether the person ever went to school or if they were educated, employed, who their family and friends are or were. The Life Course Theory has five domains and recognizes that each stage of life builds upon previous stages with the life course culminating in old age. More about Life Course Theory will be explained, but first let's look at a few earlier gerontological theories.

One of the earliest social gerontological theories is Disengagement Theory (Havighurst, 1961), which simply presumes that as individuals grow old, they gradually disengage from the world. Activity Theory (Cumming & Henry, 1961) contradicts Disengagement Theory and asserts that if a person stays engaged in their endeavors and socially active as they age, they will remain fulfilled. There is a grain of truth in each of these theories but taken alone gerontologists would agree that the entirety of the diverse experiences of life and aging cannot be described by either of these gerontological theories.

Other social theories of aging include Continuity Theory (Atchley, 1989), which argues that optimal aging occurs when a person continues living life based on preferences of adulthood or continuing one's activities and social interactions as the aging process progresses, making appropriate modifications to one's activity as one's abilities decline. Generally, the premise of productive aging is favorable and champions the value of older adults both economically and intrinsically. When older adults are engaged on a micro level by feeling connected to a life purpose and on a mezzo level to their community, they productively contribute to both the economy and the greater good.

The Life Course perspective is highly respected in the field of aging because it addresses the impact of social determinants throughout the life course on individual outcomes in later life (Elder, 1975). In the Life Course Theory, an individual's life is shaped by and can be examined through five basic principles: life span development, agency, time and place, timing, and linked lives. Each of these five psychosocial dynamics matters in a person's life course. Each older adult has felt the impact of the five areas.

- Life span development – Aging is a lifelong process that builds upon earlier actions, circumstances, and social interactions;
- Agency – The choices that an individual makes within the social and historical context shapes their life course;
- Time and place – People live within an historical and geographic context that may change over time;
- Timing – The timing of certain life events and transitions impact the life course, for example, graduating, winning an award or the birth of a child;

- Linked lives – Individual lives are "linked" to others who may be family, friends, neighbors, colleagues and these social connections shift, grow, and change throughout the life course ("Life course," n.d.).

How these five areas affect a person's life are important and signify spheres of influence that impact the protagonist and that the protagonist can impact in varying degrees.

A more recent social theory of aging, Socio-Emotional Selectivity Theory (Carstensen, 1993) emphasizes how expanding or shrinking perceptions of time influence behavior. The theory presumes goals, plans, and behavior are determined by how much time we perceive we have "left" either in our life or before a qualifying event such as a long-distance move. When a person is younger, they may believe they have plenty of time and delay certain actions. Socio-Emotional Selectivity Theory postulates that a person will make choices based on a perspective of choosing emotionally rewarding activities, over less meaningful pursuits when a person believes time is limited. This theory offers an explanation as to why older adults are more often happier and more satisfied than younger counterparts (Carstensen et al., 2020). Would a global pandemic that left older adults much more vulnerable to disease or death nullify this theory? In spring of 2020, the global pandemic presented an unprecedented and uncertain threat, especially for adults over age 64. A survey in April of 2020 found that adults over age 64 expressed greater emotional resilience than younger adults facing the same uncertain health risks posed by the early months of the Covid-19 pandemic (Carstensen et al., 2020).

Another notable theory of aging, Cumulative/Advantage Disadvantage Theory (Dannefer, 2003), has an approach that has particular significance for the Grand Challenge of Advancing Long and Healthy Lives. This theory offers a framework of understanding in which financial inequity and health inequity can be understood and addressed. This theory also gives reason for earlier intervention in the life course and offers a structure that can help to integrate other Grand Challenges with Advancing Long and Productive Lives.

Social Welfare Policy

Supporting older adults in the workforce benefits society as well as older workers themselves. Adults over age 50 contribute to the companies and small businesses in which they are employed with specialized skills, experience, and leadership. Older adults who work in jobs or careers that they enjoy and that meet their needs as they age gain mental and financial well-being. There is evidence that working past age 65 lowers the risk of cognitive decline (Population Reference Bureau, 2018). Older adults will be an important presence in the workforce in coming decades as larger numbers of older adults remain in the working past age 50 and often stay working decades past traditional retirement age.

Policies and programs that help older workers get hired, trained, or help them to retain jobs will be in great demand and this need will only grow more pressing in coming years. Because companies now include members of up to five generations, corporate programs that promote age diversity and cohesion among diverse age groups will be needed. Policies and programs that encourage best practices for a multi-generational working environments will help ensure that companies are welcoming and inclusive to older workers. Growing with Age, Unlocking the Power of the Multi-Generational Workforce is a collaborative program between American Association of Retired Persons (AARP) and the World Economic Forum that tracks and champions the advantages of age-diverse companies. Prospective policies and programs to support older adults remaining in the workforce as included and valued members of the workforce and in entrepreneurial roles will be greatly needed. It is important not to make assumptions about older workers as they are an extremely heterogeneous group; some have high levels of technical skills and others may not be as tech savvy. Supporting older workers and cohesive multi-generational workplaces will be an important part of the practice of social workers who choose to work with elders.

Volunteer or unpaid work provides many benefits to older adults and has been associated with a reduced rate of mortality, as well as physical and mental health benefits such as greater life satisfaction (Wheeler et al., 1998). Volunteering has economic benefits for the larger community and society (Gil-Lacruz et al., 2019). Volunteering has been correlated with higher rates of well-being, especially if it is meaningful (Wheeler et al., 1998). Adults who volunteer more than 200 hours a year had a 40% less chance of developing high blood pressure (Sneed & Cohen, 2013). In fact the negative outcomes of volunteering are very few and are only associated with poorly run programs. Volunteering often leads to paid work and often increases the possibility that an older adult will return to paid work after volunteering. The evidence indicates that volunteering is a positive social determinant of health, yet more research is needed on the precise circumstances in the volunteer environment that lead to positive health benefits (Gil-Lacruz et al., 2019). When older volunteers believe that they are making a difference, it is correlated with higher life satisfaction (Gil-LaCruz et al., 2019). Long-term investment in private-sector programs and government policies that support older adults' volunteer work will be well worth the costs associated with the programs. Non-profits and governmental agencies would receive the economic benefits of the unpaid work and older adults would receive the health and social benefits associated with volunteer work, not to mention the savings in health care expenses.

Understanding the benefits of intergenerational relationships will be important to social workers, regardless of the populations that they serve because people of all ages have something to gain when meaningful exchanges between older and younger people take place. Programs that include more than one generation benefit all in emotional transfer, sharing of skills, understanding new perspectives and can also have economic benefits. Pre-schools that share space and activities with members of senior homes or adult day centers have been shown to increase emotional well-being and health for both older adults and pre-K children (Femia et al., 2008). Programs that serve both youth and elders not only benefit individuals, but they can also increase social capital, elevate the practice of intergenerational reciprocity, and increase trust and harmony within a community (Murayama et al., 2019).

At Judson Manor, a senior living community, seven students from the Cleveland Institute of Music receive room and board in exchange for the title of artists in residence (Hansman, 2015). The senior residents enjoy the benefits of rich interactions with the students, as well as frequent onsite recitals. Nesterly, a home-sharing platform seeks to pair older homeowners with younger roommates, creating "mutually beneficial connections that range across generations, cultures and lived experiences" (Nesterly, 2022). By emphasizing the benefits for all generations, the start-up Nesterly capitalizes on the large number of baby boomer homeowners with spare rooms by helping them easily connect and vet prospective roommates several decades younger. Sharing your home involves trust and most rental agreements don't come with the safeguard of a monthly check in from a licensed clinical social worker, but Nesterly does just that.

Caregiving

Intrinsic rewards come with caring for a loved one or a friend; however, unlike other relationships, caregivers typically give more than they receive. Increased life expectancy means that three, four, and even five generations of the same family may be alive at the same time. Informal caregiving or family caregiving relationships have become increasingly complex, because extended life expectancy has prolonged caregiving relationships (Bengtson, 2001). Adults who simultaneously care for aging parents and give care to children or young adults are said to be part of the sandwich generation or in the United Kingdom are called sandwich carers.

Caregivers need support and need to fill up their own buckets so to speak so they may continue with their emotionally and often physically demanding work. There are many public and non-profit programs that support caregivers' mental and physical health, but they are not always easily accessible. Sometimes the caregivers do not have knowledge of support groups or other services because the programs have trouble reaching those they wish to serve. An important part of social workers that work with caregivers or those that receive care will be understanding how to access support services for caregivers.

Social Work Practice

Social workers demonstrate need an understanding of the biopsychosocial issues of elders, as well as the application of empirically supported interventions in home, community-based settings, and institutions.

Social media and the internet have created a place for speaking up about a new vision of aging. Young and old, people are voicing new and exciting views on aging in podcasts, blogs, in virtual meetings, and on social media. On www.gerowhat.com, millennial gerontologist Christina Peoples shares her self-described "goofy and energetic" ideas, opinions, and insight on growing older. Elise Marie Collins, author, speaker, and yoga teacher, interviews aging experts, academics, spiritual teachers, alternative health experts, and anti-ageism activists on her podcast, "How to Super Age." Writer, educator, and founder of "Age March," Barbara Rose Brooker represents older Baby Boomers who are redefining aging. She started the first in-person "Age March" against age discrimination and ageism in 2010 and in 2021 she created the first virtual Age March that has since gone viral (https://youtu.be/HpJfpnQjjbA).

Brooker also hosts a weekly podcast, "The Rant." Mariann Aalda, comedian, actress, and self-described Aging Anarchist hosts a weekly Clubhouse on ageism, called Ageing Shamelessly. Prominent aging experts show up to discuss and dish on the latest ageist media representations in film and television, as well as general topics on redefining what it means to grow old. Visionary activist Ashton Applewhite and her team founded www.Old School.info, an anti-ageism clearing house for resources, campaigns, and support groups which has become an indispensable tool for anyone in the aging space.

Teaching Practice: Interactions With Older Adults in and out of the Classroom

Create a blog, podcast, website, or YouTube video that addresses some of the challenges and issues facing older adults today. Interview adults over 65 years of age. What are some of the challenges they face in their lives as older adults? How has their identity impacted their choices and life course? Older adults lived at a different time in history. How has race, ethnicity, gender, sexual orientation impacted their choice and life course? Be prepared to discuss these issues with empathy.

Volunteer work has been shown to improve health and well-being for older adults, yet many older adults don't know about volunteer opportunities that welcome them.

Make a YouTube video about volunteer opportunities for older adults in your area. Create a website that explains the benefits of social interaction between generations and how and where younger people can interact and learn more about older adults in their community.

Classroom Discussion Setting the Context, the Life Course Perspective

How does historical context affect aging? Historical context and environment attitudes about race, ethnicity, sexual preference, and class create lasting impacts on older adults' lives. Think about when and where a person was born and how the attitudes of the time influenced the older adult's life.

Tom Ammiano is an American politician and LGBT activist who attended Immaculate Conception High School in Montclair New Jersey in the late 1950s. Although he did not come out as gay in high school, Ammiano was often teased and bullied at school for being different. He found that he loved running and joined the track team in high school. He continually improved as a runner and won his final race as a senior. Ammiano was thrilled to learn that he qualified to receive an award, a Varsity Letter. Yet when the awards were presented, he was left out and did not receive his Varsity Letter for athletic achievement (Pogash, 2021). Feeling hurt and upset, Ammiano realized that although he was not openly gay, his behavior or mannerism caused school authorities to fail to award him and his deserved honor due to the prejudices of the time (Bordon, 2021). After college Ammiano moved to San Francisco and became an elementary school teacher, a comedian, and a prominent politician. In 2021, after publishing his memoir, he was being interviewed by a San Francisco radio host when Ammiano told the story of being overlooked for his Varsity Letter, something that still troubled him. A listener heard his story and contacted Immaculate Conception High School in New Jersey to ask whether they would consider awarding Ammiano a Varsity Letter. In 2021 at the age of 79, some 60 plus years later, Tom Ammiano was elated to learn he would be awarded a Varsity Letter for Track and Field from Immaculate Conception High School. This story illustrates how a life course may be affected by discrimination; although unjust, it was considered acceptable at another time in history.

How can Life Course Theory or other ideas in this chapter help us to understand some of the circumstances of Tom Ammiano's life?

What can this tell us about how history and geography play a part in lives? Why would it be important to get an award later in life? How does timing impact life circumstances? Agency? Time and place? Research other stories of elders who faced prejudice, discrimination, or other unfair treatment that was not corrected.

Classroom Discussion

Think about and discuss how technology has made it easier for the aging population. Then think about and discuss how technology has created challenges for the aging population. What is the digital divide and who does it affect? Which segments of the aging population in the United States are affected by the digital divide? In the United States, Mexico, and Central America? In other continents such as Europe? Africa? Which older adults are more vulnerable to not receiving services because they don't understand technology? Which older adults are more vulnerable to not receiving services because they don't have access to technology? What are some solutions to helping older adults engage with technology? Do you know of some examples of older adults who are very tech savvy?

To live a long and healthy life, older adults need to develop the ability to relax (Collins, 2018). Yet relaxation is not typically taught in school. Many older adults who live in poverty or who are aging in stressful environments may need more support in developing lifestyle habits and practices that buffer environmental stressors. How would you help an older adult who is facing emotional challenges or environmental stressors that are beyond her/his/their control? What type of relaxing activities could you recommend or teach older adults that are facing challenges and setbacks? What are some possible programs that you could imagine if you could create one that would support older adults who are facing obstacles to aging productively?

What can we learn from those who have lived over 100 years? How can social workers use evidence-based knowledge of complementary and alternative medicine to support the aging population? What would it be like to live to be 100?

Centenarians are the fastest growing segment of the global population and many of them are thriving. In addition, it is estimated that half of all babies born in the United States in 2021 will live to be over 100 years of age. Professor Murali Nair has spent decades researching the cross-cultural habits and lifestyles of centenarians (Nair et al., 2010). Many of his studies have focused on centenarians who live in traditional cultures where social determinants of health such as healthy food, stable housing, and social support are not solely on dependent on higher incomes or socio-economic standing. His field studies can teach us how to shape policy and support for aging adults in all communities, including high-, middle-, and low-income countries. Many centenarians have avoided or postponed age-related chronic diseases (Heshmati, 2021). Dr. Nair's work brings to light cross-cultural similarities associated with centenarians' longevity and increased health span. Dr. Nair found many similar behaviors and environments amongst the centenarians he studied (Nair, 2007). Understanding what behavioral characteristics and social environments might have contributed to an exceptionally long life can help social workers effectively interact with centenarians and influence policy for older adults, especially around preventative medicine.

Teaching Advance Long and Productive Lives Course – Classroom Innovative Ideas:

- Experiential exercises (i.e., discussion, small and large group, site visits, use of arts, etc.);
- Case vignettes;
- Role plays;
- Interactions with older adults in and out of the classroom;
- Videos;
- Podcasts.

1. **Objectives**
   - Learn what is productive aging;
   - Discover how social work can lead the way with this challenge;
   - Increase understanding of the rationale, process, and challenges of evidenced-based practice and skills;
   - Apply relevant and practical empirically supported assessments and interventions to health and mental conditions or situations facing diverse older adults and their caregivers.
2. **Setting the Context**
   - Introduce the topic and engage students using best teaching practices. Best teaching practices.
3. **Highlights of Lecture Material for One Class**
   - Diversity in aging: Cultural competence of Social Work Professionals;
   - Definition – cultural diversity, culture, ethnicity, global trends;
   - Bias, prejudice, and stereotyping – older people of color;
   - Implications for services (cultural/economic barriers to utilization, cultural isolation/language differences, stigma, confusion, anger, and fear of health care professionals, lack of knowledge);
   - Spirituality/religion;
   - Cultural competence with older adults (recommendations for effective social work with racially and ethnically diverse older adults); gestures, eye contact, personal touch and space, language (working with interpreters);
   - Professional responsibility;
   - Best practice models (Explanatory, LEARN model);
   - Breakouts interspersed throughout (using art expression activities and videos throughout).
4. **Facilitating Class Discussions**
   - Tips for active participation including setting the stage (listening respectfully, assessing readiness to discuss issue(s), recognizing the diversity of students, setting a framework and objective for the discussion, providing a common base for understanding, being an active facilitator, fostering civility, dealing with tense or emotional moments, summarizing, and reflecting).

5. **Addressing Diversity: Equity, Inclusion, and Social Justice**

    - Aging populations are becoming more diverse in terms of color, culture, identity, disability, and socio-economic standing;
    - Discuss the need for culturally competent professionals and best practices;
    - Provide examples to assist investigating own biases and/or cultural experiences from a place of nonjudgment;
    - Provide a competency perspective rather than a deficit perspective.

6. **Managing Difficult Classroom Conversation**

    - Include topics of age, race, culture, gender, and/or sexual orientation;
    - Discuss the impact issues have on the dynamics of the class;
    - Discuss awareness and management of implicit bias, transference, and countertransference;
    - Provide tips and techniques for skill development (applying a framework to formulate the issue, addressing issues, facilitating discussion, providing structured opportunities for reflection and input, synthesizing, following-up, and accessing resources).

7. **Evaluation of Learning**

    - Substantive discussion and class participation;
    - Written and oral assignments;
    - Quizzes;
    - Reflections.

8. **Future Directions and Challenges**

    - Technology-enhanced services to the aged;
    - Cross-cultural and cross-national understanding of healthy aging lifestyles;
    - With limited resources and unlimited needs, handling complexity of issues.

Implications for Social Workers Interested in Working With Aging Population

The United States is the country with the largest number of centenarians in the world, followed by Japan with 87,000 centenarians. The number of centenarians around the world is projected to increase by tenfold to 1,095,000 by the year 2050. Social workers will be highly likely to work with the aging population during their career. Learning from the oldest of the old (over 85 years of age) will be an opportunity. Centenarians in traditional cultures demonstrate what is known about longevity; living a century is more than genetic predisposition and advancement in medicine. Social workers can play a major role in the field of gerontology by concentrating on the lifestyle patterns of seniors and learning from their traditions, especially outside of industrialized high-income countries. Cultural understandings of the elders are an important factor for social workers in working with the aging population.

Conclusion

The aging of the US population, longer life expectancy, and the dramatic growth of persons over age 85, as well as those identified as "Baby Boomers" have significant implications for social work practice and education in the 21st century.

Supporting the Grand Challenge of Advancing Long and Productive lives necessitates the preparation of more social workers skilled in working with older adults and their families (National Association of Social Work, 2021). There are more elders living today than any other time in history and this population will continue to grow. In 2020 there were 727 million adults over 65 living in the world and that number is projected to double by the year 2050. In the social environment, aging opportunities, challenges, policies, and experiences can vary greatly by country, state, county, and even zip code. In the United States, adults over age 65 are becoming more racially and ethnically diverse (John A. Hartford Foundation, 2018).

All other Grand Challenges support Advancing Long and Productive Lives because living a long and healthy life occurs when society supports well-being from birth to old age. Many of the other Grand Challenges address social determinants of health that addressed support health and longevity for all. For example, the Grand Challenge of ending social isolation can be helped through intergenerational programs that bring young people and older adults together in productive social environments. Young people can benefit from learning from the experience of older adults. Adopting a Life Course perspective to aging recognizes that cumulative disadvantages must be better addressed earlier in life to lessen inequality in old age (Gonzales et al., 2015).

Population health is shaped by the environment and social workers will need to work within a wide variety of settings and circumstances across the United States and in the world to deliver services and support to older adults. Social institutions are products of social environments that have yet not caught up with the rising tide of older individuals. Geriatric social workers will need to understand the necessity of acting as a member of an interdisciplinary team, especially when older adults need support with chronic illness or disability.

References

Aronson, L. (2021). *Elderhood: Redefining aging, transforming medicine, reimagining life*. Bloomsbury Publishing.

Atchley, R. C. (1989). A continuity theory of normal aging. *The Gerontologist*, *29*(2), 183–190. https://doi.org/10.1093/geront/29.2.183

Bengtson, V. L. (2001). The burgess award lecture: Beyond the nuclear family: The increasing importance of multigenerational bonds. *Journal of Marriage and Family*, *63*, 1–16.

Bordon, S. (2021, June 10) 63 years later, Tom Ammiano gets the varsity letter he was denied as a gay teen. *ESPN*. www.espn.com/espn/story/_/id/31567044/63-years-later-tom-ammiano-gets-varsity-letter-was-denied-gay-teen

Carney, G. M., & Nash, P. (2020). *Critical questions for ageing societies*. Policy Press.

Carstensen, L. L. (1993). Motivation for social contact across the lifespan: A theory of socioemotional selectivity. *Nebraska Symposium on Motivation*, *1992*(40), 209–254.

Carstensen, L. L., Shavit, Y. Z., & Barnes, J. T. (2020). Age advantages in emotional experience persist even under threat from the COVID-19 pandemic. *Psychological Science*, *31*(11), 1374–1385. doi:10.1177/0956797620967261

Collins, E. M. (2018). *Super ager, you can look younger, have more energy, a better memory, and live a long and healthy life*. Mango Publishing.

CSWE. (2022). *2022 Educational policy and accreditation standards*. www.cswe.org/accreditation/standards/2022-epas/

Cumming, E., & Henry, W. E. (1961). *Growing old: The process of disengagement*. Basic Books.

Dannefer, D. (2003). Cumulative advantage/disadvantage and the life course: Cross fertilizing age and social science theory. *Journal of Gerontology*, *58*, S327. https://doi.org/10.1093/geronb/58.6.S327

Dumez, J., & Debrew, H. (2011). *The economic crisis facing seniors of color: Background and policy recommendations, Summer Associates*. The Greenberg Institute. http://healthpolicy.ucla.edu/publications/Documents/PDF/The%20Economic%20Crisis%20Facing%20Seniors%20of%20Color.pdf

Elder, G. H. (1975). Age differentiation and the life course. *Annual Review of Sociology*, *1*(1), 65–190. https://doi.org/10.1146/annurev.so.01.080175.001121

Elder, G. H. (1998). The life course as developmental theory. *Child Development*, *69*(1), 1–12. doi:10.2307/1132065

Elliot, M. L., Caspi, A. C., Houts, R. M., Ambler, A., Broadbent, J. M., Hancox, R. J., . . . Moffit, T. E. (2021). Disparities in the pace of biological aging among midlife adults of the same chronological age have implications for future frailty risk and policy. *Nature Aging*, *1*, 295–308. https://doi.org/10.1038/s43587-021-00044-4

Femia, E. F., Zarit, S. H., Blair, C., & Jarrot, K. B. (2008). Intergenerational preschool experiences and the young child. *Potential Benefits to Development, Early Childhood Research Quarterly*, *23*(2), 272–287. https://doi.org/10.1016/j.ecresq.2007.05.001

Ferrucci, L., Gonzalez-Freire, M, Fabbri, E., Simonsick, E., Tanaka, T., Moore, Z., Salimi, S., Sierra, F., & de Cabo, R. (2020, February). Measuring biological aging in humans: A quest. *Aging Cell*, *19*(2). doi:10.1111/acel.13080.

Gil-Lacruz, M., Saz-Gil, M. I., & Gil-Lacruz, A. I. (2019). Benefits of older volunteering on wellbeing: An international comparison. *Frontiers in Psychology*, *10*, 2647. https://doi.org/10.3389/fpsyg.2019.02647

Gonzales, E., Matz-Costa, C., & Morrow-Howell, N. (2015, April). Increasing opportunities for the productive engagement of older adults: A response to population aging. *The Gerontologist*, *55*(2), 252–261. https://doi.org/10.1093/geront/gnu176

Hansman, H. (2015). College students are living rent free in a Cleveland retirement home. *Smithsonian Magazine*. www.smithsonianmag.com/innovation/college-students-are-living-rent-free-in-cleveland-retirement-home 180956930/#:~:text=Tieu%2C%20who%20is%20a%20second,of%20the%20revamped%201920s%20hotel

Havighurst, R. J. (1961). Successful aging. *The Gerontologist*, *1*(1), 8–13. https://doi.org/10.1093/geront/1.1.8

Heshmati,H.(2021).*Thecentenarians:Anemergingpopulation,geriatricupdate.* www.intechopen.com/books/update-in-geriatrics/the-centenarians-an-emerging-population

John Hartford Foundation. (2018). www.johnahartford.org

Levy, B. R., Slade, M. D., Kunkel, S. R., & Kasl, S. V. (2002, August). Longevity increased by positive self-perceptions of aging. *Journal of Personality and Social Psychology*, *83*(2), 261–270. https://doi.org/10.1037/0022-3514.83.2.261

Life Course Theory Has Five Basic Principles. (n.d.). *Glen H. Elder, Jr. University of North Carolina*. https://elder.web.unc.edu/research-projects/

Lowsky, J., Olshansky, S. J., Bhattacharya, J., & Goldman, D. P. (2014, June). Heterogeneity in healthy aging. *Journals of Gerontology Series A-Biological Sciences and Medical Sciences*, *69*(6), 640–649. doi:10.1093/gerona/glt162

Murayama, Y., Murayama, H., Hasebe, M., et al. (2019). The impact of intergenerational programs on social capital in Japan: A randomized population-based cross-sectional study. *BMC Public Health*, *19*, 156. https://doi.org/10.1186/s12889-019-6480-3

Nair, M. (2007). Interacting with centenarians. In L. M. Grobman & D. B. Bourassa (Eds.), *Days in the lives of gerontological social workers*. White Hat Communications.

Nair, M., Pesek, T., & Reminick, & R. Secrets of Long Life. (2010). Cross-cultural explorations in sustainably enhancing and promoting longevity via elders' practice wisdom. *Explore*, 6(6), 352–358.

National Association of Social Work. (2021). *Blueprint of federal social policies*. www.socialworkers.org/LinkClick.aspx?fileticket=KPdZqqY60t4%3D&portalid=0

National Institute on Aging. (2022). *What do we know about healthy aging?* www.nia.nih.gov/health/what-do-we-know-about-healthy-aging

Nelson, T. D. (2005). Ageism: Prejudice against our feared future selves. *Journal of Social Issues*, *61*(2), 207–221.

Nesterly. (2022). About us. *Nesterly*. www.nesterly.com/about-us/

Perrin, A. (2021, June 3). Mobile technology and home broadband 2021. *Pew Research Center, Report*. www.pewresearch.org/internet/2021/06/03/mobile-technology-and-home-broadband-2021/

Pogash, C. (2021, February 28). He won a varsity letter at 16. He finally got it when he was 79. *New York Times*. www.nytimes.com/2021/02/28/nyregion/tom-ammiano-gay-varsity-letter.html

Population Reference Bureau. (2018). https://scorecard.prb.org/datasheets/

Richmond-Rakerd, L. S., Righarts, A., Sugden, K., Sugden, K., Thomson, W. M., Thorne, P. R., . . . Moffit, T. E. (2021). Disparities in the pace of biological aging among midlife adults of the same chronological age have implications for future frailty risk and policy. *Nature Aging*, *1*, 295–308. https://doi.org/10.1038/s43587-021-00044-4

Sneed, R. S., & Cohen, S. (2013). A prospective study of volunteerism and hypertension risk in older adults. *Psychology and Aging*, *28*(2), 578–586. https://doi.org/10.1037/a0032718

United Nations Department of Economic and Social Affairs. (2019). *World population ageing 2019 highlights*. Department of Economic and Social Affairs. United Nations. www.un.org/en/development/desa/population/publications/pdf/ageing/WorldPopulationAgeing2019-Highlights.pdf

Villiers-Tuthill, A., Copley, A., Mcgee, H., & Morgan, K. (2016). The relationship of tobacco and alcohol use with ageing self-perceptions in older people in Ireland. *BMC Public Health*, *16*. https://doi.org/10.1186/s12889-016-3158-y

Wheeler, J. A., Gorey, K. M., & Greenblatt, B. (1998). The beneficial effects of volunteering for older volunteers and the people they serve: A meta-analysis. *The International Journal of Aging and Human Development*, *47*(1). http://dx.doi.org/10.2190/VUMP-XCMF-FQYU-V0JH

Websites, Videos and Further References:

Age Smart Employer NYC. An Initiative of the Robert N. Butler Columbia Aging Center. www.publichealth.columbia.edu/research/age-smart-employer

Ageism Is a Bully . . . Stand Up to It. (2021, June 23). TED. www.ted.com/talks/mariann_aalda_ageism_is_a_bully_stand_up_to_it

Applewhite, A. (2020). *This chair rocks: A manifesto against ageism*. Celadon Books.

Boston University Medical School of Medicine New England Centenarian Study. www.bumc.bu.edu/centenarian/overview/

Caring Across Generations. https://caringacross.org/

Cross National Field Studies on Healthy Centenarians. www.muralinair.com

Generations United. www.gu.org

The Georgia Centenarian Study. https://news.uga.edu/reaching-100-years-of-age-may-be-more-about-attitude-and-adaptation-th/

Geriatrics Career Development. https://vimeo.com/283788757 What Happens When a Nursing Center and a Day Care Center Share a Roof? PBS NewsHour. https://youtu.be/j9BfAgRa2uI

Grandparents Raising Grandchildren or Grand Families, NPR. www.youtube.com/watch?v=CInufouwJQE

Hall, A. (2021, June). Journalism showcase: SportsCenter's "SC featured" tells the story of righting a 60-year-old wrong. *ESPN Front Row*. www.espnfrontrow.com/2021/06/journalism-showcase-sportscenters-sc-featured-tells-story-of-righting-a-60-year-old-wrong/

Kaiser Family Foundation, Old and Poor: America's Forgotten. (2014). www.kff.org/medicare/video/old-and-poor-americas-forgotten/

Nair, M., & Collins, E. (2020). Centenarians: Life style for a long healthy life. In C. S. Pitchumoni & T. S. Dharmarajan (Eds.), *Geriatric gastroenterology*. Springer Publications.

Nesselroade, K. P., & Nesselroade, J. R. (2011). Emotional experience improves with age: Evidence based on over 10 years of experience sampling. *Psychology and Aging*, *26*(1), 21–33. https://doi.org/10.1037/a0021285

Okinawa Research Center for Longevity Science. https://orcls.org/about

PBS NewsHour. (2019, July 8). In Boston, a housing innovation that connects generations. [Video] PBS. www.pbs.org/video/under-one-roof-1562626755/

RAISE Family Caregiving Advisory Council. https://acl.gov/programs/support-caregivers/raise-family-caregiving-advisory-council

Solomon, P., & Estes, D. L. (2020). Why more older workers are finding themselves unemployed as retirement approaches. *PBS NewsHour*. www.pbs.org/newshour/show/why-more-older-workers-are-finding-themselves-unemployed-as-retirement-approaches

Stahl, L. (2021). New insights from the study of people 90 and above. *CBS News*. www.cbsnews.com/news/long-life-study-60-minutes-2021-05-30/

There's more than one way to age. How are you doing it? (2020). *LA Times*. www.latimes.com/science/story/2020-01-17/aging-differently-research-studies-stanford-genetics-biology

Appendix 5A

EPAS Addressed in Grand Challenge #4

Advance Long and Productive Lives

Competency 1: Demonstrate Ethical and Professional Behavior. Ethical decision-making on the part of social workers is crucial in the practice, research, and policy arenas of working with the long and productive life of people, from all backgrounds including LGBTQ elders, BIPOC elders, and elders of all races and ethnicities. In order to comprehend this phenomenon, as a base, all of us need to understand the evolution and mission of professional social work, including the principles of the code of ethics set up by the National Association of Social Workers. Identifying diverse ethical imperatives in quantitative and qualitative research methods to advance the healthy aged is very important for all helping professionals.

Competency 2: Engage Antiracism, Diversity, Equity, and Inclusion (ADEI) in Practice. Social workers are in a unique position to support antiracism, diversity, equity, and inclusion within the aging population to catalyze the Grand Challenge of Advancing Long and Productive Lives. Aging is not equitable, and an individual's social environment is one of the greatest predictor of longevity and health span. Addressing health-span and life span inequities are focal challenges in Advancing Long and Productive Lives.

Competency 3: Advance Human Rights and Social, Racial Economic, and Environmental Justice. In the technology-enhanced modern society, learning from the diverse global societies is for social workers to enhance the human rights, social, racial, and environmental justice issues of the aged population. A United Nations report states that

> we have been leading and actively contributing to the world's deep that fragility relates to rising poverty and hunger; prolonged

> conflicts and human rights crises; skyrocketing levels of inequality within and between societies; the ungoverned development of new technologies; the erosion of the nuclear disarmament regime; and the triple planetary crisis of climate change, biodiversity loss and rising levels of air and water pollution. It has never been clearer that our fates are interconnected and that the inability to solve shared problems is creating unacceptable risks.
>
> (United Nations Annual Report, 2021)

Social workers are encouraged to implement innovative programs related to aging communities. Then evaluate its impact in the wider community.

Competency 4: Engage in Practice-Informed Research and Research-Informed Practice. The American Academy for Social Work and Social Welfare set out 12 Grand Challenges for Social Work and Society, in three broad categories of individual and family well-being, social fabric, and social justice. Social workers must strive toward social progress in these categories by relying on evidence-based methods (Bent-Goodley et al., 2019). Social workers working with the aged need to review micro and macro practice-informed research and research-informed practice to enhance their delivery. It is a commitment to improve the lives of people through the purposeful and professional use of oneself (Nair & Guerrero, 2020). This is possible by introducing evidence-based research in working with the older population.

Competency 5: Engage in Policy Practice. In all levels of practice settings, social workers are trained to engage in policy practice in local, state, and federal government settings to make sure social welfare policies are enacted and implemented. Organizations such as AARP (American Association of Retired Persons: www.aarp.org) take special care to engage in policy practice related to aging in our society. Advocacy is integral aspect of policy practice.

Competency 6: Engage With Individuals, Families, Groups, Organizations, and Communities. Social work as a profession deals with diverse societal needs at micro, mezzo, and macro levels. The aged population's concerns and needs are visible at the one-on-one, family, group, organization, and community-at-large levels. Social workers are encouraged to handle these multi-level tasks, utilizing multi-disciplinary approaches.

Competency 7: Assess Individuals, Families, Groups, Organizations, and Communities. Social workers are trained to conduct ongoing and comprehensive assessment using appropriate tools as a basis for effective intervention at the individuals, families, groups, organizations, and communities levels. Understanding diagnoses in the context of comprehensive bio-psycho-social-spiritual assessment and examining implications for diverse-aged clients at the micro and macro levels are paramount for social workers. Assessment is an ongoing component of the dynamic and interactive process of social work practice with the aged.

Competency 8: Intervene With Individuals, Families, Groups, Organizations, and Communities. Social workers are aware that intervention is an ongoing component of the dynamic and interactive process of social work practice with, and on behalf of, diverse individuals, families, groups, organizations, and communities. Exploring effective interventions to assist the aged at micro and macro level is a great challenge. It can be delivered utilizing multidisciplinary and technology-enhanced approaches.

Competency 9: Evaluate Practice With Individuals, Families, Groups, Organizations, and Communities. The evaluation process in social work practice with individuals, families, groups, organizations, and communities involves using quantitative and qualitative measurements to monitor whether the services achieved the desired outcome. Engaging in practice-informed research and research-informed practice helps social workers to monitor the outcome of diverse therapeutic interventions with the diverse-aged population.

References

Bent-Goodley, T., Williams, J. H., & Teasley, M. G. S. (Eds.). (2019). *Grand challenges for society: Evidence based social work practice*. NASW Press. ISBN: 978-0-87101-536-5

Nair, M., & Guerrero, E. (2020). *Evidenced based macro practice in social work*. Gregory Publications. ISBN 978-0-911541-95-3

United Nations. (2021). *United Nations annual report, 2021*, pp. 22–23. www.un.org/annualreport/index.html

Part Two

Stronger Social Fabric

6 Eradicate Social Isolation

Harry Hunter, Jane James and Mike Gent

Introduction

This chapter considers the integration of social isolation into social work curricula to increase education about the phenomenon. Social isolation presents a Grand Challenge for Social Work and has been identified as an area of concern for health care professionals, educators, government leaders, employers, parents, and children. It is a pervasive, wicked social problem that people should be aware of and prepared to address for themselves and for individuals around them. People develop social networking skills early in life and Valtorta et al. (2016) noted that deficiencies in acquiring and maintaining these skills contribute to social isolation, and a higher risk of coronary heart disease and stroke.

Social isolation can also lead to the risk of depression, other mental health conditions, and to increased morbidity and mortality (Holt-Lunstad, 2022). Social workers are uniquely positioned to mediate social isolation and are regularly on the frontline of service provision. The continued pervasiveness of social isolation cannot go unnoticed, especially with the advent of COVID-19 that highlighted its implications. Social workers must know the risk factors for social isolation and reducing impact, calls for training to recognize its negative effects.

Social isolation can affect people regardless of socioeconomic status, ethnicity, gender, or age group (Holt-Lunstad, 2022). In early childhood, social engagement has been correlated with academic success, and adolescents who reported higher levels of social connectedness later reported better mental health and well-being (Holt-Lunstad, 2022). Social isolation is deemed to have a cumulative impact that endures as individuals age, and could exacerbate other health issues later in adulthood.

DOI: 10.4324/9781003308263-8

Emphasizing social isolation's severity as a wicked problem, Holt-Lunstad (2022) reported that being socially connected reduces the risk of early death by 50%, justifying advancing social connectedness as a public health priority. Therefore, training social workers and other helping professionals about the public health implications, requires adding social isolation in education tenets and student competency expectations. Human Behavior and the Social Environment (HBSE) course instruction on social isolation must consider the impact of enforced isolation from the COVID-19 pandemic. Holt-Lunstad (2022) found higher rates of depression and anxiety in children and adolescents after enforced isolation.

Education on social isolation requires commitment to social work values and ethics, and means helping students to increase competence in creating strategies to address social problems. Building competence involves gaining awareness about wicked problems, such as social isolation. Holt-Lunstad (2022) identified potential strategies to reduce risk and experiences of social isolation and supported innovative ideas to connect, and improve the lives of individuals, families, and communities. Innovative ideas can be developed in social work curricula that integrate instruction about social isolation and heighten skills, critical to social work practice. Training for this task must be gained from helping students identify social norms perpetuating social isolation, and preparing them to follow the change process to effectively mitigate it.

As a Grand Challenge initiative, all related professionals must be involved and know the change that can be activated through various instructions about social isolation. Instructions can include direct care worker education, public awareness campaigns, and educating health care workers. Students must understand how the educational and training framework for social isolation elevates risk, or offers pathways towards tempering these concerns. A positive impact on social isolation warrants committing it to social work curricula. To provide the best services in the field, workers must possess the critical knowledge and skills needed for effective practice.

What Is Social Isolation and Does It Matter?

Social isolation has been defined as the condition of being alone, having limited or no contact with others. For the purpose of addressing this Grand Challenge, this definition leads to social isolation being confused with loneliness. The two concepts are related, but are different (Holt-Lunstad, 2022). Hence, it is more helpful to think of social isolation as a lack of desired social connection. Social isolation can lead to loneliness in some individuals, while others can feel lonely without being socially isolated. Loneliness is the distressing feeling of being isolated and is subjective, while social isolation suggests the relative absence of social relationships, and is objective (Holt-Lunstad, 2022). People feel lonely when they perceive a lower quality in their social relationships than what they want. Cacioppo and Cacioppo (2018) described loneliness as pain from social detachment and the hunger and thirst for social bond. Feelings of loneliness stimulate connection with others, following pain from grief, thus reducing social isolation.

Lubben et al. (2015) noted that although social isolation is prevalent in many Western countries, the higher prevalence among Americans today than before provides impetus for research and analysis. However, social isolation among older adults has become more recognized as a critical issue worth studying. Lubben et al. (2015) posited that loss of friendships and perceived social alienation from the community represent two isolating factors for older adults, bearing significant outcomes and implications for social work practice.

The importance of social connections and the benefits of human relationships provide a basis for practical research into the social determinants of health. Historically, the literature was dominated by issues about socioeconomic status, race, ethnicity, gender, and sexual orientation, and offered much evidence of their importance on health and well-being (Donovan & Blazer, 2020). Current research increasingly directs attention to social isolation and loneliness, representing objective and subjective experiences of social disconnection, as two major paradigms impacting human health and well-being (Donovan & Blazer, 2020). Social isolation and loneliness are important to the physical, mental health, and longevity of older adults because circumstances such as loss of relationships, community, and aging are predisposing factors.

Aging: Stereotypes and the Impact of Social Isolation Across Generations

Social networks, particularly friendships, shrink with age. Although it is an individualized process, aging is stereotyped in Western cultures. Hunter et al. (2020) found that older adults are frequently regarded as second-class citizens who "have little to offer society, a view which often results in ageism, a bias that can affect older adults' daily lives" (p. 1). Hunter et al. (2020) also noted that societies managed by technical experts do not recognize crystalized intelligence, thereby denying that knowledge grows with age. HBSE courses can tap into developmental theory to help students understand generativity, a concept involving older adults investing in, caring for, and building the next generation. Realizing the impact of the physical environment on well-being, the World Health Organization (WHO) Global Network, which includes more than 1,333 cities in 47 countries, advocates for creating age-friendly spaces.

The WHO calls upon the health, long-term care, transportation, housing, social protection, information, and communication sectors to act in creating age-friendly spaces. The WHO deemed that combating ageism, enabling autonomy, and supporting healthy aging at all policy levels are some of many approaches that can be collectively employed by the sectors to achieve success (World Health Organization, 2022). Social work students can learn about the positive outcomes of collective behavior to promote excellence and to achieve common goals. In HBSE courses, social work students can address the global aspects of human behavior and their implication for social isolation across generations.

To do so effectively, students must be trained to recognize the relevance of culture and diversity, with a focus on acquiring knowledge to guide decisions about what practitioners must do, and how they do it. The next section presents an intersectionality framework that explains people's unique experiences of discrimination and oppression and implications for social isolation.

Intersectionality of Race, Ethnicity, Gender, and Socioeconomic Status

Intersectionality theory, coined by Kimberlé Crenshaw (2000), was developed to address the non-additivity of impacts of race/ethnicity and sex/gender. The theory can be expanded to study social isolation at different intersections of identity, social location, processes of oppression or privilege, policies, or institutional practices. Intersectionality can improve studies of older adult populations by paying more attention to the impact and underlying processes (Crenshaw, 2000), leading to social isolation. The term intersectionality can reach beyond race and gender (Crenshaw, 2000), because people experience isolation in distinct ways based on the intersection of age with other facets of their identity.

Older adults face social isolation occurring from the intersection of age with gender, race, ethnicity, socioeconomic status, sexual orientation, disability, religion, culture, and language. One of the most persistent concerns about social isolation among older adults relates to their socioeconomic status. Veenstra (2011) observed that several factors, including longer life expectancy, labor force involvement, wage disparity, social programs designed from a male or gender-neutral approach, all contribute to the prospect for older adults to experience poverty. The impetus for intersectionality theory sprang from critical race theory and Black feminism (Collins & Bilge, 2016), which jointly confront the power dynamics of diverging social locations, where structural inequalities are generated and provide prospects for social action.

With a focal point in critical analysis, intersectionality theory can provide a basis for analyzing social inequalities that contribute to social isolation among older adults. When applying intersectionality to older adults and their experiences with social isolation, social workers must understand the multiple characteristics members of this population possess, for which they may be excluded and viewed as undesirable. Relevant aspects to consider include race, ethnicity, gender, and socioeconomic status. As noted by Collins and Bilge (2016), these features interact in ways that direct the experiences an individual encounters. The pandemic's impact offered cases of and outcomes of disparity, and reason for social work respond to this.

Parent et al., (2015) stated that consolidating various social identities shape experiences, especially those connected to social and economic disparities, that can lead to social isolation. From an intersectionality angle, older adults experience social isolation emanating from the devaluation, rejection, relegation, and exclusion directed toward them, because of their race, ethnicity, and socioeconomic status (Veenstra, 2011). The outcomes of belonging to multiple stigmatized groups as it relates to social well-being, may have relevance for social workers studying social isolation with a goal to eradicating it among older adult populations.

Intersectionality and systems theories have similarities and both can inform social work students' understanding of how human beings experience the natural world. Education about social isolation must reflect the impact of identity and social context. HBSE students must acknowledge the importance of systems theory to broaden their knowledge of social isolation in context. Effective use of systems theory in social work practice requires integrating several concepts. In the next section, systems theory is laid out, highlighting its major concepts, and presented with an emphasis on the person-in-environment, to examine social isolation.

Curricula – Systems Theory Approach to Social Isolation

To better understand the link between social relationships and social isolation, ecological systems theory is introduced to explain the psychological and physical needs for relationships that exist in an individual's direct and extended environment. The notion of system has been a bastion of social science and many social work practice and human behavior textbooks have been structured around it. A systems approach serves as a framework through which human behavior can be explored. Therefore, effective social work practice addressing social isolation must rest on understanding the phenomenon within a systems framework that explains human experiences as a set of interconnected parts.

Social workers view the environment as multidimensional and are inspired by an ecological perspective. Individuals exist at the core of their own world, are impacted by, and in turn, influence the nested systems they are a part of, including structures with which they have no direct contact (Bronfenbrenner, 2000). This perspective identifies four levels of systems of influence and suggests that people thrive through regular mutual interactions that occur over time, between themselves and objects of their environment.

The first level contains *microsystems* involving direct, face-to-face contact, and relationships that occur in the individual's immediate environment, among family members and friends. As individuals age, the dynamics and reality of these relationship undergo change that may raise chances of becoming socially isolated. For instance, losing a significant other has been linked to increased social isolation.

The second level of influence, *mesosystems*, includes relationships and activities that occur between two or more microsystems representing an individual's network of microsystems (Bronfenbrenner, 2000). People are linked to others in several settings in which they participate, such as school and work. Changes within the workplace can contribute to social isolation (Umberson & Montez, 2010).

The third level of influence, *exosystems*, are connections between microsystems and larger institutions that impact the individual (Bronfenbrenner, 2000). People make connections and interact with formal and informal structures such as government, politics, culture, mass media, and in their neighborhoods. Burns et al. (2012) noted that changes such as gentrification, and changes in or lack of access to government services, can impact individuals' daily functioning and have been linked to social isolation.

The final system level, *macrosystems*, involves the broader influences of culture, subculture, and social structure. Macrosystems include stereotypes directing widely held beliefs about individuals and structures within each of the four ecological systems. Beliefs shape norms that form the foundation of our expectations of, and responses to individuals and groups. The predominant cultural and subcultural characteristics of macrosystems influence all other levels of systems, including knowledge, resources, and factors affecting lifestyle. The systems perspective views human relationships as the outcome of reciprocal interactions of people operating within linked social systems (Bronfenbrenner, 2000). The actual or perceived absence of functional and structural relationships has been associated with social isolation. Social workers must be trained to view human behavior as a result of internal and external factors transacting with each other.

Humans need strong, healthy relationships with others to survive. Recent studies show that millions of Americans are socially isolated, lonely, or both, which negatively impacts quality of life and health outcomes (Holt-Lunstad, 2022). This has implications for HBSE students to understand the human cost of social isolation and to view it as a social status. A lack of social contacts among older adults has led to an estimated $6.7 billion in additional federal spending annually (Flowers et al., 2017). The importance of public health policy to address social isolation in social service practice cannot be understated. Students of social welfare policy must acknowledge social isolation in a context of political and economic realities. The next section highlights policies, programs, and strategies that have begun to address social isolation globally.

Policies, Programs, and Strategies

The pandemic brought into focus the negative impacts and societal costs of social isolation. Evidence of social isolation's negative effects on health and mental health is also strong, and the need for expanding effective mediations and policies to reduce its harmful outcomes is dire. Notwithstanding data supporting eradicating social isolation as an urgent public health imperative, government leaders, health care providers, and private agencies are slow to champion this Grand Challenge in ways that correspond to other health priorities (Holt-Lunstad, 2022). Despite the slow pace in action, several countries across the globe are increasingly recognizing social isolation as a critical public health issue, with broad implications for policy.

In 2018, advocacy led England to identify social isolation as a health priority, to appoint a Minister of Loneliness, and to dedicate funding to address it. The United States' Surgeon General Vivek Murthy declared loneliness an epidemic and in 2021, Dr. Murthy's second nomination for Surgeon General occurred during the COVID-19 pandemic, and demanded much attention from world leaders. In France, experts discussed the importance of combatting social isolation with policymakers, and secured funding for various grassroots civic activities. Japan appointed its first Minister of Loneliness in 2021 to oversee and implement government policies dealing with loneliness and social isolation (Holt-Lunstad, 2022). In America, Cigna Health, Vodafone, centenarian non-profit groups including Big Brothers & Big Sisters, Meals on Wheels, and Boys & Girls Clubs, have committed to addressing social isolation. The Campaign to End Loneliness (2020) and the Loneliness Project have also gathered, supported, and distributed research and strategies to address this growing wicked problem.

Social isolation was a growing challenge prior to the pandemic and data suggested COVID-19 exacerbated the issue, with findings of increased loneliness and associated depression, as high as 30% (Holt-Lunstad, 2022). Challenges have been acute for certain populations, such as older adults and young adults of Generation Z, who have historically reported higher rates of social isolation (Holt-Lunstad, 2022). Addressing the persistent challenges will be critical and requires policies that directly fund attendant social services. Public health policies must be developed, adopted, and implemented to address social isolation at all societal levels. Students of public health and social welfare policy must be trained to recognize the importance of collaboration and advocacy across sectors, as social isolation has broad impacts, yet interventions are often siloed. Public health issues such as violence, drug abuse, and obesity have received significant attention (Holt-Lunstad, 2022). Evidence suggests that social isolation must be similarly tackled at all levels, with the goal of reducing risk, improving public health, and eradicating it through best practices, which are addressed in the next section.

Best Practices to Eradicate Social Isolation

Social work education must not leave students overwhelmed by macro challenges occurring from the pandemic, and teaching about social work responses to social isolation must be included in curricula. Various approaches have been employed globally to reduce the growing effects of social isolation. Effective treatment and intervention require teaching strategies of behavioral skill sets that include a best practice approach, the preferred technique for achieving a valued outcome (Mullen et al., 2013). To tackle social isolation, social work students must explore the relative efficacy of various interventions. Although the terms "treatment" and "intervention" are often used alike, students of clinical practice must know they suggest different things. A person is given treatment to alleviate symptoms of illness or disease. Interventions are designed to improve health status or encourage behavior change, and can be applied in the larger community (Mann et al., 2017). While only a few treatments have been suggested to mitigate social isolation, direct and indirect interventions have been proposed.

Direct, Indirect, and Group Interventions

Teaching about interventions can include instruction to help students discern between direct and indirect best practices to tackle social isolation. Direct interventions explicitly target social isolation and can help people overcome isolation and feelings related to relationships (Mann et al., 2017). The COVID-19 pandemic has created shifts in how organizations provide services and propelled the use of innovative and creative modes of delivery.

For instance, because young people do not respond well to social prescribing services, schools offer support and social skills training. Face-to-face contact has shifted to remote activities online, or via telephone. Social prescribing refers to measures that can link clients with established social service programs (Mann et al., 2017). Other approaches include checking in, assisting with food or medicine, group calls, or delivering arts and crafts packs, and exercise DVDs (Campaign to End Loneliness, 2020). Mindfulness and Cognitive Behavioral Therapy (CBT) are evidence-based treatment protocols used to address depression. These methods target negative thoughts that impact behavior, offer techniques that can challenge self-destructive patterns, and replace them with positive ways to respond (Campaign to End Loneliness, 2020).

Indirect interventions do not specifically aim to mitigate isolation or loneliness, but may have significant impact on an individual's perceived or objective isolation (Mann et al., 2017). For example, a physician may recommend hearing aids to assist with impaired hearing. The individual may then find it easier to interact in social environments and make connections with others, thus reducing social isolation. Socially focused support systems is another intervention that provides participants guidance to select and attend activities. The support may come from professionals, family members, or peer support workers, who can help individuals reduce levels of loneliness by helping them make their own decisions, identify needed support, and select suitable activities (Mann et al., 2017). Curricula that build skills among health care and social workers to ardently identify efforts in communities for viable referral, is paramount.

Most research on social isolation focused on older adults as the target population. Mann et al. (2017) found that lonely adults can have increased rates of morbidity and mortality, putting them at risk for Alzheimer's and other comorbidities. Interventions such as social skills training and psychoeducation can be delivered individually, in groups, or via digital technology, to help older adults alleviate loneliness (Mann et al., 2017). Social skills training aims to build self-awareness, reduce loneliness, improve social support, and includes conversational ability and body language reflection. Psychoeducation programs are diagnosis focused and offer data about the importance of social relationships to individuals, groups, and families. This approach supports social identity theory, which posits that people receive crucial parts of their identity from group membership. The premise is that older adults who receive practical advice and information are empowered to form, and maintain, meaningful connections (Mann et al., 2017).

On the other hand, interventions for younger people include mindfulness to reduce feelings of loneliness (Mann et al., 2017). For example, mindfulness is taught to school-age children in British classrooms and about 5,000 teachers have been so trained. About 370 schools in England took part in mental health trials that taught children breathing and relaxation techniques, and mindfulness exercises, to learn emotion regulation. Bristow (2019) noted that mindfulness-based interventions in the classroom can reliably influence several indicators of positive psychological, social, physical well-being, and thriving in children and youth. The need for critical pedagogy in educating social workers about best practice interventions to combat social isolation cannot be overstated. The next section considers the value of information and communication technology (ICT) as a curricula item to increase students' knowledge and appreciation for ICT's role in mediating social isolation.

Information and Communication Technology

Regardless of concerns about the use of technology-based interventions, they are being ever more employed by social workers as direct practice approaches to facilitate or deliver interventions (Waycott et al., 2019). Valuable ICT tools for tackling social isolation include smartphones, social media platforms, voice-activated virtual assistants, video conferencing, and wearable devices. These technologies are used to facilitate social interactions with others. ICT intervention is one potential solution for addressing social isolation among older adults to help them connect to a larger community, gain social support, engage in activities of interest, and boost self-confidence (Waycott et al., 2019). What remains unclear is the effectiveness of the use of ICT in nurturing and supporting meaningful social engagement, while alleviating social isolation. Social work has long been identified as a profession that accentuates personal and client-centered relationships. Growing evidence suggests that technological tools can allow for increased access and availability, greater anonymity and avoidance of stigma, extended care interventions outside the bounds of a social worker's office, and enhanced communication between the client and social worker (Ramsey & Montgomery, 2014).

Since the need to integrate ICT in social work practice was highlighted, researchers have shown interest in the potential for various forms of technology to mitigate social isolation (Ramsey & Montgomery, 2014). Social work faculty with specialized knowledge about ICT are well situated to teach students about the prospects not to only promote feelings of connectedness, but to enhance well-being. Designers of Communications courses must establish curricula reflecting ICT elements and educate students about how these systems can work to facilitate services, that mediate social isolation. Technology companies must also consider social isolation when designing products. Medical practitioners often use data from ICT to inform them about patients' heart rate, blood pressure, and sleep patterns.

The time is ripe to equally use ICT to better detect and mitigate isolation. Because of its prevalence, ICT can be easily adapted for use in intervention. Technological advances have potential to meet a critical need in reducing or eradicating social isolation. Making ICT a part of the social work curricula competency is imperative to strengthening social workers' responses to at-risk individuals. The next section shows how campaigns can help create awareness, disseminate information, and move target audiences to act in support of public health.

Campaigns

Campaigns have been successful in boosting awareness about social isolation. For instance, the National Association of Area Agencies on

Aging (n4a) together with the American Association of Retired Persons (AARP) Foundation launched a campaign to raise awareness about social isolation among older Americans (Shedrofsky, 2016). The AARP reported that prolonged social isolation can result in health risks equal to smoking 15 cigarettes daily. To address stigma around admitting to feeling socially isolated and lonely, the campaign focused on making it acceptable to admit loneliness and to seek community resources (Shedrofsky, 2016). The n4a suggested that older adults increase activities such as meeting neighbors, visiting friends or family members, and participating in community causes, to enhance connections. Community-based organizations should create volunteer opportunities for social workers, and involve them in campaigns to build strong environments for persons experiencing social isolation.

The Council on Social Work Education's Educational Policy and Accreditation Standards (EPAS) set guidelines for professional competence, guided by a person-in-environment framework, a global perspective, and respect for human diversity (CSWE, 2022). Educating social workers about campaigns will heighten their awareness of ways to engage best practices, distribute data, and to increase visibility of social problems. This will build students' ability to change public attitudes and social norms, which could in turn impact behavior change (Holt-Lunstad, 2022). Please see Appendix 6A for the EPAS that pertain to this Grand Challenge.

The EPAS (CSWE, 2022) outline the role in assessing and intervening in practice contexts and stresses the prospect that workers are trained to act as a bridge to the larger community. Assisting globally to connect providers and the larger social service community requires that social work curricula provide students tools to allocate community resources, a skill critical to success in combating social isolation.

Social workers and health care workers are crucial in efforts to prevent, and reduce negative health impacts of social isolation. Therefore, it is vital to educate them about relevant indicators. Course content can include measures in use across research in diverse disciplines. Faculty teaching clinical practice and research courses must work to increase students' knowledge and skills about valid tools used to assess social isolation. Aiming to only show a choice, the next section presents and briefly describes commonly used assessment tools.

Evaluation

Many tools exist to evaluate social isolation and loneliness but to date, most of the reputable and extensively used tools were developed for research purposes. Social isolation can be measured objectively and refers to social network size and the presence and interconnections among different social ties. Loneliness is subjective and refers to a person's self-perceived lack of social support and companionship.

Historically, research using assessment tools focused on defining the prevalence, the risk factors, and the health impacts of social isolation and loneliness. Recently, the attention has shifted to assessing the effectiveness of interventions by using measures of social isolation and loneliness as outcomes. Assessment and intervention occur within the intersection of multiple factors, including age, class, culture, and disability, to name a few. Focusing on these factors reinforces the value of understanding the influence of social determinants of health on individuals' lifelong development (CSWE, 2022).

Some regularly used measures to assess social isolation include the Steptoe Social Isolation Index which involves a five-point scale, with one point being assigned for each of the following factors: 1) Unmarried/not cohabiting, 2) Less than monthly contact (including face-to-face, by telephone, or in writing/email) with children; 3) Less than monthly contact (including face-to-face, by telephone, or in writing/email) with other family; 4) Less than monthly contact (including face-to-face, by telephone, or in writing/email) with friends; and 5) No participation in social clubs, resident groups, religious groups, or committees. People with a score of 2 or more were defined as being socially isolated (Steptoe et al., 2013).

A second measure is the UCLA Loneliness Scale developed by Daniel Russell (1996), a 20-item tool designed to determine one's subjective feelings of loneliness and of social isolation. Participants rate items on a scale from 1 (Never) to 4 (Often). A third measure is the Campaign to End Loneliness Measurement Tool built as a three-item device to assess loneliness. Guidance for using the tool suggests an aim to measure changes that occur after intervention to address loneliness (Campaign to End Loneliness, 2020). People are asked to respond to the following questions: 1) I am content with my friendships and relationships. 2) I have enough people I feel comfortable asking for help at any time, and 3) My relationships are satisfying as I would want them to be. The score is a total of responses to the three statements, based on scored responses of strongly disagree (4)/disagree, (3)/neutral, (2)/agree, (1)/strongly agree (0). The higher the score, the greater the degree of loneliness.

Social workers and the programs that educate them must understand the social determinants of health of the populations they help. Therefore, social work education institutions must integrate them in the design and implementation of the program curricula. The EPAS outlines a social work role in assessment and intervention within a practice context that includes working with individuals and families (CSWE, 2022). These competencies highlight the prospect that social workers are trained to pay attention to social and emotional needs of adolescents, young and older adults, and their families, within health and social service settings. We have established that the EPAS sets guidelines for professional competence. The next section explores effective teaching strategies that build competence, while fostering social connectedness.

Teaching Practices in the Classroom

Social connectedness is a valuable protective factor for students and critical to health and mental well-being. Connectedness refers to the extent to which a person or group is mutually close, interconnected, or shares resources with other individuals or groups (Holt-Lunstad, 2022). A didactic approach in the classroom may potentially engulf students with an excess of information and may not promote connectedness. To enhance this method, an instructor may use small group discussions, problem-solving exercises, short videos, and case studies. These strategies can increase sharing and help students engage in retrospection (Moulton et al., 2017).

A key strategy to strengthen social connectedness in the classroom is the use of active learning as a pedagogical approach. Active learning is characterized by a departure from the traditional lecture format that transmits information passively to students (Moulton et al., 2017). A crucial factor in active learning is the level of student engagement, meaning that there is a shift from the instructor acting as the knowledge provider to being the guide, who gently directs students in their intellectual journey (Mello & Less, 2013).

Active learning strategies include collaborative, cooperative, and problem-based learning. Collaborative and cooperative learning focus on interactions between students as members of small groups. The goal of collaborative and cooperative learning is to shift students away from solitary learning activities to engagement in group activities. These strategies promote a high level of student interaction. Problem-based learning occurs when the instructional strategy is to express the material as a problem to provide context for subsequent instruction. Mello and Less (2013) recommended that to strengthen social connectedness among students, the cooperative learning approach is preferred, because it emphasize less student competition and more teamwork as a group to meet goal expectations.

Demonstrating the Necessary Evidence-Based Research Practice Knowledge

It is established that systems theory can be used to help social workers become effective change agents at micro, mezzo, and macro levels. Social work is rewarding, but challenging. It requires developing strategies and skills necessary to be resilient to provide the most effective service (Weinberg & Murphy, 2013). Resiliency is considered an important variable to be analyzed in the context of social work and is supported by factors in the individual, factors residing in the organizational context, and factors linked with the educational preparation of social work practitioners (Weinberg & Murphy, 2013). To be efficient in their work, social workers must understand and use research to render their practice evidenced based. Evidenced-based practice (EBP) is not a cookie-cutter approach, but a review process needing critical thinking, to come up with effective solutions for social problems, such as social isolation.

To effectively eradicate social isolation, practice decisions and change efforts based on research evidence, is paramount. To increase understanding of social isolation and attendant perceptions of older adults, social workers must learn the conditions leading to social isolation and work toward translating research into sustainable methods of practice. On their website, the National Association of Social Workers (NASW, 2021) asserted that social workers increasingly are seeking information about EBPs.

This can be construed as social workers are seeking to enhance their understanding of EBP and sounds promising, considering their presence in the field of practice. Nevertheless, augmenting the use of EBP among social workers is critical. After all, they are at the frontline of working with individuals with mental illness. Despite their dominance in the field of mental health and the Code of Ethics emphasis on research-based service, most social workers do not draw on research findings to inform practice.

Jeffrey (2013) found that 25% of licensed social workers reported not reading scholarly journal articles on social work and more than 50% did not receive any formal supervision. These findings are troubling and cast doubt on the value of social work interventions, if they are devoid of an evidence base. Efforts toward effectively eradicating social isolation will collapse, absent evidence-based research as a catalyst. The EPAS clearly states the expectation that social workers will distinguish, review, and integrate multiple sources of research-based knowledge in their work (CSWE, 2022). This behooves social workers to proactively build on their knowledge of EBP, as no shortage exists in attendant journal articles. Research over the past 20 years has appeared in social work journals, and this research endures (Jeffrey, 2013).

Touted as a profession with expertise driven by values and ethics, and aimed at tackling wicked problems, social work demands that social work leaders, educators, and practitioners support their work with multiple sources of research-based knowledge. Effective eradication of social isolation compels social work research curricula to commit to actively train social workers, to strengthen their ability to conduct evidence-based research, that translates into viable EBP.

Setting the Context

Single dimensional learning where students passively receive information with emphasis on simply acquiring knowledge is increasingly finding a place in the past. The 21st century has recognized a shift in the way learning is approached. It is accessible, flexible, and innovative (Tseng et al., 2016). That students bring their own life experiences to the learning environment must be considered in the classroom, as a basis for enriching learning. Training social workers for practice with vulnerable populations must be student-centered, requires planning with the student in mind, and places them at the center of the learning process.

In essence, instruction is designed for the student and learning is cooperative, collaborative, and community oriented (Tseng et al., 2016). We have established that using vignettes, case studies, and other illustrative tools to help students connect foundational concepts with their personal and professional lives, adds value to learning. Therefore, students' experiences should support their intellectual efforts. This educational approach does not suggest that teachers abandon initiative, responsibility, and leadership. Rather, it offers logic about students' obligations and instructors' execution of their roles of a shared purpose.

Conclusion

Humans are social beings and our social connectedness allows us to flourish. Facing prolonged loneliness is linked to great risk of irritability, depression, suicidal ideation, substance abuse, and a reduction in life span (Holt-Lunstad, 2022). Research by Cacioppo and Cacioppo (2018), and by others mentioned in this chapter, have provided evidence of the triggers and consequences of social isolation and loneliness. Social work education plays a critical role in preparing social workers to lead efforts that improve health for youth, adolescents, families, and young and older adults. Instruction must focus on teaching the skills needed to conduct research, and to identify risk factors and outcomes of social isolation and loneliness. Social work students should be educated about programs, policies, and strategies, assessment tools, and effective interventions to address social isolation. Social workers must be taught to use the current and evolving evidence base with a focus to inform practice. Failing to act is not an option.

References

Bristow, J. (2019). *Mindful: Healthy mind, healthy life*. www.mindful.org/why-schools-in-england-are-teaching-mindfulness/

Bronfenbrenner, U. (2000). Ecological systems theory. In A. E. Kazdin (Eds.), *Encyclopedia of psychology* (pp. 129–133). American Psychological Association. doi:10.1037/10518-046

Burns, V. F., Lavoie, J., & Rose, D. (2012). Revisiting the role of neighborhood change in social exclusion and inclusion of older people. *Journal of Aging Research*, 1–12. doi:10.1155/2012/148287

Cacioppo, J. T., & Cacioppo, S. (2018). The growing problem of loneliness. *The Lancet*, *391*(10119), 426. doi:10.1016/S0140-6736(18)30142-9

Campaign to End Loneliness. (2020). *Promising approaches revisited: Effective action on loneliness in later life*. www.campaigntoendloneliness.org/wp-content/uploads/Promising_Approaches_Revisited_FULL_REPORT.pdf

Collins, P. H., & Bilge, S. (2016). *Intersectionality*. John Wiley & Sons.

Crenshaw, K. W. (2000). *Background paper for the expert group meeting on the gender-related aspects of race discrimination*. www.wicej.addr.com/wcar_docs/crenshaw.html

CSWE. (2022). *Educational policy and accreditation standards*. www.cswe.org/accreditation/standards/2022-epas/

Donovan, J., & Blazer, D. (2020). Social isolation and loneliness in older adults: Review and commentaries of a national academies report. *American Journal of Geriatric Psychology*, *28*(12), 1233–1244. doi:10.1016/j.jagp.2020.08.005

Flowers, L., Houser, A., & Noel-Miller, C. (2017). *Medicare spends more on socially isolated older adults*. www.aarp.org/ppi/info-2017/medicare-spends-more-on-socially-isolated-older-adults.html

Holt-Lunstad, J. (2022). Social connection as a public health issue: The evidence and a systemic framework for prioritizing the "social" in social determinants of health. *Annual Review of Public Health*, *43*, 193–213. https://doi.org/10.1146/annurev-publhealth-052020–110732

Hunter, H., O'Leary, V., Denes, S., & Ginn, L. D. (2020). More than meals: An international innovative social impact project for France. *Health & Social Work*, *45*(3), 1, 59–61. https://doi.org/10.1093/hsw/hlz032

Jeffrey, J. (2013). *Use of social work research among clinicians*. https://sophia.stkate.edu/msw_papers/201

Lubben, J., Gironda, M., Sabbath, E., Kong, J., & Johnson, C. (2015). *Social isolation presents a grand challenge for social work*. American Academy for Social Work and Social Welfare. https://federation.net.ucf.edu/adfs/ls/?client-request-id=652ecc5e-88f4–4b6e-991d

Mann, F., Bone, J. K., Lloyd-Evans, B., Frerich, J., Pinfold, V., Ma, R., Wang, J., & Johnson, S. (2017). A life less lonely: The state of the art in interventions to reduce loneliness in people with mental health problems. *Social Psychiatry and Psychiatric Epidemiology*, *52*(6), 627–639. https://doi.org/10.1007/s00127-017-1392-y

Mello, D., & Less, C. A. (2013). Effectiveness of active learning in the arts and sciences. *Humanities Department Faculty Publications & Research*, *45*. https://scholarsarchive.jwu.edu/humanities_fac/45

Moulton, S. T., Turkay, S. T., & Kosslyn, S. M. (2017). Does a presentation's medium affect its message? PowerPoint, Prezi, and oral presentations. *PLoS One*, *12*(7), e0178774. https://doi.org/10.1371/journal.pone.0178774

Mullen, E. J., Bellamy, J. L., & Bledsoe, S. E. (2013). *Best practices*. https://oxfordre.com/socialwork/view/10.1093/acrefore/9780199975839.001.0001/acrefore-9780199975839-e-32

National Association of Social Workers. (2021). *Evidenced-based practice*. www.socialworkers.org/News/Research-Data/Social-Work-Policy- Research/Evidence-Based-Practice

Parent, M. C., De Blaere, C., & Moradi, B. (2015). Approaches to research on intersectionality: Perspectives on gender, LGBT, and racial/ethnic identities. *Sex Roles*, *68*, 11–12. doi:10.1007/s11199-013-0283-2

Ramsey, A. T., & Montgomery, K. (2014). Technology-based interventions in social work practice: A systematic review of mental health interventions. *Social Work Health Care*, *53*(9), 883–899. doi:10.1080/00981389.2014.925531

Russell, D. W. (1996). UCLA loneliness scale (version 3): Reliability, validity, and factor structure. *Journal of Personality Assessment*, *66*(1), 20–40. doi:10.1207/s15327752jpa6601_2

Shedrofsky, K. (2016, November 16). Campaign helps seniors suffering from social isolation & loneliness. *USA Today*. www.usatoday.com/story/news/politics/2016/11/16/campaign-helps-seniors-suffering-social-isolation-and-loneliness/93920672/

Steptoe, A., Shankar, A., Demarkakos, P., & Ward, J. (2013). *Social isolation, loneliness, and all-cause mortality in older men and women*. https://doi.org/10.1073/pnas.12196861

Tseng, H., Gardner, T., & Yeh, H. (2016). Enhancing students' self-efficacy, elaboration and critical thinking in a collaborative educator preparation program. *The Quarterly Review of Distance Education*, *17*(2), 1–14.

Umberson, D., & Montez, J. K. (2010). Social relationships and health: A flashpoint for health policy. *Journal of Health and Social Behavior*, *51*(Suppl), S54–S66. https://doi.org/10.1177/0022146510383501

Valtorta, N. K., Kanaan, M., Gilbody, S., Ronzi, S., & Hanratty, B. (2016). Loneliness and social isolation as risk factors for coronary heart disease and stroke: Systematic review and meta-analysis of longitudinal observational studies. *Heart*, *102*(13). doi:10.1136/heartjnl-2015-308790

Veenstra, G. (2011). Race, gender, class, and sexual orientation: Intersecting axes of inequality and self-rated health in Canada. *International Journal of Equity Health*, *10*, 3. https://doi.org/10.1186/1475-9276-10-3

Waycott, J., Velere, F., & Ozanne, E. (2019). Building social connections: A framework for enriching older adults' social connectedness through information and communication technologies. *Ageing and Digital Technology*, 65–82. doi:10.1007/978-981-13-3693-5_5 Harvard University.

Weinberg, A., & Murphy, M. (2013). Stress in social work. In A. Worsley, T. Mann, A. Olsen, & E. Mason-Whitehead (Eds.), *Key concepts in social work practice*. Sage. http://sk.sagepub.com.libezproxy.open.ac.uk/books/key-concepts-in-social-work-practice/n56.xml

World Health Organization. (2022). *Age-friendly world*. https://extranet.who.int/agefriendlyworld/network/

Appendix 6A

EPAS Addressed in Grand Challenge #5

Eradicate Social Isolation

Competency 1: Demonstrate Ethical and Professional Behavior. Social workers understand frameworks of ethical decision-making and how to apply the principles of critical thinking to those frameworks in the practice, research, and policy arenas. Ethical issues pertaining to intervention are addressed. Social workers are urged to understand the profession's history and mission, along with their roles and responsibilities in addressing the wicked problem of social isolation. Social isolation, which presents a Grand Challenge for social work, has been broadly recognized as an area of opportunity and concern for professionals of all backgrounds. Because social isolation is a wicked problem, social workers are advised to be aware of and prepared to address the seriousness and prevalence of social isolation and its association with increased morbidity and mortality when compared to other well- known risk factors such as heavy smoking and obesity.

Competency 2: Engage Antiracism, Diversity, Equity, and Inclusion (ADEI) in Practice. Social workers understand how diversity and differences characterize and shape the human experience and are critical to the formation of identity. Social workers are urged to recognize that social isolation is a pervasive wicked social problem that can affect individuals from all backgrounds, regardless of age group, socioeconomic circumstances, race, ethnicity, or gender. Social workers are advised to understand and apply intersectionality theory to help to confront the power dynamics of diverging social locations, where structural inequalities are generated and provide prospects for social action. Social workers are reminded of their ethical imperative to recognize and intervene on behalf of people experiencing social isolation across all backgrounds and age groups.

Competency 3: Advance Human Rights and Social, Racial Economic, and Environmental Justice. Social workers understand that all human beings, regardless of position in society, should have such fundamental rights as freedom, safety, privacy, adequate standard of living, health care, and education. Social workers are encouraged to apply an ecological perspective to interventions and are impelled to understand how their personal experiences and affective reactions influence their professional judgment and behavior. Hunter et al. (2020) found that "older adults often are treated as second-class citizens who have little to offer society. This negative view of older adults can result in ageism, a type of bias that can affect their daily lives" (p. 1). Reducing social isolation requires that social workers take an inclusive approach to practice and be capable of interacting with people from different racial, ethnic, or socioeconomic backgrounds. Social workers are encouraged to take a global approach to practice and to acquire knowledge about the theories of human need, social justice, and strategies to promote social and economic justice and human rights (CSWE, 2022).

Competency 4: Engage in Practice-Informed Research and Research-Informed Practice. Social workers understand that evidence that informs practice derives from multidisciplinary sources and multiple ways of knowing. They also understand the processes for translating research findings into effective practice. To be efficient in their work to eradicate social isolation, social workers must understand and use research to ensure that their practices are evidence based. To eradicate social isolation effectively, it is paramount that practice decisions and change efforts be based on research evidence. To increase understanding of social isolation and the attendant perceptions of older adults, it is imperative to understand the circumstances that lead to social isolation. Social workers are encouraged to work toward translating research on social isolation into sustainable methods of social work practice.

Competency 5: Engage in Policy Practice. Social workers understand the history and current structures of social policies and services, the role of policy in service delivery, and the role of practice in policy development. Social workers are encouraged to recognize the need to advocate for and implement public health policies to address social isolation at the macrolevel. Public health issues such as violence, drug abuse, and even obesity have received a significant investment of resources in the past and ample evidence suggests that social isolation needs to be similarly tackled at all levels, with the goal of reducing risk, improving public health, and even eradicating social isolation (Holt-Lunstad, 2022).

Competency 6: Engage With Individuals, Families, Groups, Organizations, and Communities. Social workers understand that engagement is an ongoing component of the dynamic and interactive process of social work practice with and on behalf of diverse individuals, families, groups, organizations, and communities. Social workers are encouraged to engage with people experiencing social isolation, their families, the organizations with which they interact, and the communities in which they reside.

Competency 7: Assess Individuals, Families, Groups, Organizations, and Communities. Social workers understand that assessment is an ongoing component of the dynamic and interactive process of social work practice with and on behalf of diverse individuals, families, groups, organizations, and communities. Social workers are urged to learn about and understand theories of human behavior and the social environment, and critically evaluate and apply this knowledge in the assessment of clients presenting with social isolation. Social workers are encouraged to apply appropriate therapeutic approaches as part of evidence-based treatment protocols for people experiencing social isolation.

Competency 8: Intervene With Individuals, Families, Groups, Organizations, and Communities. Social workers are knowledgeable about evidence-informed interventions to achieve the goals of clients and constituencies, including individuals, families, groups, organizations, and communities. Social workers are prompted to explore promising interventions to help older adults to alleviate social isolation. These interventions can be delivered individually, in groups, or by way of digital technology.

Competency 9: Evaluate Practice With Individuals, Families, Groups, Organizations, and Communities. Social workers understand that evaluation is an ongoing component of the dynamic and interactive process of social work practice with and on behalf of diverse individuals, families, groups, organizations, and communities. Evaluation of practice helps social workers to assess and monitor whether their work to eradicate social isolation is helpful. Social workers are impelled to assess and monitor their work with social isolation by employing measures to evaluate processes and outcomes to advance practice, policy, and service delivery effectiveness. Several tools and measurements are suggested to guide social workers in process and practice evaluations. Social workers must understand the use of qualitative and quantitative methods to evaluate outcomes and practice effectiveness.

References

Council of Social Work Education (CSWE) (2022). *2022 Educational policy and accreditation standards*. www.cswe.org/accreditation/standards/2022-epas/

Holt-Lunstad, J. (2022). Social connection as a public health issue: The evidence and a systemic framework for prioritizing the "social" in social determinants of health. *Annual Review of Public Health*, *43*, 193–213. https://doi.org/10.1146/annurev-publhealth-052020–110732

Hunter Jr, H., O'Leary, V., Denes, S., & Ginn, L. D. (2020). More than meals: An international innovative social impact project for France. *Health & Social Work*, *45*(1), 59–61. https://doi.org/10.1093/hsw/hlz032

7 End Homelessness

Jeffrey S. Yarvis, Andreja N. Lukic and David W. Babbs

The Diverse Experiences of Homelessness

Global Scope

Homelessness is a wicked social problem that negatively impacts populations across the globe. Homelessness and substandard living substantially change the entire world too much that the United Nations (UN) (1991) declared adequate housing a universal human right. The UN (2005) and UN-Habitat (2016) comprehensive studies estimated that 1.6 billion people (nearly one-fifth of the world's population) lack adequate housing, and about 100 million people worldwide are homeless.

US Prevalence

According to the 2019 Annual Homeless Assessment Report (AHAR) submitted to the US Congress by the US Department of Housing and Urban Development (HUD), approximately 568,000 people were experiencing homelessness. The AHAR also showed that the states of California, New York, Texas, Florida, Washington, and Massachusetts comprise nearly half of the US homeless population (HUD, 2019).

Literature Review

Contributing Factors

The literature supports that lack of affordable and supportive housing and poverty are the primary causes of homelessness (NLCHP, 2015; Joint Center for Housing Studies, 2019). Additional factors causing homelessness include lack of access to affordable health care, racial

DOI: 10.4324/9781003308263-9

disparities, mental health, substance abuse, escaping violence, and natural disasters (U.S. Conference of Mayors, 2016; National Alliance to End Homelessness, 2020).

STIGMA

Societies have negative perceptions about populations facing intractable social problems like poverty, homelessness, and mental illness. Stigmas often have a profound impact on holding that social problem in the place (Weisz & Quinn, 2018). Weisz and Quinn (2018) concluded in a study that "a person experiencing homelessness can attribute some of their health problems due to being targets of stigma." Homeless populations face group and individual discrimination (Johnstone et al., 2015). Society often views the homeless population as less than human (Gerring, 2018; Farha, 2015). Society often blames the victim for being homeless, instead of looking at what decisions the government and community may have made that have contributed to their homelessness (Farha, 2015). Stigmas can create barriers that attribute to the length of one's time spent homeless (Weisz & Quinn, 2018).

RISK FACTORS

Some homeless suffer from trauma including sexual, physical, and mental trauma and problematic termination from work. Also, economic adversity and social isolation are known to increase risk of becoming homeless (Tsai et al., 2017; United States Interagency Council on Homelessness, 2018).

Homelessness and Human Behavior and the Social Environment

Homelessness is a complex social problem with a variety of underlying economic and social factors such as poverty, lack of affordable housing, uncertain physical and mental health, addictions, and community and family breakdown. As a social construct it is important for social workers to understand that homelessness is the result of personal challenges, such as substance abuse and social disaffiliation, whereas structural interpretations suggest that it is the result of systemic factors, such as lack of affordable housing and employment opportunities. Causal factors of homelessness among unaccompanied individuals are 1) lack of affordable housing, 2) unemployment, 3) poverty, 4) mental illness and the lack of needed services, and

(5) substance abuse and the lack of needed services. Homelessness and poverty are inextricably linked. When individuals or families are unable to generate enough income to pay for housing, food, child-care, health care, and education, necessities with a high cost burden sometimes fall to the wayside.

Social Work Curricula Pertaining to Homelessness

The forces which affect homelessness are complex and often interactive in nature. Social forces such as addictions, family breakdown, and mental illness are compounded by structural forces such as lack of available low-cost housing, poor economic conditions, and insufficient mental health services. Together these factors impact levels of homelessness through their dynamic relations. Historic models, which are static in nature, have only been marginally successful in capturing these relationships.

1. Objectives
    a. Students will gain an understanding of homelessness as a social justice issue.
    b. Students will identify the unique challenges and opportunitics of veterans impacted by homelessness.
    c. Students will identify interventions for homelessness and innovative ideas for interventionists, clinicians, and policy makers to understand.
    d. Students will observe and explain homelessness through the lens of change theory.
    e. Students will evaluate evidence-based outputs.

Additionally, please see the Educational Policy and Accreditation Standards (EPAS, CSWE, 2022) in Appendix 7A for the application of competencies to this Grand Challenge.

Current Interventions

Homelessness and the stigma related to transitional and independent living program services continue to impact current service delivery. Transitional Living Programs (TLP) are group home models of planned care that provide housing and aging out services or after discharge from large institutions. TLP are believed to be a vital part of addressing homelessness for foster youth, veterans, and institutionalized mentally ill. TLPs were vital for identification and development for clients who have experienced homelessness and identified a sense of family, connection, community, and preparedness.

Housing First

The Housing First model "provides noncontingent housing"; once the person attains housing, the intervention includes supportive services and treatments, resulting in "significantly improved outcomes" (O'Toole & Pape, 2015). The Veterans Affairs (VA) model of Housing First consists of three parts; "a) removing traditional preconditions to the housing such as completing treatment or proving continuous sobriety, b) providing extensive support for recovery, and c) delivering recovery-oriented services according to the consumer's choice" (Kertesz et al., 2015). Several studies support strong evidence of Housing First's success in reducing homelessness, increasing housing stability, and reducing hospital utilization amongst both veteran and non-veteran populations (Montgomery et al., 2013; Stergiopoulos, Hwang Gozdzik, et al., 2015). The Housing First model is not without its critics; a comparative analysis by Kertesz et al. (2015) found that some veterans that entered the HUD-VASH program that follows HF principals had "poorer outcomes" than those who were "receiving community treatment as usual." However, Kertesz et al.'s (2015) secondary analyses were limited because it could not determine if those participating in the HUD-VASH program had the "same access to the kind of community treatment" as those who were not in the program.

The analysis of Kertesz et al. (2015) is essential because it suggests that persons not actively receiving treatment or some form of program intervention are not as likely to overcome addictions and homelessness as those who are actively receiving treatment.

The problem with these traditional models is that they may exacerbate trauma and stigma. Therefore, clients continue to view the "housing first" model as a speculative model of care. While there are a number of innovatively sound designs for addressing homelessness, more research needs to provide insight on the one-stop shop service initiatives and housing vouchers with at-risk populations from a national perspective. People exiting systems such as the military, temporary shelters, prisons, and mental institutions face deleterious consequences from being systematically oppressed, which is a crime of moral turpitude. It is inconceivable to believe that people exiting systems without support and the basic skills needed for survival would not be at risk for negative outcomes. These individuals are at substantial risk for dropping out of school, homelessness, unemployment, poor mental health, substance abuse, health issues, and victimization. While systems will argue that every concern about the homeless population has been and is being addressed, it is clearly far from the truth for at-risk populations who have to live, struggle, and survive under these conditions after leaving institutional systems.

Most homeless interventions are categorized as street outreach or emergency shelters, transitional housing or supportive housing, and permanent supportive housing (PSH) (VA, 2019a; Homeless Hub, 2020). This review focuses on permanent supportive housing (PSH) because PSH programs are known to be the most successful as a homeless intervention.

HUD-VASH

HUD-VASH is HUD's program that issues housing vouchers from HUD for permanent supportive housing (PSH) that includes full-time case management for eligible individuals. Participants also receive health care services that include mental health and substance abuse programs (Kertesz et al., 2017; Monet, 2019). According to Monet (2019), the HUD-VASH program has "well-documented success" and is "largely responsible for the 48% decline in Veterans homelessness from 2009–2018." PSH programs vary, and individuals are housed in single-site, mixed housing, or scattered-site housing (Veterans Center for Homelessness Among Veterans, 2015). Virginia Supportive Housing (VSH) (2020) is a 30-year provider of supportive housing that places emphasis on community connection, and "work[s] with tenants to ensure a strong sense of connectedness in the apartment community as well as with the larger community." VSH (2020) reported that "95% of their clients do not return to homelessness." Presently, it is not known if community connections influence VSH's program success rate.

Tiny Homes

Recently tiny homes have gained popularity as an affordable housing solution (Xle, 2017). In Texas, where "land still is still abundant and affordable," the 400 square foot cottages were constructed by Hickory Crossing, a PSH provider in Dallas (Xle, 2017). In California, real estate is "expensive and scarce," and "micro-dwellings as small as 50 square foot" were built by the "My Tiny House Project LA" (Coleman, 2018). Another example is the Veterans Community

Project (VCP) (2020) that provides supportive transitional housing in tiny homes for free to veterans. They focus on "community, camaraderie and familiar culture" (Hirschfeld, 2019). The VCP has already expanded into six states and the organization is barely three years old, which is a good indication of project success, but measures were not found to substantiate their operation's success on reducing veterans' homelessness.

3D Printed Homes

The first successful 3D printed inhabitable home was built in Austin, Texas, in 2016 by ICON (ICON, 2019; Mims, 2018). In the winter of 2019, construction started on a 3D home village in Mexico, and houses are built with only 24 hours of print time for less than $4,000 in construction cost (ICON, 2019). ICON's (2019) plans are to deviate from "traditional homebuilding and construction" methods to create "affordable and dignified housing available to everyone on earth." The 3D printing industry can disrupt construction methods and significantly increase the availability of affordable homes, which could lead to a decrease in poverty and homelessness.

Village Sustainable Housing is a novel initiative that provides a new version of permanent supportive housing called Village Sustainable Housing (VSH). The goal of VSH is to decrease participants' chances of returning to homelessness through community connectivity with low environmental impact. The VSH objectives are threefold: increase the social safety network of its residents, improve the quality of life of all Village participants, and enhance neighborhoods. VSH achieves this through social architecture designed to increase opportunities for people to interact socially and organically form relationships, and to provide essential amenities that communities desire or may lack. The Village Sustainable Housing designs include eco-friendly villages that encompass parks, outdoor fitness zones, gardens, green space, recreational and educational opportunities, and retail space. All are desired amenities by emerging or thriving communities (Knight, 2019). The VSH model assumes that when neighborhoods that normally oppose supportive housing and low-income developments are offered amenities that are highly desired, they will become less opposed to the development.

According to Henwood et al. (2015) "innovative thinking" about "housing and sustainable income combined with political influence" is necessary to "reduce risk factors" for people experiencing homelessness and ultimately decrease the number of homeless persons.

The Village Sustainable Housing model provides opportunities for residents and community members to participate in recreational therapy and work on-site in an eco-friendly village. According to Dr. J. Savage, "programs shared" with (homeless intervention) "residents and community members in an environmentally friendly village way have not been done" to his knowledge (personal communication, April 3, 2019).

Homeless programs such as the ones noted earlier require the interplay of multiple services to achieve success, such as gardens, parks, walking and cycling tracks, art programs, outdoor fitness parks, educational classes, dog parks, and laundry services. All programs and facilities will be open to the residents and surrounding community members. An example of successful synergies between services is supported by the Veteran-Centered Therapeutic Model. The Veteran-Centered Therapeutic Model (Appendix 7A), and the VA's motto for therapy is "Changing Lives through Recreation Therapy and Creative Arts Therapies" (Peterson, 2016; VA, 2020). The VA and therapeutic teams achieve positive outcomes by improving the knowledge skills and ability of those participating in the activities (Peterson, 2016; VA, 2020). The successful programs perform four functions: to educate, to empower, to heal, and to connect.

Change Theory

Successfully ending homelessness follows Maslow's (1943) Hierarchy of Needs principles that include five levels of human needs. First, the basic physiological and secure needs of the residents are provided by any of the aforementioned interventions. According to Maslow (1943), "the most basic human life necessities included: security, safety, food, water, shelter, warmth, and rest." Those fundamental necessities are keys to addressing the physical and psychological needs of homeless individuals and need to be foundational elements of any successful program. The newly housed residents' psychological needs come from support staff, refereed resources, and programs. Theoretically, as residents stabilize and acclimate to their new living conditions, their motivation to participate and socialize to fulfill a sense of belonging will increase (Maslow, 1943). As participants actively partake in programs and increase interpersonal relationships, their self-esteem and sense of belonging should increase, subsequently fulfilling psychological needs (Maslow, 1943).

Each proposed service for at-risk populations will be introduced and given a "face" by introducing a case emblematic of that unique at-risk group. Please see Appendix 7D for lectures on other vulnerable populations.

Veterans

US veterans are at higher risk for homelessness as compared to the general population and are reported to be overrepresented within the homeless population (Balshem et al., 2011; Peterson et al., 2015). According to the 2020 Annual Homeless Assessment Report (AHAR) to Congress, the US Department of Housing and Urban Development reported that in January 2020, 37,252 veterans were experiencing homelessness on one given night, which equates to be 8% of all homeless adults (US Department of Housing and Urban Development, 2020). It further reports that out of every 10,000 veterans in the United States, approximately 21 are experiencing homelessness. These numbers have been steadily declining over the years and are almost half of what they were in the 2009 report, which indicated that approximately 73,367 veterans were homeless. In 2020, the AHAR reported that African Americans were disproportionately represented and constituted for approximately one-third of the overall amount of veterans experiencing homelessness. Another alarming statistic in the 2018 report by the United States Interagency Council on Homelessness found that nearly 6 out of 10 veterans experiencing homelessness were aged 51 and older, and that the number of elderly veterans aged 62 and older increased 54.2% between 2009 and 2016. There are speculations that older adults will be a majority of the population that experience or are at risk for homelessness in the coming years due to the complex nature of their age-related needs and medical conditions combined with costs associated with those needs.

According to Tsai and Rosenheck (2015), veterans have been overrepresented in the homeless population since 1980. One of the most identified risk factors for homelessness among veterans is substance abuse and mental health issues. Specifically, psychotic disorders such as schizophrenia and alcohol and drug use disorders have been found to be associated with homelessness (Tsai & Rosenheck, 2015). These findings are consistent with that of overall homeless populations. Although many believe that posttraumatic stress disorder (PTSD) and TBI (traumatic brain injury) contribute to homelessness among this population, research has not found much evidence to support these claims. Many other factors have been found to contribute to the likelihood or increase of homelessness in veterans, such as poverty, unemployment or economic hardships, trauma, mental health disorders, substance use disorders, family conflict, disruptions in connections to social connections, social isolation, and incarceration (United States Interagency Council on Homelessness, 2018). Among veterans seeking treatment for opioid disorders, the rate of homelessness (10.2%) was more than 10 times the rate for the general population receiving care at the VA (United States Interagency Council on Homelessness, 2018).

As noted earlier, the number of homeless veterans has been steadily declining. This is in part due to combined efforts at federal, state, and local levels to increase opportunities for veterans to access permanent housing and through the development of various programs to help address their complex needs. Nonetheless, it is important to continue to develop adequate services to reach this population in need. After all, these veterans serve our country and put their life on the line, only to be left vulnerable and without access to services.

Homelessness as a Diversity and Equity Issue

Equity is a strategy to address disparities and achieve fairness for all. Social workers must understand that all of the problems of at-risk populations are exacerbated by inequity and disparity issues. Therefore, intervening social workers must partner with communities and people with lived experience. We must incorporate person-centered, recovery-oriented, and trauma-informed approaches to understand factors that drive inequities and achieve transformative outcomes.

People of color are disproportionately more likely than White people to experience homelessness in the US. Systemic discrimination and racism have resulted in disparities in the ways housing programs and homeless services impact diverse populations. When people of color experience homelessness, trauma, substance use, and mental health challenges, their housing stability is further undermined by racism, discrimination, and stigma.

Black, Indigenous, and Hispanic and Latinx people experiencing housing instability and homelessness need access to effective, culturally responsive, racially equitable services and supports.

Managing Difficult Conversations in the Classroom

It is hard to have conversations on cross-cultural and social justice issues. We recommend that professors and students engage in a values clarification exercise such as the Alligator-River Story (Oakland.

edu, n.d.) to highlight the challenges of having conversations on topics such as homelessness even when all parties believe they are open-minded and without bias. The following steps are good to keep in mind preceding a difficult class discussion.

Prepare

Clearly, this only works when you know that the difficult conversation is coming and you are the one who will be facilitating it, but really this can be in regards to any interaction. Take some time to think things through – what are the main points you really want to make? If time permits, write down those ideas, keeping them basic. If you know the person isn't going to agree with you, also prepare some examples and factual information to support what you are stating. Be prepared for pushback and disagreement and know that it is okay to acknowledge the difference of opinions.

Practice

Again, this one requires a little bit of prep time. I typically have the conversation in my head several times before it actually happens (yet in my head it still seems to go better than in person!). Often for me, this "practice time" is in the car on the ride to meeting with the Managing Difficult Conversations. This will help to make sure that you do get the main points across that you plan to make. In the moment, if it is tense, it's natural for your communication to speed up or for the words you want not to come, but if you've thought through what you want to say (and you take some deep breaths to calm yourself), you are more likely to remain a clear communicator.

During the conversation – share what you need to and then *listen*, and *be empathetic*. Be open to the other person's view and interpretation of the situation. Remember that perception is a good portion of reality – and so you and whomever you are having the difficult conversation with may have very different perceptions (and realities). You can both learn from one another if you take the time to listen. Sometimes I think we worry too much about proving that we are right and someone else is wrong. We are more likely to reach a place of agreement if we approach the conversation with empathy, acknowledging the feelings that someone else has, and allowing those to be expressed without judgment. Listening empathetically doesn't equate agreement (and I think sometimes we forget that).

Allow silence

We are so used to filling every moment with something that often silence makes us uncomfortable. But when having difficult conversations which may cause all kinds of emotions, allowing silence is sometimes key. You can use that time to refocus and center yourself – breathe and allow that time for processing and keeping yourself calm. Try counting in your head to three, while noticing your breath before responding – especially if you aren't sure what to say or aren't sure if you should or shouldn't be giving a response.

Decide on *clear next steps*. Almost always with difficult conversations, there is a "now what?" that needs to be answered. Sometimes that is as simple as "let's both take some time to think through what we each shared and come back in x amount of time to decide next steps." Other times, more specific next steps are warranted (especially if you are delivering bad news). I find it helpful to end a difficult conversation focusing on the future and giving the person you are talking with as clear of a picture as possible about what happens next.

Additionally, a primer video about veterans and homelessness titled "Homeless to Homeowner Project" (Glynn, n.d.) is a helpful tool for introducing the issue in the classroom. Primer video: www.youtube.com/watch?v=U2Hj_iNI5QY

Therapy and Healing

The goals of homeless treatment programs are to educate, empower, heal, and connect. The programs will achieve this by providing additional support for the residents through recreational therapy, creative arts, healing, and leisure activities located at the Village. All the programs could be delivered under the new Whole Health Model (Appendix 7B) that is a health and well-being program that places the client at the center of their health and is personalized based on the values, needs, and goals of the individual (VA, 2020).

Art Therapy

Homeless populations become "resourceful living on the streets because it is a matter of survival" (Abate, 2016). Future residents likely have experienced resourcefulness in repurposing and reusing discarded goods. The resourcefulness trait blends naturally with art therapy programs that create desirable items from items that were no longer desirable. The previous plastic program will reduce plastic waste by recycling plastic into new products such as phone cases, kitchenware, and wearables.

Evidence-Based Therapy

Some of the world's largest health care organizations, including the United Nations' World Health Organization (WHO) and the VA's health care system, support "creative or expressive art" as an accepted form of therapy (VA, 2019b; WHO, 2019). "Art is a wound that turns into light," 20th-century artist Georges Braque once said.) The homeless certainly have treatment needs, and a variety of programs must be implemented to assist in healing their wounds. Collectedly, successful art therapy programs typically achieve positive responses in psychological, physiological, social, and behavioral areas (VA, 2019b; WHO, 2019).

Transorganizational

Organizations that address wicked social problems like homelessness must solicit stakeholders, government, non-government organizations, corporate, and private citizens, to form alliances that collaborate to reduce or eliminate the problem. Collaborative efforts that share the same common goal of change are called "transorganizational" (Cummings & Worley, 2014, p. 605). Transorganizational strategies can provide resources that individual efforts cannot achieve (Cummings & Worley, 2014, p. 606).

Once a housing organization is formed, it would internally strategize a plan to achieve a transorganizational effort that would make a veteran's village for the formerly homeless a reality. Fortunately, in Fort Worth, Texas, a transorganizational attempt to end homelessness already exists. It includes over 40 agency partnerships and is called the Tarrant County Homeless Coalition (TCHC) (2020).

Not all organizations or individuals will join a broad coalition, such as TCHC. However, they can contribute resources and become allies that emphasize assistance for homeless veterans, which could be helpful. Communities that have achieved successful campaigns to combat homelessness "involved a wide variety of stakeholders, beyond the usual suspects" (United States Interagency Council on Homelessness, 2018). This includes gaining the most valuable insight from those who have or are experiencing homelessness. This can be achieved through published stories, secondary data, and conducting focus groups that provide a formative process for gathering information.

Internal stakeholders include formal partnerships, organization board members, staff, village residents, and communities who participate in the villages programs. Inclusion will start with communication designed for all stakeholders. The organization will follow best practices for communicating, such as via social media. Some best practices include tailoring communication for the audience and providing specific, authentic, engaging, frequent creative content and prioritizing storytelling over marketing (but being donor-centric) (Nonprofit Tech for Good Tech, 2014; Lombardi, 2019).

Continuum of Care (CoC) Systems Performance and Removing Barriers (Appendix 7D)

The HUD-VASH (2020) program goals are to assist individuals and their families to gain stable housing while promoting full recovery and independence in their community, thereby ending homelessness.

Outputs

The role and responsibilities of the case managers (CM) are to use clinical skills to support housing stability, link people to services from the community, and maintain confidentiality/privacy (HUD, 2020). The outputs of the CMs are identifying clients' needs and prioritizing issues; developing a feasible plan; coordinating patient-centered care; identifying barriers, strengths, and abilities to achieve goals; accompanying veterans to appointments; facilitating the exchange of information; promoting understanding; facilitating the development of self-management and independent living skills; arranging and connecting veterans to social needs; providing ongoing monitoring and assessment.

Outcomes

Case management-based programs have reported significant positive evidence-based outcomes in physical and mental health, service utilization, housing, and cost (Kane, 2014). Additional results include reduced use of drugs and alcohol, reduced psychiatric symptoms, reduced social isolation, increased use of Hep A and B vaccines, improved quality of life, and removed employment barriers (Kane, 2014). Typical results for service utilization include reduced emergency department visits, reduced hospital stays, increased access to substance use disorder treatment, and increased insurance coverage (Kane, 2014). Typical results include increased housing stability, reduced time spent homeless, and success of homeless prevention and rapid re-housing programs (Kane, 2014).

Furthermore, there is anticipated reduced hospital cost, reduced cost associated with shelter services, and costs suggested to offset the economic impact of homelessness (Kane, 2014; Stergiopoulos, Hwang, Gozdzik, et al., 2015). The reduced cost to the public of providing supportive housing over shelters or doing nothing is essential information that will be communicated with the public during the project implementation phase to gain public approval.

Integrated treatment, recreational and creative art programs are designed to promote "independence in life activities based upon patient/residents needs and goals" with the intended outcomes of improved motivation, improved mental and physical health, increased motor sensor skills, and increased knowledge and skills, healing and community reentry (VA, 2020).

Technology of Person in the Environment

Social media and the Internet of Things (IoT) is a growing market in which "hundreds of billions of sensors are embedded in a vast array of networked physical objects" (Wired, 2017). Currently, the connected world is expanding with Wi-Fi 6 (connected via local area internet network) and 5G (connected via the cellular network) technologies that will significantly increase the speed and amount of data that can transfer between sensors that lead to systems for monitoring, analyzing, and using Artificial Intelligence (AI) (Looper, 2020; Wired, 2017). In today's technologically driven environment, new programs must explore the options for data collection and analyzing, including AI, to gain valuable insight on the person-to-person and person-to-facility usage. Examples of desired data would include frequency, length of time, and other interactions. This technology would be helpful for users and staff to accurately monitor the activity of facility amenities. This equipment would be less invasive; however, with facial recognition AI, it is possible to track community connectivity. Organizations working in the fight against homelessness could seek partnerships with technology companies to develop and pilot sensors and software that measures the person in the environment. The data collected could be a game-changer in the way communities and supportive housing programs are designed and delivered.

Conclusion

It is easy to get wrapped up in societal views and opinions; however, respect is an all-encompassing and foundational theme woven throughout the National Association of Social Workers (NASW) Code of Ethics. This starts with the core value of Dignity and Worth of the Person and continues within the ethical principle: Social workers respect the inherent dignity and worth of the person (NASW Code of Ethics, n.d.). Therefore, it is imperative that educators and social work students alike learn about the biases and stigmas associated with homelessness and the vulnerable populations that are at a higher risk of being homeless, such as foster youth, veterans, LGBTQ youth, and victims of domestic violence and sexual violence. Throughout this chapter we aimed to provide readers with a better understanding of contributing factors to homelessness; common stigmas and barriers the homeless face; interventions utilized for homeless populations; and an integration of relevant theories that help better explain the challenges of homelessness. As social workers we have a duty to advocate for and protect vulnerable populations. We hope that by taking a deeper look into the Grand Challenge to End Homelessness that our readers will have a better understanding of homelessness and that one by one we can start making changes not only from a societal standpoint, but also through policy changes, ultimately eradicating this problem that is plaguing our country.

References

Abate, C. (2016, May 13). How homeless recyclers make a living redeeming recyclables. *PBS*. www.pbs.org/independentlens/blog/how-homeless-recyclers-make-living-redeeming-recyclables/

Baker, C. K., Billhardt, K. A., Warren, J., Rollins, C., & Glass, N. E. (2010). Domestic violence, housing instability, and homelessness: A review of housing policies and program practices for meeting the needs of survivors. *Aggression and Violent Behavior*, *15*(6), 430–439.

Balshem, H., Christensen, V., Tuepker, A., & Kansagara, D. (2011). A critical review of the literature regarding homelessness among veterans. In *A critical review of the literature regarding homelessness among veterans*. US Department of Veterans Affairs.

Berberet, H. M. (2006). Putting the pieces together for queer youth: A model of integrated assessment of need and program planning. *Child Welfare*, *85*(2), 361–384.

Byrne, C. A., Resnick, H. S., Kilpatrick, D. G., Best, C. L., & Saunders, B. E. (1999). The socioeconomic impact of interpersonal violence on women. *Journal of Consulting and Clinical Psychology*, *67*(3), 362–366.

Castellanos, H. D. (2016). The role of institutional placement, family conflict, and homosexuality in homelessness pathways among Latino LGBT youth in New York City. *Journal of Homosexuality*, *63*(5), 601–632.

Coleman, R. (2018, August 28). *Are tiny houses useful and feasible for addressing the homelessness crisis? Turner center for housing innovation*. UC. https://ternercenter.berkeley.edu/blog/are-tiny-houses-useful-and-feasible-for-addressing-the-homelessness-crisis

Collins, M. E., Spencer, R., & Ward, R. (2010). Supporting youth in the transition from foster care: Formal and informal connections. *Child Welfare*, 125–143. https://www.jstor.org/stable/45400625

CSWE. (2022). *Educational policy and accreditation standards*. www.cswe.org/accreditation/standards/2022-epas/

Cummings, T. G., & Worley, C. G. (2014). *Organization development and change* (10th ed., pp. 605–606). West Pub.

Farha, L. (2015, December 21). Homeless people are not cockroaches or vermin – they are human and have rights. *The Guardian*. www.theguardian.com/housing-network/2015/dec/21/homeless-people-not-vermin-cockroaches-human-rights

Forge, N., & Ream, G. L. (2014). *Homeless lesbian, gay, bisexual and transgender (LGBT) youth in New York City: Insights from the field*. Georgia State University. https://scholarworks.gsu.edu/cgi/viewcontent.cgi?article=1062&context=ssw_facpub

Gerring, M. (2018, June 18). How to be a better neighbor to homeless people: A guide to treating everyone who lives on your block with compassion. *Better Humans*. https://betterhumans.coach.me/how-to-be-a-better-neighbor-to-homeless-people-5ab230d2c738

Glynn, C. (n.d.). *Homeless to homeowner project*. www.youtube.com/watch?v=U2Hj_iNI5QY

Henwood, B. F., Wenzel, S. L., Mangano, P. F., Hombs, M., Padgett, D. K., Byrne, T., . . . & Uretsky, M. C. (2015). The grand challenge of ending homelessness (No. 9). Working paper. American Academy of Social Work & Social Welfare.

Hirschfeld, A. (2019, December 2019). Can villages of tiny homes help America's homeless veterans? *Ozy Media*. www.ozy.com/the-new-and-the-next/can-villages-of-tiny-homes-help-americas-homeless-veterans/242432/

Homeless Hub. (2020). Retrieved March 14, 2020, from www.homelesshub.ca/solutions/affordable-housing/nimby-not-my-backyard

Housing and Urban Development (HUD). (2019). *The 2019 annual homeless assessment report (AHAR) to congress*. https://files.hudexchange.info/resources/documents/2019-AHAR-Part-1.pdf

Housing and Urban Development (HUD) (2020). www.hudexchange.info/programs/hdx/pit-hic/

ICON. (2019, December 11). *ICON+ new story+ ECHALE unveil first homes in 3D printed community*. www.iconbuild.com/updates/first-3d-printed-home-community

Institute for Children and Poverty. (2002). *The hidden migration: Why New York City shelters are overflowing with families*. Institute for Children and Poverty.

Johnstone, M., Jetten, J., Dingle, G. A., Parsell, C., & Walter, Z. C. (2015). Discrimination and well-being amongst the homeless: The role of multiple group membership. *Frontiers in Psychology*, 6, 739. doi:10.3389/fpsyg.2015.00739

Joint Center for Housing Studies of Harvard University. (2019). *State of the nation's housing report*. www.jchs.harvard.edu/sites/default/files/Harvard_JCHS_State_of_the_Nations_Housing_2019.pdf

Kane, V. (2014). *Housing first: Veterans centered care helping to end veterans homelessness*. www.blogs.va.gov/VAntage/16408/housing-first-veteran-centered-care-helping-to-end-veteran-homelessness/

Kertesz, S. G., Austin, E. L., Holmes, S. K., DeRussy, A. J., Van Deusen Lukas, C., & Pollio, D. E. (2017). Housing first on a large scale: Fidelity strengths and challenges in the VA's HUD-VASH program. *Psychological Services*, *14*(2), 118–128. doi:10.1037/ser000012)

Kertesz, S. G., Austin, E. L., Holmes, S. K., Pollio, D. E., & VanDeusen Lukas, C. (2015). Housing first and the risk of failure: A comment on Westermeyer and Lee (2013). *The Journal of Nervous and Mental Disease*, *203*(7), 559–562. https://doi.org/10.1097/NMD.0000000000000328

Knight, D. (2019, December 17). Top new amenities in new-home neighborhoods. *New Home Source*.

Lombardi, L. (2019, March 11). 9 best practices for communications that stand out. *Network for Good*. www.networkforgood.com/nonprofitblog/9-best-practices-for-donor-communications/

Looper, C. (2020, January 24). *What is 5G?* www.digitaltrends.com/mobile/what-is-5g/

Maslow, A. H. (1943). A theory of human motivation. *Psychological Review*, *50*(4), 370–396.

Mims, C. (2018, April 1). 3-D printed buildings are a tech twist on ancient construction techniques. *The Wall Street Journal*. www.wsj.com/articles/3-d-printed-buildings-are-a-tech-twist-on-ancient-construction-techniques-1522580400

Monet, K. (2019). Veterans Affairs supportive housing vouchers. *National Coalition for Homeless Veterans*. https://nlihc.org/sites/default/files/AG-2019/04-06_VASH-Vouchers.pdf

Montgomery, A. E., Hill, L. L., Kane, V., & Culhane, D. P. (2013). Housing chronically homeless veterans: Evaluating the efficacy of a housing first approach to HUD-VASH. *Journal of Community Psychology*, *41*(4), 505–514. doi:10.1002/jcop.21554

National Alliance to End Homelessness. (2020). https://endhomelessness.org/homelessness-in-america/what-causes-homelessness/housing/

National Association of Social Workers (NASW) (n.d). *Code of ethics*. https://www.socialworkers.org/About/Ethics/Code-of-Ethics

National Resource Center on Domestic Violence (n.d.). *The intersection of homelessness and domestic violence*. www.youtube.com/watch?v=gVnwGFqyEcQ

Nonprofit Tech for Good. (2014, September 14). *9 must-know best practices for distributing your nonprofit's content on social networks*. www.nptechforgood.com/2014/09/14/9-must-know-best-practices-for-distributing-your-nonprofits-content-on-social-networks/

Oakland.edu (n.d.) *Alligator-River Story*. https://www.oakland.edu/Assets/upload/docs/Instructor-Handbook/The-Alligator-River-Story.pdf

Olsen, L., Rollins, C., Billhardt, K., & Med, E. (2013). *The intersection of domestic violence and homelessness*. Washington State Coalition Against Domestic Violence.

O'Toole, T., & Pape, L. (2015, November–December). Innovative efforts to address homelessness among veterans. *North Carolina Medical Journal*, *76*(5), 311–314. doi:10.18043/ncm.76.5.311

Page, M. (2017). Forgotten youth: Homeless LGBT youth of color and the runaway and homeless youth act. *Northwestern Journal of Law & Social Policy*, *12*(2), 17.

Peterson, H. (2016, February 9). The success of recreation therapy for veterans. *Veterans' Health Administration*. www.va.gov/HEALTH/NewsFeatures/2016/February/The-Success-of-Recreation-Therapy-for-Veterans.asp

Peterson, R., Gundlapalli, A. V., Metraux, S., Carter, M. E., Palmer, M., Redd, A., et al. (2015). Identifying homelessness among veterans using VA administrative data: Opportunities to expand detection criteria. *PLoS One*, *10*(7), e0132664. doi:10.1371/journal.pone.0132664

Ray, N. (2006). *An epidemic of homelessness*. National, Gay and Lesbian Task Force Policy Institute, National Coalition for the Homeless.

Ream, G. L., & Forge, N. R. (2014). Homeless lesbian, gay, bisexual, and transgender (LGBT) youth in New York City: Insights from the field. *Child Welfare*, *93*(2), 7–22. https://www.jstor.org/stable/48623427

Shelton, J., DeChants, J., Bender, K., Hsu, H. T., Maria, D. S., Petering, R., . . . Barman-Adhikari, A. (2018). Homelessness and housing experiences among LGBTQ young adults in seven US cities. *Cityscape*, *20*(3), 9–34.

Stergiopoulos, V., Hwang, S. W., Gozdzik, A., et al. (2015, March). Effect of scattered-site housing using rent supplements and intensive case management on housing stability among homeless adults with mental illness: A randomized trial. *Journal of the American Medical Association*, *313*(9), 905–915.

Tarrant County Homeless Coalition. (2020). Retrieved March 27, 2020, from https://ahomewithhope.org/education/

Thompson, M. H., Wojciak, S. A., & Cooley, E. M. (2018). The experience with independent living services for youth in care and those formerly in care. *Children and Youth Services Review*, *84*, 17–25.

Tsai, J., Hoff, R. A., & Harpaz-Rotem, I. (2017). One-year incidence and predictors of homelessness among 300,000 US Veterans seen in specialty mental health care. *Psychological Services*, *14*(2), 203–207. www.ncbi.nlm.nih.gov/pubmed/28481605

Tsai, J., & Rosenheck, R. A. (2015). Risk factors for homelessness among US veterans. *Epidemiologic Reviews*, *37*(1), 177–195.

United Nations. (1991, September 13). CESCR general comment no. 4: The right to adequate housing (art. 11 (1) of the covenant). *Office of the High Commissioner for Human Rights*. www.refworld.org/pdfid/47a7079a1.pdf

United Nations. (2005, March 3). *Report of the special rapporteur on adequate housing as a component of the right to an adequate standard of living*. Economic and Social Council. Commission on Human Rights. Sixty-First Session.

United Nations. (2017). *LGBT homeless youth: IDAHOT*. www.youtube.com/watch?v=jSVrDuXFTtM

UN-Habitat. (2016). *World cities report 2016*. United Nations Human Settlements Program. https://unhabitat.org/sites/default/files/download-manager-files/WCR-2016-WEB.pdf

United States Interagency Council on Homelessness. (2018, June). *Homelessness in America: Focus on veterans*. www.usich.gov/resources/uploads/asset_library/Homelessness_in_America._Focus_on_Veterans.pdf

U.S. Conference of Mayors. (2016, December). *Report on hunger and homelessness*. https://endhomelessness.atavist.com/mayorsreport2016

Veterans Affairs (VA). (2019a). *Homeless veterans*. www.va.gov/HOMELESS/pit_count.asp

Veterans Affairs (VA). (2019b). *Evidence map of art therapy. Evidence synthesis program (ESP) Center west Los Angeles VA medical center*. www.hsrd.research.va.gov/publications/esp/art-therapy.pdf

Veterans Affairs (VA). (2020) *Rehabilitation and prosthetic services*. www.rehab.va.gov/rectherapy/

Veterans Center for Homelessness Among Veterans. (2015, December). Permanent supportive housing resource guide. *Department of Veterans Affairs*. www.va.gov/HOMELESS/nchav/docs/Permanent-Supportive-Housing-Resource-Guide-FINAL.PDF

Veterans Community Project. (2020). Retrieved February 18, 2020, from www.veteranscommunityproject.org/

Virginia Supportive Housing. (2020). Retrieved March 14, 2020, from www.virginiasupportivehousing.org/about/

Weisz, C., & Quinn, D. M. (2018). Stigmatized identities, psychological distress, and physical health: Intersections of homelessness and race. *Stigma and Health*, *3*(3), 229–240. https://doi-org.ezproxy.uta.edu/10.1037/sah0000093

Wired. (2017). The sensor based economy. *Brand Lab*. www.wired.com/brandlab/2017/01/sensor-based-economy/

World Health Organization. (2019). *What is the evidence on the role of the arts in improving health and well-being? A scoping review*. By Daisy Fancourt, Saoirse Finn. Health Evidence Network synthesis report 67. www.

euro.who.int/en/data-and-evidence/evidence-informed-policy-making/publications/2019/what-is-the-evidence-on-the-role-of-the-arts-in-improving-health-and-well-being-a-scoping-review-2019

Xle, J. (2017, July 18). 10 Tiny house villages for the homeless across the U.S. Case studies for a trending idea. *Curbed. Vox Media.* www.curbed.com/maps/tiny-houses-for-the-homeless-villages

Young, R. (2020). *Ending homelessness: Evolution of quad prep academy.* DSW Student Capstone Project submitted to the University of Southern California.

Appendix 7A
EPAS Addressed in Grand Challenge #6

End Homelessness

Competency 2: Advance Human Rights and Social, Racial, Economic, and Environmental Justice. Social workers understand that every person regardless of position in society has fundamental human rights. Social workers advocate and engage in strategies to eliminate oppressive structural barriers to ensure that social resources, rights, and responsibilities are distributed equitably and that civil, political, economic, social, and cultural human rights are protected. Social workers are urged to recognize the importance of recognizing and advocating for the human rights of those who are homeless.

Competency 3: Engage in Anti-Racism, Diversity, Equity, and Inclusion (ADEI) in Practice. Social workers understand how oppression shapes human experiences and how this influences practice at the individual, family, group, organization, and community level. Social workers understand that this intersectionality means that a person's life experiences may include oppression, poverty, marginalization, and alienation as well as privilege and power. Social workers understand the societal and historical roots of social and racial injustices and the forms and mechanisms of oppression and discrimination (CSWE, 2022). With this knowledge and awareness, we can ultimately help end homelessness.

Competency 5: Engage in Policy Practice. Social workers work to identify social policy at local, state, and federal levels that affects well-being, human rights and justice, service delivery, and access to services. Social workers are aware of the impact that policies have on vulnerable populations and how beneficial it can be to advocate for policy changes. Ending homelessness can help put individuals, including disabled or otherwise disenfranchised people, and families on a trajectory towards inclusion, integration, health and well-being (Henwood et al., 2015). There are many policies out there to help address the needs of the homeless; however, there is always room for changes. Though innovation is necessary to end homelessness, meeting this challenge will require interdisciplinary or cross-sector collaboration that includes a focused, organized response from social work researchers, clinicians, and policy makers (Henwood et al., 2015).

Competency 7: Assess Individuals, Families, Groups, Organizations, and Communities. Social workers understand that assessment is an ongoing component of the interactive process of social work. It is important to be able to adequately assess individuals, families, groups, organizations, and communities and recognize the implications of the larger practice context. Through proper assessment the needs and strengths of the homeless population can be better identified and more programs and policies can be developed to ultimately help our Grand Challenge of ending homelessness.

Competency 8: Intervene With Individuals, Families, Groups, Organizations, and Communities. Social workers understand theories of human behavior, person-in-environment, and other interprofessional conceptual frameworks, and they critically evaluate and apply this knowledge in selecting culturally responsive interventions with clients and constituencies, including individuals, families, groups, organizations, and communities. Homelessness and housing instability are substantial problems that afflict a diverse group of subpopulations such as families, youth, veterans, and chronically homeless single adults who may require tailored interventions that are responsive to specific individualized needs (Henwood et al., 2015). Social workers are equipped to handle these unique needs. It is imperative that as social workers we intervene when necessary and help end homelessness. To eradicate all forms of homelessness in ten years, interdisciplinary and cross-sector collaboration will be necessary for accurately assessing the scope of the problem; improving data; establishing innovative and clear solutions to family, youth, and other subpopulation homelessness; and disseminating existing effective solutions (Henwood et al., 2015).

References

CSWE. (2022). *2022 educational policy and accreditation standards*. www.cswe.org/accreditation/standards/2022-epas/

Henwood, B. F., Wenzel, S. L., Mangano, P. F., Hombs, M., Padgett, D. K., Byrne, T., . . . & Uretsky, M. C. (2015). The grand challenge of ending homelessness (No. 9). Working paper. American Academy of Social Work & Social Welfare.

Appendix 7B

Suggested Course Assignments:

1. Reaction Paper.

Watch the short film and describe your reactions to the film, what insights about the homeless you gained from the film, and what made the film effective. www.youtube.com/watch?v=R8ead6CvOPk. Then watch "The Case of Paul" and describe how Paul changed your understanding of homeless individuals.

https://drive.google.com/file/d/12-UYXVu4Fw0xPjRYCfwuczuFYsaH9v82/view

Greene, P. (2020). Short-form video and the case of Paul. YouTube Uploaded August 6, 2020. Student project. University of Southern California, Los Angeles, CA.

2. Create a Homeless Grand Challenge Short Form Video (20%).

We live in a world of "short form video." Any number of social causes and non-profit organizations will feature persuasive short videos of "Our Story," "Reducing Stress," "Bike Ride," presenting highlights of successful projects completed during the summer, at Halloween, etc. We will see plenty of examples of these messages.

Many short-form videos are two to four minutes long. Speed of speech should be fairly quick, but not hurried. You will want to speak fluidly, clearly, and you want to engage your audience. The organization needs to be easy to follow, like "problem-solution" or "chronologically ordered." Most successful short-form videos are cast as positive and up-beat with sympathy communicated for victims/survivors and a clear focus on successfully overcoming a problem. Inspirational messages are often the ones most liked and more often forwarded to others. The professor and class members will critique and provide feedback.

3. Grand Challenges Homeless Campaign Paper.

Part I: Students will write a review of a campaign or movement associated with the Grand Challenge of Homelessness and one of the at-risk populations.

Example: "Foster Youth and Homelessness" and much more. Students can look at the 100+ campaigns housed within the Ad Council. If possible, select a campaign that has won awards. Award-winning campaigns are listed in Effie.org (for Effective Campaigns), or in the WARC database. There is usually more material written on award-winning campaigns than other campaigns. Many campaigns (even corporate ones) appeal to values, like "Save a Child by 5," and P&G's projects on fighting labels and working toward equality.

Outline for Part I:

I. An introduction, statement of the problem, reason for the campaign;
II. How the campaign was conceived and researched (we call this "formative" research) and elements selected – using what media, targeting what audience, how were messages designed, etc.;
III. How the campaign was launched, how it was assessed, and with what outcomes;
IV. Conclusion: what worked, what did not work, what is proposed as the next step.

Outline for Part II:

I. Why is your new campaign needed?;
II. Description of your new campaign;
III. What do you know about the target group (your receivers; beneficiaries)?;
IV. How is your new campaign different from your researched campaign?;
V. For your new campaign:

   a) What is the message(s) and appeal (logic, emotional; which emotions)?;

b) Who are the speakers or sources (celebrities, average people, experts, etc.)?;
c) Which channels/media are used (TV, social media, radio, internet, direct mail, etc.)?

Part II is intended for the doctoral student to design a campaign to market, advertise, disseminate, educate, and inform mass audiences about their Grand Challenge initiative and/or innovation. This is their communication plan/strategy and informs their final capstone paper.

Grading for this assignment is influenced by:

a) Quality and organization of writing (clarity, concise writing) (33%);
b) Reasonable comprehension of details about the need, designed message strategy, including message appeals and source characteristics) (33%); and
c) A clear, brief exposition of the outcomes; why was or wasn't the researched campaign successful; and, why could the proposed campaign be successful on one or more group of receivers; relatedness to student's Grand Challenge.

The paper is to be no less than eight full pages to ten pages of text in length; APA format, 12-point New Times Roman font. The first page is a cover page, the last page or section is the works cited page; add a header and page numbers.

4. Innovative Idea In-Class Rehearsal.

   A professional sales pitch or infomercial recorded and uploaded for this assignment should last 5 to 6 minutes and follow the self-presentational and public speaking principles discussed in the readings and discussed in the grading of previous Talks noted above. Students are encouraged to provide detailed and constructive feedback to one another throughout the semester. Everyone in the class is a member of a learning community of social change agents committed to the greater good. Everyone in this class is expected to be helpful, to give advice, share material, and insights. Classmates are your future friends, colleagues, and collaborators (and sometimes your future employers). *View: How to look your best for online meetings and recordings (https://youtu.be/ACNGhPKnmok).

5. Short Form Marketing Video (20%).

This final original short form video – two minutes – will be recorded and uploaded as your final product for public relations or marketing of your ideas. This SFV is intended for you to communicate your ideas succinctly to mass audiences. This talk is intended to be viewed by a much larger and diverse audience and may be placed on your website. The grading is still based on speed of delivery, fluency, clarity, and flow.

Appendix 7C

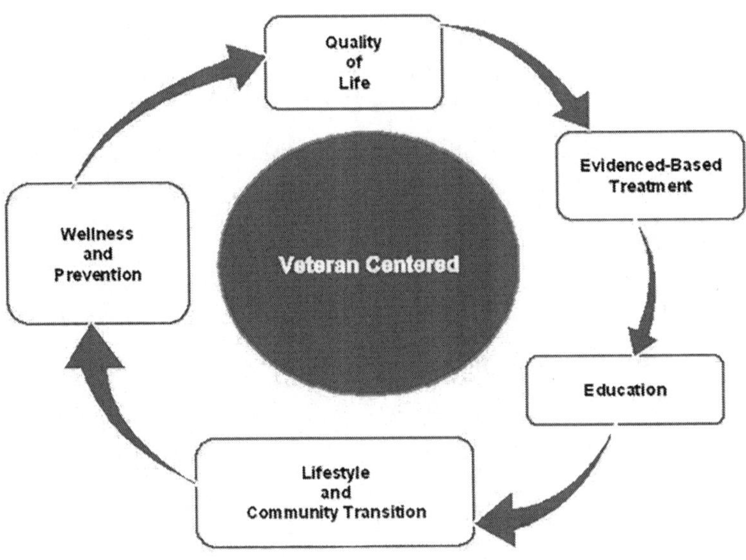

Figure 7.1 National Recreation Therapy Service

Appendix 7D

Table 7.1 Continuum of Care (CoC) Systems Performance Measures

Measurement 1. The length of time persons remains homeless.
Desired outcome is a reduction in the average and median length of time persons remain homeless.
Measurement 2a. The extent to which persons who exit homelessness to permanent housing destinations return to homelessness within 6 to 12 months.
Desired outcome is a reduction in the percent of persons who return to homelessness.
Measurement 2b. The extent to which persons who exit homelessness to permanent housing destinations return to homelessness within two years.
Measurement 3. The number of homeless persons in PIT count.
Desired outcome is a reduction in sheltered and unsheltered homeless persons PIT count.
Measurement 4. The employment and income growth for homeless persons in CoC program-funded projects.
Desired outcome is increases in the percent of adults who gain or increase employment or non-employment cash income over time.
Measurement 5. Reduction in the number of persons who become homeless for the first time.
Desired outcome is the reduction in the number of persons who become homeless for the first time.
Measurement 6. Preventing returns to homelessness within 24 months.
Desired outcome is the reduction in the percent of persons defined as homeless over 24 months.
Measurement 7. The successful placement in or retention of permanent housing.
Desired outcome is increases in the percent of persons who exit to or retain permanent housing.

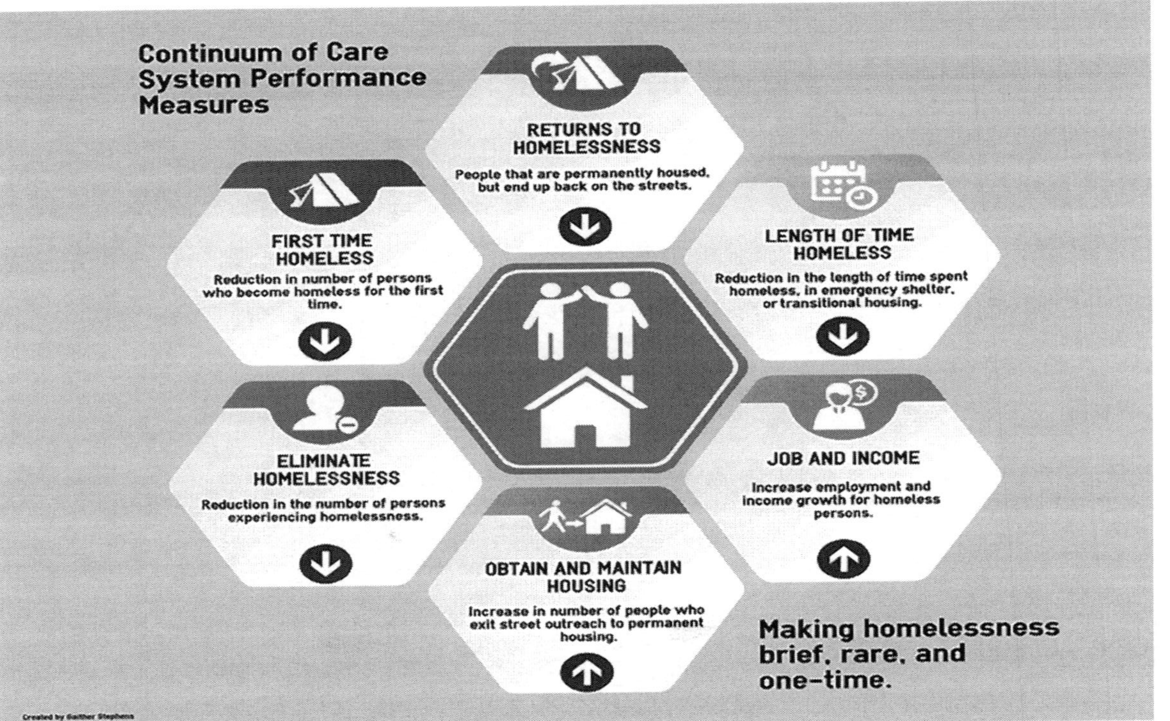

Figure 7.2 Performance measures graph

Appendix 7E
Lectures for Other Vulnerable Groups

LGBT Youth

> A primer video is available for classroom use titled: LGBT Homeless Youth: IDAHOT www.youtube.com/watch?v=jSVrDuXFTtM (United Nations, 2017)

LGBTQ young adults are disproportionately represented among the population of youth experiencing homelessness in the United States (Shelton et al., 2018). Over 1.5 million youths are homeless every year with sexual minority youth being overrepresented in most geographic areas (Castellanos, 2016). The National Gay and Lesbian Task Force Policy Institute and the National Coalition for the Homeless estimate that between 20% and 40% of all homeless youth identify as LGBTQ (Castellanos, 2016; Ray, 2006). Disclosure of sexual orientation is often cited as the chief cause of homelessness among LGBT youth (Castellanos, 2016; Ray, 2006). Studies have found that approximately 20% of youth leave home because their family members disapprove of their coming out or are uncomfortable with their sexual orientation (Page, 2017). Some LGBTQ youth run away prior to disclosing their sexual orientation for fear of rejection, stress, or getting kicked out of their homes. Other factors that may contribute to why LGBTQ youth are homeless may include substance abuse, physical abuse, sexual abuse, mental health issues, early development of sexual orientation, family poverty, aging out of foster care or juvenile justice systems, and financial or emotional neglect from family members (Page, 2017).

Studies find that homeless LGBTQ are at a higher risk of succumbing to extreme survival strategies, such as being forced into sexual exploits to provide for their basic needs of food and shelter (Page, 2017). Homeless LGBTQ youth also face harassment, victimization, and stigmatization (Page, 2017). As an at-risk population, LGBTQ youth have higher rates of school-related problems, such as fights, using drugs, and often experience more problems with sexual assault, physical abuse, and mental health issues than their heterosexual counterparts (Page, 2017). It is also noted that homeless LGBTQ youth are at greater risk for sexual risk behaviors as well as suicidality compared to heterosexual homeless youth (Ream & Forge, 2014). It is reported that most currently homeless LGBTQ youth did not go from familial homes straight to the streets but were once involved in the child welfare system and had stayed at other shelters (Berberet, 2006; Ream & Forge, 2014). It is imperative that we do not allow populations like this to "slip through the cracks." Funding, policies, appropriate training, and adequate resources are needed to address this concern.

Domestic Violence and Sexual Assault Victims

> A primer video is available for classroom use titled: The Intersection of Homelessness and Domestic Violence: www.youtube.com/watch?v=gVnwGFqyEcQ
> (National Resource Center on Domestic Violence, n.d.)

Approximately 1 in 5 women report being physically assaulted by an intimate partner at some point in their lifetime (Baker et al., 2010). Evidence suggests that domestic violence is among the leading causes nationally for homelessness among women and children (Institute for Children's Poverty, 2002; Baker et al., 2010). It is reported that as women attempt to secure housing away from their abusers, they face many barriers. Byrne and colleagues (1999) found that past exposure to domestic violence has been shown to be linked to future unemployment and poverty for women. Other difficulties to securing stable housing can include poor rental history; lack of affordable housing; criminal history; and evictions and credit problems due to having trouble paying rent on their own.

"Federal cuts in subsidized housing have greatly limited access to affordable housing for low-income people, among them millions of DV survivors and their children struggling with housing instability and compromised safety" (Olsen et al., 2013, p. 2). Studies show that many women who fell through the cracks of the DV system's eligibility triage ended up in homeless shelters when the DV shelters were full. Homeless shelters were often uncomfortable sheltering these victims due to their complex safety needs and potential violence of abusive partners (Olsen et al., 2013). Housing policies that specifically address the unique needs of survivors of domestic violence need to be implemented. It is also recommended that domestic violence providers become more aware about housing options in their communities and help advocate for their clients to help them find stable and safe housing options.

Foster Youth

A primer video is available for classroom use on the challenges of foster youth: www.youtube.com/watch?v=qqNsjHiIsa8
(Young, R., 2020)

Homelessness plays a major dysfunctional and disruptive role in subpopulations, such as youth aging out of foster care. A vital problem related to youth exiting the foster care system is that youth are literally unprepared for life after foster care and are still in need of essential services and guidance in adulthood. Documented exposure to trauma increases the vulnerability of individuals who have been in foster care (Young, 2020). Entry into foster care is a traumatic event compounded by the reason for entry into foster care (Collins et al., 2010). In addition to the compacted traumatic events that foster care youth experience is the endless suffering endured by youth who have languished in the system with little to no help for years. Youth become institutionalized and labeled as having severe mental and behavioral health needs, as well as being hard to place due to substance abuse and criminal history. Many youth have been in more than 15 placements over the span of being in foster care. For a country who claims to love its children, we provide little innovation, love, or justice for them in the foster care system (Collins et al., 2010). Both the system that is designed to help and the youth sever ties when they turn 18. The problems youth face when they voluntarily sign out of care after reaching the age of emancipation are insurmountable. Youth exit the system and enter a world of independence lacking the skills necessary to be independent, and face homelessness instantaneously. Difficulty transitioning to adulthood is amplified for young adults who leave foster care at 18 years of age since they are less stable than their peers who are vulnerable for other reasons. Youth who were bought up in foster care characteristically do not have the stability that comes from attachment to a family that other disadvantaged youth do (e.g. high school dropouts, the poor). Throughout their young life, they have had various placements, schools, health care providers, and caregivers. Inevitably, when they turn 18, the cycle continues – making the beginning of adulthood hardly a celebration and more the beginning of an obstacle course (Collins et al., 2010).

All youth formerly in foster care share a heightened risk of inadequate access to health care, involvement with the criminal justice system, becoming incarcerated, living in poverty, becoming pregnant unexpectedly, experiencing homelessness, or having difficulty obtaining employment (Thompson et al., 2018). The problems highlighted need to be addressed as no youth should be leaving a system of care unprepared. Youth need housing and in-depth training to be truly recognized as independent. The stigma that traditional placements and experiences that youth had in care calls for a non-traditional approach to address both housing and sustainable living proprieties for foster care youth. To be liberated beyond foster care calls for appropriate housing, independent living skills training, a high school diploma, certifications, and sustainable employment.

8 Create Social Responses to a Changing Environment

Melissa Indera Singh, Kelly Smith and Murali Nair

The authors of this chapter are gathered on the unceded land of the Seminole, Merricks, Matinecocks, Fernandeño Tataviam, and Chumash people. I ask you to join me in acknowledging the Seminole, Merricks, Matinecocks, Fernandeño Tataviam, and Chumash communities, their elders both past and present, as well as future generations. This acknowledgment demonstrates a commitment to beginning the process of working to dismantle the ongoing legacies of settler colonialism.[1]

Social Work Grand Challenge: Create Social Responses to a Changing Environment

The Grand Challenge to Create a Social Response to the Changing Environment by The Academy of Social Work and Social Welfare is a major step toward solidifying the role social workers can play in addressing hazardous environmental issues, which disproportionately burden vulnerable groups. Social workers are called to incorporate the physical environment to advance justice while elevating ecological concerns to their rightful place as an essential and significant component of current and future social work practice and scholarship (Mason et al., 2017). The Grand Challenge initiative invites social workers to better respond to the complex challenges of social justice and their ethical responsibilities to environmental plights.

Social workers are often established in the communities most negatively affected by the climate crisis and have a unique skill set across the micro, mezzo, and macro levels. Social work practitioners may work with individuals who experience solastalgia, ecological grief, or eco-anxiety (as defined in Appendix 8A). Researchers and practitioners react to environmental concerns environmental concerns, notably highlighting lived experiences at the individual and community level

DOI: 10.4324/9781003308263-10

of practice (Boddy et al., 2022). The Grand Challenge calls attention to such disparities and encourages the discipline to address the disproportionate consequences of acute and pervasive environmental dilemmas on communities centering inequitable power and resource allocation.

Grand Challenge in the Curricula

Human Behavior in the Social Environment

The profession of social work values the social environment to understand human behavior. The Grand Challenge calls for social workers to act on the threats of adverse environmental impacts which increase vulnerability (Fong et al., 2018). Thus, the traditional definition of the social environment should be expanded to include the natural world and the relationship that an individual has to place. According to Akesson et al. (2017), there should be an emphasis on place, specifically territoriality and place attachment and identity, within social work. The human-nature dichotomy limits social work's efficacy that can be advanced by recognizing interconnectivity and interdependence (de Mol van Otterloo et al., 2018). With the broader incorporation of the environment, social workers can improve their holistic assessment of an individual.

Social work curricula often incorporate a person-in-environment (PIE) approach, which conceptualizes an individual impacted by their environment (Richmond, 1917). Bronfenbrenner further defined PIE using an ecological systems model to develop an individual grounded in Ecosystems Theory (Bronfenbrenner, 1989). The strengths perspective (Saleebey, 2006) is also a foundational concept in social work practice. Since the late 20th century, the expansion of social work scholarship through a person-in-environment framework emphasizes the deep intersections between ecological and social wellness (Krings et al., 2020). Simultaneously, this expansion further advances social work's ethical obligations to attend to environmental justice and protection (Bowles et al., 2018). A PIE approach, ecosystems theory, and a strengths perspective position the social work profession to impact environmental justice.

Social work education equips students to engage, assess, and intervene in chronic and acute crises, often using case studies. In the case of COVID-19 social workers faced a syndemic, combining the words synergy and epidemics to describe the phenomenon of communities impacted by a new epidemic often facing an existential threat to health

(Singer, 1996). Singer (1996) researched HIV in North America during the 1990s and determined that syndemics are not simply co-occurring but rather perpetuating and adding to existing problems, especially in communities of color. Wilson et al. (2014) researched HIV as a public health crisis affecting Latino and Black men by exploring how social, biological, and structural factors interact and found a complex systems analysis, multi-disciplinary collaboration, and diverse public health practitioners are necessary to further understand social marginalization. Similarly, social work education and practice bring a micro, mezzo, and macro perspective to syndemics to understand the individual and systems analysis and advance an interdisciplinary approach.

In 2010, Singer added an environmental perspective to a syndemic and created an ecosyndemic, a synergistic interaction based on hu(man) made environmental changes. An ecosyndemic framework includes the possibility of interactions between psychological stress, vector-borne infections, and sexually transmitted infections and highlights the need for an interdisciplinary approach (Tallman et al., 2020). Social worker practitioners may be trained at each level of education to incorporate a person and environment framework to create a more comprehensive assessment of clients and communities.

By practicing social work using a person and environment (PAE) model, social workers can improve their holistic assessment of an individual. According to Akesson et al. (2017), there should be an emphasis on place, specifically territoriality and place attachment and identity, within social work. The traditional definition of the social environment should be expanded to include the natural world and the relationship that an individual has to their place. Hutchison (2019) integrates the physical environment within the fluid PAE model. Lewicka (2011) studied place attachment, the bond between geographical areas of residence and individuals and groups, including families. Bernardo and Palma-Oliveira (2016) confirmed that place identity, a fusion of place into self-identity, also influences social categorization and impacts how people think, feel, and act.

Social Work Policy

The National Association of Social Work (NASW) Code of Ethics roots environmental justice as a core component of social work's ethical responsibility. According to the document, social workers have ethical responsibilities to the broader and endeavor to:

> Promote the general welfare of society, from local to global levels, and the development of people, their communities, and their

> environments. Social workers should advocate for living conditions conducive to the fulfillment of basic human needs and should promote social, economic, political, and cultural values and institutions that are compatible with the realization of social justice.
> (NASW, 2017, Standard 6.01)

Additionally, social workers are called to action to "provide appropriate professional services in public emergencies to the greatest extent possible" (NASW, 2017, Standard 6.03). As the climate crisis accelerates and continues to cause significant environmental and social disruptions worldwide, social workers are mandated to use their skills in response to these myriad impacts.

Social work employs a humanizing lens, so integrating this skill set and knowledge at the macro level of practice offers opportunities to accelerate responses to climate change. Advancing education and policy centered on a right-based approach rather than on climate impact timelines and statistics will likely contribute to more rapid and effective behavioral changes (The Editorial Board, 2018). Acknowledging and adhering to social work ethical responsibilities helps close the vast gap between current and needed planning, mitigation, and coalition building for resilience in facing environmental injustice.

Environmental Justice in Social Work Education

A person and environment (PAE) framework can describe a multidimensional approach in social work education, which suggests that the PAE dimensions are intertwined (Hutchison, 2019). Environmental justice incorporates the dynamic and complex intersectional history of identities such as but not limited to race, class, and gender, which are deeply connected to inequitable impact on individuals, communities, countries, and the world. Social work educators are tasked to combine perspectives from multiple disciplines to understand how climate change impacts people in the classroom. This teaching practice will focus on the social work practice domain.

Learning and Engagement

Generally, individuals do not expect one another to take actions that mitigate climate change (Leiserowitz et al., 2018). However, the increasing frequency and widening geographic scope of climate change events and disasters are shifting these norms. Classroom-based peer working groups that engage students with climate change can build upon social worker skill sets to employ harm reduction techniques through climate crisis competency. Fostering community is also an essential component to successfully integrate environmental justice into curriculum.

A considerable need exists for evidence-based response strategies and curriculum development for social workers to mitigate the daily consequences of climate change (Mason et al., 2017). Largely, surveyed social workers reported feeling unprepared to address environmental impacts on clients, citing a lack of resources and training (Nesmith & Smyth, 2015). Further, gaps between social work education and deeper understanding of the interconnections between social work and the environment are consistently identified as an area of growth for the profession (Beltrán et al., 2016; Miller & Hayward, 2014). Furthermore, developing positive peer pressure among social workers that the climate crisis bears their attention and skills can further shift the beliefs and substantiate claims that environmental concerns lie well within the scope of the profession's obligation and reach (Gordon, 2017; Schmitz et al., 2010). Employing positive peer pressure supports environmental justice as a core component of equality in social work, which will build inclusive, responsive practices that confront the multifaceted problems connected to the climate crisis.

Advancing the Social Work Curriculum

Powers et al. (2019) introduce two models for implicit and explicit ecosocial work education: the infusion and integration models. The infusion model transforms social work education to include ecosocial work as the base for social work education, whereas the integration model embeds ecosocial work, when possible, into the existing curriculum (Powers et al., 2019). Chonody et al. (2020) found that 28% of social work students defined environmental justice within a context of general environmental harm, and less (15%) described the disproportionate exposure to marginalized populations. These findings suggest that social work students need further educational opportunities to raise awareness of environmental injustice (Chonody et al., 2020). Social workers need to learn how to work in transdisciplinary teams to create adaptable, scalable solutions and elicit change across communities.

The Council on Social Work Education (CSWE), Center for Diversity and Social & Economic Justice created a curricular guide for environmental justice in 2020 based on the CSWE 2015 Educational Policy and Accreditation Standards (EPAS). The curricular guide contains suggested readings, activities, and assignments mapped to knowledge, values, skills, cognitive and affective processes, and CSWE EPAS (CSWE, 2022). The 2022 EPAS that could be applied to this Grand Challenge are presented in Appendix 8A (CSWE, 2022). Additionally, conceptual questions, frameworks and tools, and learning goals based on BSW, MSW, and doctoral degree levels to advance the social work curricula are available in Appendix 8C. Classroom discussion prompts (see Appendix 8D) and pedagogical considerations (see Appendix 8E) provide opportunities to introduce environmental justice dialogue into the classroom. These suggestions are not exhaustive but rather a beginning to consider creating social responses to a changing environment.

Equity, Diversity, Inclusion, and Social Justice

Environmental racism is an imperative issue across social work. The consistent marginalization of certain groups by historical systems of intersecting oppressions, including racial, economic, and gendered inequities, are well documented and further exacerbated by changes associated with environmental degradation and the climate crisis. Additionally, slower yet more persistent environmental effects, such as air pollution or environmental toxicity, may not immediately rise to the observation level; they perpetuate incremental and deferred destruction with impacts as severe as acute climate consequences (Clayton et al., 2017). These issues are felt more significantly by marginalized communities and highlight the expanding gap between those with the resources to cope with or avoid environmental hazards, and those who then experience worsening poverty, loss of food and water security, and forced migration as a result of environmental harms (Alston, 2015). These circumstances increase vulnerability and have complicated and substantial impacts on human rights, public health, and equity efforts.

Social work must continue critically examining and explicitly naming environmental injustice as a core component within systems of oppression and racism. Disciplinary acceptance of race and class as primary factors of inequality should expand to include environmental injustice as an additional perpetuating and multifaceted factor expansion of inequity (Dewane, 2011). Research in social work and other disciplines consistently demonstrates that in the United States, racial minorities, especially those living in poverty, face substantially more negative environmental exposures in daily life than wealthier, white individuals (Beltrán et al., 2016). Holding these multiple and layered marginalizations, including environmental injustice, encourages a deeper understanding of vulnerability and can create opportunities to better develop and employ appropriate social work interventions from the micro through macro levels.

Managing Difficult Classroom Conversations

Acknowledging the settler/colonist history between social work and marginalized populations, including Indigenous communities, in social work classrooms including explorations of environmental justice is essential within ecosocial work. Marginalized populations are impacted differently than other communities, and it is crucial to incorporate these truths into classroom discussions. Significant exploitation by Western institutions and non-Indigenous social workers during attempts at collaboration on environmental issues is one area deserving of academic acknowledgment and critique. Justifiably, some Indigenous partners and communities may have concerns regarding tokenization and limited leadership or input in collaborative planning initiatives (McBeath et al., 2019).

Building this awareness among social work students on the myriad ways to center and prioritize beneficial Indigenous-led solutions may reinforce tribal capacity, and community goals can support successful social work interventions that attend to the challenges brought forth by the changing environment while centering social justice (Billiot et al., 2019). Embedding culturally inclusive narratives and scholarship from diverse populations throughout the curriculum may serve as bridges that establish long-term community benefits by advancing environmental justice (Schmitz et al., 2010). There is a multitude of classroom tools to create a classroom environment and manage difficult conversations (see Appendix 8F).

Evaluation of Learning

Supporting student success in the environmental justice curriculum using trauma-informed teaching practices such as collaboration, problem-solving, and inclusion in decision-making regarding assessments can foster growth and meaningful practice skill-building. Checking to understand the connections between environmental principles to other areas of social work scholarship and practice will further advance the applicability of these principles for students. Instructors can employ formative and summative assessments and support students by elaborating on the purpose, process, and criteria for success on each task (see Appendix 8F). Students can become active participants in measuring their learning as instructors build choice into assessments, encouraging students to set learning objectives that speak to their professional goals. To further assess understanding and processing of the complex concepts embedded within the curriculum, students can complete short personal reflections on the course content, drawing connections to texts, experiences, and social justice.

Future Directions and Challenges

Challenges to future social work practice from correlations between the exploitation of the earth and rising social injustices abound. The rapidly developing climate crisis threatens the loss of the last half-century's worldwide social justice and equality gains. The situation creates a distinct call to action and reckoning within the profession. Largely, social work engagement with environmental justice leans toward studies of acute events and their corresponding mental health implications, whereas a need remains for scholarship on effective and needs-based planning and preparation (Hayes et al., 2018). Revisioning the climate crisis and environmental degradation as an opportunity to realign social works' historic aims may create space to expand social work capacity by applying disciplinary competencies and skills to these present and emerging problems.

Through interdisciplinary engagement and leadership, social work has opportunities to move away from focusing resources solely on post-disaster responses and instead better support more effective planning and preparation for climate consequences (Hayes et al., 2018). Social work may significantly contribute to such collaborative efforts in concert by centering and elevating historically marginalized individuals and communities, which may otherwise be overlooked or superseded by other concerns.

Note

1 This land acknowledgment was adapted from the statement provided by http://landacknowledgements.org/.

References

Akesson, B., Burns, V., & Hordyk, S. (2017). The place of place in social work: Rethinking the person-in-environment model in social work education and practice. *Journal of Social Work Education*, *53*(3), 372–383. https://doi.org/10.1080/10437797.2016.1272512

Alston, M. (2015). Social work, climate change and global cooperation. *International Social Work*, *58*(3), 355–363.

Arao, B., & Clemens, K. (2013). From safe spaces to brave spaces. *The Art of Effective Facilitation: Reflections from Social Justice Educators*, 135–150.

Beech, P. (2020, July 31). What is environmental racism and how can we fight it? *World Economic Forum*. www.weforum.org/agenda/2020/07/what-is-environmental-racism-pollution-covid-systemic/

Beltrán, R., Hacker, A., & Begun, S. (2016). Environmental justice is a social justice issue: Incorporating environmental justice into social work practice curricula. *Journal of Social Work Education*, *52*(4), 493–502. https://doi.org/10.1080/10437797.2016.1215277

Bernardo, F., & Palma-Oliveira, J. M. (2016). Urban neighbourhoods and intergroup relations: The importance of place identity. *Journal of Environmental Psychology*, *45*, 239–251.

Billiot, S., Beltrán, R., Brown, D., Mitchell, F. M., & Fernandez, A. (2019). Indigenous perspectives for strengthening social responses to global environmental changes: A response to the social work grand challenge on environmental change. *Journal of Community Practice*, *27*(3–4), 296–316.

Boddy, J., Johns, L., Frost, C. D., Lynch, M., & Stevens, F. (2022). Understanding simulated learning and its relationship to field education. In R. Baikady, Sajid S. M., V. Nadesan, M. R. Islam (Eds.), *The Routledge handbook of field work education in social work* (pp. 218–232). Routledge.

Bowles, W., Boetto, H., Jones, P., & McKinnon, J. (2018). Is social work really greening? Exploring the place of sustainability and environment in social work codes of ethics. *International Social Work*, *61*(4), 503–517.

Bronfenbrenner, U. (1989). Ecological systems theory. *Annals of Child Development*, *6*, 187–249.

Carello, J., & Butler, L. D. (2015). Practicing what we teach: Trauma-informed educational practice. *Journal of Teaching in Social Work*, *35*(3), 262–278.

Clayton, S., Manning, C. M., Krygsman, K., & Speiser, M. (2017). *Mental health and our changing climate: Impacts, implications, and guidance*. American Psychological Association and Eco America. www.apa.org/news/press/releases/2017/03/mental-health-climate.pdf

Chonody, J. M., Sultzman, V., & Hippie, J. (2020). Are social work students concerned about the environment? The role of personal beliefs. *Journal of Social Work Education*, *56*(4), 809–824.

Council of Social Work Education (CSWE) (2022). *2022 Educational policy and accreditation standards (EPAS)*. Author. https://www.cswe.org/getmedia/94471c42-13b8-493b-9041-b30f48533d64/2022-EPAS.pdf

Council on Social Work Education. (2020). *Specialized practice curricular guide for environmental justice. 2015 EPAS curricular guide resource series*. Council on Social Work Education.

de Mol van Otterloo, N., Yun, J., & Nair, M. (2018). Healing power of the environment: Traditional dimensions. *International Research Journal of Environmental Sciences*, *7*(9).

Dewane, C. (2011). Environmentalism & social work: The ultimate social justice issue. *Social Work Today*, *11*(5), 20. www.socialworktoday.com/archive/092011p20.shtml

Dominelli, L. (2012). *Green social work: From environmental crisis to environmental justice*. Polity Press.

Dominelli, L. (Ed.). (2018). *The Routledge handbook of green social work*. Routledge.

The Editorial Board. (2018, November 28). Humanising health and climate change [Editorial]. *The Lancet*, *392*(10162), 2326–2326. https://doi.org/10.1016/S0140-6736(18)33016-2

Environmental Protection Agency (n.d.). *Environmental justice*. Environmental Protection Agency. https://www.epa.gov/environmentaljustice/learn-about-environmental-justice

Fong, R., Lubben, J., & Barth, R. (2018). *Grand challenges for social work and society*. Oxford University Press.

Gaba, A. (2021). *APA at the United Nations–2021 annual report*. Diss. United Nations.

Gordon, H. L. (2017). Climate change and food: A green social work perspective. *Critical and Radical Social Work*, *5*(2), 145–162.

Hardy, K. (2016). Antiracist approaches for shaping theoretical and practice paradigms. *Strategies for Deconstructing Racism in the Health and Human Services*, 125–142.

Hayes, K., Blashki, G., Wiseman, J., Burke, S., & Reifels, L. (2018). Climate change and mental health: Risks, impacts and priority actions. *International Journal of Mental Health Systems*, *12*(1), 1–12.

Hutchison, E. D. (2019). *Dimensions of human behavior: Person and environment* (6th ed.). SAGE Publications.

Intergovernmental Panel on Climate Change. (2018). *Global warming of 1.5°C*. www.ipcc.ch/sr15/

Kivel, P. (2017). Social service or social change. In *The revolution will not be funded: Beyond* the *non-profit industrial complex* (pp. 129–149). Duke University Press.

Krings, A., Victor, B. G., Mathias, J., & Perron, B. E. (2020). Environmental social work in the disciplinary literature, 1991–2015. *International Social Work*, *63*(3), 275–290.

Leiserowitz, A., Maibach, E., Rosenthal, S., Kotcher, J., Ballew, M., Goldberg, M., & Gustafson. (2018). *Climate change in the American mind: December 2018*. Yale University and George Mason University. Yale Program on Climate Change Communication.

Lewicka, M. (2011). Place attachment: How far have we come in the last 40 years? *Journal of Environmental Psychology*, *31*(3), 207–230.

Mason, L. R., Shires, M. K., Arwood, C., & Borst, A. (2017). Social work research and global environmental change. *Journal of the Society for Social Work and Research*, *8*(4), 645–672.

McBeath, B., Tian, Q., Xu, B., & Huang McBeath, J. (2019). Human service organization-environment relationships in relation to environmental justice: Old and new approaches to macro practice and research. *Human Service Organizations: Management, Leadership & Governance*, *43*(4), 299–313.

McInroy, L. B., Byers, D. S., Kattari, S. K., & CSWE Council on Sexual Orientation and Gender Expression. (2019). *The NAME Steps: How to name and address anti- LGBTQIA2S+microaggressions in social work classrooms*. Council on Social Work Education.

Miller, S. E., & Hayward, R. A. (2014). Social work education's role in addressing people and a planet at risk. *Social Work Education*, *33*(3), 280–295.

National Association of Social Workers. (2017). *Code of ethics of the national association of social workers*. www.socialworkers.org/About/Ethics/Code-of-Ethics/Code-of-Ethics-English

Nesmith, A., & Smyth, N. (2015). Environmental justice and social work education: Social workers' professional perspectives. *Social Work Education*, *34*(5), 484–501.

Nipperess, S., & Boddy, J. (2018). Greening Australian social work practice and education. In *The Routledge handbook of green social work* (pp. 547–557). Routledge.

Oxford Learners Dictionaries. (n.d.). Climate crisis. In *Oxford learners dictionaries*. www.oxfordlearnersdictionaries.com/us/definition/english/climate-crisis

Powers, M. C. (2016). Transforming the profession: Social workers' expanding response to the environmental crisis. In *Ecosocial transition of societies: Contribution of social work and social policy*. Routledge.

Powers, M. C., Schmitz, C., & Beckwith Moritz, M. (2019). Preparing social workers for ecosocial work practice and community building. *Journal of Community Practice*, *27*(3–4), 446–459.

Richmond, M. E. (1917). *Social diagnosis*. Russell Sage Foundation.

Saleebey, D. (2006). Strengths perspective in social work practice, 4/e (197–220). *Allan Bacon*, *75*.

Schmitz, C. L., Stinson, C. H., & James, C. D. (2010). Community and environmental sustainability: Collaboration and interdisciplinary education. *Critical Social Work*, *11*(3).

Singer, M. (1996). A dose of drugs, a touch of violence, a case of AIDS: Conceptualizing the SAVA syndemic. *Free Inquiry in Creative Sociology*, *24*(2), 99–110.

Singer, M. (2010). Ecosyndemics: Global warming and 21st century plague. In D. A. Herring & A. C. Swedlund (Eds.), *Plagues and epidemics: Infected spaces past and present* (pp. 21–37). Berg.

Singer, M., Bulled, N., Ostrach, B., & Mendenhall, E. (2017). Syndemics and the biosocial conception of health. *The Lancet (British Edition)*, *389*(10072), 941–950. https://doi.org/10.1016/S0140-6736(17)30003-X

Tallman, P. S., Riley-Powell, A. R., Schwarz, L., Salmón-Mulanovich, G., Southgate, T., Pace, C., . . . Lee, G. O. (2020). Ecosyndemics: The potential synergistic health impacts of highways and dams in the Amazon. *Social Science & Medicine*, 113037.

Teixeira, S., & Krings, A. (2015). Sustainable social work: An environmental justice framework for social work education. *Social Work Education, 34*(5), 513–527.

Villanueva, E. (2018). *Decolonizing wealth: Indigenous wisdom to heal divides and restores balance.* Berrett-Koehler Publishers, Inc.

Warren, K. J. (2015, April 27). *Feminist environmental philosophy.* Stanford Encyclopedia o Philosophy. https://plato.stanford.edu/entries/feminism-environmental/#EpiPer.

Wilson, P. A., Nanin, J., Amesty, S., Wallace, S., Cherenack, E. M., & Fullilove, R. (2014). Using syndemic theory to understand vulnerability to HIV infection among Black and Latino men in New York City. *Journal of Urban Health*, *91*(5), 983–998.

Appendix 8A

EPAS Addressed in Grand Challenge #7

Creating Social Response to a Changing Environment

Competency 1: Demonstrate Ethical and Professional Behavior. Ethical decision-making on the part of social workers is crucial in the practice, research, and policy arenas of working with individuals, families, groups, organizations, and communities. To comprehend these phenomena as a base, we all need to understand the evolution and mission of professional social work, including the principles of the code of ethics set up by the National Association of Social Workers. Such ethical decision-making must include environmentally just and equitable use of resources such as land, water, air, and food.

Competency 2: Advance Human Rights and Social, Racial Economic, and Environmental Justice. In the technology-enhanced modern society, learning from the diverse global societies is for social workers to enhance the human rights, social, racial, and environmental justice issues of diverse populations. A United Nations report states that

> we have been leading and actively contributing to the world's deep fragility relates to rising poverty and hunger; prolonged conflicts and human rights crises; skyrocketing levels of inequality within and between societies; the ungoverned development of new technologies; and the triple planetary crisis of climate change, biodiversity loss and rising levels of air and water pollution. It has never been clearer that our fates are interconnected and that the inability to solve shared problems is creating unacceptable risks.
>
> (Gaba, 2021)

Competency 3: Engage Antiracism, Diversity, Equity, and Inclusion (ADEI) in Practice. Social workers are uniquely positioned to support antiracism, diversity, equity, and inclusion within all population groups to catalyze the Grand Challenges of our society. Therefore, social workers must expand their antiracist capacities and understand and confront the historical and ongoing impacts of environmental racism while affirming diversity and frontline voices to address environmental injustices.

Competency 4: Engage in Practice-Informed Research and Research-Informed Practice. Social workers need to review micro and macro practice-informed research and research-informed practice to enhance the delivery system at the micro and macro level. It is a commitment to improving the lives of people through the purposeful and professional use of oneself. Such a circular model allows social workers to consider better the intersections between practice and policy initiatives regarding environmental justice. Through day-to-day practice, research, policy advocacy, and curriculum development, an opportunity exists for social workers to respond to environmental injustices and advance new solutions that better serve the populations climate change most dangerously threatens.

Competency 5: Engage in Policy Practice. In all practice settings, social workers are trained to engage in policy practice in local, state, and federal government settings to make certain social welfare policies are enacted and implemented. Training social workers for policy-level practice and leadership increases effectiveness in promoting policies that reflect social work's ethical values and commitment to social justice. Expanding such training to include environmental justice can expand social workers' reach by increasing their political activity across campaigns and supporting legislation that expands environmental protections. Furthermore, social workers can better recognize and resolve the pervasive impacts of policies that contribute to environmental racism.

Competency 6: Engage With Individuals, Families, Groups, Organizations, and Communities. Social work as a profession deals with diverse societal needs at the micro, mezzo, and macro level. Social workers are encouraged to handle these multi-level tasks, utilizing multi-disciplinary approaches. Social workers also must recognize the disproportionate impacts of environmental injustice, including the repercussions of the climate crisis that expands inequities, responding with equity-based approaches that elevate the needs and voices of historically underrepresented populations. Social work responses rely upon participatory interventions that advance meaningful solutions (Dominelli, 2012).

Competency 7: Assess Individuals, Families, Groups, Organizations, and Communities. Social workers are trained to conduct an ongoing and comprehensive assessment using appropriate tools as a basis for effective intervention for individuals, families, groups, organizations, and communities. Social workers can utilize an ecosyndemic (Singer, 2010) framework, problem-and-environment framework (Hutchison, 2019) to comprehensively assess individuals, families, groups, organizations, and communities to understand how the person and environment impact each other.

Competency 8: Intervene With Individuals, Families, Groups, Organizations, and Communities. Social workers know that intervention is an ongoing component of the dynamic and interactive process of social work practice with, and on behalf of, diverse individuals, families, groups, organizations, and communities. Social work practitioners and advocates understand the connection between the natural environment, quality of life, and the micro, mezzo, and macro systems. Therefore, social workers should focus on capacity building through empowerment and access to resources through advocacy.

Competency 9: Evaluate Practice With Individuals, Families, Groups, Organizations, and Communities. The evaluation process in social work practice with individuals, families, groups, organizations, and communities involves using quantitative and qualitative measurements to monitor whether the services achieved the desired outcome. Social work evaluation tools on the micro, mezzo, and macro levels should include environmental aspects to promote sustainability and environmental justice.

Appendix 8B

Table 8.1 Frameworks and Definitions

Terminology	*Definition Relating to Environmental Justice*
Climate crisis	"A situation characterized by the threat of highly dangerous, irreversible changes to the global climate" (Oxford Learners Dictionaries, n.d.).
Environmental degradation	Deterioration of the environment, primarily from human disturbances heavily influenced by issues of consumption, population, and urbanization with adverse impacts on the natural world.
Environmental justice	"The fair treatment and meaningful involvement of all people regardless of race, color, national origin, or income with respect to the development, implementation, and enforcement of environmental laws, regulations, and policies. Fair treatment means that no population, due to policy or economic disempowerment, is forced to bear a disproportionate share of the negative human health or environmental impacts of pollution or environmental consequences resulting from industrial, municipal, and commercial operations or the execution of federal, state, local and tribal programs and policies" (Environmental Protection Agency, n.d., para. 1).
Environmental racism	"Racial discrimination in environmental policy-making, the enforcement of regulations and laws, the deliberate targeting of communities of color for toxic waste facilities, the official sanctioning of the life-threatening presence of poisons and pollutants in our communities, and the history of excluding people of color from leadership of the ecology movements" (Chavis, 1982, as cited in Beech, 2020, para. 3).

(*Continued*)

Table 8.1 (Continued)

Terminology	*Definition Relating to Environmental Justice*
Ecofeminist epistemology	Within social work, an ecofeminist approach is a rights-based framework that integrates gender by incorporating feminist theory and critical masculinity studies (Nipperess & Boddy, 2018). Ecofeminist epistemology explores gender influences on conceptions of knowledge, the knower, and methods of inquiry and justification (Warren, 2015).
Ecosocial work	Ecosocial work expands the person in environment framework to recognize that the ecological environment impacts individuals, families, and communities (Powers, 2016, as cited in Powers et al., 2019).
Green social work	"Specifically address environmental issues from a social work perspective, advocating for and strengthening the voice of social workers who support people during disasters at policymaking and practice levels, however and wherever these take place . . . transcend[ing] the concerns of ecological social work, which is a systems-based approach to the mainstream social work preoccupation with the person in their environment" (Dominelli, 2012, p. 3).
Person and environment	A multidimension approach of incorporating globalization, diversity, human rights, and social, economic, and environmental justice along with time into the person in environment framework (Hutchison, 2019)
Sustainable social work	"Integrates global social work standards with environmental justice principles . . . based on global standards for social work set forth by The International Federation of Social Workers (IFSW) and the International Association of Schools of Social Work (IASSW)" (Teixeira & Krings, 2015, p. 514).
Syndemic	"The adverse interaction between diseases and health conditions of all types (e.g., infections, chronic non-communicable diseases, mental health problems, behavioral conditions, toxic exposure, and malnutrition) and are most likely to emerge under conditions of health inequality caused by poverty, stigmatization, stress, or structural violence" (Singer et al., 2017, p. 941).

Terminology	*Definition Relating to Environmental Justice*
Transdisciplinarity	"Encourages student engagement with a wide range of expertise necessary for operationalizing social, economic, and environmental justice into disaster interventions, and include people from other disciplines and professions in their multi-stakeholder partnerships for sustainable social development and disaster interventions" (Dominelli, 2018, p. 18).

Appendix 8C

Table 8.2 Advancing the Social Work Curricula

	Conceptual Questions	*Suggested Frameworks and Tools*	*Goals*
BSW	How does environmental justice intersect with social work? How do we define key concepts relating to environmental justice? Understanding the environmental justice implications for social work practice at the micro, mezzo, and macro levels.	Green social work Asset Mapping PA Policy Framework for Environmental Justice	Defining principles Local context
MSW	How can you apply environmental justice into social work practice? How do we incorporate environmental justice into social work practice? Expand environmental justice work within field practice. How can social workers advocate for just environmental policies at various levels of government?	Sendai Framework Eco mapping EPA Environmental Justice Assessment Methodology Phase 1 – Problem Formulation Phase 2 – Data Collection Phase 3 – Assessment of the Potential for "Adverse" Environmental and Human Health Effects or Impacts Phase 4 – Assessment of the Potential for "Disproportionately High and Adverse" Effects or Impacts	Practical Applications & Advocacy

	Conceptual Questions	*Suggested Frameworks and Tools*	*Goals*
DSW/ PhD	What research can support environmental justice in social work? How do we evaluate social work environmental justice interventions/ practice? What role can/does social work play in interdisciplinary efforts for environmental justice?		Research, evaluation, and interdisciplinary extensions

Appendix 8D

Table 8.3 Classroom Discussions

	Discussion Prompts
BSW	• What are some of the key terms related to environmental justice? • How does environmental justice impact the work of social workers? • How are marginalized populations and disenfranchised communities impacted by environmental justice?
MSW	• Where do social work and environmental justice intersect? • What social work practices can support marginalized populations and disenfranchised communities impacted by environmental justice? • What are environmental justice strategies on a micro, mezzo, and macro level?
DSW/ PhD	• What are the intersections between physical, built, and social environments for various communities? • How can we synthesize community-engaged research in environmental health disparities? • What tools support investigations into social and environmental determinants of health disparities? • How can social work advance environmental justice in collaboration with other disciplines?

Appendix 8E

Table 8.4 Pedagogical Considerations

Activity	*Description*
Introduce a land acknowledgment	The purpose of land acknowledgments is to increase awareness and demonstrate respect to Indigenous peoples. While land acknowledgment is important and a good first step it is important to decolonize the social work curriculum and include the voices of Indigenous people.
Decolonize social work	Addressing the needs of individuals reeling from the personal and devastating impact of institutional systems of exploitation and violence while challenging the root causes of the exploitation and violence (Kivel, 2017).
Separate economy and political systems	Exploits natural resources and most of the planet's inhabitants for the profit of a few. Separation-based political systems create arbitrary nation-states with imaginary boundaries with laws and institutions that oppress some groups and privilege others (Villanueva, 2018).
Infuse environmental justice into existing social work curriculum	Educators will consider their curriculum establishing intersections with issues relating to environmental justice (Powers et al., 2019). This critical evaluation of current coursework will better prepare students for changing dynamics at the macro, mezzo, and micro level due to increases in environmental degradation and compounding problems both now and in the future.
Prepare the lesson plan	As an educator, take the required time to be prepared and craft a lesson plan around the environmental justice topic keeping in mind disenfranchised populations.

(*Continued*)

Table 8.4 (Continued)

Activity	*Description*
Create a classroom environment	Consider creating brave spaces (Arao & Clemens, 2013) as well as community and discussion agreements with the students, so that students know how to engage and what to expect. Also, develop and agree upon a plan of action if a rule or agreement is broken.
Utilize small group discussions	While large group discussions provide an opportunity for all students to hear each other, utilize small groups to apply knowledge and for creation.
Reflect upon synchronous sessions	Reflection is key for both students and educators whether it is in the session or after the session ends. Attempt to create intention spaces for students to write, think, or dialogue around what happened during the session. Educators should also reflect upon their unconscious bias, intersectionality, and positionality within the classroom and how it impacted the discussion.
PAST model	Power/privilege-sensitive framework designed to defuse contentious conversations and to facilitate constructive engagement across divides of race and other dimensions of diversity (Hardy, 2016).
Trauma-informed teaching principles	"To be *trauma-informed*, in any context, is to understand the ways in which violence, victimization, and other traumatic experiences may have impacted the lives of the individuals involved and to apply that understanding to the design of systems and provision of services so they accommodate trauma survivors' needs and are consonant with healing and recovery" (Butler et al., 2011; Harris & Fallot, 2001; N. J. Smyth, 2008, as cited in Carello & Butler, 2015).

Appendix 8F

Table 8.5 Tools to Prepare the Classroom Environment

Challenging Discussions	• http://cet.usc.edu/challenging-discussions/
Community Agreements	• www.nationalequityproject.org/tools/developing-community-agreements • https://crlt.umich.edu/examples-discussion-guidelines
Managing Difficult Dialogues	• https://cft.vanderbilt.edu/guides-sub-pages/difficult-dialogues/
N.A.M.E. Microaggressions	• Notice/Acknowledge/Make Space/Engage the Group (McInroy et al., 2019) • www.cswe.org/CSWE/media/CSOGIE/6861_cswe_CSOGIE_TheNAMESteps_Guide_WEB72_REV2.pdf
Teaching Controversial Topics	• https://serc.carleton.edu/NAGTWorkshops/affective/controversial.html
Trauma Informed Online Teaching	• www.socialworker.com/feature-articles/education – credentials/trauma-informed-online-teaching-essential-coming-academic-year/ • https://fieldeducator.simmons.edu/article/virtual-academic-challenges-to-real-time-trauma/

Appendix 8G

Table 8.6 Assessment Resources

Assessment Suggestions	• www.seattleu.edu/cejs/what-you-can-do/ej-teaching-resources/assessments-and-assignments-summary/ • https://serc.carleton.edu/integrate/workshops/envirojustice2013/activities.html
Curricular Guide for Environmental Justice	• www.cswe.org/Education-Resources/2015-Curricular-Guides/2015-Environmental-Justice-Guide-Web-Version.aspx
More Equitable Assignments	• https://sites.tufts.edu/teaching/2021/03/04/four-high-impact-practices-for-designing-more-equitable-assessments/
Power, Trauma, and Grading	• https://academiccommons.columbia.edu/doi/10.7916/d8-4fh7-zm92

9 Harnessing Technology in Social Good

Kenneth Scott Smith, Katherine Chism Selber and Cathy Newman Thomas

Introduction

In 2016, the American Academy of Social Work and Social Welfare (AASWSW) launched a major initiative to identify, analyze, and impact a series of Grand Challenges for the social work profession. The intent was to focus resources on solving some of the most difficult social problems using science to drive progress. One of these Grand Challenges includes Harnessing Technology for the Social Good (AASWSW, 2021). The goal of this challenge is to influence the transformation of the social work profession with respect to use, adaptation, and its relationship to technology. The challenge's strategy is to use data from interdisciplinary fields and across sectors to drive innovation and to use technology to improve social programming effectiveness, enhance the pace of innovation, and reduce inequalities (AASWSW, 2021). Although progress is being made, social work has been slower to adapt technology than some other professions (Berzin et al., 2015). The question is – can schools of social work and especially practice and field education address and integrate this Grand Challenge in both the academic classroom and field settings?

Berzin et al. (2015) state that there are three reasons why the social work profession is limited in its response to the use and benefits of technology. The first is that there is limited education and training to prepare practitioners on how to utilize technology (Mishna et al., 2015). The latest NASW Technology Standards (2017) offers updated guidance for thinking about the use of technology in social work practice, but it is still not clear how many programs are addressing this need and to what extent. Second, social workers have limited exposure to innovative applications of technology such as in practice or in class (Langlois, 2011). For new skills to be transferred into effective practice, future social workers must understand the underlying theory,

DOI: 10.4324/9781003308263-11

see the practices modeled, experience opportunities for practice, and receive expert coaching to improve their practice both in class and field (Joyce & Showers, 2002). Social work must develop and evaluate technological efforts to advance curriculum and training. To move to the level of adoption requires not only embracing the Grand Challenge, but also a roadmap to guide progress for schools of social work. Lastly, innovations outpace research (Bloomberg, 2015), increasing the challenges in deciding what technology has the most significant impacts and what should be adopted. In all cases, technology should result in outcomes that are as effective or more effective than they would be without technology.

Social workers in both educational and practice settings and their clients are attempting to integrate technology throughout their lives (Reamer, 2019). In spite of significant potential advantages, both are struggling, as there is no formal effort to bring each up to speed with current best practices. Technical literacy should be addressed in the Grand Challenges and should be viewed as a cultural competency that we teach in our BSW/MSW programs (Belluomini, 2016). Classes should require coursework that prepares our students on how to utilize technology in an effective way in their practice. However, first, social work educators must themselves acquire technological pedagogical content knowledge and skills (Schropshire, 2019).

The Pace of Distance Education and Online Education in Social Work

Distance and online education in social work have evolved, driven by technological advances such as broadband, interactive video conferencing, software, and web-based platforms (Kurzman, 2019). A 2018 survey revealed that about 80% of BSW and MSW programs offer part of their program in an online and hybrid format (Kurzman, 2019), and online education is quickly outpacing on-campus enrollment in social work (Allen & Seaman, 2013). These advances present opportunities to greatly enhance social work education and practice outcomes (Kurzman, 2019). If social work education is to remain at the forefront of such fields as mental health, it will need to fully embrace this Grand Challenge both in university online education as well as in the more challenging arenas of field education and practice. The question is how can universities in a post-COVID environment provide the training, resources, and structure needed to enhance online delivery methodologies and keep pace with the ever-changing landscape of technology?

The Grand Challenge of Technology Within Social Work Education and Its Curriculum Domains (Human Behavior and Social Environment, Policy, and Practice/Field Education)

Technology can be utilized across all curriculum domains of social work education. The following discussion examines the pace of online education and distance education and the implications of technology use and limitations across the domain. This chapter will assist social work educators towards developing content and pedagogy around technology in our classrooms, providing information on best practices, and discussing relevant policies regarding technology, and certain technological efforts being deployed in the classroom and field. In addition, it will provide a sample learning module within a social work educational setting as an exemplar to address some of these gaps. The path forward will require resources and collaborations across academic and field settings. Furthermore, please see Appendix 9A for the application of Council of Social Work Education's (CSWE, 2022) *2022 Educational Policy and Accreditation Standards* (EPAS) and how these can be used to develop learning competencies in relation to this topic.

Adapting Technology in Practice and Field Education

Social work practice in general, and field education in particular, struggle to keep pace with changing technology. This is primarily due to social work practice and field education's traditional reliance on a face-to-face approach. Field education has long been considered the heart and hallmark of social work education and the signature pedagogical tool for educating social work students (Wayne et al., 2010). However, for the first time in decades, that may be changing (Clarke & Morley, 2020); field instruction, once heavily dependent on social interaction between student intern and agency field instructor, now can exist with a new definition of what constitutes direct engagement, employing technology to deliver services and provide supervision.

From the beginning of social work education in the charity's movement of the late 19th century to the heavily digitized world of today where social work students take many or all courses online, social work education and field education have pushed to keep up. From working across digital platforms for coursework, receiving field agency supervision through videoconferencing, to working with clients using telehealth, traditional modes of field education are continually changing. The COVID-19 pandemic further pushed the changes to rapidly transform social work, "opening the gate" to employ technology (Csoba & Diebel, 2020, p. 1095). The starkness of this change can be seen when we consider that in a generation or two, social work students may graduate never having had a face-to-face meeting with a client or a supervisory meeting throughout their entire social work education experience.

Standards for Teaching Practice in Field Education

In 2017, major social work professional associations collaborated on a set of standards for the use of technology in practice and education (National Association of Social Workers [NASW], Council on Social Work Education, Association of Social Work Boards, and the Clinical Social Work Association, 2017). These standards included field education standards to support supervisory access and assessment of interns and for teaching how to use technology for field education. Standards addressed the use of supervision platforms and suggested topics for field instructors to discuss with students, including 1) technology use in agency settings; 2) securing electronic records; 3) social media policies; 4) the impact of personal and professional social media; 5) regulations and laws that impact technology applications; 6) ethical standards; and 7) agency confidentiality and technology policies (Reamer, 2019).

However, the extent that the standards are utilized within social work education is unclear (Barsky, 2019). Slowness to adopt may be mitigated as a new wave of professors enter the profession with new technology knowledge and skills. However, the issue of use within the agencies where field education is conducted must be considered. For example, non-profits often lack resources to purchase and train on new technologies, and this should be a concern for field internships (Zorn et al., 2011). As well, public agencies often lag behind private sector in technology updates and usage. This unevenness of field education has always been, and will continue to be, a challenge for social work educators (Apgar, 2019). The extent to which social work educators view technology as crucial and teachable is debatable. The issue is more complex due to the multiple stakeholders who collaborate – agencies, social work educators and administrators within their universities, and students (Colvin & Bullock, 2014). Although social work is changing rapidly, field education, supervision, and training have not kept pace with technology and its innovations, even in online social work programs.

Potential Technologies to Support Practice and Field Education

Practice and field education can advance student outcomes by using innovative technologies for teaching and supervision. For example, caseworkers in one study used video clips of interaction with young clients to send to supervisors to then be used in an online web-based supervisory session (Antczak et al., 2019). Clips are viewed together to situate discussions about such topics as intern rapport with clients, progress in relationship building skills, goal setting, and other practice concepts. Topics such as how to handle confidentiality issues, build trust and credibility with online platforms, legal issues, and risks such as privacy concerns can also be woven into a supervision session (Dombo et al., 2014). Bug-in-ear is another technology useful in internship training. Built on simple livestream technology, the supervisor provides prompts to the intern in real time while the intern is providing services, giving feedback to help model and guide practice. Research indicates that this technique builds more permanent skills and enthusiasm among interns (Will, 2019). Electronic interactive whiteboards, such as Jamboard, are also helpful ways of building engagement with supervisors (Campbell et al., 2019), increasing student input and creativity for brainstorming, for exercises in logic model development, and to open discussion of concepts and tasks for input by more participants. From online teaching, video conferencing and streaming, geographical information mapping, virtual reality training, avatars, and phone-based apps for service delivery, technology is pushing further into the classrooms and field settings.

Strengths and Limitations of Technology in the Practice and Field Education Domain

It is important to consider the strengths and limitations of technology utilization to understand how to best harness potential for classroom and field settings. One review of studies on technology integration across many professions (Wretman & Macy, 2016) recognized strengths including 1) ease of access, 2) creation of opportunities such as access to online education across rural areas, 3) integrating many tools into teaching, 4) enhanced student motivation, and 5) ease of use within any curriculum. In addition, the research identified an advantage of applying technology across clinical, macro, and all levels of practice in many different fields of practice, not just social work. In terms of barriers the article mentioned 1) expense, 2) heavy training needs, and 3) time required to update knowledge, skills, and tools. Within field education it is important to understand what universities require, and conversely, universities must understand the capacities of social work intern settings.

Adapting Technology in the Human Behavior and Social Environment (HBSE) Domain

Social workers use their knowledge of human behavior to advocate at the individual case, group, and systems level for social, economic, and environmental improvements to enhance their clients' quality of life, and to improve the organizations that serve them. Whether working to address case specific issues of goal setting and outcomes, group methodologies such as building peer support, or working to improve client well-being and support systems, advances in technology can be applied to this domain.

Cultural Topics

One key aspect of HBSE content is understanding cultural issues of client systems and how those impact our understanding of clients and plan for interventions. Exploration of identity – gender, race, class, age, sexual orientation, and geographic setting – can help reflect on how students/clients/providers use technology and their perspectives on its use. Technologies can be seen through a HBSE lens and an exploration of a specific technology such as the use of Twitter or Facebook can be compared in terms of their cultural profiles – what kind of users and community and purposes do these technologies have? Understanding culture is key to service provision.

Issues of Access

Another key issue in applying technology to the HBSE domain is accessibility, especially for diverse users. The proliferation of smartphones and their apps across large sections of populations makes client and service provider access more feasible in the classroom and field (Reamer, 2019). While it is possible to provide expert instruction and supervision anywhere, anytime, to remote and under-resourced areas (Dede et al., 2009), technology access is tied to a plethora of social justice issues around working with populations with limited resources, such as clients with disabilities, and other special needs populations (Sanders & Scanlon, 2021).

Use of Social Media

Social media can be used as a platform for pushing knowledge about services and how to access these for clients. Relationships between professors and students, among university peers, and among clients in a group can also be strengthened using social media. Apps such as Storify can help peers connect with each other by building stories about their lives that can help others gain insight and awareness of how environmental factors impacted the course of their lives. At the organizational level, social media can keep organization members and stakeholders informed about current events, connect like-minded networks of organizations, and build bridges to new constituents. Social work students and professors can work together on PSAs, projects to solve social problems, and strengthen team engagement and learning. Podcasts can help clients feel a part of a community and develop supportive relationships across a geographical community or a community of those with like lived experiences.

Use of Virtual Reality

Virtual reality is another tool that has gained momentum as a learning technology. It allows for simulating certain mental health situations, practicing interview skills, motivational interviewing, and diversity training (Huttar & BrintzenhofeSzoc, 2019). The use of a head-mounted display like Oculus Quest can fully immerse the student within a learning environment. Virtual reality provides a safe place to offer simulations for students around diversity, assessment of mental health disorders, and allows students to see how they perform, make corrections, and receive real-time feedback about their performance without any impact on real clients, and with extended opportunities for supervisor support (Lee, 2014).

Strengths and Limitations of Technology in the Human Behavior and Social Environment Domain

Although a variety of technologies are now used to positive effect in social work, many social workers still seem hesitant to fully embrace them. Too few social workers have considered the elements of digital literacy, and especially, to the cultural and environmental context aspects of digital literacy. Technology platforms have limitations in their use and exploring how those can both support but also limit a client's developmental roles and tasks such as relationship development and community building is an example of connecting HBSE content. Training of social work educators, practitioners, and clients on advancing technologies remains the key to early adoption across the curriculum.

Implications for Adapting Technology in Policy

Numerous policy issues are implicit using technology use, including the call to consider pedagogy theory in teaching and training (NASW et al., 2017; Schropshire, 2019), implementation of Universal Design for Learning, access for diverse learners, including those with disabilities, the growing digital divide (Sanders & Scanlon, 2021).

Specific Uses

There are many avenues to include the Grand Challenge of Technology within the policy practice domain. There are several federal laws and policies related to technology in social worker preparation and in service delivery that need to be addressed in this curriculum domain. Some relevant policies deal with access, such as the Individuals with Disabilities Education Act (2004) and the Americans with Disabilities Act (1990). The core of these policies is to define protections that ensure that technologies used in schools, including in higher education and in workplaces are accessible to all. Accessibility of technology is related to social work values and thus should be addressed in the policy domain.

Additionally, considerations for adhering to issues of privacy and confidentiality such as the Health Insurance Portability and Accountability Act of 1996 (HIPAA) and Family Educational Rights and Privacy Act of 1974 (FERPA) laws while using technology for education, service delivery, or data management purposes are essential to discuss in the policy domain. These policies can be used within this domain for a policy analysis assignment that can provide insight into the unique privacy and confidentiality issues inherent for use with technology in social work. The gathering, storage, and sharing of information are all enhanced by technology and must be clearly addressed in an organization's policies and training of staff. Students must be trained in these issues as well. Clients should be given information pertinent to these issues so that they can understand how their own data will be used by the organization. Finally, in response to the pandemic, funding to ensure equitable access to technology was addressed by the CARES Act (2020), an intensive effort to increase connectivity and to support remote learning. Funding through distance learning and telemedicine grants support innovation and development programs that reach underserved communities. Also, the CARES Act has been suggested as an important step in narrowing the digital divide with implications beyond the pandemic that made these funds immediately necessary (Edgerton & Cookson, 2020). Finally, ethic issues around privacy and confidentiality in social work are expressly addressed in the NASW Code of Ethics Standards for the Digital Age (Reamer, 2019).

Strengths and Limitations of Technology in the Policy Domain

While technology has the capacity to provide security, and be secure, there are critical risks and limitations that should be taught about technology use and security in the policy area. For data management, it is important that policies cover issues such as hacking of an organization's emails and website and illegally accessing data, email, and electronic records sent to the wrong person by mistake, and breaches of privacy. As privacy and confidentiality practices differ across settings, regions, and states, multiple practice sites might be involved in both educational and practice settings, and policies should address these potential differences.

Given This Background Information, Next, a Teaching Module Is Presented as a Model for Training

Teaching Practices: The Practice Domain: An Example Learning Module

Learning Objectives

The purpose of this module is to prepare students to analyze how to critically consider digital apps for use with clients for mental health assessment and intervention. The authors suggest the following learning objectives on technology for this module:

The student will be able to:

1. Describe a minimum of three ways in which smartphone applications are impacting field practices in social work for clients (Technology Standard 1–4).

2. Identify smartphone applications that are relevant to client needs by applying the APA framework.
3. Recommend analysis from relevant frameworks including Bakker et al. (2016), MARS (Hides et al., 2014), and UDL (CAST, 2018).
4. Analyze decisions about ethics and accessibility that meet professional standards and federal guidelines, including rationale for such decisions.
5. Demonstrate cultural competence in app selection and use, defining and matching critical characteristics such as language, access, and preferences.
6. Submit a plan for collecting client data to evaluate the effectiveness of the smartphone applications for its intended purpose.

Setting the Context and Preparation of Students for Learning

An important application of technology for field education and social work practice is its capacity to support clients and offer improved outcomes. Online mental health services, telehealth, and the impact of smartphone applications have transformed how we consume information and receive treatments (Dowling & Rickwood, 2013). It is not clear how many social workers are using teletherapy and smartphone apps in their practice (Mishna et al., 2012), and in what ways technology is a useful support. Currently, there are 10,000 mental health-related smartphone apps (Torous & Roberts, 2017). Unfortunately, teletherapy and smartphone applications are not well researched, and in some cases apps have been harmful (Wilson et al., 2016). It is critical to teach our students not only how to identify evidence-based platforms but also how to decipher what is effective for their clients. It is important to demonstrate when and how technology should be incorporated in treatment or as a case management tool. Educators must tackle both classroom practice and field education settings if we are to gain momentum applying technology in social work.

Estimates suggest at least 25% of people worldwide have some form of mental health event in their lifetime, and that only about a third seek treatment due to stigma, access, and costs. Over 76% state willingness to use apps to improve mental health/health issues, probably due in part to protection of privacy with the use of self-help applications. Given the lack of adequate numbers of mental health professionals and the reluctance of some disadvantaged populations to access mental health care, apps have the power to provide access (Akgün et al., 2019).

Highlights of Lecture Material

- One or more class sessions;
- Focus on evidence-based practice or practice-based evidence.

While smartphone apps are being used for various reasons, it is not clear how effective they are at addressing specified symptoms. One study determined that only 19 of 165 reviewed smartphone apps conducted research on effectiveness (Weisel et al., 2019). Another study reviewed 208 apps and found that more than half did not report effectiveness (Radovic et al., 2016). The lack of evidence-based practice and guidelines for app use in social work practice further complicates these issues.

Assignment Purpose

The purpose of this assignment is to provide social work learners with the opportunity to identify useful smartphone apps and build competencies around evaluating smartphone app effectiveness.

Evaluation Models and Tools

One evaluation model from the American Psychiatric Association (APA) breaks criteria for evaluation into five objectives: 1) access and background, 2) privacy and safety, 3) clinical foundation, 4) usability, and 5) therapeutic goal (APA, 2021). The first step is to determine whether or not there is enough information available to make conclusions about the app. For example, does the app come from a trusted source; what operating system is required? Next, how are data privacy and security protected? Next, a focus on clinical foundation to evaluate if the app has been researched, if it does what it says it will do, and if there is foundational knowledge and theory driving the app development and strategies. The final two criteria focus on usability and therapeutic goals. Is the app customizable, easy to use, and does it reinforce engagement? Is the app for individual use or to be used in collaboration with a provider? Does the app have the ability to export or transfer data securely? Most importantly, does the app lead to any positive behavior change or skill acquisition?

Bakker et al. (2016) conducted a literature review, scrutinizing research across diverse fields and identified 16 recommendations to guide smartphone app development (see Table 9.1). Recommendations cover everything from mental health knowledge to recording of thoughts and feelings to gamification to real-time engagement. These recommendations are a beneficial add-on with the APA model and should be used when considering the utility of a smartphone app.

Another useful tool is the Mobile Application Rating Scale (MARS) which was recently developed to enable clinicians and consumers to make informed decisions about smartphone-based support (Hides et al., 2014). MARS is a 23-item multidimensional measure that evaluates apps on the following criteria: 1) engagement, 2) functionality, 3) aesthetics, 4) information quality, and 5) app subjective quality (Hides et al., 2015). MARS demonstrated excellent internal consistency (alpha = .90) and interrater reliability (ICC = .79). MARS is helpful for determining client progress and treatment.

Facilitating Discussion and Class Exercise(s)

To introduce the assignment, instructors may wish to activate students' prior knowledge and make connections to their personal experience with smartphone/tablet apps. Instructors may pose questions during class or small group discussion, via discussion board, or even as a writing reflection to prepare students to engage in the critical thinking this assignment will require.

Managing Difficult Classroom Conversations

Important, yet potentially difficult conversations may present themselves in class discussion on the topic of use of mobile apps for mental health concerns. One such question is the ethical issue of the rights of the client to use applications in comparison to how professionals may view how the app is being used, and if indeed the client's goals are improving with its use. Client rights and safety issues may be disparate. In addition, discussing issues of privacy is very important. Having students consider factors such as who owns the data, who it is shared with, for what purposes, and how privacy is protected is important.

There is also a potential issue that student self-disclosures in the classroom can share too much information, violating privacy, and potentially, confidentiality among peers and outside entities within the university such as certain disclosures that require reporting. Federal regulations and guidelines such as HIPAA (1996) and FERPA (2011) can raise further difficult dilemmas for instructors to consider. The evaluation criteria of usefulness, usability, and integration and infrastructure can also raise areas of sensitive discussion when the evaluation of the app is uneven, less clear, or runs contrary to what students believe in their own use (Chan et al., 2015). Attitudinal issues besides structural factors such as privacy, workflow, and safety may also produce divergence of views in class discussions (Chan et al., 2015; Weisel et al., 2019). Attitudinal issues such as fear of stigmatization and a preference for self-reliance can clash with professional opinions (Weisel et al., 2019).

Evaluation of Learning

This assignment is designed to guide future training and in-service training for social workers through the process of selecting a smartphone/tablet application that will enhance client services, while learning the standards and ethical care of excellence in social work. Instructors should utilize the rubric found in Tables 9.3 and 9.4.

Conclusion and Final Considerations

Although technology is increasingly utilized in the social work education and practice, little comprehensive research has been conducted on its uses, successes, best practices, and outcomes. One systematic review of the literature indicated how knowledge in social work and its very nature is being transformed from social to informational with technology use (López Peláez & Marcuello-Servós, 2018). Digital tools have impacted research interventions, therapy, social networks, and how field settings go about their administrative and human resources work. The use of these technologies brings an urgent focus on the ethical and legal issues in their utilization such as confidentiality and privacy. Another important question to be explored is how social work education and practice, including field education, can develop adequate curriculum to train for these technologies and the challenging issues that come with their use. Upholding social work values of the profession within face-to-face interactions in the classroom and practice must now transition to exploring how to uphold them online and on technology-driven platforms where face-to-face interactions are not possible, feasible, or desirable. This challenge of infusing values into these new teaching and training modalities must be addressed so that as a profession we can embrace the inevitable change these technologies bring and have input into how our profession likewise changes (López Peláez & Marcuello-Servós, 2018). Social work educators must embrace these changes and build on the recent momentum forced onto the field – both in educational and field practice settings – by the COVID-19 pandemic which required an online presence and high levels of innovation and creativity to meet the crisis. Field educators and university faculty must be focused on this Grand Challenge to develop a roadmap for driving further gains throughout schools of social work and their field education partnerships and later through all fields of practice.

Social workers have spent the last half century perfecting and developing models of practice for in-person service delivery (Huttar & BrintzenhofeSzoc, 2019). We are a profession that embraces the power of human relationships, and technology is still often viewed as a barrier to that process (La Mendola, 2010). This does not have to be the case. As we begin to understand how this pandemic has impacted our profession it is important to realize we are spending more time now than ever connecting without being in person. Post-pandemic will provide an opportunity to continue the advances and innovations that technology has enabled, and to resume the irreplaceable face-to-face interactions that are the center of quality social work.

As technology washes over the world, it engulfs social work education and practice as well. Questions still need to be addressed through research: *When is technology used for the greater good? Can social work education develop a plan to guide design and use in all areas of the curriculum so that the profession and its stakeholders benefit from its use?* A research and practice roadmap for schools of social work is essential to meet the Grand Challenges.

References

Akgün, B. D., Aktaç, A., & Yorulmaz, O. (2019). Mobile applications in mental health: A systematic review of efficacy. *Psikiyatride Guncel Yaklasimlar*, *11*(4), 519–530.

Allen, I. E., & Seaman, J. (2013). *Changing course: Ten years of tracking online education in the United States*. The Sloan Consortium.

American Academy of Social Work & Social Welfare. (2021). *Progress and plans for the grand challenges*. University of Maryland.

American Psychiatric Association. (2021). *App advisor: An American psychiatric association initiative*. www.psychiatry.org/psychiatrists/practice/mental-health-apps

Americans with Disabilities Act of 1990. (1990). 42 U.S.C. § 12101 et seq.

Antczak, H. B., Mackrill, T., Steensbæk, S., & Ebsen, F. (2019). What works in video-based youth statutory caseworker supervision – caseworker and supervisor perspectives. *Social Work Education*, *38*(8), 1025–1040. https://doi: org.libproxy.txstate.edu/10.1080/02615479.2019.1611757

Apgar, D. (2019). Conceptualization of capstone experiences: Examining their role in social work education. *Social Work Education*, *38*(2), 143–158. https://doi-org.libproxy.txstate.edu/10.1080/02615479.2018.1512963

Bakker, D., Kazantzis, N., Rickwood, D., & Rickard, N. (2016). Mental health smartphone apps: Review and evidence-based recommendations for future developments. *JMIR Mental Health*, *3*(1), e7. https://doi.org/10.2196/mental.4984

Barsky, A. (2019). Technology in field education: Managing ethical issues. *Journal of Technology in Human Services*, *37*(⅔), 241–254. doi:10.1080/15228835.2019.1578326

Belluomini, E. M. (2016). Digitally immigrant Social Work faculty: Technology self-efficacy and practice outcomes. *Walden Dissertations and Doctoral Studies*, 3280. https://scholarworks.waldenu.edu/dissertations/3280

Berzin, S., Singer, J., & Chan, C. (2015). *Practice innovation in technology in the digital age: A grand challenge for social work*. American Academy of Social Work and Social Welfare.

Bloomberg, J. (2015). Innovation takes the exponential express. *WIRED*. www.wired.com/insights/2015/01/innovation-takes-the-exponential-express/

Campbell, M., Detres, M., & Lucio, R. (2019). Can a digital whiteboard foster student engagement? *Social Work Education*, *38*(6), 735–752. https://doi-org.libproxy.txstate.edu/10.1080/02615479.2018.1556631

CARES Act. (2020). S. 2440 (115th).

Chan, S., Torous, J., Hinton, L., & Yellowlees, P. (2015). Towards a framework for evaluating mobile mental health apps. *Telemedicine Journal and E-Health: The Official Journal of the American Telemedicine Association*, *21*(12), 1038–1041. https://doi-org.libproxy.txstate.edu/10.1089/tmj.2015.0002

Clarke, J., & Morley, C. (2020). From crisis to opportunity? Innovations in Australian social work field education during the COVID-19 global pandemic. *Social Work Education*, *39*(8), 1048–1057. https://doi-org.libproxy.txstate.edu/10.1080/02615479.2020.1836145

Colvin, A. D., & Bullock, A. N. (2014). Technology acceptance in social work education: Implications for the field practicum. *Journal of Teaching in Social Work*, *34*(4), 496–513. https://doi.org/10.1080/08841233.2014.952869

Council of Social Work Education (CSWE). (2022). *2022 Educational policy and accreditation standards (EPAS)*. Author. www.cswe.org/accreditation/standards/2022-epas/

Csoba, J., & Diebel, A. (2020). Worldwide closed! Social worker field practice during the "lockdown" period. *Social Work Education*, *39*(8), 1094–1106. https://doi-org.libproxy.txstate.edu/10.1080/02615479.2020.1829580

Dede, C., Jass Ketelhut, D., Whitehouse, P., Breit, L., & McCloskey, E. M. (2009). A research agenda for online teacher professional development. *Journal of Teacher Education*, *60*(1), 8–19. doi:10.1177/0022487108327554

Dombo, E. A., Kays, L., & Weller, K. (2014). Clinical social work practice and technology: Personal, practical, regulatory, and ethical considerations for the Twenty-First Century. *Social Work in Health Care*, *53*(9), 900–919. https://doi-org.libproxy.txstate.edu/10.1080/00981389.2014.948585

Dowling, M., & Rickwood, D. (2013). Online counseling and therapy for mental health problems: A systematic review of individual synchronous interventions using chat. *Journal of Technology in Human Services*, *31*, 1–21. www.researchgate.net/deref/http%3A%2F%2Fdx.doi.org%2F10.1080%2F15228835.2012.728508

Edgerton, J. K., & Cookson, P. W., Jr. (2020). Closing the digital divide: The critical role of the federal government. *Learning Policy Institute*. https://learningpolicyinstitute.org/blog/covid-closing-digital-divide-federal-government

Family Educational Rights and Privacy Act (FERPA). (2011). 34 C.F.R. § 99.

Health Insurance Portability and Accountability Act (HIPAA). (1996). Pub.L. 104–191, 110 Stat. 1936.

Hides, L., Kavanagh, D., Stoyanov, S., Zelenko, O., Tjondronegoro, D., & Mani, M. (2015). *Mobile application rating scale (MARS)*. Young and Well Cooperative Research Centre.

Huttar, C. M., & BrintzenhofeSzoc, K. (2019). Virtual reality and computer simulation in social work education: A systematic review. *Journal of Social Work Education*, *56*(1), 131–141.

Joyce, B. R., & Showers, B. (2002). *Student achievement through staff development* (3rd ed.). Association for Supervision & Curriculum Development (ASCD).

Kurzman, P. A. (2019). The current status of social work online and distance education. *Journal of Teaching in Social Work*, *39*(4–5), 286–292.

La Mendola, W. (2010). Social work and social presence in an online world. *Journal of Technology in Human Services*, *28*(1/2), 108–119. doi:10.1080/15228831003759562

Langlois, G. (2011). Meaning, semiotechnologies, and participatory media. *Culture Machine*, *12*.

Lee, E. O. (2014). Use of avatars and a virtual community to increase cultural competence. *Journal of Technology in Human Services*, *32*, 93–107.

López Peláez, A., & Marcuello-Servós, C. (2018). e-Social work and digital society: Re-conceptualizing approaches, practices and technologies. *European Journal of Social Work*, *21*(6), 801–803.

Mishna, F., Bogo, M., Root, J., Sawyer, J.-L., & Khoury-Kassabri, M. (2012). "It just crept in": The digital age and implications for social work practice. *Clinical Social Work Journal*, *40*(3), 277–286. https://doi.org/10.1007/s10615-012-0383-4

Mishna, F., Bogo, M., & Sawyer, J.-L. (2015). Cyber counseling: Illuminating benefits and challenges. *Clinical Social Work Journal*, *43*(2), 169–178. https://doi.org/10.1007/s10615-013-0470-1

National Association of Social Workers [NASW], Council on Social Work Education [CSWE], Association of Social Work Boards [ASWB], and the Clinical Social Work Association [CSWA]. (2017). *Technology in social work practice*. NASW Press.

Radovic, A., Vona, P. L., Santostefano, A. M., Ciaravino, S., Miller, E., & Stein, B. D. (2016). Smartphone applications for mental health. *Cyberpsychology,*

Behavior, and Social Networking, *19*(7), 465–470. https://doi.org/10.1089/cyber.2015.0619

Reamer, F. G. (2019). Social work education in a digital world: Technology standards for education and practice. *Journal of Social Work Education*, *55*(3), 420–432. https://doi-org.libproxy.txstate.edu/10.1080/10437797.2019.1567412

Sanders, C. K., & Scanlon, E. (2021). The digital divide is a human rights issue: Advancing social inclusion through social work advocacy. *Journal of Human Rights and Social Work*, *6*(2), 130–143.

Schropshire, N. (2019, March). Introducing SW-TPACK. In K. Graziano (Ed.), *Society for Information Technology & Teacher Education International Conference* (pp. 2517–2523). Association for the Advancement of Computing in Education (AACE).

Torous, J., & Roberts, L. W. (2017). Needed innovation in digital health and smartphone applications for mental health: Transparency and trust. *JAMA Psychiatry*, *74*(5), 437–438. https://doi.org/10.1001/jamapsychiatry.2017.0262

Wayne, J., Bogo, M., & Raskin, M. (2010). Field education as the signature pedagogy of social work. *Journal of Social Work Education*, *46*(3), 327–339. https://doi.org/10.5175/JSWE.2010.200900043

Weisel, K. K., Fuhrmann, L. M., Berking, M., Baumeister, H., Cuijpers, P., & Ebert, D. D. (2019). Standalone smartphone apps for mental health – A systematic review and meta-analysis. *NPJ Digital Medicine*, *2*(118). https://doi.org/10.1038/s41746-019-0188-8

Will, M. (2019, February 26). With bug-in-ear coaching, teachers get feedback on the fly. *Education Week*. www.edweek.org/leadership/with-bug-in-ear-coaching-teachers-get-feedback-on-the-fly/2019/02

Wilson, H., Stoyanov, S. R., Gandabhai, S., Baldwin, A., & Garnes, B. (2016). The quality and accuracy of mobile apps to prevent driving after drinking alcohol. *JMIR mHealth and uHealth*, *4*(3), e98. doi:10.2196/mhealth.5961.

Wretman, C. J., & Macy, R. J. (2016). Technology in social work education: A systematic review. *Journal of Social Work Education*, *52*(4), 409–421. https://doi-org.libproxy.txstate.edu/10.1080/10437797.2016.1198293

Zorn, T. E., Flanagin, A. J., & Shoham, M. D. (2011). Institutional and non-institutional influences on information and communication technology adoption and use among nonprofit organizations. *Human Communication Research*, *37*(1), 1–33. https://doi.org/10.1111/j.1468-2958.2010.01387.x

Appendix 9A

EPAS Addressed in Grand Challenge #8

Harnessing Technology for Social Good

Competency 1: Demonstrate Ethical and Professional Behavior. The only competency in which CSWE directly mentioned technology is in the ethical use of technology in practice. Although the use of technology is of huge importance in practice, it is aligned in all competencies even though not mentioned. This competency requires social workers to recognize the importance of developing and updating their skills in the use of technology to ensure that their practice remains useful and relevant. Most importantly, social workers are called on to understand the ethical use of technology. To assess the use of different digital apps used on smartphones for client assessment remains a growing trend in mental health and well-being areas. In a fast-changing field such as technology, social workers must be committed to engaging in continued educational efforts both in their graduate training and after in their practice to keep pace with the changing use of technology to help clients and develop effective agencies. In addition, schools of social work must have adequate technology resources to pursue their missions and to educate students both in the classroom and most importantly in their agencies during their field education. This bridge between classroom and field can be enhanced by use of technology in tracking students throughout their degrees, placing student in an ever-changing field practice environment, as well as in enhancing supervision within the agency settings and communicating educational outcomes expected across agencies.

Competency 2: Advance Human Rights and Social, Racial, Economic, and Environmental Justice. Issues of access to technology both in practice and in training on campus are aligned with this competency. The use of technology in agencies that serve clients of diverse backgrounds is unevenly applied and budget issues also impact the implementation of technology. Although advances have been made in recent years nonprofits and state-run agencies often lack both budgets and IT staff to provide the needed resources. Likewise, in schools of social work, budget issues have made it difficult for faculty and staff to train to use the latest technology and to make sure to teach this to students. Since students in social work also must be able to arrive on the doorstep of schools with some knowledge and access to technology to be successful.

Competency 3: Engage Anti-Racism, Diversity, Equity, and Inclusion (ADEI) in Practice. Understanding the use of technology is advantageous in terms of advancing practice outcomes and developing professional knowledge, expertise, and opportunities. It is crucial that all populations and groups be trained and equipped with technology in order to develop to their highest potential in the profession and in terms of advancing skills for helping clients most efficiently.

Competency 4: Engage in Practice-Informed Research and Research-Informed Practice: Engage in Policy Practice. Technology is increasingly used by all disciplines to advance research in practice which then informs policy development and advocacy. The rest of the world has advanced in technology faster than in social work which jeopardizes our ability to be on the national stage with other disciplines, thus limiting our professional influence. Social work must do more in keeping up with the challenge of new technology in order to remain relevant in the helping professions.

Competency 5: Engage in Policy Practice. Advocacy of policy positions and bridging practice to policy requires a command of technology across various platforms such as social media, software for helping develop and implement research and acquire data for supporting policy positions. Public health issues, such as during the COVID-19 epidemic requires data gathering and tracking in real time to inform changing policies.

Competency 6: Engage With Individuals, Families, Groups, Organizations, and Communities. Social workers need technology to be able to keep up with practice, especially in accessing clients and tracking progress. Technology allows us to amplify access and delivery to give clients more options for treatment across diverse communities.

Competency 7: Assess Individuals, Families, Groups, Organizations, and Communities. Social workers must use technology to assess and track clients and to efficiently run organizations that serve these clients. Our clients span ever-increasing areas of geography and time zones thus technology can help both deliver services and assess client needs. This can be helpful in making our practice more client based and relevant to the communities in which clients live.

Competency 8: Intervene With Individuals, Families, Groups, Organizations, and Communities. Social workers must also use the advances in technology-driven telehealth to be able to provide services and that implies the knowledge and skills in technology platforms used for working remotely with clients as well as apps in the mental health arena, for example.

Competency 9: Evaluate Practice With Individuals, Families, Groups, Organizations, and Communities. Social workers also must use technology such as software and practice apps prevalent on smartphones to help drive the evaluation process for working across individuals, families, groups, organizations, and communities. Practice evaluation at the macro level also depends on the use of software and technology for monitoring outcomes at the organizational level so that funding can be maintained, clients can continue to be served, and effective supervision be utilized.

Appendix 9B

Table 9.1 Recommendations for Future Mental Health Apps

Evidence	*Recommendation*	*Details*
Demonstrably effective, but more research needed in MHapp field	1. Cognitive behavioral therapy based	Start with an evidence-based framework to maximize effectiveness
	2. Address both anxiety and low mood	Increases accessibility and addresses comorbidity between anxiety and depression. Also compatible with transdiagnostic theories of anxiety and depression
Probably effective, but more research needed in MHapp field	3. Designed for use by nonclinical populations	Avoiding diagnostic labels reduces stigma, increases accessibility, and enables preventative use
	4. Automated tailoring	Tailored interventions are more efficacious than is rigid self-help
	5. Reporting of thoughts, feelings, or behaviors	Self-monitoring and self-reflection to promote psychological growth and enable progress evaluation
	6. Recommend activities	Behavioral activation to boost self-efficacy and repertoire of coping skills
	7. Mental health information	Develop mental health literacy
	8. Real-time engagement	Allows users to use in moments in which they are experiencing distress for optimum benefits of coping behaviors and relaxation techniques

(*Continued*)

Table 9.1 (Continued)

Evidence	*Recommendation*	*Details*
Supported by theory and indirect evidence but focused research needed	9. Activities explicitly linked to specific reported mood problems	Enhances understanding of cause-and-effect relationship between actions and emotions
	10. Encourage non-technology-based activities	Helps to avoid potential problems with attention, increase opportunities for mindfulness, and limit time spent on devices
	11. Gamification and intrinsic motivation to engage	Encourage use of the app via rewards and internal triggers, and positive reinforcement and behavioral conditioning. Also links with flourishing
	12. Log of past app use	Encourage use of the app through personal investment. Internal triggers for repeated engagement
	13. Reminders to engage	External triggers for engagement
	14. Simple and intuitive interface and interactions	Reduce confusion and disengagement in users
	15. Links to crisis support services	Helps users who are in crisis to seek help

Note. Bakker et al., 2016, www.ncbi.nlm.nih.gov/pmc/articles/PMC4795320/

Table 9.2 Practice Assignment Worksheet: Using This Worksheet, Examine Alignment Across Frameworks, Identifying Similarities, Differences, and Gaps

The APA Model	*Describe Alignment With Standards and Frameworks*				
	NASW Standards	*MARS*	*Bakker et al., 2016*	*Cultural Competence*	*UDL*
Step 1. Access and Background: Does the app . . . 1. Identify ownership? 2. Identify funding sources, conflicts of interest?					

The APA Model	*Describe Alignment With Standards and Frameworks*				
	NASW Standards	*MARS*	*Bakker et al., 2016*	*Cultural Competence*	*UDL*
3. Come from a trusted source?					
4. Claim to be medical?					
5. Include additional or hidden costs?					
6. Work offline?					
7. Identify technological platforms required?					
8. Compatible with, includes accessibility features					
9. Updated within the previous 180 days?					
Step 2. Privacy and Security: Does the app . . .					
1. Share a privacy policy that is clear and transparent before use?					
2. Declare the data use policy and purpose?					
3. Tell whether Personal Health Information is de-identified or anonymous? How is it used?					
4. Allow users to opt out of and delete data?					
5. Disclose if data is maintained on the device or in the cloud?					

(*Continued*)

Table 9.2 (Continued)

The APA Model	*Describe Alignment With Standards and Frameworks*				
	NASW Standards	*MARS*	*Bakker et al., 2016*	*Cultural Competence*	*UDL*
6. Explain the security systems in place?					
7. Collect, use, or transmit sensitive data? Is this secured? How?					
8. Share data with any third parties?					
9. Have a system to respond to potential harms or safety concerns, if appropriate					
Step 3. Clinical Foundations: Does the app . . .					
1. Appear to do what it claims to do?					
2. Include content that is correct, well-written, and relevant?					
3. Share relevant sources or references supporting the app use cases?					
4. Provide evidence of specific benefit from academic institutions, publications, end user feedback, or research studies?					
5. Report evidence of effectiveness/ efficacy?					

The APA Model	*Describe Alignment With Standards and Frameworks*				
	NASW Standards	*MARS*	*Bakker et al., 2016*	*Cultural Competence*	*UDL*
6. Document attempts to validate app usability and feasibility?					
7. Have a clinical/ recovery foundation relevant to intended use?					
8. Does the app appear to do what it claims to do?					
Step 4. Usability: What about . . .					
1. The main engagement styles of the app?					
2. Its alignment with the needs and priorities of the user?					
3. Its capacity for customization?					
4. A clearly defined functional scope?					
5. Its ease of use?					
Step 5. Data Integration Towards Therapeutic Goal: Is it easy to identify . . .					
1. Does the user own their own data?					
2. How can data be shared and interpreted consistent with the app's stated purpose?					

(*Continued*)

Table 9.2 (Continued)

The APA Model	*Describe Alignment With Standards and Frameworks*				
	NASW Standards	*MARS*	*Bakker et al., 2016*	*Cultural Competence*	*UDL*
3. The ability to share data with Emergency Medical Services and other data tools (e.g. Apple Healthkit, FitBit, etc.)?					
4. If it is intended for individual use or to share data with a provider?					
5. If it is intended to share data with a provider, does the app have the ability to export or transfer data?					
6. Should/will the app lead to positive behavior change or skill acquisition?					
7. Might the app lead to an improved therapeutic alliance between the patient and the provider?					

Note. Table developed using the American Psychiatric Association App Evaluation Model. See www.psychiatry.org/psychiatrists/practice/mental-health-apps/the-app-evaluation-model

Table 9.3 App Evaluation Assignment and Grading Rubric

The APA Model	*Response to Query*		*Comments*
	Yes	*No*	
Screening			
Step 1. Access and Background: Does the app . . . 1. Identify ownership? 2. Identify funding sources, conflicts of interest? 3. Come from a trusted source? 4. Claim to be medical? 5. Include additional or hidden costs? 6. Work offline? 7. Identify technological platforms required? 8. Compatible with, includes accessibility features 9. Updated within the previous 180 days? **Step 2. Privacy & Security:** Does the app . . . 1. Share a privacy policy that is clear and transparent before use? 2. Declare the data use policy and purpose? 3. Tell whether Personal Health Information is de-identified or anonymous? How is it used? 4. Allow users to opt out of and delete data? 5. Disclose if data is maintained on the device or in the cloud? 6. Explain the security systems in place? 7. Collect, use, or transmit sensitive data? Is this secured? How? 8. Share data with any third parties? 9. Have a system to respond to potential harms or safety concerns, if appropriate			

(*Continued*)

Table 9.3 (Continued)

The APA Model	*Response to Query*		*Comments*
	Yes	*No*	
Screening			
Step 3. Clinical Foundations: Does the app . . .			
1. Appear to do what it claims to do?			
2. Include content that is correct, well-written, and relevant?			
3. Share relevant sources or references supporting the app use cases?			
4. Provide evidence of specific benefit from academic institutions, publications, end user feedback, or research studies?			
5. Report evidence of effectiveness/efficacy?			
6. Document attempts to validate app usability and feasibility?			
7. Have a clinical/recovery foundation relevant to intended use?			
8. Does the app appear to do what it claims to do?			
Step 4. Usability: What about . . .			
1. The main engagement styles of the app			
2. Its alignment with the needs and priorities of the user?			
3. Its capacity for customization?			
4. A clearly defined functional scope?			
5. Its ease of use?			
Step 5. Data Integration Towards Therapeutic Goal			
Is it easy to identify . . .			
1. Does the user own their own data?			
2. How can data be shared and interpreted consistent with the app's stated purpose?			

The APA Model	*Response to Query*		*Comments*
	Yes	*No*	
Screening			
3. The ability to share data with Emergency Medical Services and other data tools (e.g. Apple Healthkit, FitBit, etc.)?			
4. If it is intended for individual use or to share data with a provider?			
5. If it is intended to share data with a provider, does the app have the ability to export or transfer data?			
6. Should/will the app lead to positive behavior change or skill acquisition?			
7. If the app might lead to an improved therapeutic alliance between the patient and the provider?			

Note. Table developed using the American Psychiatric Association App Evaluation Model. See www.psychiatry.org/psychiatrists/practice/mental-health-apps/the-app-evaluation-model

Table 9.4 Grading Rubric

APA Criteria	*Evaluation Quality*		
	Excellent	*Adequate*	*Insufficient*
	Responses are accurate, ethical, professional, complete	*Responses may be partially accurate, ethical, professional, or complete*	*Responses are, on one or more markers, inadequate or unacceptable*
Access and Background	9		
Privacy and Security	9		
Clinical Foundation	7		
Usability	5		
Data Integration Toward Therapeutic Goal	7		
Alignment With Standards	4		
Relation to Other Frameworks	3		
Cultural Considerations	3		
Limitations and Benefits	3		
Total points possible	50		

Constructive Feedback to Improve Future App Evaluation:

Part Three

A Just Society

10 Eliminate Racism

Todd Vanidestine, Candida Brooks-Harrison, Sandra Bernabei, Onaje Muid, Joyce James and Robin Benton

Introduction

Grand Challenge of Eliminating Racism

The stark reality of White supremacy and structural racism (also known as institutionalized or systemic racism) goes to the very core of our country's soul. The first act of the first US Congress in 1790 was the Naturalization Act, which clearly defined White men, women, and children as citizens (López, 2006; Teasley et al., 2021). Over approximately the next 160 years this act was in place, almost every single institution and system was developed by, and for, White people. Fast-forward to the present-day US racial context; there are extralegal killings of Black, Indigenous, and People of Color (BIPOC) and glaring racial health inequities magnified by a global pandemic. Further evidence of ongoing racism and White supremacy lies in the inequitable racial outcomes across numerous intersecting systems including employment, health care, legal, housing, and education, to name a few (National Association of Social Workers [NASW], 2021). This requires social work education to explicitly conceptualize the inequitable racial outcomes as a result of systemic and institutional processes steeped in racism and White supremacy carried out by witting or unwitting individuals.

The authors want to emphasize the importance of strengthening relationships, accountability, and collective transformative power through organizing within classrooms, communities, institutions, and systems (Editors, 2015; Tolliver & Burghardt, 2016). We are a multiracial, anti-racism group of people representing overlapping roles that include organizers, educators, consultants, practitioners (micro, mezzo, macro), community residents, leaders, and researchers. We appreciate the opportunity to share our collective insights using social

DOI: 10.4324/9781003308263-13

work education as a vehicle to interrogate the consequences of racism and White supremacy. Many of our insights evolved from our work with the People's Institute for Survival and Beyond (PISAB) in communities, including schools of social work and our own families. We are indebted to PISAB for the Undoing Racism®/Community Organizing workshop, which provided invaluable insights, guidance, and leadership development that supported our collective anti-racism organizing within our personal and professional spaces (PISAB, n.d.).

This chapter will offer insights and ideas for teaching about racism and White supremacy. The chapter is divided into three sections. The first section focuses on the Grand Challenge of Eliminating Racism (GCER), social work's history of attempting to address racism, and challenges to addressing racism in social work. The second section focuses on situating the GCER in the foundational domains of the curricula; human behavior in the social environment (HBSE), practice, and policy. Finally, the third section provides examples of teaching practices within the policy curricula in order to emphasize the importance of an anti-racism, macro-level analysis to unearth the racial power dynamics at the root of many unjust racial outcomes in US society and to ultimately inform actions to eliminate racism.

Background

Since its inception in 2013, the Grand Challenges for Social Work (GCSW) emerged as a volunteer group of practitioners, academics, organizations, and other interested entities under the auspices of the American Academy of Social Work and Social Welfare (AASWSW) to identify and address major social issues (GCSW, 2021a). Although the GCSW Committee originally declared their commitment to ending racism by infusing it into all the original Grand Challenges, the historical and present-day realities of racism and White supremacy required a stronger emphasis (GCSW, 2020; Rao et al., 2021). On June 26, 2020, the GCER became a stand-alone challenge, which included an outline of actions that resulted in six guiding objectives:

- Focus on evidence- and practice-based research that cultivates innovation to improve conditions of daily life of people impacted by racism and facilitates systemic change in the individual, organization, community, and societal levels;
- Advance community empowerment and advocacy for eradicating racism and White supremacy through solutions that create sustainable changes;

- Foster the development of an anti-racist social work workforce that promotes access to resources and opportunities and encompasses transdisciplinary collaboration;
- Promote teaching and learning within social work education programs that examines structural inequalities and White privilege, and their impact on individual and group outcomes;
- Develop a policy agenda for eradicating racism and White supremacy from institutions and organizations, where structural racism is evident and causes the most damage;
- Examine the profession of social work itself with respect to rooting out racist policies and practices (GCSW, 2021b).

It is important to highlight the following concepts found in these objectives: structural racism, White supremacy, White privilege, and anti-racist (anti-racism). Historically, they have received limited attention by social work, including its approach to educating future social work practitioners and educators (Abrams & Moio, 2009; Corley & Young, 2018; McMahon & Allen-Meares, 1992; NASW, 2007; Social Work Policy Institute [SWPI], 2014; Whitaker et al., 2021). Although these concepts are currently receiving greater attention, anti-racism educational approaches must also include collective, accountable, and sustained actions. The following section will discuss social work's history of simultaneously perpetuating and attempting to address racism and White supremacy.

History of Addressing Racism and White Supremacy

Social work's history addressing racism and White supremacy within the profession and society has fluctuated between supporting and resisting the processes underlying inequitable, racialized outcomes. This paradoxical relationship is exemplified in the early 20th-century settlement house movement where social work focused on supporting immigrant communities living in poverty and concurrently reinforced segregationist policies, institutional racism, and xenophobia of the times (Reisch & Andrews, 2002). The social work profession also reinforced other forms of macro-level racism by supporting the eugenics movement, forced sterilizations, and the implementation of internment camps for Japanese Americans during World War II (LaPan & Platt, 2005; Park, 2008).

Conversely, the social work profession offered calls-to-action and supported national movements to address racial injustices. During the 1960s Civil Rights movement and racial uprisings, the National

Advisory Commission on Civil Disorders was created and identified "White racism" as a cause of societal unrest (National Advisory Commission on Civil Disorders, 2016). This influenced the NASW and CSWE to call for an end to White racism (Reisch & Andrews, 2002). Social workers took direct action by supporting protests focused on the Vietnam War and the oppressive conditions affecting communities of color, to varying degrees (Schiele & Hopps, 2009). Notwithstanding, social work was still immersed in an ongoing intra-profession racial struggle as seen with the formation of the National Association of Black Social Workers (NABSW) because the NASW, a White-dominated professional organization, was not effectively addressing White racism within Black communities and the social work profession (NABSW, 1968). Although White racism temporarily emerged as a common social injustice for the country and social work, the concept never really gained the necessary long-term attention within social work.

Throughout the 1970s–1990s, social work education began implementing diversity-related theoretical approaches to educate social workers about racial and ethnic differences. CSWE put forth several diversity educational standards, which included the dual perspective, the ethnic sensitivity and awareness approach, and cultural competence (Devore & Schlesinger, 1981; Lum, 1999; Norton, 1978). Cultural competence became an essential part of social work's attempt to understand race and ethnicity, along with related practice approaches such as cultural awareness, knowledge acquisition, skills development, and inductive learning (Lum, 2005), which are necessary but not sufficient for anti-racism social work practice. Framing concepts such as racism and White supremacy within frameworks such as cultural competency and diversity further minimized social work's ability to effectively analyze racism and take actions to eliminate it (Abrams & Moio, 2009; Graham & Schiele, 2010).

Over the last 20 years, the social work profession highlighted racism as an ongoing issue that required attention at multiple levels of society, including within the profession itself. In 2005, the Social Work Congress brought together over 400 leaders within the field to establish a long-term strategic vision of how to address pressing issues over the following five years, including two imperatives focused on racism (Clark et al., 2006). Then the NASW (2007) published a document titled *Institutional Racism & the Social Work Profession: A Call to Action* that emphasized how racism manifests in social systems and provided concrete action steps to create a more racially just vision for our profession. Social workers continued organizing within the profession, and across disciplines, to strengthen the profession's ability to analyze the consequences of racism. In November 2013, the NASW and the SWPI held a racial equity "think tank" that led to a subsequent report titled *Achieving Racial Equity: Calling the Social Work Profession to Action.*

Challenges to Addressing Racism

Eliminating racism and White supremacy within the social work profession and society demands transformative change rather than transactional change. A transformative change requires a complete overhaul of the system, institution, or profession in question whereas transactional change only requires minor adjustments while leaving the fundamental structure and culture of an entity in place (Barndt, 2007). Furthermore, social and racial justice require "the transformation of people and systems; transformation of the individual and elements of the collective society" (Teasley & Archuleta, 2015, p. 612). However, social work's current approach to racism and White supremacy oftentimes mirrors its historical approach and revolves around transactional responses such as writing position statements and calls-to-action in response to national tragedies and/or uprisings (e.g. George Floyd, Breonna Taylor, Black Lives Matter, among others; see also Perez, 2021; Santiago & Ivery, 2020). While these efforts contain critical insights and important suggested actions, the follow through of, and accountability to, proposed policy changes can often remain unfulfilled.

During his presidential plenary speech at the Society for Social Work and Research (SSWR), Dr. Larry E. Davis (2016) provided insights about the barriers to eliminate racism. He stated,

> Meaningful discussions on topics of race [and racism] get lost in the more comfortable and less anxiety-arousing discussion of diversity . . . diversity celebrations and diversity programs have not proven to be helpful for analyzing racism or for developing effective policy recommendations.
>
> (p. 398)

There are numerous factors creating barriers to establishing clear, consistent anti-racism curriculum and pedagogy that affects social work's efficacy to eliminate racism such as the lack of approaches to critically analyze race, limited preparation to teach about racism and anti-racism, minimal interrogation of whiteness, and insufficient understanding of social work's historical relationship to racism and White supremacy (Gregory, 2021; Ortiz & Jani, 2010; Perez, 2021; Whitaker et al., 2021). However, we will focus on two related challenges connected to Dr. Davis's quote earlier: 1) unclear conceptualizations of racism through race-neutral discourse without critically analyzing whiteness; and 2) de-emphasizing macro-level analyses of structural racism and White supremacy that in turn limits collective, strategic actions to change laws, policies, and other guidance within the social work profession and society as a whole.

Transformational change to eliminate racism and White supremacy must include critical discourse and language related to their manifestations and outcomes; without clear multi-level analyses of these concepts, effective actions and comprehensive solutions are less likely to happen. Discourse represents a social practice (discursive practice) where meaning is produced and reproduced across social relations (Fairclough & Wodak, 1997), including through disciplinary discourses such as social work and other helping professions (Vanidestine & Aparicio, 2019). Additionally, discursive practices serve as connectors between knowledge and power to (re)produce meaning for any number of concepts (Foucault, 1979), including racism and White supremacy. By subsuming racial concepts within approaches such as "cultural competence," "diversity," and "inclusion" (Abrams & Moio, 2009; Constance-Huggins & Davis, 2017; Ortiz & Jani, 2010; Pon, 2009), social work education runs the risk of reproducing the racism and White supremacy it is attempting to address. These concepts also serve to diminish the outcomes of racism and reproduce color-blind racism, which represents the maintenance of structural racial order within apparently non-racial practices, language, and attitudes (Bonilla-Silva, 2010; Constance-Huggins & Davis, 2017).

The second part of Dr. Davis's quote ("diversity celebrations and diversity programs have not proven to be helpful [or effective] for analyzing racism or for developing effective policy recommendations") highlights another challenge to eliminating racism, which is de-emphasizing macro-level analyses and actions (Hill et al., 2017; Reisch, 2016; Specht & Courtney, 1994). Social work's ethical commitment to the broader society (macro-level) is clearly laid out in Section 6.04 Social and Political Action of the *Code of Ethics of the* NASW (2017) with phrases related to macro-practice such as "engage in social and political action," "advocate for changes in policy and legislation," "promote policies that safeguard rights," and "act to prevent and eliminate domination of, exploitation of, and discrimination against any person, group, or class." Although these ethical mandates are invaluable to eliminate racism and White supremacy, social work has struggled to fully embody these macro-level mandates.

The curricula content and pedagogy for social and political action is limited in content, faculty commitment, and emphasis. The Association for Community Organization and Social Action (ACOSA) conducted a survey in 2010–2011 of its members, mainly social work macro practitioners, to understand challenges they faced in the classroom (Rothman, 2012). The responses revealed barriers to including macro-level content such as minimizing macro-level practice, clinical and administration colleagues resisting macro content, lack of funding, and minimal focus on recruiting macro-level faculty members. Similarly, Hill et al. (2017) found challenges to macro social work education included limited field placements, lack of institutional support and resources, and students' feeling challenged to gain employment by focusing on macro-practice. Because there is an association between macro-practice and the ability to integrate social justice into social work education (Funge et al., 2020), de-emphasizing macro-level analyses and actions further compounds social work's tendency to conceptualize racism as predominantly interpersonal beliefs, values, and attitudes located primarily in micro-level interactions.

Combining the resistance to macro-level practice with a lack of conceptual clarity of race, racism, and White supremacy reinforces a micro-level understanding of racial injustices, thus limiting the scope and efficacy of actions (Corley & Young, 2018). This often results from limited experience (or unwillingness) with incorporating structural racial concepts into clinical social work content (Quiros et al., 2019; Varghese, 2016), interrupting the "scaffolding" of White supremacy as an act of liberation (Pewewardy & Almeida, 2014), and promoting "structural solutions to systemic inequalities and various forms of oppression that go beyond individual adaptation and resilience" (Reisch, 2016, p. 261). Doing so then widens the divide between micro- and macro-practice as well as professionalism and social/racial justice practice (Kam, 2014; Olson, 2007), thus diminishing social work's ability to eliminate racism.

Grand Challenge and Social Work Curricula

CSWE is the guiding social work entity that provides educational policy and standards for all BSW and MSW programs in the US. The current CSWE (2015) *Educational Policy and Accreditation Standards* (EPAS) omits any explicit reference to racism, White supremacy, or anti-racism. Instead, there is a reliance on framing race ambiguously under "diversity and difference," "human rights," and "justice" (p. 7). However, CSWE's first draft revision of the *2022 EPAS* (2021), which includes more explicit language regarding racism, equity, and anti-racism in Competency 2's title, "Engage Anti-Racism, Diversity, Equity and Inclusion in Practice." The proposed revisions also include specific concepts such as "white supremacy/superiority," "power," and "anti-racist practice." Translating social work's educational policy into actions will require commitment and accountability across the curricula, faculty, and profession. The GCER can potentially function as a conduit to do so by strengthening the macro-level discourse related to racism and White supremacy, coupled with anti-racism principles and actions. The following section will situate the GCER within the three overlapping curricula domains of the EPAS, which include HBSE, practice, and policy. For the application of the current 2022 EPAS per CSWE, please see Appendix 10A. At the time of this writing, the EPAS were being revised from the 2015 version to the 2022.

Human Behavior in the Social Environment (HBSE)

The EPAS (2015) highlights HBSE in four of the nine social work competencies by stating, "apply knowledge of human behavior and the social environment, person-in-environment, and other multidisciplinary theoretical frameworks" to engage, assess, intervene, and evaluate various aspects of individuals and constituencies (pp. 8–9). HBSE content in social work curriculum attempts to facilitate students learning "about the interrelationships between individual behavior and the larger social environments" via various theories (Rogers, 2019, p. 2). Although there is an overwhelming emphasis on the person-in-environment and ecological theoretical approaches, the bio/psycho/social of the individual (micro and mezzo) is the focus of many theories with lesser attention paid to the macro-level (Jani & Reisch, 2011; Payne, 2005). Additionally, scholars have critiqued many of the theoretical models as being Eurocentric and hegemonic knowledge underlying social work practice (Del-Vilar, 2021; Graham, 2000; Schiele, 2017), which aligns with previously discussed challenges to eliminate racism.

Moving forward, HBSE holds important opportunities to strengthen social work's commitment to a systemic analysis of racism and include more anti-racism and race critical theories to guide practice such as critical race theory (CRT) and anti-racism principles from the PISAB (Abrams & Moio, 2009; Aldana & Vazquez, 2020; Ortiz & Jani, 2010; PISAB, n.d.). Additionally, the social work profession will benefit from interrogating many of its dominant theories written by White men and ultimately steeped in White supremacy (Ortega-Williams & McLane-Davison, 2021). In other words, social work education must emphasize critical, macro-level theoretical analyses of racism and White supremacy to strengthen our anti-racism practice at the micro- and mezzo-levels of society.

Social Work Practice

Social work practice forms the basis of what we do as a profession by operationalizing the theories learned in HBSE with practice knowledge and competencies. NASW (n.d.) defines practice as

> the professional application of social work values, principles, and techniques to one or more of the following ends: helping people obtain tangible services; counseling and psychotherapy with individuals, families, and groups; helping communities or groups provide or improve social and health services; and participating in legislative processes,

which encompasses the educational goals of social work curriculum. CSWE EPAS (2015) transitioned from a content-driven curriculum to a competency-based approach, which emphasizes "what students demonstrate in practice" and assessed via learning outcomes (p. 6). Additionally, field education is explicitly referred to as the "signature pedagogy of social work" in order to guide practitioners "to think, to perform, and to act ethically and with integrity" (p. 12). Given the prominence of practice in social work's curriculum, understanding anti-racism principles will be imperative to eliminate racism.

Because the 2022 EPAS (2021) draft revisions are preliminarily calling for explicitly "anti-racist social work practice," NASW, CSWE, and the GCER will need to define and operationalize what exactly this will entail. By developing a collective strategy among the various professional entities, and with the communities we serve, social work education can influence the profession's overall commitment to eliminating racism in service of fulfilling social work's social justice ethical value.

Social Welfare Policy

Policy is listed as Competency 5, Engage in Policy Practice in CSWEs (EPAS, 2015). Fulfilling the policy competency includes understanding "that human rights and social justice . . . are mediated by policy and its implementation at the federal, state, and local levels" along with applying "critical thinking to analyze, formulate, and advocate for policies that advance human rights" and other forms of justice. In an effort to strengthen the macro content of social work curricula related to the competencies identified in the 2015 *EPAS*, CSWE and the Special Commission to Advance Macro Practice wrote the *Specialized Practice Curricular Guide for Macro Social Work Practice* (2018) to emphasize policy practice, community organizing, and administration and management.

To further emphasize the critical need for all social workers to acquire policy practice skills, the NASW recently released a *Blueprint of Federal Social Policy Priorities: Recommendations to the Biden-Harris Administration and Congress* (BFSPP, 2021), which is aligned with the Grand Challenges for Social Work. Each section of the report references policies, laws, and court cases that affect intersecting systems where social workers practice, further highlighting the connection between analyzing policy, policy practice, and addressing the racism found throughout US institutions and systems. Specific to eliminating racism, the NASW BFSPP (2021) explains that inequitable outcomes for BIPOC are a result of "centuries-old institutions of racial oppression" and "insufficient structural redress" where "we must commit to transforming the entrenched systems" whereby "instances of racism and discrimination must be recognized, taken seriously, and addressed directly" (pp. 22–23). The policy focus of the curriculum provides an arena for critical theories and concrete practices to strengthen social work education's commitment to eliminating racism. The next section will focus on teaching practices and content related to supporting this effort.

Teaching Practices

We believe the re-energized commitment from GCER, NASW, and CSWE to anti-racism practice could offer opportunities to fulfill the overlapping efforts to eliminate racism and White supremacy in social work and society as a whole. However, individual faculty must not only be open to reinforcing a macro-level understanding of race, racism, White supremacy, and all forms of racial power but also model a willingness to interrogate the profession, educational institutions, and personal preconceived notions associated with these concepts. Additionally, social work educators can more effectively facilitate this content by understanding the historical context of racism and White supremacy (Werkmeister-Rozas & Miller, 2009). The following section will focus on suggested learning objectives, lecture materials, content for class discussions, strategies to manage difficult conversations, and an assignment to critically analyze racism and White supremacy from a macro-level perspective.

Learning Objectives

Prior to the class(es) these objectives will focus on, ask the class to read the documents identified in Appendix 10B, under the "Suggested Class Readings" section. These will provide an overview of the historical, political, and social context of racism and White supremacy. The following learning objectives will guide the focus of the class(es):

- Students will have an opportunity to critically reflect on their own racial identity and the relationship to historical manifestations of racism and White supremacy;
- Students will gain a macro-level understanding of race-related concepts (race, racism, whiteness, White privilege, White supremacy) and their relationship to social justice and anti-racism social work practice;
- Students will examine the interconnectedness of race-related concepts, various systems, and the resulting outcomes.

To further clarify what will be covered, faculty members can share a copy of the written assignment (see Appendix 10C) so students can synthesize their insights from class discussions into content for the assignment. After presenting the learning objectives, ask students to share their name, area of practice interest, when they first became aware of race, and why it is urgent to address racism. This will allow the instructor to gain a sense of each student's perspective.

Managing Classroom Discussions

Once introductions are completed, consider reviewing the community/class norms if they were established during the first class by the instructor and/or students. Whether the community/class norms already exist or not, the faculty member could use this as an opportunity to emphasize the importance of community/class norms to support a productive learning community and manage difficult classroom discussions, especially when discussing race-related concepts. It is helpful to ask students to identify relevant values that can support a communicative and critical thinking learning community. As they are sharing these, start making a list and also consider asking each participant who shares a norm to expand on their interpretation of its meaning. This provides an opportunity to highlight the differences and similarities related to commonly identified values such as respect. Additional examples of community/class norms include respect, active and open listening, speaking from "I" rather than "you," stepping up/stepping back (paying attention to how much each individual is participating), and "ouch" if someone says something that offends another person; then the faculty member will pause the class in order to facilitate a discussion about what was said and how to learn from the situation.

After the list of norms is complete, ask the entire class to raise their hands if they can commit to the norms. If the faculty member would like to include specific group norms (after the class has made their list), explain the suggested norm(s) to the class and ask if people are okay with adding them to the list. Also, encourage students to contact you via email if they're uncomfortable sharing concerns about the community norms in a group setting. Once the community norms are completed, emphasize that the learning community will use the norms as an accountability mechanism to increase the likelihood of a supportive, critical thinking space.

Lecture Material

Effective class facilitation requires faculty members and students to critically reflect on their socialized understanding of race, racism, and White supremacy in addition to the historical manifestations of these concepts. The formation of the United States provides an important starting point to better understand how the conflict of national values can reveal early manifestations of racism and White supremacy. For example, create a PowerPoint slide with the following question: "how do we reconcile our country's founding on paradoxical concepts such as life, liberty, freedom, and justice with kidnapping/enslavement of Africans, the genocidal treatment of Native Americans, and creating a foreign status for Mexican/Mexican Americans by stealing their land?" (See Appendix 10B, Suggested Class Readings and Resources for historical references.) First, ask the class how they would explain this paradox and encourage people to share. Once some people have shared, then ask the class to comment on how this paradox has influenced present-day oppressive conditions and how the collective manifestations of this paradox could influence their work in marginalized communities. As each student shares insights, the faculty member should be prepared to provide additional historical context as necessary and tie that context to present-day outcomes across various systemic outcomes (see NASW, 2021 for additional information regarding systemic outcomes among racial and ethnic groups). Focusing first on these paradoxical concepts offers an opportunity to make an explicit connection between the past and the present. countering the common tropes such as "racism is a thing of the past" or we're now in a "post-racial" society since former President Obama's two-term presidency. Conversely, the discussion should highlight that enslavement, genocide, and land appropriation/theft are foundational strains of DNA inherent to our country's creation and continued existence.

Although the previous question may develop into a productive discussion, there will likely be students who are unwilling, distrustful, or uncomfortable to share about these issues in a large group setting for various reasons. The faculty member can transition to a small group exercise by asking students to identify when they first became aware of their own race and write or type a brief definition of "race," "racism," and "White supremacy." Encourage participants to write freely without overthinking what the definitions should be; write what first comes to mind. Then divide the class into small groups (two to four people depending on the size of class), ask the groups to introduce themselves to each other, share answers to these questions, and ensure everyone has a fair amount of time to speak. After approximately 12–20 minutes (depending on size of groups), allow group participants to report their collective insights to the entire class. Some helpful prompts to highlight key aspects of the exercise include asking how it felt to discuss these concepts? What made it easier or more challenging? Ask whether the definitions were all the same; if not, how does that affect our actions/interventions in addressing unjust outcomes? If the definitions focused on interpersonal forms of racism or White supremacy, what happens to unexamined systemic and institutional processes guiding individuals' actions (including the social welfare system and the social work profession)? Beyond posing these questions in a classroom setting, we recommend faculty to reflect on these questions, in addition to doing so with our colleagues, family members, and other groups of people in our spheres of influence. This critical reflection will provide us with vital insights to improve our ability to discuss, and take action to resist, racism and White supremacy across our spheres of influence.

Oftentimes the discussion will organically evolve as participants build on the critical, collective insights of their colleagues. After allowing each group to share their experiences, show the following definitions on a PowerPoint slide:

- **Race** – "is an arbitrary (specious, false) socio/biological construct created by Europeans [White] during the time of world-wide colonial expansion and adapted in the political and social structures of the United States, to assign human worth and social status, using themselves as the model of humanity, for the purpose of legitimizing White power and White skin privilege"[1] (Barndt, 2007, p. 72);
- **Racism** – Race prejudice plus the inequitable use of legitimate, state-sanctioned power through systemic and institutional processes (Barndt, 2007; Chisom & Washington, 1997);
- **Whiteness** – No credible biological evidence; social and legal construction operating as a societal organizing tool, producing real outcomes; a form of property based on the historical enslavement of Black people (free labor) and appropriating land (free land) from Native Americans (Harris, 1993; Leonardo, 2004);
- **White privilege** – Unearned advantage, entitlement based on whiteness (McIntosh, 1990; Whitaker et al., 2021);
- **White supremacy** – "a political, economic, and cultural system in which whites overwhelmingly control power and material resources, conscious and unconscious ideas of white superiority and entitlement are widespread, and relations of white dominance and non-white subordination are daily reenacted across a broad array of institutions and social settings" (Ansley, 1989, p. 1024; see also Whitaker et al., 2021).

Again, we strongly emphasize the importance of faculty members processing what these definitions mean to them and how they manifest in our families, profession, and society.

After encouraging the students to reflect on their experience with this exercise, discuss the challenges and significance of identifying common definitions as it relates to creating effective anti-racism change actions. To further enrich the discussion, the faculty member can ask students how these definitions relate to commonly used social work concepts to frame race and racism such as diversity, cultural competence, or inclusion. Another helpful prompt for this discussion is to ask how or if these frameworks relate to inequity or social power imbalances as found in various systemic outcomes. The use of those frameworks can oftentimes veil the institutional and systemic manifestations of racial power to reinforce the relative positions of racial domination and subordination (Ortiz & Jani, 2010; Pon, 2009). Finally, ask about how these frameworks manifest in, and influence, laws/policies that in turn produce racialized (inequitable) outcomes produced by systems, institutions, and the people working in them. As the discussion wraps up, the instructor can encourage students to review the written assignment instructions, ask if there any questions, and provide time to write relevant insights in the corresponding sections of the assignment.

Learning Assessment

The evaluation of learning should encompass various aspects of the course; classroom discussions, small group exercises, reflections of relevant readings, consistently reviewing content related to eliminating racism, and written assignments. Appendix 10C offers an example of a written assignment for faculty to use as an evaluation tool of the content covered in this chapter. The assignment encourages students to examine systems, intervention outcomes, and compare cultural competence, diversity, racism, and White supremacy in social work. Depending on the faculty member's approach to completing assignments, students often appreciate time during the class to discuss challenges about completing the assignment and providing peer support in small groups.

Conclusion

As discussed earlier in the chapter, social work's history with racism and White supremacy is complicated because both "are ingrained within American institutions and systems and have therefore affected social work ideology and practice for generations" (NASW, 2020). Social work education and educators (both in-class and internships) represent translators between ideologies and practice. Depending on how racism and White supremacy are conceptualized and presented to students, the efficacy of subsequent anti-racism practice will hinge on individuals' willingness to first interrogate their own understanding of, and relationship to, racism and White supremacy that often act as barriers to teaching this content (Perez, 2021; Olcoń et al., 2020). Then, secondly to engage in intra-profession and intra-organizational (schools of social work) activism (Bent-Goodley, 2015; Jeyapal, 2017). This will include social work professional organizations, administrations, faculty, staff, students, and alumni working strategically together to institutionalize an anti-racism commitment to eliminate racism and White supremacy. Oftentimes these efforts relied on PISAB (n.d.) principles to undo racism and White supremacy. These included liberated gatekeeping, analyzing power, understanding internalized oppression (racial inferiority and superiority), and accountability (Riley et al., 2021; Tolliver & Burghardt, 2016). Leaning into the challenges of teaching about racism and White supremacy requires an even stronger commitment to continually learn about our own personal, institutional, and systemic relationships to those power-ladened concepts, which can ultimately support social work's commitment to eliminate racism.

Note

1 This definition of race evolved from Dr. Maulana Karenga's original wording through the trainings of People's Institute for Survival and Beyond and Crossroads Ministry. In particular, the collaboration between Dr. Karenga and Dr. Michael Washington of the People's Institute for Survival and Beyond.

References

Abrams, L. S., & Moio, J. A. (2009). Critical race theory and the cultural competence dilemma in social work education. *Journal of Social Work Education*, *45*(2), 245–261. https://doi.org/10.5175/JSWE.2009.200700109

Aldana, A., & Vazquez, N. (2020). From colour-blind racism to critical race theory: The road towards anti-racist social work in the United States. In G. Singh & S. Masocha (Eds.), *Anti-racist social work: International perspectives* (pp. 129–148). Red Globe Press.

Ansley, F. L. (1988/1989). Stirring the ashes: Race, class, and the future of civil rights scholarship. *Cornell Law Review*, *74*, 993–1077. https://scholarship.law.cornell.edu/clr/vol74/iss6/1

Barndt, J. (2007). *Understanding and dismantling racism: The twenty-first century challenges to white America*. Fortress Press.

Bent-Goodley, T. B. (2015). *A call for social work activism. Social Work*, *60*(1), 101–103. https://doi.org/10.1093/sw/swv005

Bonilla-Silva, E. (2010). *Racism without racists: Color-blind racism and racial inequality in contemporary America*. Rowman & Littlefield.

Chisom, R., & Washington, M. (1997). *Undoing racism: A philosophy of international social change*. People's Institute Press.

Clark, E. J., Weismiller, T., Whitaker, T., Waller, G. W., Zlotnik, J. L., & Corbett, B. (Eds.). (2006). *2005 social work congress-final report*. NASW Press.

Constance-Huggins, M., & Davis, A. (2017). Color-blind racial attitudes and their implications for achieving race-related grand challenges. *Urban Social Work*, *1*(2), 104–116. https://doi.org/10.1891/2474-8684.1.2.104

Corley, N. A., & Young, S. M. (2018). Is social work *still* racist? A content analysis of recent literature. *Social Work*, *63*(4), 317–326. https://doi.org/10.1093/sw/swy042

Council on Social Work Education. (2015). *2015 educational policy and accreditation standards*. Author. www.cswe.org/getattachment/Accreditation/Standards-and-Policies/2015-EPAS/2015EPASandGlossary.pdf.asp

Council on Social Work Education. (2018). *Specialized practice curricular guide for macro social work practice*. Author. https://cswe.org/getattachment/Education-Resources/2015-Curricular-Guides/2015-Macro-Guide-Web-Version.pdf.aspx

Council on Social Work Education. (2021, Spring). *Draft 1 2022 educational policy and accreditation standards*. Author. https://cswe.org/getattachment/Accreditation/Information/2022-EPAS/EPAS-2022-Draft-1-April-2021-(2).pdf.aspx

Council of Social Work Education. (2022). *2022 Educational policy and accreditation standards (EPAS)*. Author. www.cswe.org/accreditation/standards/2022-epas/

Davis, L. E. (2016). Race: America's grand challenge. *Journal of the Society for Social Work and Research*, *7*, 395–403. https://doi.org/10.1086/686296

Del-Vilar, Z. (2021). Confronting historical White supremacy in social work education and practice: A way forward. *Advances in Social Work*, *21*(2/3), 636–653. https://doi.org/10.18060/24168

Devore, W., & Schlesinger, F. G. (1981). *Ethnic sensitivity social work practice*. CV Mosby.

Editors. (2015). Students at UC turn the tables on a racist professor. *The Bold Italic*. https://thebolditalic.com/students-at-uc-berkeley-turn-the-tables-on-a-racist-professor-the-bold-italic-san-francisco-7d725a3c8229

Fairclough, N., & Wodak, R. (1997). Critical discourse analysis. In T. A. van Dijk (Ed.), *Discourse as social interaction* (pp. 258–284). Sage.

Foucault, M. (1979). *Discipline and punish: The birth of the prison*. Vintage.

Funge, S. P., Crutchfield, R. M., & Jennings, L. K. (2020). The challenge of integrating social justice content into social work education: Making the abstract more concrete. *Journal of Social Work Education*, *56*(1), 41–55. https://doi.org/10.1080/10437797.2019.1656566

Graham, M. (2000). Honouring social work principles – Exploring the connection between anti-racist social work and African-centered worldviews. *Social Work Education*, *19*(5), 421–436. https://doi.org/10.1080/026154700435959

Graham, M., & Schiele, J. H. (2010). Equality-of-oppressions and anti-discriminatory models of social work: Reflections from the USA and UK. *European Journal of Social Work*, *13*(2), 231–244. https://doi.org/10.1080/13691451003690882

Grand Challenges for Social Work. (2020). *Announcements*. https://grandchallengesforsocialwork.org/grand-challenges-for-social-work/announcing-the grand-challenge-to-eliminate-racism/

Grand Challenges for Social Work. (2021a). *About*. https://grandchallengesforsocialwork.org/about/

Grand Challenges for Social Work. (2021b). *Progress and plans for the grand challenges: An impact report at year 5 of the 10-year initiative.* https://grandchallengesforsocialwork.org/publications/grand-challenges-5-year-impact-report/

Gregory, J. R. (2021). Social work as a product and project of whiteness, 1607–1900. *Journal of Progressive Human Services*, *32*(1), 17–36. https://doi.org/10.1080/10428232.2020.1730143

Harris, C. I. (1993). Whiteness as property. *Harvard Law Review*, *106*, 1707–1791. https://harvardlawreview.org/1993/06/whiteness-as-property/

Hill, K. M., Erickson, C. L., Plitt-Donaldson, L., Fogel, S. J., & Ferguson, S. M. (2017). Perceptions of macro social work education: An exploratory study of educators and practitioners. *Advances in Social Work*, *18*(2), 522–542. https://doi.org/10.18060/21455

Jani, J., & Reisch, M. (2011). Common human need, uncommon solutions: Applying a critical framework to perspectives on human behavior. *Families in Society*, *92*(1), 13–20. https://doi.org/10.1606/1044-3894.4065

Jeyapal, D. (2017). The evolving politics of race and social work activism: A call across borders. *Social Work*, *62*(1), 45–52. PMID: 28395038

Kam, P. K. (2014). Back to the "social" of social work: Reviving the social work profession's contribution to the promotion of social justice. *International Social Work*, *57*(6), 723–739. https://doi.org/10.1177/0020872812447118

LaPan, A., & Platt, T. (2005). 'To stem the tide of degeneracy': The eugenic impulse in social work. In S. A. Kirk (Ed.), *Mental disorders in the social environment: Critical perspectives* (pp. 139–164). Columbia University Press.

Leonardo, Z. (2004). The color of supremacy: Beyond the discourse of 'white privilege'. *Educational Philosophy and Theory*, *36*(2), 137–152. https://doi.org/10.1111/j.1469-5812.2004.00057.x

López, I. H. (2006). *White by law: The legal construction of race*. New York University Press.

Lum, D. (1999). *Culturally competent practice: A framework for growth and action*. Thomson Brooks/Cole.

Lum, D. (2005). *Cultural competence, practice stages, and client systems: A case study approach*. Thomson Brooks/Cole.

McIntosh, P. (1990). *White privilege: Unpacking the invisible knapsack*. https://nationalseedproject.org/Key-SEED-Texts/white-privilege-unpacking-the-invisible-knapsack

McMahon, A., & Allen-Meares, P. (1992). Is social work racist? A content analysis of recent literature. *Social Work*, *37*, 533–539. https://doi.org/10.1093/sw/37.6.533

National Advisory Commission on Civil Disorders. (2016). *The Kerner report*. Princeton University Press.

National Association of Black Social Workers. (1968). *Our roots: Position statement of the national association of black social workers*. https://cdn.ymaws.com/www.nabsw.org/resource/collection/E1582D77-E4CD-4104-

996A-D42D08F9CA7D/NABSW_30_Years_of_Unity_-_Our_Roots_Position_Statement_1968.pdf

National Association of Social Workers. (2007). *Institutional racism & the social work profession: A call to action.* www.socialworkers.org/diversity/InstitutionalRacism.pdf

National Association of Social Workers. (2017). *Code of ethics of the national association of social workers.* www.socialworkers.org/About/Ethics/Code-of-Ethics/Code-of-Ethics-English

National Association of Social Workers. (2020). *Social workers must help dismantle systems of oppression and fight racism within the social work profession.* www.socialworkers.org/News/News-Releases/ID/2219/Social-Workers-Must-Help-Dismantle-Systems-of-Oppression-and-Fight-Racism-Within-Social-Work-Profession

National Association of Social Workers. (2021). *Blueprint of federal social priorities: Recommendations to the Biden-Harris administration and congress.* www.socialworkers.org/LinkClick.aspx?fileticket=KPdZqqY60t4%3d&portalid=0

National Association of Social Workers. (n.d.). *Practice.* www.socialworkers.org/Practice

Norton, D. (1978). *Dual perspectives: The inclusion of ethnic minority content in social work curriculums.* Council on Social Work Education.

Olcoń, K., Gilbert, D. J., & Pulliam, R. M. (2020). Teaching about racial and ethnic diversity in social work education: A systematic review. *Journal of Social Work Education*, *56*(2), 215–237. https://doi.org/10.1080/10437797.2019.1656578

Olson, J. J. (2007). Social work's professional and social justice projects: Discourses in conflict. *Journal of Progressive Human Services*, *18*(1), 45–69. https://doi.org/10.1300/J059v18n01_04

Ortega-Williams, A., & McLane-Davison, D. (2021). Wringing out the "whitewash": Confronting the hegemonic epistemologies of social work canons (Disrupting the reproduction of the white normative. *Advances in Social Work*, *21*(2/3), 566–587. https://doi.org/10.18060/24475

Ortiz, L., & Jani, J. (2010). Critical race theory: A transformational model for teaching diversity. *Journal of Social Work Education*, *46*(2), 175–193. https://doi.org/10.5175/JSWE.2010.200900070

Park, Y. (2008). Facilitating injustice: Tracing the role of social workers in the World War II internment of Japanese Americans. *Social Service Review*, *82*(3), 447–483. https://doi.org/10.1086/592361

Payne, M. (2005). *Modern social work theory* (3rd ed.). Lyceum Books.

People's Institute for Survival and Beyond. (n.d.). *Principles.* https://pisab.org/our-principles/

Perez, E. N. (2021). Faculty as a barrier to dismantling racism in social work education. *Advances in Social Work*, *21*(2/3), 500–521. https://doi.org/10.18060/24178

Pewewardy, N., & Almeida, R. V. (2014). Articulating the scaffolding of white supremacy: The act of naming in liberation. *Journal of Progressive Human Services*, *25*(3), 230–253. https://doi.org/10.1080/10428232.2014.940485

Pon, G. (2009). Cultural competency as new racism: An ontology of forgetting. *Journal of Progressive Human Services*, *20*(1), 59–71. https://doi.org/10.1080/10428230902871173

Quiros, L., Varghese, R., & Vanidestine, T. (2019). Disrupting the single story: Challenging dominant trauma narratives through a critical race lens. *Traumatology*, *26*(2), 160–168. https://doi.org/10.1037/trm0000223

Rao, S., Woo, B., Maglalang, D. D., Bartholomew, M., Cano, M., Harris, A., & Tucker, T. B. (2021). Race and ethnicity in the social work grand challenges. *Social Work*, *66*(1), 9–17. https://doi.org/10.1093/sw/swaa053

Reisch, M. (2016). Why macro practice matters. *Journal of Social Work Education*, *52*(3), 258–268. doi:10.1080/23303131.2016.1179537

Reisch, M., & Andrews, J. (2002). *The road not taken: A history of radical social work in the United States*. Brunner-Routledge.

Riley, A. T., Bewley, K., Butler-King, R. L., Byers, L. G., Miller, C. R., Dell, J. E., & Kendrick, C. J. (2021). Finding shelter in the storm: Undoing racism in a predominantly white school of social work. *Advances in Social Work*, *21*(2/3), 898–919. https://orcid.org/0000-0003-0308-8944

Rogers, A. T. (2019). *Human behavior in the social environment: Perspectives on development and the life course* (5th ed.). Routledge.

Rothman, J. (2012). *Education for macro intervention: A survey of problems and prospects*. Association for Community Organizations and Social Administration.

Santiago, A. M., & Ivery, J. (2020). Removing knees from their necks: Mobilizing community practice and social action for racial justice. *Journal of Community Practice*, *28*(3), 195–207. https://doi.org/10.1080/10705422.2020.1823672

Schiele, J. H. (2017). The Afrocentric paradigm in social work: A historical perspective and future outlook. *Journal of Human Behavior in the Social Environment*, 27(1/2), 15–26. https://doi.org/10.1080/10911359.2016.1252601

Schiele, J. H., & Hopps, J. G. (2009). Racial minorities then and now: The continuing significance of race. *Social Work*, *54*(3), 195–199. PMID: 19530566

Social Work Policy Institute. (2014). *Achieving racial equity: Calling the social work profession to action*. National Association of Social Workers.

Specht, H., & Courtney, M. E. (1994). *Unfaithful angels: How social work has abandoned its mission*. The Free Press.

Teasley, M. L., & Archuleta, A. J. (2015). A review of social justice and diversity content in diversity course syllabi. *Social Work Education*, *34*(6), 607–622. https://doi.org/10.1080/02615479.2015.1037828

Teasley, M. L., McCarter, S., Woo, B., Conner, L. R., Spencer, M. S., & Green, T. (2021). *Eliminate racism* (Grand Challenges for Social Work Initiative

Working Paper No. 26). American Academy of Social Work & Social Welfare.

Tolliver, W., & Burghardt, S. (2016). Education and training of a race-conscious workforce. In A. J. Carten, A. B. Suskind, & M. Pender Greene (Eds.), *Strategies for deconstructing racism in the health and human services* (pp. 33–50). Oxford University Press.

Vanidestine, T., & Aparicio, E. M. (2019). How social welfare and health professionals understand "race," racism, and whiteness: A social justice approach to grounded theory. *Social Work in Public Health*, *34*(5), 430–443. https://doi.org/10.1080/19371918.2019.1616645

Varghese, R. (2016). Teaching to transform? Addressing race and racism in the teaching of clinical social work practice. *Journal of Social Work Education*, *52*(S1), S134–S147. https://doi.org/10.1080/10437797.2016.1174646

Werkmeister-Rozas, L. M., & Miller, J. (2009). Discourses for social justice education: The web of racism and the web of resistance. *Journal of Ethnic & Cultural Diversity in Social Work*, *18*(1/2), 24–39. https://doi.org/10.1080/15313200902874953

Whitaker, T., Alfrey, L., Gates, A. B., & Gooding, A. R. (2021). *White supremacy*. https://oxfordre.com/socialwork/view/10.1093/acrefore/9780199975839.001.0001/acrefore-9780199975839-e-1586

Appendix 10A

EPAS Addressed in Grand Challenge #9

Eliminate Racism

An explicit Grand Challenge to Eliminate Racism and a newly revised Council of Social Work Education (CSWE) *2022 Educational Policy and Accreditation Standards* (*EPAS*) focuses on eliminating racism and White supremacy and offers the social work profession reinforcing clarity about this social injustice and necessary change actions. Chapter 10, Eliminate Racism, highlights the importance of clearly defining racism and White supremacy through the discourse of structural racial, economic, and political power. Additionally, the chapter emphasizes how macro-level conceptual clarity will improve the likelihood of collective, macro-level actions to change policies, laws, and organizations. The Eliminate Racism chapter aligns with the following competencies in the revised *2022 Educational Policy and Accreditation Standards*:

1. Demonstrate ethical and professional behavior.
2. Advance human rights and social, racial, economic, and environmental justice.
3. Engage anti-racism, diversity, equity, and inclusion (ADEI) in practice.
5. Engage in policy practice.

Competency 1: Demonstrate Ethical and Professional Behavior, should complement the implementation of human rights, anti-racism, and anti-oppression principles that are becoming more prominent in the social work profession. Chapter 10 reinforces an ongoing vigilance to examine the challenges of reconciling ethical and professional behaviors with human rights/anti-racism/anti-oppression practice because the former concepts can often provide a false sense of a priori presence of the latter, without clearly understanding the meanings related to those latter concepts and actions necessary to fulfill them. Social justice is the most obvious ethical value related to eliminating racism; however, historically racism and White supremacy have been noticeably missing when discussing the fulfillment of social justice. This chapter encourages a more explicit connection among social justice, anti-racism, and eliminating racism and White supremacy.

Competency 2: Advance Human Rights and Social, Racial, Economic, and Environmental Justice, explicitly connects human rights with various forms of justice, including racial justice. The eliminate racism chapter emphasizes the importance of incorporating a macro-level analysis to implement macro-level actions to fulfill our ethical commitments more effectively. Additionally, the chapter highlights the structural aspects (intersecting systemic manifestations) of racism and White supremacy, which reflects the intersectional spirit of this competency.

Competency 3: Engage Anti-Racism, Diversity, Equity, and Inclusion (ADEI) in Practice, includes various concepts related to understanding how "racism and oppression" produces inequitable outcomes at multiple levels of our society. Chapter 10 discusses the need for analyzing racial power as manifested in processes, policies, laws, and racialized outcomes, which should form the basis of anti-racism social work practice and importantly distinguish this concept from DEI. A particularly crucial aspect of eliminating racism underscored in the chapter is avoiding conceptual conflation whereby anti-racism takes on the meanings (and chosen change actions) of diversity, equity, and inclusion. In other words, DEI efforts are complementary, and even necessary, to do anti-racism social work practice but they are not sufficient to comprehensively challenge and resist racism and White supremacy.

Competency 5: Engage in Policy Practice, focuses on the social workers' ability to analyze, and change social policy at various levels of society (local, state, federal, and global). Chapter 10 highlights the policy content of social work curriculum as a critical area to strengthen the profession's commitment to eliminate racism. Through an emphasis on clearly defining racism and White supremacy through the language of intersecting structures, systems, institutions, and power, the policy practice to eliminate racism becomes more effective in fulfilling this mandate.

The Eliminate Racism chapter offers suggestions to social work educators and practitioners about actions we can use to complement the new *2022 EPAS* and its focus on anti-racism. In combination with other social work calls-to-action and professional organizations' commitment to ending racism, individual social workers must form collective groups and networks across the profession to support efforts to consistently define, analyze, and resist the outcomes of racism and White supremacy more effectively. The strength and power of achieving this necessary goal will come from social work students, staff, faculty, and administrators collectively participating in institutional spaces and geographical locales to eliminate racism. Ultimately, social work's anti-racism and anti-oppression commitment to eliminate racism, White supremacy, and other forms of oppression must be accountably integrated throughout all nine social work competencies.

Appendix 10B
Suggested Class Readings and Resources

Suggested Class Readings

Social Work Policy Institute. (2014). *Achieving racial equity: Calling the social work profession to action.* www.antiracistalliance.com/SWPIRacialEquityReport.pdf

Teasley, M. L., McCarter, S., Woo, B., Conner, L. R., Spencer, M. S., & Green, T. (2021). *Eliminate racism* (Grand Challenges for Social Work Initiative Working Paper No. 26). https://grandchallengesforsocialwork.org/wp-content/uploads/2021/05/Eliminate-Racism-Concept-Paper.pdf

Whitaker, T., Alfrey, L., Gates, A. B., & Gooding, A. R. (2021). *White supremacy.* https://oxfordre.com/socialwork/view/10.1093/acrefore/9780199975839.001.0001/acrefore-9780199975839-e-1586

Resources

Anti-Racist Alliance. (n.d.). *Anti-racist alliance.* www.antiracistalliance.com/

Barndt, J. (2007). *Understanding and dismantling racism: The twenty-first century challenges to white America.* Fortress Press.

Carten, A. J., Siskind, A. B., & Pender Greene, M. (Eds.). (2016). *Strategies for deconstructing racism in the health and human services.* Oxford University Press.

Chisom, R., & Washington, M. (1997). *Undoing racism: A philosophy of international social change.* People's Institute Press.

Council of Social Work Education. (2018). *Specialized practice curricular guide for macro social work practice.* Author. https://cswe.org/getattachment/Education-Resources/2015-Curricular-Guides/2015-Macro-Guide-Web-Version.pdf.aspx

Garran, A. M., Werkmeister Rozas, L., Kang, H. K., & Miller, J. (2021). *Racism in the United States: Implications for the helping professions* (3rd ed.). Springer Publishing Company.

Gregory, J. R. (2021). Social work as a product and project of whiteness, 1607–1900. *Journal of Progressive Human Services, 32*(1), 17–36.

National Association of Social Workers. (2007). *Institutional racism & the social work profession: A call to action*. www.socialworkers.org/diversity/InstitutionalRacism.pdf

National Association of Social Workers. (2021). *Blueprint of federal social priorities: Recommendations to the Biden-Harris administration and congress*. www.socialworkers.org/LinkClick.aspx?fileticket=KPdZqqY60t4%3d&portalid=0

People's Institute for Survival and Beyond. (n.d.). *Principles*. https://pisab.org/our-principles/

Racial Equity Tools. (n.d.). *Racial equity tools*. www.racialequitytools.org/

Yearwood, C., Barbera, R. A., Fisher, A. K., & Hostetter, C. (Eds.). (2021). Dismantling racism in social work education. *Advances in Social Work*, *21*(2/3), 217–1063. http://journals.iupui.edu/index.php/advancesinsocialwork/index

Appendix 10C
Suggested Assignment

The following assignment offers students an opportunity to critically investigate, examine, and compare various concepts related to inequitable, racialized outcomes within a particular system that the people we serve often rely on.

- **Choose a system and then do a Google Scholar search in order to identify one (1) article for each of the following:**
    - **Identify a system (e.g. "healthcare system," "education system," "social welfare system," "legal system," etc.) and the terms "diversity" or "cultural competency"** within the past five years in the US. For example, type in the search "healthcare system and diversity" (or "cultural competency"), then identify a five-year period prior to the current date, and focus on US articles. These should be published in peer-reviewed journals.
    - **Identify a system (same as the identified one above) and the terms "racism" or "White supremacy"** within the past five years in the US. For example, type in the search "healthcare system and racism" (or "White supremacy"), then identify a five-year period prior to the current date and focus on US articles. Again, these should be published in peer-reviewed journals.
- **Critically read and review each article in order to discuss the following questions in a 5–6-page paper:**
    - **Introduction** (short paragraph).
    - **How are the race-related outcomes defined in each article?** More specifically, how is "diversity" or "cultural competency" defined in relationship to racial outcomes of your

identified system? And how is "racism" or "White supremacy" defined in relationship to racial outcomes of your identified system (1–2 pages)?

- **What intervention(s) (micro-, mezzo-, and/or macro-level of practice) are identified in each article?** Provide a brief explanation of the intervention(s) (if more than one, include a brief explanation of each one). If there are no interventions explicitly mentioned, use the definitions of "diversity," "cultural competency," "racism," and "White supremacy" to infer what actions would be taken to address racialized outcomes of your chosen system (approx. 1 page).
- **Critically reflect and discuss how this assignment will inform your approach** to social justice and anti-racism social work practice. Identify specific insights that will make you more effective in addressing racial injustices and fulfilling our social justice/anti-racism ethical mandate (1–2 pages).
- **Conclusion** (short paragraph).

11 Smart Decarceration

A Multi-Prong Approach to Healing With the Incarcerated

Robert Anthony Hernandez, Steven Kim and Deepa Karmakar

An Introduction of Mass Incarceration

The American Academy of Social Work and Social Welfare in 2009 unveiled 12 Grand Challenges for the field to address thus prompting social work researchers and practitioners to act. In recent years, the American Academy has added a 13th Grand Challenge, "eliminate racism". As will be discussed throughout this chapter, the United States foundation was predicated on violence and racist discriminatory practices and policies. The 13 Grand Challenges requires an examination of a host of social problems in need of attention. This effort encourages collaboration at all levels to seek to resolve the identified challenges through research. Identified as one of the Grand Challenges, Smart Decarceration addresses the social justice crisis that has manifested from mass incarceration. The process in moving towards Smart Decarceration is guided by specific outcomes, which include reducing the incarcerated population and addressing racial, economic, and behavior disparities among system-involved individuals while also enhancing both public safety and community restoration.

Human Behavior in the Social Environment (HBSE): Life Course Perspective

Mass incarceration has impacted largely communities of color (Pettit & Western, 2004). By the end of the 21st century, 1.3 million men of color were held in state and federal prison (2004). The work of Freeman (1996) indicates that imprisonment has become an expected and standard experience of early adulthood for men of color. Studies explore the disadvantaged education system, deindustrialization, housing segregation, wealth inequality, low wages, high rates of unemployment, fragmented institutions, high rates of recidivism, and barriers to

DOI: 10.4324/9781003308263-14

community engagement; all of which are labor market consequences of incarceration that deteriorates the ability for equity to exist within urban communities (Western et al., 2001). Hayasaki (2016) also notes that brain development is impacted by housing discrimination, unsafe living environments, racism, and underfunded schools. Studies reveal that unaddressed trauma for communities of color has detrimental effects on youth and families, which then manifests itself as underachievement in schools, high rates of drug use/abuse, dangerous sexual behavior, delinquency, and violence exposure (Substance Abuse and Mental Health Services Administration, 2017). Furthermore, the National Center of Post-Traumatic Stress Disorder (PTSD) indicates that 30 to 35% of urban youth develop PTSD (Saigh, 1991). Further studies by Gillespie and colleagues (2009) show that at least 90% of urban, low-income residents exposed to community trauma develop a 40% higher rate of PTSD than the general population.

Unaddressed trauma can have detrimental effects on the body and overall psychosocial functioning. Recent studies show a strong connection to physiologic disruptions associated with chronic disease (Shonkoff & Garner, 2012) as a result of organ and regulatory breakdown starting in childhood. Furthermore, the work of Glaze and Maruschak (2010) highlights that individuals experiencing familial incarceration have added concern for physical and mental health issues. A high degree of stress is correlated with further adversity; therefore, it is not surprising to find that people with childhood histories of trauma, abuse, and neglect make up almost the entire criminal justice population in the United States (Jäggi et al., 2016).

Policy

Discriminatory practices influenced policies, which in turn negatively impacted communities of color. The 'super-predator' concept, commonly used in criminology, took the position that youth were out of control and savage-like by nature, showing no remorse as they willingly committed violent acts (Bernstein, 2014). Popular in the 1990s, this new founded myth of the super predator brought forth the rhetoric echoed by so many politicians. The type of 'law and order' that was born out of this discourse spearheaded a full assault on communities of color, further exacerbating what has been referred to as mass incarceration.

Discriminatory Policies

Despite a decline in illicit drug use, President Richard Nixon launched a War on Drugs in a message that was relayed to Congress on July 14,

1969 (King, 2008). Political initiatives, law enforcement grants, strategic reorientation of policing methods and punitive legal outcomes; all of which were tailored to combat the War on Drugs that largely targeted communities of color. Aggressive street-level enforcement of drug laws and harsh sentencing of drug offenders created historically high levels of prison populations throughout the 1990s (Roberts, 2004). Several of these policies (Sentencing Reform Act of 1984, mandatory minimum sentencing laws, the Anti-Drug Abuse Act, and the 1994 Crime Bill) negatively impacted communities of color.

Practices

Similar to the changes that were taking place within the judicial system, law enforcement agencies adopted new policing strategies as a means to combat both the use and sale of illicit drugs on the street level. In 1984, the Drug Enforcement Agency established Operation Pipeline, which provided training to state and local law enforcement agencies to be strategic in their encounters with civilians. The outcome of such policing efforts resulted in an increase of annual drug arrests by threefold between 1980 and 2005 (Alexander, 2012). More than 31 million people have been arrested for drug offenses since the War on Drugs was launched.

Systemic Barriers and Institutional Failures

The criminal justice system is besieged with systemic barriers and institutional failures, thus perpetuating a vicious cycle of system involvement for poor communities of color. Inadequate resources restrict peoples from accessing legal representation, which can lead to plea bargains and consequently, lengthier sentences. It is estimated that 90 to 95% of federal and state cases are resolved through plea bargaining (Bureau of Justice Statistics, 2005). Bail practices are often discriminatory as Black and Latino men are charged 35% more towards bail payments compared to 19% of their white counterparts for similar crimes (Onyekwere, 2021). Nearly half a million people in the US are currently being detained pretrial, which means that they are awaiting trial and are legally innocent. Forty-three percent of the pretrial population is African American and the average yearly income of an individual who cannot afford bail is estimated to be $16,000 (Ring & Gill, 2017). Poverty is not only a predictor of incarceration, but continues to exacerbate the outcome as criminal history generates debt and reduces employment opportunities (Rabuy & Kopf, 2016). It is these racist practices that continue to oppress communities of color.

In order to uplift the Grand Challenge of Smart Decarceration, it is recommended that the teaching pedagogy includes a curriculum that is comprehensive, holistic, and seeks to uncover the root causes of what has been termed mass incarceration.

Teaching Practices in One (1) of the Targeted Domains

The practice domain will serve as the platform to provide social work faculty with a hands-on experience for students so that the Grand Challenge of Promoting Smart Decarceration can be integrated into their teaching curricula. More specifically, practice-policy will be highlighted as an informed practice approach for the Grand Challenge of Smart Decarceration. To begin, the following articulation of learning objectives provides clear and specific statements as it relates to what the student will learn in the classroom setting under the practice domain for Smart Decarceration.

- Objective 1: Synthesize and integrate a hands-on, experience-based learning opportunity with knowledge gained in other domains of the course to prepare students to consider how they can contribute to the topic of Smart Decarceration.
- Objective 2: Apply and integrate classroom knowledge with community agency site visits and guest speakers centered on reentry.
- Objective 3: Examine prominent informed-practice approaches for the justice-involved population and demonstrate an understanding of their use.

Fundamental knowledge including a strong framework of historical context and theory will enhance students' understanding about the complexities of mass incarceration. Due to recent pressure placed on the government through advocacy work, there has been a shift to a *Care First, Jails Last* approach when working with system-impacted individuals. Furthermore, several practice modalities will be considered and referenced as informed practice evidence. The course should be concerned with how research has been translated into actual practices, as well as the proof of success or weaknesses of such programs when working with justice-involved individuals. The Grand Challenge of Smart Decarceration advocates for outcome goals that include reducing the population of individuals behind bars, addressing racial, economic, and behavioral health disparities amongst this population and overall community safety and well-being (Hawkins & Jenson, 2017). Exploring these outcome goals with students will allow them to see the big picture of an agenda that seeks to champion social progress and tackle our nation's toughest social problem: mass incarceration. Additionally, the Council of Social Work Education's (CSWE, 2022) *2022 Educational Policy and Accreditation Standards* (EPAS) are outlined in Appendix 11A.

Setting the stage for student engagement will consist of a brief exercise that incorporates words from renowned founder and director of Homeboy Industries, Father Greg Boyle. Homeboy Industries is the world's largest gang-intervention, reentry, and rehabilitation program for justice-impacted individuals. Through the use of short 4–5-minute YouTube video clips, Father Greg Boyle shares the "Thought of the Day" with the audience. These YouTube clips of Father Greg Boyle provide a safe space that invites students into a place of reflection with the justice-involved population. This promotes self-introspection, which allows for the viewer to challenge preconceived notions about the population. Please refer to Appendix 11B to access some of the links to Father Greg Boyle's Thought of the Day YouTube clips. The instructor can use the "Thought of the Day" video clips as a tool to facilitate a larger class discussion with students, which further promotes a healthy public discourse both about the population and the criminal system. This provides the instructor with a baseline of students' existing knowledge on the topic of Smart Decarceration, their understanding of the population, and any preconceived notions they may have about the subject matter. Appendix 11C includes a 60-minute outline of the first class session that prepares students for learning and engagement. In addition, PowerPoints for this session can be accessed in Appendix 11C (Figure 11.1).

Community as the Classroom

Active and experiential project-based learning allows for students to gain practice-based knowledge to enhance evidenced-based interventions and theories grounded in academia. The Association of Experiential Education (2015) defines Experiential Education as a philosophy that informs many methodologies in which educators purposefully engage with learners in direct experience and focused reflection in order to increase knowledge, develop skills, clarify values, and develop people's capacity to contribute to their communities (para. 2). Experiential learning allows students to expand learning opportunities from the community to the classroom. It facilitates learning by engaging with the community (Dewey, 1915), reflective thinking, and learning from experience (Dewey, 1933). Learning is fostered through didactic presentations, small and large group discussions, videos, experiential exercises, and guest speakers. These various learning outlets provide students the ability to learn creatively, authentically, and present experiences and opportunities that integrate non-formal learning in an intentional, purposeful, and meaningful way (Dewey, 1938).

The use of field-site visits, either virtually or in person, allows students to make real-world connections (Jacobson et al., 2011) that bridge communication and connections with their local community and around the globe (Smith & Brown, 2017). Students gain insight through the interactions in the community and have the opportunity to bring back their experiences into the classroom. Students can share their experiences with other students and make further meaning while creating future content (Smith & Brown, 2017). Partnerships, specifically with community-based organizations who have an expertise in working with system-impacted individuals, provide the means to accommodate such learning opportunities. Reentry organizations such as Project Kinship, a non-profit organization in Orange County, CA that provides reentry and intervention services for individuals and families impacted by incarceration, violence, trauma, and gangs is an ideal partner for such a class. Project Kinship provides students the educational space to engage with clients and staff who have been formerly incarcerated. Students gain firsthand experience and exposure to service delivery and programming while gaining valuable life narratives of the people who have been directly impacted by mass incarceration. These educational experiences both create and further enhance rich classroom discussions. For more information on Project Kinship please refer to Appendix 11D.

Facilitating Classroom Discussions and Use of Guest Speakers

Facilitating class discussions provides students a space to expand their knowledge through the use of peer-to-peer learning and meaningful dialogue. The instructor can lead discussions or create scenarios to invite students to express their thoughts about the subject matter. These conversations allow for students to wrestle through opinions on opposite sides of the spectrum while creating the opportunity to meet somewhere in the middle. For example, after meeting with formerly incarcerated individuals at Project Kinship, students had the opportunity to engage in a facilitated discussion on controversial issues such as the death penalty, punitive and rehabilitative approaches within carceral settings, and services provided to victims. The discussion drew from theoretical content along with practice-based approaches and field-site visits. Students were able to weave in all three variables, which enhanced and carved new avenues of learning.

The use of guest speakers provides opportunities for students to hear from individuals who challenge the dominant narrative of marginalized populations that are so often shaped by the media. Individuals from Project Kinship and other community based-organizations such as The Professional Community Intervention Training Institute (PCITI), and Champions In Service (CIS), all based in California and committed to supporting system-impacted individuals, provide education through personal stories of transformation, healing, and reintegration back into the community after incarceration. Students gain insight into personal and intimate challenges as well as barriers and roadmaps to success from the guest speakers. This valuable information and interchange of discussion humanizes the academic content and enhances practices from the community into the classroom.

Given the mission and purpose of social work, the course needs to integrate content on the values and ethics of the profession as they pertain to justice-involved individuals. Special attention must be given to the influence of diversity as characterized by, but not limited to, age, gender, class, race, ethnicity, culture, sexual orientation, disability and religion. It is recommended that the course makes important linkages between course content and social work practice, policy, research, and field practice.

Diversity, Equity, and Inclusion

The classroom can be a place where the next generation of social workers are challenged to enter the field with a heightened sense of sensitivity to the challenges of marginalized populations and a lifelong commitment to advocacy efforts geared towards diversity, equity, and inclusion. This educational space is a catalyst to future generations that will mold the direction and standard of both our community and our country. The classroom creates a community that is a melting pot of various ideas, experiences, cultures, and values. We must also recognize the need for greater diversity, equity, and inclusion of marginalized populations to be included in such spaces. Gay (2000, p. 25) joins in this respect, "If educators continue to be ignorant of, ignore, impugn, and silence the cultural orientations, values, and performance styles of ethnically different students, they will persist in imposing cultural hegemony, personal denigration, educational inequity, and academic underachievement upon them". Accepting the validity of these students' cultural socialization and experiences will help to reverse achievement trends. There is no such thing as a *neutral* educational process. Education either functions as an instrument that is used to facilitate the integration of the younger generation into the logic of the present system and bring about conformity to it, *or* it becomes the "practice of freedom", the means by which individuals deal critically and creatively with reality and discover how to participate in the transformation of their world (Shaull, 1970).

Systemic racism and other forms of oppressive actions that create a caste system for minority populations continues to rear its ugly head of injustice, oppression, and inexcusable harm in our country. We have seen this illuminated through the calling out of multiple incidents and acts of violence among marginalized populations through various media outlets. Educators hold a responsibility to facilitate and promote the integration of deeper understanding as it relates to diversity, equity, and inclusion.

Diversity, equity, and inclusion through a social justice lens is essential in understanding root causes and must play key roles in molding the future of Smart Decarceration. As mentioned earlier in this chapter, we have seen the devastating impact of demonizing policies and practices that have led to inhumane treatment of individuals who enter the system. America has witnessed long-lasting systemic inequities that have created permanent scarlet letters of criminal records, thus displacing individuals long after completing their time served, whether behind bars or stipulations of probation and parole. Terrance, who is formerly incarcerated, shares that the ongoing implications of his past record affect his family and their ability to obtain equity and inclusion. He states, "My wife and children experience the same consequences I do. When I am denied housing, they are denied too" (Repairing the Road to Redemption in California, 2021). It is our hope that this generation of educators and students will advance the historical movements of equity while embracing diversity and advocating for the inclusion of marginalized and oppressed populations.

Managing Difficult Classroom Conversations

Discussing sensitive topics such as the level of disproportionality that exists within the legal system can become polarizing and uncomfortable. It is important that a safe and healthy class environment is established. In doing so, class parameters need to be created and sustained. This begins with starting on time, ending on time, and providing an agenda at the start of each class. Guidelines and expectations must be agreed upon with the class to promote a healthy learning environment. This engenders trust, which can promote an inclusionary environment where there are opportunities for reflection. In order for this to occur, discussions need to be meaningful, purposeful, and productive. This means that it is necessary for students to voice their thoughts, and ideologies in a manner that critically analyzes the course material by incorporating data to further validate their assertions as it lessens the personalization of such topics. The instructor becomes the facilitator by monitoring the discussion closely through active listening while identifying microaggressions and dismissive content, if and when it is necessary to do so. This can be done in a way that maintains a high level of respect by asking for clarity in responses and questions rather than making assumptions. In addition to reframing questionable comments, monitoring body language and use of language is important. Follow up is also a useful strategy, which can include the utilization of office hours or key breaks to further explore disagreements to advance the classroom discussion all the while tending to individual student concern to increase safe and brave spaces for students.

Evaluation of Learning

Class discussion is an integral part of the learning process; reviewing the terminology, concepts, and frameworks and their application to the criminal justice system is a way to discover students' comprehension of the class material. This allows the instructor to provide prompt feedback to their in-classroom discussions, ensuring goals and objectives of the class are maintained and achieved. Furthermore, connections are made to the learning outcomes of each class session during these in-classroom discussions and at the close of each class session. To further enhance instructional quality, it is encouraged that all assignments be reviewed in detail with students during class sessions. Use of examples can be incorporated when reviewing each assignment with students in order to enhance their production of quality work. The use of real-world case studies, and/or situations with course material allows for students to critically analyze difficult concepts and course material in general with the ability to reflect and observe their learning process beyond the classroom setting. This allows students the opportunity to master course material and engage in group discussions and debates as well as develop a sense of leadership organically. Reflection tools, papers, in-class discussions, and presentations can serve as ways to monitor students' comprehension of the course material. Demonstration briefs and project-based presentations to key community stakeholders can further serve as creative, innovative ways to monitor student grasp of the course content while promoting community engagement.

Conclusion and Areas for Further Teaching and Curricular Considerations

Mass incarceration is finally being recognized as a Grand Challenge that has unjustly affected communities of color. Further foundational knowledge is needed to address the social norms that continue to hold the problem of mass incarceration in place. Furthermore, the concern as to how research has been translated into actual practices as well as the proof of success or weaknesses of such programs to best serve the population must be examined. Sadly, studies do reveal that earlier engagement with the criminal justice system, especially for youth of color can end with more frequent secure placement found in confinement (Pope et al., 2002). Hinton (2016) indicates this being a prime example of systemic racism where the relationship between race and well-being is impacted, resulting in psychological barriers for the population. This in and of itself leads to the re-traumatization of the population by the retriggering of complex traumas found in the prison systems design that promotes racial disproportionality (Estrada et al., 2017). Herein lies a critical variable to address when supporting the justice-involved population: their exposure to cultural trauma, which is viewed differently from psychological and physical trauma, as it is more likely to result in a "dramatic loss of identity" (Eyerman et al., 2004). Much of the criminal justice literature neglects to examine this piece when working with the justice-involved population, which can serve as the impetus to building a successful reentry plan with the population, like what programs such as Project Kinship are attempting to achieve. Implementing a curriculum from a teaching pedagogy that is flexible and non-traditional as found in this chapter, "community-centered", can prepare students to advance relevant practice, research, and policy when working with justice-involved individuals to assist in designing successful reentry models with the population's voice and their experiences as the agent of change.

References

Alexander, M. (2012). *The new Jim Crow: Mass incarceration in the age of colorblindness*. New Press.

The Association of Experiential Education Conference. (2015). *Social Justice: Creating Change*, Oct 22–25, Portland.

Bernstein, N. (2014). *Burning down the house: The end of juvenile prison.* New Press.

Bureau of Justice Statistics. (2005). *State court sentencing of convicted felons.* U.S. Department of Justice.

Council of Social Work Education (CSWE). (2022). *2022 Educational policy and accreditation standards (EPAS).* Author. www.cswe.org/accreditation/standards/2022-epas/

Dewey, J. (1915). The school and society. In *The school and society and the child and the curriculum* (2nd ed., pp. 5–65). Digireads.com Publishing, 2010.

Dewey, J. (1933). *How we think: A restatement of the relation of reflective thinking to the educative process.* D.C. Heath & Co Publishers.

Dewey, J. (1938). *Experience and education.* Macmillan Company.

Estrada, J. N., Hernandez, R. A., & Kim, S. (2017). Considering definitional issues, cultural components, and the impact of trauma when counseling vulnerable youth susceptible to gang involvement. In *Handbook of multicultural counseling* (4th ed.). Sage.

Eyerman, R., Alexander, J., Giesen, B., Smelser, N., & Sztompka, P. (2004). Cultural trauma: Slavery and the formation of African American identity. In *Cultural trauma and collective identity* (pp. 60–111). University of California Press. www.jstor.org/stable/10.1525/j.ctt1pp9nb.6

Foster, H. I., & Hagan, J. (2007). Incarceration and intergenerational social exclusion. *Social Problems*, *54*(4), 399–433. https://doi.org/10.1525/sp.2007.54.4.399

Freeman, R. B. (1996). Why do so many young American men commit crimes and what might we do about it? *Journal of Economic Perspectives*, *10*, 25–42.

Gay, G. (2000). *Culturally responsive teaching: Theory, research, and practice.* Teachers College Press.

Gillespie, C. F., Bradley, B., Mercer, K., Smith, A. K., Conneely, K., Gapen, M., Weiss, T., Schwartz, A. C., Cubells, J. F., & Ressler, K. J. (2009). Trauma exposure and stress-related disorders in inner city primary care patients. *General Hospital Psychiatry*, *31*, 505–514.

Glaze, L. E., & Maruschak, L. M. (2010). *Parents in prison and their minor children.* Bureau of Justice Statistics. www.bjs.gov/index.cfm?ty=pbdetail&iid=823

Hawkins, D. J., & Jenson, J. (Eds.) (2017). American Academy of Social Work & Social Welfare. *Grand challenges for social work: Promote smart decarceration.* https://grandchallengesforsocialwork.org/promote-smart-decarceration/

Hayasaki, E. (2016). Tech & science: How poverty affects the brain. *Newsweek.* www.newsweek.com/2016/09/02/how-poverty-affects-brains-493239.html

Hinton, E. (2016). *From the war on poverty to the war on crime.* Harvard University Press.

Jacobson, J., Oravecz, L., Falk, A., & Osteen, P. (2011). Proximate outcomes of service-learning among family studies undergraduates. *Family Science Review*, *16*(1), 22–33.

Jäggi, L. J., Mezuk, B., Watkins, D. C., & Jackson, J. S. (2016). The relationship between trauma, arrest, and incarceration history among black Americans: Findings from the National Survey of American Life. *Society and Mental Health*, 6(3), 187–206.

King, R. S. (2008). *Disparity by geography: The war on drugs in America's cities*. The Sentencing Project.

Nellis, A. (2016). *The color of justice: Racial and ethnic disparity in state prisons*. The Sentencing Project. www.sentencingproject.org/wp-content/uploads/2016/06/The-Color-of-Justice-Racial-and-Ethnic-Disparity-in-State-Prisons.pdf.

Onyekwere, A. (2021). *How cash bail works: The cash bail systems are unfair to low-income people and people of color, but there are ways to fix it*. Brennan Center For Justice. www.brennancenter.org/our-work/research-reports/how-cash-bail-works

The Open Health Services and Policy Journal, 3: 80–100 Trauma Center at JRI 1269, Beacon Street Brookline, MA 02446, USA.

Pettit, B., & Western, B. (2004). Mass imprisonment and the life course: Race and class inequality in U.S. incarceration. *American Sociological Review*, 69(2), 151–169. https://doi.org/10.1177/000312240406900201

Pope, C. E., Lovell, R., & Hsia, H. M. (2002). *Disproportionate minority confinement: A review of the research literature from 1989 through 2001*. Department of Justice.

Public Safety Performance Project. (2008). *One in 100: Behind bars in America 2008*. The Pew Center on the States.

Rabuy, B., & Kopf, D. (2016). *Detaining the Poor: How money bail perpetuates an endless cycle of poverty and jail time*. Prison Policy Initiative. www.prisonpolicy.org/reports/incomejails.html

Ring, K., & Gill, M. (2017). *Using time to reduce crime: Federal prisoner survey results show ways to reduce recidivism*. Families Against Mandatory Minimums (FAMM). www.prisonpolicy.org/scans/famm/Prison-Report_May-31_Final.pdf

Roberts, D. E. (2004). The social and moral cost of mass incarceration in African American communities. *Faculty Scholarship at Penn Law*, *583*. https://scholarship.law.upenn.edu/faculty_scholarship/583

Saigh, P. A. (1991). The development of posttraumatic stress disorder following four different types of traumatization. *Behaviour Research and Therapy*, *29*, 213–216.

Sawyer, W., & Wagner, P. (2020, March 24). *Mass incarceration: The whole pie 2020*. Prison Policy Initiative. www.prisonpolicy.org/reports/pie2020.html#slideshows/slideshow1/2

Shaull, R. (1970). *Introduction to pedagogy of the oppressed*. Seabury.

Shonkoff, J. P., Garner, A. S., Committee on Psychosocial Aspects of Child and Family Health, Committee on Early Childhood, Adoption, and Dependent Care, & Section on Developmental and Behavioral Pediatrics. (2012).

The lifelong effects of early childhood adversity and toxic stress. *Pediatrics*, *129*(1), e232–e246. https://doi.org/10.1542/peds.2011-2663

Smith Budhai, S., & Brown Skipwith, K. (2017). *Best practices in engaging online learners through active and experiential learning strategies* (1st ed.). Routledge. https://doi-org.libproxy1.usc.edu/10.4324/9781315617503

Substance Abuse and Mental Health Service Administration. (2017). www.samhsa.gov/

Western, B., Kling, J. R., & Weiman, D. F. (2001). The labor market consequences of incarceration. *Crime & Delinquency*, *47*(3), 410–427. https://doi.org/10.1177/0011128701047003007

Appendix 11A

EPAS Addressed in Grand Challenge #10

Promote Smart Decarceration

Competency 2: Advance Human Rights and Social, Racial, Economic, and Environmental Justice. Social workers share a close relationship with human justice as the profession itself adheres to values such as respect, dignity, and social justice. This illustrates that all human beings are deserving of fundamental rights regardless of their social, racial, economic, or environmental status. Mass incarceration and its long-standing effects threatens every facet of human experience, which further accentuates that social workers apply the life-course perspective to interventions and the way in which system-impacted individuals are treated. To forge the process of Smart Decarceration, social workers must address the racial, economic, behavioral, and environmental disparities that are present amongst system-impacted individuals.

Competency 3: Engage Antiracism, Diversity, Equity, and Inclusion (ADEI) in Practice. Social workers consider how intersectionality is a driving force in determining an individual's experience of oppression and discrimination. When social workers champion for equity for all human beings, it is of equal importance that marginalized populations who have faced systemic injustice are brought to the forefront. The Grand Challenge of Promoting Smart Decarceration includes looking at minority populations that have consistently been overrepresented in the United States Criminal Justice system. To have a society that promotes antiracism, diversity, equity, and inclusion means to both challenge and dismantle any practice that is intended to keep oppressed populations further bound.

Competency 4: Engage in Practice-Informed Research and Research-Informed Practice. Social workers often commit to lifelong learning, which incorporates looking at evidence to inform both new and current practices. When social workers evaluate their own practices and conduct program evaluations, it leaves room to improve practice, policy, and service delivery. Due to recent pressure placed on the government through advocacy work, there is a shift in the way the carceral system views punitive and rehabilitative approaches. With this shift, social workers must look at what has been successful and unsuccessful as research will continue to translate what will lead to evidence-based practices.

Competency 5: Engage in Policy Practice. Like how the War on Drugs and the War on Terror birthed several policies that have led to an over-inundated carceral system, there are a number of policies that make it difficult throughout the process and thereafter when an individual is attempting to reintegrate back into society. Social workers can advocate for policy change to dismantle the carceral system as it exists. Social workers take on the commitment to combat injustices that impact various populations at the macro, mezzo, and micro level. Policy reform makes it possible to affect change as policy often informs the quality, accessibility, and delivery of services.

Competency 6: Engage With Individuals, Families, Groups, Organizations, and Communities. Social workers realize a holistic perspective on the needs of the populations that they serve and a part of this comes from ensuring meaningful engagement with communities. System-impacted individuals are not solely affected by mass incarceration; we see the continuance of intergenerational trauma when minority populations are disproportionately impacted by mass incarceration. At the end of the 21st century, 1.3 million men of color were imprisoned in state and federal institutions (Pettit & Western, 2004). What isn't highlighted in that number is the families of those that have been incarcerated; therefore social workers are implored to consider ways in which the field can engage with not only the families, but the marginalized communities in which these instances occur.

Appendix 11B

Integrating the Grand Challenges Content Into the Social Work Curricula and Classroom

Smart Decarceration: A Multi-Prong Approach to Healing the Incarcerated

Teaching Tools

Thought of the Day with Father Greg Boyle of Homeboy Industries

https://youtu.be/T1kU-v0O5N0
https://youtu.be/xYFCDOV4HVg
https://youtu.be/jXM_rO-ktp8
https://youtu.be/3S4CDiKPWos
https://youtu.be/PfV27HovIIM

Appendix 11C

- 0:00 to 0:05 minute YouTube video clip – Father Greg Boyle's "Thought of the Day";
- 0:05 to 0:15 Students, reflection, and feedback regarding Father Greg Boyle's "Thought of the Day";
- 0:15 to 0:30 Discussion, common perceptions about justice-involved individuals;
- 0:30 to 0:50 Scope of the problem – ethno-historical considerations, demographic data-sharing highlighting the population, impact of prisons, and disproportionality that exist within America's prisons;
- 0:50 to 0:60 Position the following question, what is mass incarceration?

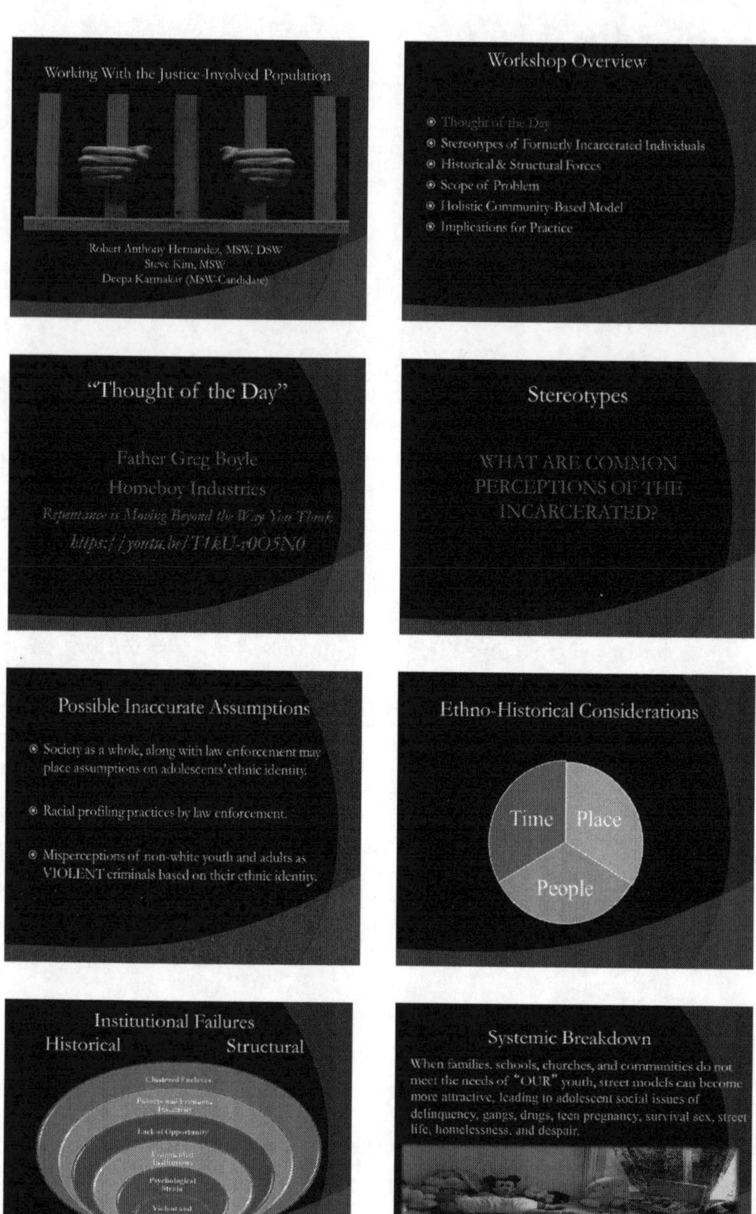

Figure 11.1 PowerPoint of student engagement – Session 1

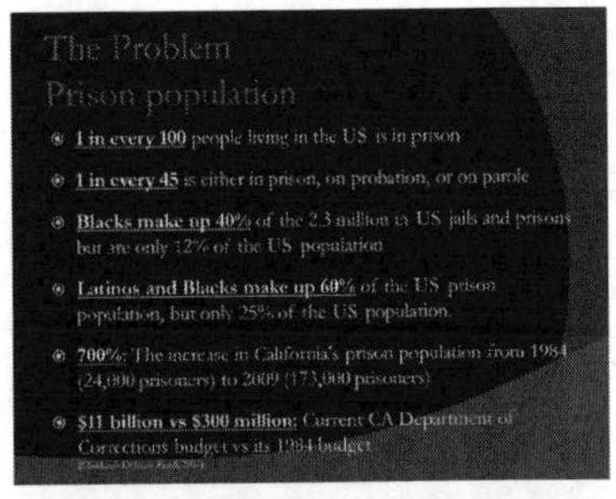

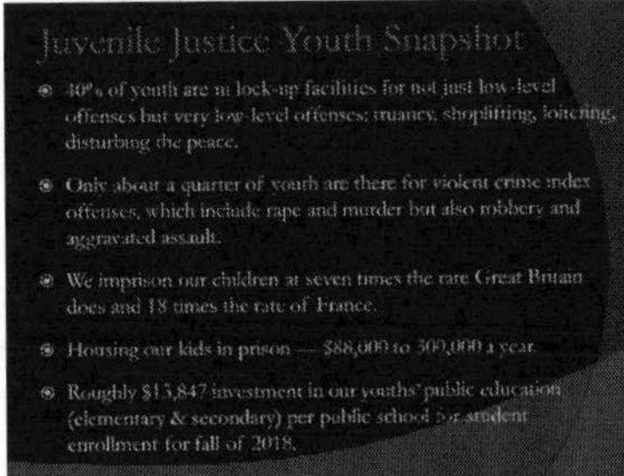

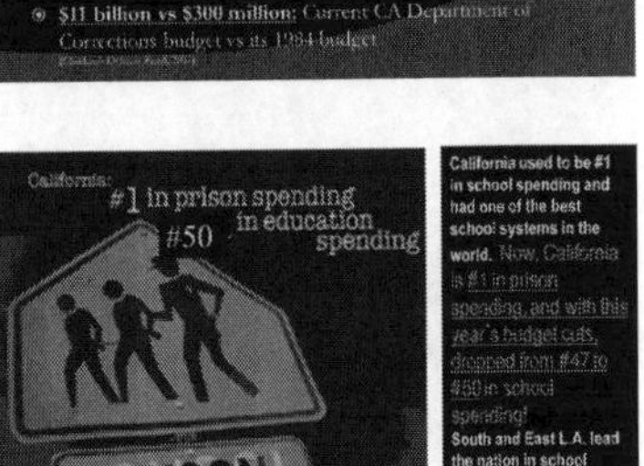

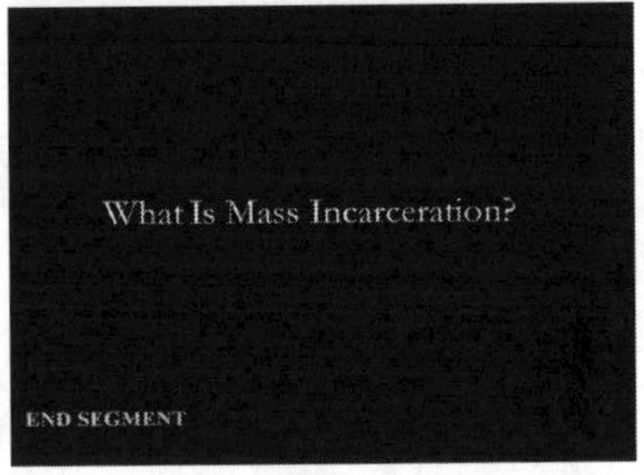

Figure 11.1 (Continued)

Appendix 11D

Project Kinship

Project Kinship is a non-profit organization in Orange County, CA that provides reentry and intervention services for individuals and families impacted by incarceration, violence, trauma, and gangs. Reentry services are grounded in trauma-informed and culturally sensitive practices. Project Kinship's mission is to provide support and training to lives impacted by incarceration, gangs, and violence through hope, healing, and transformation. Project Kinship envisions a world where hope lives and the cycle of despair ends and works to promote hope, encourage healthy life decisions, lower recidivism, provide education for re-employment, and offer rehabilitation services that seek healing and restorative justice in the community. Project Kinship is currently one of the leading agencies in Orange County serving as a drop-in reentry center for those being released from jails. Project Kinship's services include Medi-Cal/CalFresh Enrollment Assistance; Job Employment Program for reentry transitional-aged youth (16–26 years old); School-Based Restorative Practices and gang intervention; recovery and community support services for reentry adults; and mental health services, advocacy and training services.

Over time, Project Kinship has earned a reputation for excellent programming and has been able to expand its services growing from what was initially two staff members to now over 60 employees within a six-year span. In addition to the need for services, there are four core areas that have contributed to the accelerated growth of Project Kinship, which include the hiring and training of formerly incarcerated individuals to provide service delivery and shape programming, inclusion of trauma-informed care, community of kinship and inclusion, and self-care.

12 Building Financial Capability and Assets for All

Elena Delavega, Kari L. Fletcher and Melissa Hirschi

Introduction and Background of Building Financial Capacity

Over the past century, Grand Challenges have evolved into a collaborative, innovative, and creative process with the potential to strengthen communities and have been embraced across multiple disciplines and countries (Grand Challenges Canada, 2011). Within the field of social work, the American Academy of Social Work and Social Welfare introduced the initial 12 Grand Challenges during 2014, emphasizing how our profession's strengths (e.g., inquiry, innovation, technology) may address the following key social problems:

> Ensure healthy development for all youth; close the health gap; stop family violence; advance long and productive lives; eradicate social isolation; end homelessness; create social responses to a changing environment; harness technology for social good; promote smart decarceration; reduce extreme economic inequality; build financial capability for all; achieve equal opportunity and justice.
>
> (American Academy of Social Work and Social Welfare, n.d.)

A 13th Grand Challenge to include eliminating racism was added in 2020 as a standalone Grand Challenge.

How Building Financial Capability Is Situated Within Social Work Curricula

Promoting economic justice and engaging in practices that seek to give every person an environment of economic justice and economic inclusion are core social work values. In our discipline, Council on

DOI: 10.4324/9781003308263-15

Social Work Education (CSWE) accreditation standards influence how the building financial capability Grand Challenge is situated within social work curricula. Beyond stipulating that accredited social work programs' curriculum shall attend to the economic context from the micro to the macro levels.

Throughout this chapter, we share the vignette of "Morgan" to help illustrate the important role social work education plays in helping students learn about building financial capability for all. The case scenario is placed in italics for clarity.

Morgan is a social work student at an urban university in Texas, where she also works as a waitress. She struggles financially but is very committed to her education. Life is hard for her and she must count every penny to make ends meet. She does not have any children, but sometimes helps her sister Karla, a single mother of three children. This semester, Morgan is enrolled in a required policy and economics course and she is not excited about it. She does not really care for the subject, which she finds boring and difficult. She wants to be a therapist and feels the policy and economics course is a waste of her time.

As Morgan participated in classroom conversations specific to building financial capability, she was surprised to learn that social work is rooted in economic struggles and that so many of the social work "mothers" worked to change economic policy that hurt the poor and marginalized. She still felt, however, that while interesting, the subject matter had nothing to do with her future life as a therapist.

Human Behavior in the Social Environment

As a profession that has historically emphasized the Person in Environment (PIE), financial capability and the understanding of how the economy works is fundamental for social work. As the largest context in which social work operates, the economy – and in this context, financial social work – has arisen to address this very important and yet often forgotten piece of PIE. As the social work profession has emerged, it has focused upon the issues of economic inequality and poverty.

Policy

From Hull House to the National Consumers League (Blumberg, 1966; National Consumers League [NCL], n.d.) to the 1938 Fair Labor and Standards Act, the earliest social workers were involved in economic issues. Included in the 1938 Fair Labor and Standards Act, which "provides for minimum standards for both wages and overtime entitlement, and spells out administrative procedures by which covered worktime [*sic*] must be compensated," were child labor, equal pay, and portal-to-portal activities-related provisions (U.S. Office of Personnel Management [OPM], n.d., ¶7).

Practice

The practice of social work is rooted in addressing economic justice. Worsening economic conditions for the majority of people, together with rising income inequality, erosion of the middle class, and increased opposition to social welfare programs result in greater need of social workers who understand economics and finance, and public resistance to funding social welfare (Gillen & Loeffler, 2012; Interprofessional Education Collaborative Expert Panel, 2011; Reich, 2015). Economics impact every facet of life. Financial capability affects access, outcomes, and even power relations. Social workers, regardless of area of specialization, must understand economic context. While social work students are often assumed to be disinterested in finances or economics (Anderson & Harris, 2015), it may simply be that they do not understand or feel confident engaging around this topic (Dooley et al., 2009). Social work curriculum can, and should, include curriculum that addresses financial capability.

The Curriculum

Economics Curriculum

While social work competencies instruct social work educators to teach *about* economics and financial capability, they do not specify *what* to teach. In order to prepare our students for lives post-graduation and a real-world practice that will involve the world of finance and economics, we (the authors) propose that all social work students be taught economic concepts. Years of study, research, and teaching (Delavega, 2016; Doran & Bagdasaryan, 2018; Frey et al., 2017; Loke et al., 2017; Reich, 2015; Sachs, 2017; Wheelan, 2010) suggest concepts taught should include supply and demand, including the concept of utility, marginal utility, and marginal costs; trade and tariffs; incentives, and how incentives can be perverse; the business cycle and shocks; markets and market failures; stocks and bonds; investment and return on investment; labor market, including wages (and the minimum wage), labor contracts, labor rights and responsibilities, unemployment, and the role of trade organizations and unions; the US budget, the deficit, and the national debt; the role of taxes and regulation in the economy; the Earned Income Tax Credit (EITC); and inflation, deflation, and stagflation.

In the freezing storm that devastated Texas and left millions without power Morgan was hit hard. As she huddled together with her sister and her children in a freezing house, it was so cold that the walls felt like ice. When the pipes froze a few hours later and they lost access to water as well, the family shivered and tried to survive for days on the bottled water they could get. Just before the storm, Morgan's class had focused on the market, market failures, and regulation. When she was able to return to class, she told the teacher, "I understand now what happened. Texas has an independent power grid to avoid regulation, but that means the electricity providers had not wanted to spend the money needed to winterize the grid, so it failed!" (Fordham, 2021). "Yes," commented her instructor, "regulation would have helped prevent this." Morgan continued, "And, because energy is provided by private companies, not the national grid, there was no way they could have gotten more power from somewhere else. The worst thing," Morgan continued, "is that because of supply and demand, power asymmetries, and market failures, my bill is going to be thousands of dollars that I cannot afford. I think I am starting to understand why learning all this stuff is important."

Personal Finance Curriculum

It is also important to teach social work students about personal finance – this is closer to our understanding of financial capability as we understand the role of the larger economy is fundamental to financial capability. In terms of personal finance, social work students should be able to understand banking, the banking industry, as well as different types of bank accounts, their purposes, and management; personal budgets and balance sheets; cash and checks; savings, emergency savings funds, long-term savings, and savings for a goal; credit, credit scores, credit reporting agencies, and the rights of citizens regarding their credit; secured and unsecured loans (credit cards and other forms of credit such as mortgages and car loans); debt, debt repayment, principal, balance, and penalties; interest (fixed and adjustable rates), compound interest; rental contracts, when to rent, and when to buy; taxes and how to file taxes; and assets, liabilities, and ways to build wealth.

Morgan was very happy that she had learned about the Earned Income Tax Credit and could not wait to tell her sister about it.

"I thought I hated taxes," she told the instructor, "but I think I like them." Morgan had a lot of questions about credit scores and interest. She was particularly surprised that the payday loan place she had been using charged such high interest rates. She vowed never to use that lender again.

There are many resources that social work instructors can use to teach financial capability, but this list should provide a starting point for developing a strong curriculum in financial capability. Additionally, in Appendix 12A the reader will find the Council of Social Work Education's (CSWE, 2022) *2022 Educational Policy and Accreditation Standards* (EPAS) that can be applied to the topic of this chapter.

Teaching Practices

Context and Student Preparation for Learning and Engagement

As educators, we are responsible for offering context and preparing students for engagement and classroom learning.

NASW Code of Ethics

As a frequent resource educators draw upon, the National Association of Social Workers (NASW) Code of Ethics helps students better understand educational concepts related to our discipline (Greenfield et al., 2018; National Association of Social Workers [NASW], 2017). As it pertains more specifically to the Grand Challenges in Social Work, the NASW Code of Ethics' mission and values reinforce this professional code as it pertains to building financial capability.

In addition to the NASW Code of Ethics, Greenfield et al. (2018) suggest six other "educational best practices" that can be applied to guide instructors to prepare students to learn about building financial capability:

- Establish class norms (e.g., how discussions will take place, the rules for engaging in discussion, and how to respectfully listen and engage).
- Engage in respectful critique of leaders (e.g., having open discussions about leaders including decisions that may be controversial, and exploring critical thinking and questioning in order to have a deeper understanding and stronger rationale for opinions that might differ).

- Use "tough" words (e.g., including words that may be uncomfortable such as racism, sexism, elitism, and power. Shirking from using actual words inhibits our ability to engage in difficult conversations. If, for example, we are not willing to use the word racist, our ability to have a conversation about racism is impacted, p. 431).
- Engage in reflective practice (e.g., modeling for students reflective practice such as asking reflective questions of students to help them think critically about their experiences and move more deeply into the experience).
- Clearly lay out modes of assessment (e.g., such as what the assignments are in the course, how each will be assessed, and being up front with students about what the expectations are for graded work and participation assessments).
- Open multiple methods of communication (e.g., including holding regular office hours, allowing students to set up office hours that fall outside of those, allowing students to communicate with the instructor using discussion boards, email, and telephone, pp. 430–432).

The NASW Code of Ethics is foundational to our profession (Greenwood, 1956; NASW, 2017). This Code of Ethics guides our profession, our practice, our values, and the education of our future social workers. Although the NASW Code of ethics is crucial, it may often be so core to who we are and what we do, that we as educators do not take time to be intentional with teaching our students. As Greenfield et al. (2018) have encouraged, making explicit connections between relevant principles of the Code of Ethics will not only reinforce the importance of the code, but will also demonstrate the applicability across curriculum and practice. Although class discussions and content can cover the range of social work values and ethical standards, a few key starting points related to financial capability for social work students may include social justice; competence; our ethical responsibilities to clients; and our ethical responsibilities in practice settings, as professionals, to the larger profession, and broader society (NASW, 2017).

In order to more effectively incorporate the NASW Code of Ethics and build a classroom environment that is conducive for students to learn and be actively engaged, it is imperative to establish classroom norms (Greenfield et al., 2018). Early in the educational relationship, for example, at the beginning of a new semester, students and educators should collaboratively work to establish the rules and norms for the class. While some rules or norms may not be negotiable such as ethical violations, threats of harm, etc., other aspects have more flexibility and should be mutually agreed upon. Having a shared responsibility for the larger group is a key element of fostering motivation for adult learners (Brookfield, 1996). Students also benefit from knowing up front what is okay, what is not okay, and that the shared space is a safe space to explore, learn, and practice. The climate of the classroom is vitally important for building a space that students can learn (Raghallaigh & Cunniffe, 2013).

For Morgan, sharing her experiences was hard at first. She was ashamed of being poor and did not want to disclose anything. But as she began to understand not only her own personal finances but the larger economy, she began to understand where the system had failed her. She started getting angry at the system, and then she got ready to change policy.

Critical Thinking

With a safe classroom climate, students will be more likely to take risks and explore difficult subject matter, including engaging in respectful critique of leaders and using "tough" words (Greenfield et al., 2018, p. 431). Critical thinking is valued in education, yet it can be challenging to teach students how to practice critical thinking. Asking questions and encouraging students to ask questions is one way to begin this process. Additionally, helping students to use their voice and take risks is another way (Oliver et al., 2017). Exploring ways to respectfully question also builds skills for social work students who can use those when advocating for social justice and vulnerable populations. Along with asking questions, helping students to learn that it is okay to use strong words or words that may be uncomfortable for some is important (Greenfield et al., 2018). It may be uncomfortable to openly talk about some topics, especially depending on the audience, but helping students engage openly and safely in the classroom to navigate conversations about racism, sexuality, gender, power, wealth, health inequity, trauma, abuse, police brutality, and other topics will set a precedent for our students to feel more comfortable having these conversations with classmates, educators, policy makers, clients, and our communities.

Reflective Practice

Helping students to engage with content and develop skill in reflective practice (Ferguson, 2018; Greenfield et al., 2018; Kwong, 2020) is also important in creating an educational space for students to be prepared for learning about content and practicing methods that may be uncomfortable or unfamiliar. Breaking down reflective practice, for example walking students through our own process as an educator for how we arrived at a particular conclusion or made a specific decision in a situation, can help students learn how to be reflective in their approach. Slowing the process down in order to look at the pieces that went into the decision, including the context, our thoughts, what we were feeling, and being able to have a self-awareness to look at things from a 1,000 foot view rather than up close (Ferguson, 2018), are ways we can practice and model reflective work.

The final two suggestions to guide the preparation of the classroom environment to teach challenging concepts such as financial capability to social work students, are setting clear guides around assessment and multiple methods of communication (Greenfield et al., 2018). Similar to ensuring clear rules and norms for the class, having concrete guidelines and expectations on what is assessed and how will allow students to be more open to taking risks for assessment in the classroom which is important. For example, letting students know that what is said in discussion is not graded, but active participation in discussion is part of their grade. Finally, having multiple methods that students can communicate with the instructor and one another is valuable (Greenfield et al., 2018). Various methods to engage with course content such as class discussions in person, electronic discussion boards in the learning management system, opportunities for written reflection and discussion submitted to the instructor and avenues to connect with the instructor via email, phone, and virtual platforms. Intentionally incorporating these best practices (Greenfield et al., 2018) will help to set the context and help prepare social work students to learn and engage with uncomfortable and unfamiliar content, including building financial capability.

Managing Difficult Classroom Conversations and Evaluation of Learning

Difficult conversations are just that, "difficult," and engaging in them can take courage (Oliver et al., 2017; Staller, 2014). Navigating difficult conversations in the classroom is an important pedagogical component for teaching social work students across diverse topics, including building financial capacity. Holding space for and encouraging difficult conversations in the classroom is one method to help students learn knowledge and engage with concepts through critical thinking and conversation. Additionally, modeling difficult conversations in the classroom can help students learn through experience how to have these conversations in the field.

An overarching premise for navigating conversations is to approach from a talking "with" rather than "at" (Staller, 2014) perspective. Kim and Prado (2019) have developed an eight-step model that can be applied to difficult conversations. These steps are:

1. Identify a grounded goal (e.g., being responsible for knowing and listening to our bodies and our cues for when we are becoming uncomfortable or upset and that everyone is responsible for their role in the class or that everyone is working on pushing themselves out of their comfort zone in order to actively participate and engage in the discussion).
2. Locate and acknowledge barriers (e.g., helping students identify and see barriers to having difficult conversation such as differences in experience, culture, ideas, and values).
3. Set a value-driven intention (e.g., taking time to explore one's own values to then determine the value or set of values such as humility, respect, compassion, and courage that will guide the work being done in the classroom related to difficult conversations).
4. Set the stage (e.g., using our values to guide or practice, including using our voice to practice talking to each other and not just having conversations in our own minds).
5. Take action (e.g., actually engaging in the conversation, including being mindful of who you want to talk with and why, being open to your own experience during the conversation, and being intentional about what you are asking of the other person).
6. Listen (e.g., this crucial step requires listening with more than just our ears, but also being mindful of the words that are not spoken and the body language that is also used).
7. Respond (e.g., when we are engaging in critical conversations, often about sensitive topics, it is important to respond to those who take risks, even if we don't know what to say, acknowledging and responding demonstrates that we are listening and invested in the conversation).
8. Do it again (e.g., repeating the steps over and over in order to practice and strengthen skills in this area will help our students become more capable of doing this outside of the classroom as well).

Assessing learning can be challenging outside of concrete deliverables. In order to help students learn through conversation and discussion, it is important to set the standards for assessment from the beginning and be clear about the expectations. Methods for assessment may include

- Self-reflective assignments (e.g., having students respond to questions that guide them through being self-reflective such as describing their thoughts, feelings, sensations in their body);
- Self-administered assessments of engagements (e.g., allowing students to assess their own level of engagement with large or small group discussions will help students learn to notice their involvement and take a more active role in their interactions); and/or
- Being open as an educator to allowing students flexibility in how and what assessment and learning might look like for them individually (e.g., having discussions early on in the course about different options for assessment and allowing students a choice for one or multiple aspects of the assessment).

Working with students and meeting them where they are at can help build a trusting relationship that will foster safety and encourage students to engage in difficult conversations (Staller, 2014). Instructors may also use knowledge assessment quizzes and tests, as these have value in evaluating whether students have learned the core concepts that are fundamental to economics and financial capability. Taking steps and being intentional as educators is pivotal to helping students learn in a safe environment. If we are able to help students learn skills, practice, and engage when it is safe, we can strengthen them to have the necessary foundation to build on in the field as social work interns and our future social work colleagues.

Facilitating Class Discussions and Any Class Exercises

In addition to readings and teaching concepts, experiential exercises and gamification are excellent ways to teach financial capability. Participatory learning is an excellent way to achieve higher-order learning in many areas of knowledge (Abdulwahed & Nagy, 2009; Askeland, 2003; Huerta-Wong & Schoech, 2010; Kolb & Kolb, 2009). Kolb (1984) described an experiential learning cycle that involves concrete experience, reflective observation, abstract conceptualization, and active experimentation in a recursive cycle of doing-thinking-conceptualizing-applying (Kolb & Kolb, 2009). In higher education, in-class simulations and other experiential learning activities expose students to difficult concepts and promote critical thinking through the examination of the concepts and analysis of the experience (Angelini, 2016; Backlund & Hendrix, 2013; de Smale et al., 2015; McLoughlin & Lee, 2008). They also provide practice with complex tasks through reflective practice (Kolb & Kolb, 2009). When used together with readings, concept development, and discussion, in-class simulations or experiential exercises are particularly useful in teaching complex economics concepts and making learning a subject that may be distasteful a lot more palatable. Several experiential exercises developed to teach economics concepts are described next.

In the game "Candy and Taxes" the entire national income of the United States is converted into 100 pieces of candy and divided according to the percent of the national income each quintile has (see Appendix 12A). The students are then randomly assigned to a quintile and provided the appropriate amount of candy. There are several students in each quintile, depending on class size. The instructor then implements different tax schemes, from very regressive to very progressive, so the students can experience how these affect different people and the economy in general.

To teach about the asymmetries inherent in the economy, I (lead author) have used a game in which students randomly take tokens from bags and are expected to achieve high points by trading. What the students do not know is that the bags and the tokens are not random, and that indeed, a few students have been given chips of much greater value. Adding the number of points from the first round to the score of the second round also ensures that those with the most points remain with the most points. The game is used as a springboard to discuss the economy and the role of power and privilege.

Students can learn about the challenges of poverty and lack of financial capability through any number of experiential exercises that expose students to the life of a person in poverty. There is a popular commercial poverty simulation exercise in which they have to "live" like a poor person for a "month." Students begin the program by role-playing *a month in the life* of low-income families, from single parents trying to care for their children to senior citizens trying to maintain their self-sufficiency on Social Security. Over the four 15-minute *weeks*, students experience the challenges of providing food, shelter, and other basic necessities in an environment with limited transportation, social supports, and community resources. Another simulation in which students experience the challenges of people in poverty requires them to apply in person for various local services by relying solely on public transportation. Students then debrief about their experiences.

Yet another simulation assigns students a limited monthly food budget and instructs them to create a full month of meals and snacks on that limited amount of money. The amount of money allocated to food is based on the minimum wage. A variation of this exercise assigns different amounts of money to different students, allowing some of them to "purchase" more or more varied food and create easier meal plans. Students then compare notes and talk about their experiences.

For Morgan, many of the experiential exercises were just like the struggles of her life. For other students, the exercises were a little melodramatic. Morgan told the class "the way that the poor suffer in this game is real. I have lived it – it is true." Her comments helped solidify the learning experience for more privileged students.

A truly immersive experiential learning activity requires students to become certified as Volunteer Income Tax Assistance (VITA) tax preparers and to volunteer a number of hours helping low-income people file their taxes with the Internal Revenue Service (IRS). The experiential activity provides a depth of financial understanding that would be impossible to achieve otherwise.

Doing taxes scared Morgan. She was particularly terrified of doing taxes for other people. "I am going to screw something up," she told the instructor, "I cannot really think like that." The instructor told her to practice and use her critical thinking skills, and that the social work competencies of assessment and intervention are useful problem-solving skills when it comes to taxes. Morgan kept at it, and eventually became one of the best VITA volunteers. At the end of the tax season that semester she told the instructor, "I did my taxes by myself, too, but the best part of all was that I helped my sister with her taxes and she got the EITC!"

It is crucial to mention the role of debriefing in all immersive, experiential, and simulative activities. Understanding the connection between theory and practice is essential for these activities to achieve higher-order learning goals (Kolb & Kolb, 2009).

Addressing Diversity, Equity, and Inclusion

The 2022 EPAS very clearly connect economic justice to social justice and emphasize inclusion. Economic exclusion is as severe a form of exclusion as racial or sexual exclusion. People who lack access to the economic life of their community and to the goods and services connected there are as excluded as those who lack access due to discriminatory or segregationist laws and policies. Lack of financial capability expose people to exploitation and oppressive practices in their quest for mere survival; the lives of people in poverty are often expendable and are valued much less than the lives of the rich. This has clearly been shown with the 2020 pandemic, in which the poor have much less access to the resources necessary for the protection of life, and much less opportunity to work from home and avoid the spaces in which contagion is most likely (Reeves & Rothwell, 2020). In the same manner, because of high costs the poor have had much less access to timely testing and access to medical services (Reeves & Rothwell, 2020). As a result, those who lack the financial capability to protect themselves or their families fall to this disease much more often, and are more likely to die from it (Reeves & Rothwell, 2020). Economic exclusion and lack of financial capability are quite literally matters of life or death. The social work profession is ethically committed to correcting the injustices created by economic exclusion and lack of financial capability (Delavega & Reyes, 2019).

At the end of the semester, Morgan was very pleased she had taken the class. She understood a lot more about her own finances and the economy, and she felt confident that she could have a better financial future because of it. Most importantly, she now knew exactly what policies she needed to advocate for. She still wanted to become a therapist, but she understood that the economy is something that affects every aspect of her life and the lives of her clients.

Conclusion and Areas for Further Teaching/Curricular Considerations

Financial capability builds the financial well-being that is fundamental for human dignity, freedom, and the exercise of self-determination that are core values for social work (Delavega & Reyes, 2019; Sachs, 2017). Amartya Sen has said that people who cannot meet their basic needs lack basic freedoms. Teaching social workers how to build financial capability is within our scope of practice and purview, and it is an important piece of PIE. Traditionally, social workers have been reluctant to engage in economics and finances (Anderson & Harris, 2005; Dooley et al., 2009), but understanding these and intervening in the economic context are critical to building financial capability (Delavega & Reyes, 2019), as is being able to differentiate between best practices and dangerous misconceptions that promote oppressive practice (Servon, 2017). Teaching financial capability concepts can be challenging, but it can be done with a little planning and guidance. Experiential exercises may be particularly useful in reaching students and helping them understand concepts that are non-intuitive. In this chapter, we have aimed to do just that.

References

Abdulwahed, M., & Nagy, Z. K. (2009). Applying Kolb's experiential learning cycle for laboratory education. *Journal of Engineering Education*, *98*(3), 283–294.

Askeland, G. A. (2003). Reality-play – experiential learning in social work training: A teaching model. *Social Work Education*, *22*(4), 351–362.

American Academy of Social Work and Social Welfare. (n.d.). *Grand challenges for social work*. http://aaswsw.org/grand-challenges-initiative/

Anderson, D. K., & Harris, B. M. (2015). Teaching social welfare policy: A comparison of two pedagogical approaches. *Journal of Social Work Education*, *41*(3), 511–526. www.cswe.org/CSWE/publications/journal/

Angelini, M. L. (2016). Integration of the pedagogical models "simulation" and "flipped classroom" in teacher instruction. *SAGE Open*, *6*(1). doi:10.1177/2158244016636430

Backlund, P., & Hendrix, M. (2013). Educational games-are they worth the effort? A literature survey of the effectiveness of serious games. *Games and Virtual Worlds for Serious Application (VS-GAMES)*, *5*, 1–8.

Brookfield, S. D. (1996). *Understanding and facilitating adult learning: A comprehensive analysis of principles and effective practices*. Open University Press.

Council of Social Work Education (CSWE). (2022). *2022 Educational policy and accreditation standards (EPAS)*. Author. www.cswe.org/accreditation/standards/2022-epas/

Crawford, C., Valentine-Phillips, V., Delavega, E., & Blackwell, N. (2013, October 31–November 3). *Candy and taxes: Teaching tax policy in the social work curriculum*. Poster presented at the Annual Program Meeting, Council on Social Work Education.

de Smale, S., Overmans, T., Jeuring, J., & van de Grint, L. (2015). The effect of simulations and games on learning objectives in tertiary education: A systematic review. In *Games and Learning Alliance 4th International Conference*. GALA.

Delavega, E. (2016). The earned income tax credit: Estimating non-claims rates among eligible participants and why it matters to social workers. *Journal of Policy Practice*, *15*(3), 145–161.

Delavega, E., & Reyes, K. (2019). The ethics of financial social work. *Journal of Social Work Values and Ethics*, *16*(2).

Dooley, J., Sellers, S., & Gordon-Hempe, C. (2009). Lemons to lemonade: How five challenges in teaching macro practice helped to strengthen our course. *Journal of Teaching in Social Work*, *29*, 431–448.

Doran, J. K., & Bagdasaryan, S. (2018). Infusing financial capability and asset building content into a community organizing class. *Journal of Social Work Education*, *54*(1), 122–134. doi:10.1080/10437797.2017.1404523

Ferguson, H. (2018). How social workers reflect in action and when and why they don't: The possibilities and limits to reflective practice in social work.

Social Work Education, *37*(4), 4150427. doi:10.1080/02615479.2017.14 13083

Fordham, E. (2021, February 15). Deadly Texas winter storm leaves millions without power amid frigid temperatures. *Fox News*. www.foxnews.com/us/ texas-winter-storm-power-outage-snow-temperatures

Frey, J. J., Sherraden, M., Birkenmaier, J., & Callahan, C. (2017). Financial capability and asset building in social work education. *Journal of Social Work Education*, *53*(1), 79–83. doi:10.1080/10437797.2016.12 56170

Gillen, M., & Loeffler, D. N. (2012). Financial literacy and social work students: Knowledge is power. *Journal of Financial Therapy*, *3*(2), 28–38.

Grand Challenges Canada/Grand Défis Canada. (2011). *The grand challenges approach*. www.grandchallenges.ca/wp-content/uploads/2011/02/thegran dchallengesapproach.pdf

Greenfield, J. C., Ash, B. A., & Plassmeyer, M. (2018). Teaching social work and social policy in the era of hyperpartisanship. *Journal of Social Work Education*, *54*(3), 426–434.

Greenwood, E. (1956). Attributes of a profession. *Social Work*, *2*(3), 45–55.

Huerta-Wong, J. E., & Schoech, R. (2010). Experiential learning and learning environments: The case of active listening skills. *Journal of Social Work Education*, *46*(1), 85–101.

Interprofessional Education Collaborative Expert Panel. (2011). *Core competencies for interprofessional collaborative practice: Report of an expert panel*. Interprofessional Education Collaborative.

Kim, A. S., & Prado, A. (2019). *It's time to talk (and listen): How to have constructive conversations about race, class, sexuality, ability & gender in a polarized world*. New Harbinger Publications.

Kolb, A. Y., & Kolb, D. A. (2009). The learning way: Meta-cognitive aspects of experiential learning. *Simulation Gaming*, *40*(3), 297–327.

Kolb, D. A. (1984). The process of experiential learning. In Kolb, D. A. (Ed.), *Experiential learning: Experience as the source of learning and development*. Taylor and Francis (pp. 20–38).

Kwong, K. (2020). Teaching microaggressions, identity, and social justice: A reflective, experiential and collaborative pedagogical approach. *International Journal of Higher Education*, *9*(4), 184–198.

Loke, V., Birkenmaier, J., & Hageman, S. A. (2017). Financial capability and asset building in the curricula: Student perceptions. *Journal of Social Work Education*, *53*(1), 84–98. doi:10.1080/10437797.2016.1212751

McLoughlin, C., & Lee, M. J. W. (2008). The three P's of pedagogy for the networked society: Personalization, participation, and productivity. *International Journal of Teaching and Learning in Higher Education*, *20*(1), 10–27.

National Association of Social Workers. (2017). *NASW code of ethics*. www. socialworkers.org/About/Ethics/Code-of-Ethics/Code-of-Ethics-English

National Consumers League. (n.d.). *A brief look back on a hundred years of advocacy*. www.nclnet.org/about/history.htm

Oliver, C., Jones, E., Rayner, A., Penner, J., & Jamieson, A. (2017). Teaching social work students to speak up. *Social Work Education*, *36*(6), 702–714.

Reeves, R. V., & Rothwell, J. (2020). *Class and COVID: How the less affluent face double risks*. Brookings Institution. www.brookings.edu/blog/up-front/2020/03/27/class-and-covid-how-the-less-affluent-face-double-risks/

Reich, R. (2015). *Saving capitalism: For the many, not the few*. Vintage.

Sachs, J. (2017). *Building the new American economy: Smart, fair, and sustainable*. Columbia University Press.

Servon, L. (2017). *The unbanking of America*. Houghton Mifflin Harcourt.

Staller, K. M. (2014). Difficult conversations: Talking *with* rather than talking *at*. *Qualitative Social Work*, *13*(2), 167–175.

Wheelan, C. J. (2010). *Naked economics: Undressing the dismal science*. W. W. Norton.

Appendix 12A
EPAS Addressed in Grand Challenge #11

Building Financial Capability for All

The social work competencies for the 2022 Educational Policy and Accreditation Standards (EPAS) are the curricular guide for social work education. The inclusion of economics and financial capability as topics of study in social work is supported by three of the competencies described in the 2022 EPAS, Competency 2, Competency 3, and Competency 5. These social work education competencies promote understanding economics and the economic environment in research and practice at the micro and macro levels in various ways.

Competency 2, Competency 3, and Competency 5 are transcribed next, in *italics*, with relevant sections in bold. We then provide an explanation of the relevance of each competency to the inclusion of economics and financial capability in social work education.

> **Competency 2: Advance Human Rights and Social, Racial, Economic, and Environmental Justice.** *Social workers understand that* ***every person regardless of position in society has fundamental human rights.*** *Social workers are knowledgeable about the global intersecting and ongoing injustices throughout history that result in* ***oppression*** *and racism, including social work's role and response. Social workers critically evaluate the distribution of power and privilege in society in order to promote social, racial,* ***economic,*** *and environmental justice* ***by reducing inequities*** *and ensuring dignity and respect for all. Social workers advocate for and engage in strategies* ***to eliminate oppressive structural barriers to ensure that social resources, rights, and responsibilities are distributed equitably*** *and that civil, political,* ***economic,*** *social, and cultural human rights are protected.*

Social workers:

a. advocate for human rights at the individual, family, group, organizational, and **community system levels***; and*

b. engage in practices that advance human rights to promote social, racial, **economic***, and environmental justice.*

Competency 2 emphasizes the importance of social workers' ability to understand the ways in which economic theory and the economic context affects the Person in the Environment, as well as the ways and practices with which to demolish barriers, exploitation, and oppression, and advance the rights and opportunities of all people.

Competency 3: Engage Anti-Racism, Diversity, Equity, and Inclusion (ADEI) in Practice. *Social workers understand how racism and oppression shape human experiences and how these two constructs influence practice at the individual, family, group, organizational, and* **community levels** *and in* **policy** *and research. Social workers understand the pervasive impact of White supremacy and privilege and use their knowledge, awareness, and skills to engage in anti-racist practice. Social workers understand how diversity and intersectionality shape human experiences and identity development and affect equity and inclusion. The dimensions of diversity are understood as the intersectionality of factors including but not limited to age, caste, class, color, culture, disability and ability, ethnicity, gender, gender identity and expression, generational status, immigration status, legal status, marital status, political ideology, race, nationality, religion and spirituality, sex, sexual orientation, and tribal sovereign status. Social workers understand that this intersectionality means that a person's life experiences may include* **oppression, poverty, marginalization***, and alienation as well as* **privilege and power***. Social workers understand the* **societal and historical roots of social and racial injustices and the forms and mechanisms of oppression and discrimination***. Social workers understand cultural humility and recognize the extent to which a culture's structures and values, including social, economic, political, racial, technological, and cultural exclusions, may create privilege and power resulting in systemic oppression.*

Social workers:

a. demonstrate anti-racist and anti-oppressive social work practice at the individual, family, group, organizational, ***community****, research, and* ***policy*** *levels; and*

b. demonstrate cultural humility by applying ***critical reflection****, self-awareness, and self-regulation to manage the influence of bias,* ***power****, privilege, and values in working with clients and constituencies, acknowledging them as experts of their own lived experiences.*

Competency 3 highlights the importance of social workers' ability to recognize that people in poverty and who lack financial capability exist as a group with special needs and conditions, and recognize the challenges and limitations, as well as the perceptions of people who lack access to economic justice. Social workers seek to include them as part of practice of inclusion and valuing of diversity. Competency 3 compels social workers to understand the racist foundations of unfair economic practices, and how racism can lead to economic injustice such as covert redlining, undervaluing persons of color, the impact of racism on credit scores, and how economic practices that oppress the poor have their origin in racism, sexism, and xenophobia.

Competency 5: Engage in Policy Practice. *Social workers identify social policy at the local, state, federal, and global level that affects wellbeing, human rights and justice, service delivery, and access to social services. Social workers recognize the historical, social, racial, cultural,* ***economic****, organizational, environmental, and global influences that affect social policy. Social workers understand and critique the history and current structures of social policies and services and the role of policy in service delivery through* ***rights-based****, anti-oppressive, and anti-racist lenses.* ***Social workers influence policy formulation, analysis, implementation, and evaluation*** *within their practice settings with individuals, families, groups, organizations, and communities.* ***Social workers actively engage in and advocate for anti-racist and anti-oppressive policy practice to effect change in*** *those settings.*

Social workers:

*a. use social justice, anti-racist, and anti-oppressive lenses to assess how **social welfare policies affect the delivery of and access to social services**; and*

*b. **apply critical thinking to analyze, formulate, and advocate for policies that advance human rights and social, racial, economic, and environmental justice.***

Competency 5 promotes the importance of social workers' ability to understand the ways in which policies may exclude and oppress people, as well as the manner in which social workers may intervene in policy practice at all levels in order to protect the rights of all people and inclusion for all people in the fullness of economic life. Competency 5 connects economic policy to social welfare policy and to oppressive structures. Council on Social Work Education (EPAS 2022).

Appendix 12B

Candy and Taxes: Teaching Tax Policy in the Social Work Curriculum

Purpose

The Candy and Taxes (Crawford et al., 2013) game is designed to utilize cognitive-affective teaching techniques to demonstrate the different taxation schemes and their effect on various segments of the population.

Materials Needed

- 100 to 300 pieces of candy;
- Gallon-size and sandwich-size zipper baggies (depending on number of students/packets needed);
- Luck quintile cards;
- Distribution table (for instructor);
- Tax handouts for students.

Instructions

Each student in a MSW policy class is randomly assigned to a tax quintile, with the number of students in each quintile dependent on class size. Each quintile then receives a specific number of pieces of candy (representing income) based on the income distribution statistics in the US. See the distribution table, included, for the specific numbers of candy each student receives. Following the candy distribution different tax schemes (progressive, regressive, flat, "fair," etc.) are exemplified by taking and redistributing pieces of candy. Also note how many pieces of candy "the government" (you) keeps in order to provide services such as the military, roads, clean water, etc. Students are encouraged to express their opinions and feelings as each tax scheme is "implemented." Social work values and ethics need to be included in the discussion as well as basic concepts of economics. Point out that the students in the bottom quintile are not contributing their fair share of taxes many times, so have the class call them "moochers." At the end of the exercise, after you have completed the progressive tax scheme, point out that the students who started with the largest number of candies STILL have the largest number of candies, but now every student has at least four, and that the government has sufficient pieces to serve the community.

Before class buy candy (the better kinds are more effective because students want the candy and become emotionally involved) and distribute into Ziploc bags. You will need two (2) gallon-size bags and eight (8) or more sandwich-size bags depending on group size. Place a quintile assignment card into each bag as appropriate. On the day of class have students randomly pick a card and then distribute the candy from the top down. When students see the large bag the top student receives they become excited. They become disappointed soon after.

Appendix 12C

Candy Distribution Tables

Table 12.1 Candy Distribution Table – This Is How I Distributed 100 Pieces of Candy for a Class With Ten Students

Income			*Candies*		*Flat Tax*			*Proportional Tax*			*Progressive Tax*			*Redistribution*		*Wealth Inequality*	
Group	*Distribution (%) per Quintile*		*Per Quintile*	*Per Student*	*Candies Taken*	*Percent Tax*	*Candies Left*	*Candies Taken*	*Percent Tax*	*Candies Left*	*Candies Taken*	*Percent Tax*	*Candies Left*	*Candies Given*	*Candies Left*	*Wealth %*	*Candies*
1 Top 10%	51.2	27.5	28	28	1	4	27	7	25	21	16	57	12	0	12	86	258
2 Top Quintile B		23.7	24	24	1	4	23	6	25	18	13	54	11	0	11		
3 Second Quintile A	23.2		23	13	1	8	12	4	31	9	6	46	7	0	7	10	30
4 Second Quintile B				10	1	10	9	3	30	7	4	40	6	0	6		
5 Third Quintile A	14.3		14	8	1	13	7	2	25	6	3	38	5	0	5	3.7	11
6 Third Quintile B				6	1	17	5	2	33	4	2	33	4	0	4		
7 Fourth Quintile A	8.2		8	4	1	25	3	1	25	3	0	0	4	0	4	0.2	0.6
8 Fourth Quintile B				4	1	25	3	1	25	3	0	0	4	0	4		
9 Bottom Quintile A	3.1		3	2	1	50	1	0	0	2	0	0	2	2	4	0.1	0.3
10 Bottom Quintile B				1	1	100	0	0	0	1	0	0	1	3	4		
Total	100	51.2	100	100	10			26			44			5	39	100	300

Table 12.2 Candy Distribution Table – This Is How I Distributed 300 Pieces of Candy for a Class With Ten Students

Income			*Candies*		*Flat Tax*			*Proportional Tax*			*Progressive Tax*			*Redistribution*		*Wealth Inequality*	
Group	*Distribution (%) per Quintile*		*Per Quintile*	*Per Student*	*Candies Taken*	*Percent Tax*	*Candies Left*	*Candies Taken*	*Percent Tax*	*Candies Left*	*Candies Taken*	*Percent Tax*	*Candies Left*	*Candies Given*	*Candies Left*	*Wealth %*	*Candies*
1 Top 10%	51.2	27.5	84	84	3	4	81	25	30	59	53	63	31	0	31	86	258
2 Top Quintile B		23.7	72	72	3	4	69	21	29	51	43	60	29	0	29		
3 Second Quintile A	23.2		69	40	3	8	37	12	30	28	22	55	18	0	18	10	30
4 Second Quintile B				29	3	10	26	9	31	20	13	45	16	0	16		
5 Third Quintile A	14.3		42	24	3	13	21	7	29	17	9	38	15	0	15	3.7	11
6 Third Quintile B				18	3	17	15	5	28	13	4	22	14	0	14		
7 Fourth Quintile A	8.2		24	14	3	21	11	4	29	10	1	7	13	0	13	0.2	0.6
8 Fourth Quintile B				10	3	30	7	3	30	7	0	0	10	3	13		
9 Bottom Quintile A	3.1		9	6	3	50	3	2	33	4	0	0	6	7	13	0.1	0.3
10 Bottom Quintile B				3	3	100	0	1	33	2	0	0	3	10	13		
Total	100	51.2	300	300	30			89			145			20	125	100	300

Table 12.3 Quintile Cards for Random ("Lucky") Assignment of Students to Quintiles

TOP 10%	TOP QUINTILE B
SECOND QUINTILE A	SECOND QUINTILE B
THIRD QUINTILE A	THIRD QUINTILE B
FOURTH QUINTILE A	FOURTH QUINTILE B
BOTTOM QUINTILE A	BOTTOM QUINTILE B
TOP QUINTILE C	SECOND QUINTILE C
THIRD QUINTILE C	FOURTH QUINTILE C
BOTTOM QUINTILE C	RANDOM QUINTILE CARDS

Make two copies, one for random assignment of students to quintiles, and another for the prepared candy bags.

Note there are additional cards marked "C" for large groups, but in that case, you will need to work the math.

Attachment 3

Tax Handouts for Students

Taxes are the money people pay the government and which fund the functions and services a country, state, or city provide.

"Taxes are what we pay for civilized society." Supreme Court Justice Oliver Wendell Holmes, Jr. (1841–1935).

The Federal Income Tax was instituted through the 16th Amendment in 1913.

Everyone Pays Taxes

The 47% don't pay taxes Mitt Romney famously said in 2012. This is not true. All people pay taxes: sales taxes, fees, property taxes, and federal taxes in the form of payroll taxes even when the effective tax rate on income is zero.

Types of Taxes

Proportional Taxes – Everyone pays the same percentage of income regardless of how much or how little income a person makes.

Progressive Taxes – Those people with larger incomes pay a greater percentage of their income in taxes.

Regressive Taxes – Every person pays the same amount, but those who have less income end up paying a much larger percentage of their income in taxes, while those with larger incomes pay a smaller percentage of their income in taxes.

Some Terms You Need to Know

- *Tax Rate* – The percentage (of income, of price, etc.) that is paid in taxes.
- *Statutory Tax Rate* – The official percentage that must be paid as tax. What is written.
- *Marginal Tax Rate* – The tax rate that applies to the next unit above a given threshold. The higher tax rate only applies to the portion of income, for instance, that is above a certain amount. Income below a certain amount is taxed at a lower tax rate.
- *Effective Tax Rate* – The final tax rate that is paid after all deductions and adjustments are made. Usually lower than the statutory tax rate.
- *Flat Tax* – A proportional tax rate.
- *Capped Flat Tax* – A flat tax that applies until a certain threshold is reached. After that, the tax stops, which results in a regressive tax.
- *Tax Deductions* – A reduction on the income subject to tax. A tax deduction of $11,000 reduces the taxable income a person must

base the tax on by $11,000, which may place the person in a lower tax bracket.

- *Tax Bracket* – A level from a certain income to a certain income for the purpose of imposing a progressive tax rate.

Common Taxes

- *Income Tax* – Tax paid on income earned.
- *Sales Tax* – A percentage of the purchase price of something that is paid on purchases above the price of the item.
- *Use Tax* – A sales tax that the seller does not collect but the buyer is obligated to report and pay (e.g., on interstate internet purchases).
- *Property Tax* – A tax paid on the value of a property. A percentage of the value of a property that must be paid as tax.
- *Excise Tax* – A sales tax imposed on the manufacturer or seller of something, who is then expected to raise the price of the product. This is different from a sales tax in that the tax is included in the price.
- *Payroll Taxes* – Taxes employers and employees pay as a percentage of wages, like Medicare or Social Security.
- *Estate Tax* – A percentage of the value of the estate a person leaves upon death that must be paid as tax. Most people are exempt because they are not rich enough. Also called a "death tax" to emphasize negative connotations, although it is probably the fairest type of tax.
- *Gift Tax* – A tax a person who makes a gift pays.
- *Licenses and Fees* – A form of tax in which a flat rate is paid to establish a business, obtain a license (driving, hunting), or have access to land or other property or resources. Highly regressive.
- *Transient Occupancy Taxes* – Hotel taxes.
- *Severance Taxes* – Taxes paid to extract a natural resource that is a public good.
- *Capital Gains Tax* – A tax imposed on the value gained by an asset (the difference between purchase price and current value). A tax mostly on investments, stocks, bonds, gold, and the like.
- *Corporate Tax* – A tax imposed on the assets or profits of a corporation established as such.
- *Value Added Tax* – Excise tax that is paid by the ultimate consumer in the form of higher prices. From the perspective of the seller, the VAT only adds to the price (value) of a product or service but is not a tax.

The Earned Income Tax Credit (EITC): A 2021 Primer

Compiled by Dr. Elena Delavega, Professor, University of Memphis School of Social Work

What Is the EITC and Who Qualifies for FY 2021 (Jan. 1, 2021, to Dec. 31, 2021) July9–2 The Earned Income Tax Credit (EITC) is a refundable tax credit American citizens or permanent residents can receive if they have earned any income in a fiscal year (any kind of work for which they have received payment. Must be work **$10,000** or less), and the filer must be either a head of household or married filing jointly, and not having been claimed as a dependent on another return. If the filer does not have dependent children, he or she must be between the ages of 25 and 65.

Minimum Requirements to Claim the EITC

- You must be a citizen of the United States and must live in the US for more than half of the year;
- You must have earned income for the tax year and a valid Social Security number (SSN);
- You can't be a qualifying child on another return;
- You can't use the married filing separate (MFS) filing status (see 2021 Exception later).*

Income Thresholds to Receive the EITC for FY 2021

- $51,464 ($57,414 married filing jointly) with three or more qualifying children;
- $47,915 ($53,865 married filing jointly) with two qualifying children;
- $42,158 ($48,108 married filing jointly) with one qualifying child;
- $21,430 ($27,380 married filing jointly) with no qualifying children;
- *Investment income* must be *$10,000* or less for the year;
- Legal Same-Sex Marriages Will Be Recognized for Federal Tax Purposes.

Tax Year 2021 Maximum Credit

- *$6,728* with three or more qualifying children;
- *$5,980* with two qualifying children;
- *$3,618* with one qualifying child;
- *$1,502* with no qualifying children.

To Claim the EITC

- Filer with a qualifying child must use Form EIC and attach it to Form 1040A or 1040.
- Filer with no qualifying children and between the ages of 25 and 65 must use **Form 1040EZ** or the 1040A or 1040.
- Taxpayers claiming the EITC who file Married Filing Separately must meet the eligibility requirements under the special rule in the American Rescue Plan Act (ARPA) of 2021.

Warning

- If filer claims the EIC when not eligible, filer will be barred from claiming the EITC for up to ten years. If error was due to "reckless or intentional disregard of the EIC rules," filer will be penalized for two years even if otherwise eligible to claim the EITC. If action is found to be fraudulent, exclusion from EITC will be ten years and other penalties may apply.
- If EIC claim was disallowed or reduced for reasons other than math or clerical errors after 1996, filer may need to file Form 8862 before the Internal Revenue Service allows filer to use the credit again.

Information retrieved from: www.irs.gov/credits-deductions/individuals/earned-income-tax-

13 Reduce Extreme Economic Inequality

Mary E. Fortson-Harwell and Lauren Marlotte

Introduction

The wealth gap between the richest and poorest Americans more than doubled from 1989 to 2016 (Horowitz et al., 2020). With its relationship to social mobility across generations, this wealth gap has become so extreme that the term the "Great Gatsby Curve" is often used to describe the phenomena (Krueger, 2012). Indeed, advantages and disadvantages afforded to Americans are becoming increasingly determined by the wealth of one's childhood caregivers. Access to social mobility and opportunity is moving farther and farther out of reach for those on the end of the Great Gatsby Curve. For example, the top 1 percent of wealth holders in the United States have at least three times as much wealth as the bottom 80 percent (Wolff, 2015). Of the over 328 million people living in the United States (US), 38.1 million are living in poverty (United States Census Bureau, 2019a). These economic disparities disproportionately affect families of color, particularly Black households, who earned ten times less than Caucasian/white households in 2016 (McIntosh et al., 2020), amongst other disparities. When comparing all Black men to all white men, Black men earn 51 cents for every dollar white men earn, which represents a gap that has remained constant since 1950 (Bayer & Charles, 2018). Working cisgender women earn just 82 cents for every dollar cisgender men earn and the gap between women of color is larger than for white women (United States Census Bureau, 2019b). Of course, wages and employment are among the many factors that impact economic inequality.

Thirteen Grand Challenges for Social Work

The Grand Challenges for Social Work identify the need to reduce extreme economic inequality as essential to building a just society

DOI: 10.4324/9781003308263-16

(Uehara et al., 2014). First published in 2014, "the Grand Challenges for Social Work are designed to focus a world of thought and action on the most compelling and critical social issues of our day" (Uehara et al., 2014, p. 2). In the years since its publication, advances in the Grand Challenges have been driven by educational and policy initiatives at the local, state, and national levels. Members of this Grand Challenge called for strategies to reduce extreme economic inequality through the expansion of job creation, access to childcare, support for the Earned Income Tax Credit, and cash transfer programs (Grand Challenges in Social Work [GCSW], 2021). Members also advocated for strengthening labor standards and creating new policies to encourage inclusive, progressive wealth building (GCSW, 2021).

Social work curricular is rich with opportunities to incorporate ways to develop "a new social contract to reduce inequalities in wealth and income, and to close the financial gaps among racial groups, and between men and women" (GCSW, 2021, p. 32). The current chapter situates the Grand Challenge into generalist practice social work courses including Human Behavior in the Social Environment (HBSE), social welfare policy, and Social Practice courses. Practical tools are presented to help educators incorporate evidence-based methods to reduce extreme economic inequality into lectures, activities, assignments, coursework, and classroom discussions. In doing so, the authors of this chapter address diversity, equity, and inclusion within content delivery, and conclude with a discussion of evaluation and assessment for the topic.

Background

The official poverty measure in the United States was developed in the 1960s during President Lyndon B. Johnson's *War on Poverty* (Semega et al., 2019). Although the percentage of people living in poverty has declined since that time,[1] the war on poverty has certainly not been won. Staggering income inequality has continued to grow, despite these reductions.

Extreme income inequality is not a new phenomenon in the United States. In 1915, the top 0.01 percent of income earners recorded more than 400 times the income of the average wage earner (Piketty & Saez, 2003). More than a century later, in 2017, that earning gap has risen to 517 percent (Dungan, 2020). This inequality of economic conditions is not only seen in wages, however. The availability of employment that pays a living wage and employment that provides retirement, health, and sick leave benefits is also unequally doled out across the American population.

In August 2020, Black Americans were nearly twice as likely to be unemployed than white Americans, at 13 percent and 7.3 percent, respectively (Bureau of Labor Statistics, 2020). This same report also showed higher rates of unemployment for Asian and Latinx populations, with unemployment at around 10.6 percent for both demographic groups. Unemployment also unevenly impacts income categories, a factor felt acutely during the COVID-19 pandemic. Findings from a Pew Research Center survey made available in April 2020 indicated that 44 percent of upper income respondents reported a household member having recently lost their job or had their wages cut, while 80 percent of lower income respondents indicated the same (Parker et al., 2020). Women were more significantly impacted by job loss in response to the COVID-19 pandemic, particularly Latinx and Black women (Bureau of Labor Statistics, May 2020). Black and Latinx men were also disproportionally impacted by unemployment considering the pandemic (Falk et al., 2021).

Income has impacts beyond finances. Adverse Childhood Experiences (ACEs), which are associated with a host of mental and physical health challenges, are more likely to be experienced by children living in lower-income households (Walsh et al., 2019). Income inequality has long been shown to account for an increase in mortality rates across ages and geographic areas (Daly et al., 1998; Lynch et al., 1998; Ross et al., 2000; Shi et al., 2003). In addition to increased mortality rates, there are also psychological effects of income inequality. Income inequality has a detrimental effect on overall well-being and sense of trust in society (Buttrick & Oishi, 2017), in addition to general happiness (Oishi et al., 2011; Sommet et al., 2018). These psychological effects tend to translate into health effects over time. For example, income inequality is strongly correlated with coronary heart disease, malignant neoplasms, and infant mortality, in addition to total mortality rates (Kawachi et al., 1997). Furthermore, income inequality has detrimental effects across generations, reducing mobility and flexibility intergenerationally (Aiyar & Ebeke, 2020).

Income Inequality and Social Work Curricula

According to the Council on Social Work Education (CSWE), generalist social work practice "is grounded in the liberal arts and the person-in-environment framework" (2022, p. 13). Social work education and practice consists of a variety of skills, theories, and prevention and intervention methods to assess, engage, and intervene with "diverse individuals, families, groups, organizations, and communities based on scientific inquiry and best practices" (CSWE, 2022, p. 13). To accomplish this goal, social work curricula often include generalist practice courses such as Human Behavior and the Social Environment (HBSE), social welfare policy, and Social Work Practice courses. The following three sections will situate the Grand Challenge of reducing extreme income inequality within these curricula.

Human Behavior and the Social Environment

This course generally provides students with critical perspectives on a variety of theoretical frameworks used to understand regularities and irregularities in human development and functioning across the life span. One important focus of the curriculum, and an area where discussions of the Grand Challenge of reducing extreme economic inequality could be introduced, is the ecological-developmental approach. The ecological-developmental approach emphasizes the ways in which culture and the broader social environment shape human behavior and identity, both in terms of general patterns and unique configurations (Bronfenbrenner, 1979, 1986).

Reducing extreme economic inequality can be seamlessly introduced into HBSE in a variety of ways. For example, as particular attention in HBSE is paid to culture, race, class, gender, and sexual orientation as dynamic social constructions, these concepts, particularly those of socio-economic status and the inequality of poverty across race/ethnicity and gender, can be introduced as sources of both oppression and strength at all levels of social systems. Additionally, as a second focus of HBSE generally includes the biological, psychological, and spiritual person and the interrelatedness of emotion and cognition, neurobiology, and the social environment, discussions regarding the association of income inequality and health and well-being indicators are at home in HBSE curricula.

Social Welfare Policy

Social work courses on social welfare policy tend to provide an overview of United States social welfare policies and programs, which may begin with the New Deal and progress to the study of major current social welfare issues. Social welfare policy type courses can also explore the political and social contexts in which social policies and programs are developed and implemented, and the conflicts and reform efforts that arise throughout policy making processes. As explored in the teaching practices section of this chapter, the Grand Challenge of reducing extreme economic inequality is particularly well suited for integration within social welfare policy curricula through exploration of economic policies and their impact on poverty.

Social Work Practice Courses

Social Work Practice courses typically focus on the development of knowledge and practice skills necessary to understand planned change and use impactful, solution-focused problem-solving methods. Practice courses are often designed to socialize students into the social work profession, prepare students to enter their field experience courses, and promote the development of professional values, ethics, behaviors, and competence. Providing a concrete opportunity for students to integrate, synthesize, and apply classroom learning in the practice environment, Social Work Practice courses can provide multiple opportunities to explore the Grand Challenge of reducing extreme economic inequality. For example, instructors may choose to explore how socio-economic status impacts access to and delivery of social work services, in addition to underscoring the relationship between reducing economic disparities with the social work value of social justice (National Association of Social Workers [NASW], 2017).

Teaching Practices

As introduced in the previous section, the Grand Challenge of reducing extreme economic inequality is particularly well suited for integration within social welfare policy curricula. Educators may seamlessly incorporate this Grand Challenge into the social welfare policy curriculum within modules discussing poverty and public assistance policy. In the sections that follow, the authors will discuss specific ways to incorporate the Grand Challenge of reducing extreme economic inequality into social welfare policy curricula through exercises, class discussions, and didactic lectures. In addition, the following sections will explore considerations for preparing students to engage in the topic as well as matters of diversity, equity, and inclusion.

Grand Challenge-Incorporated Learning Objectives

The following learning objectives are examples of ways in which educators may incorporate economic justice-focused language into their courses. Sample learning objectives include, but are not limited to:

- Identify and analyze historical policies that have exacerbated extreme economic inequalities (e.g., redlining);
- Contrast the major governmental approaches to poverty and their implications for public policy and poverty reduction;
- Discuss the effectiveness of federal approaches to address diversity and recognize bias in public assistance and social insurance policies and programs;
- Reflect on the role of power and privilege in creating, exacerbating, and addressing economic inequality throughout society and within one's own personal experiences.

Additionally, the reader is referred to Appendix 13A for the Council of Social Work Education's *2022 Educational Policy and Accreditation Standards* (EPAS) as these could be applied to this chapter.

Preparing Students for Learning and Engagement

When introducing the Grand Challenge of reducing extreme income inequality, instructors should engage students by using best teaching practices and while creating a trauma-informed learning environment (Felitti et al., 1998). As student learning is generated and sustained by their own motivation (Ambrose et al., 2010), engaging and motivating students to invest in reducing income equality will be beneficial. Motivation may be achieved through connecting the Grand Challenge with the core values of the social work profession, as presented by the NASW Code of Ethics (NASW, 2017). Particularly, reducing extreme income inequality can be explicitly linked with the NASW values of service and social justice, making concrete for students the ways in which engaging with policy to reduce extreme income inequality aligns with the goals of the social work profession to help people in need, address social problems, and challenge social injustice (2017).

In Teaching Tolerance (n.d.), the Southern Poverty Law Center recommends that the instructor evaluate their own identity, power, privilege, and biases to thoughtfully engage students in difficult discussions and in creating a trauma-informed classroom. This classroom resource may also be adapted to suggest that one way to start this evaluation is to assess one's comfortability with talking about economic privilege, the hardest part of talking about economic privilege, and the most beneficial part of talking about economic privilege. The instructor will benefit from some degree of comfortability and willingness to approach difficult topics, although there may be a need to consult the literature beyond this chapter and/or seek out additional consultation and support if the instructor, themselves, feel increasing discomfort when approaching these discussion topics.

Creating a trauma-informed classroom, while broaching difficult topics explored when introducing the Grand Challenge of reducing extreme economic inequality, may be informed by the Substance Abuse and Mental Health Services Administration's (SAMHSA) guiding principles of a trauma-informed approach (2014). These principles emphasize safety; trust; collaboration; empowerment; choice; cultural, historical, and gender issues; and acknowledgment of power differentials. Instructors should be clear about expectations and assignments, such as how students will and will not be evaluated. If the instructor asks students to present or write about their cultural background, including their economic status, students should be made aware that they will not be evaluated on the degree to which they process the impact of power and privilege on their cultural identity, but that they will be evaluated on completion of the assignment. Emphasis on choice within assignments should be provided for students. For example, students should be given agency to choose how much to share about their personal background and experiences.

Addressing Diversity, Equity, and Inclusion

Diversity, equity, and inclusion characterize and shape the human experience and are critical to the formation and development of identity. For clients and systems impacted by poverty and economic injustice, the intersectionality of multiple factors shapes clients' lived experiences and exacerbates challenges. Yet, these same factors also form the foundation for resilience building and identity development. When teaching social work students ways to reduce extreme income inequality, it is critical that students become aware that economic inequality is experienced differently across demographic categories, particularly impacting women and people of color and Indigenous People most severely.

While learning to practice with cultural humility to engage clients and constituencies as experts of their own experience, students should be encouraged to explore aspects of their own identity, which may impact their learning. Instructors are encouraged to be mindful of the diverse experiences of students within the learning environment and approach discussions from a competency perspective, rather than a deficit perspective, anchoring classroom exercises and activities in the CSWE 2022 Educational Policy Competency 2, Engage Diversity, Equity, and Inclusion in Practice (see Appendix 13A).

Lecture Material Highlights

Although social welfare policy courses often rank amongst students' least favorite classes (Popple & Leighninger, 1998; Wolk et al., 1996), research suggests that connecting social welfare policy to students' field experiences may help make the connection between policy and practice more salient (Anderson & Harris, 2005). Considering this evidence base, lecture materials infusing the Grand Challenge of reducing extreme income inequality into social welfare policy courses should highlight the link between policy and students' work with clients and client systems in their field practice experience as well as in the future.

When setting the stage for the discussion of income inequality and policy in the United States, it is important that instructors begin with a review of the dynamics and history of poverty and economic vulnerability within America. Income inequality has deep roots in the United States. The wealth gap between the richest and poorest Americans, while a more prominent discussion in recent years, has more than doubled from 1989 to 2016 (Horowitz et al., 2020). In fact, the vast gap in wages has persisted and expanded over the past century (Piketty & Saez, 2003; Dungan, 2020).

One topic that could both resonate with students and also portray economic inequality is student loan debt. Student loan debt is a problem facing more students today than ever before. In the past 20 years, student loan debt has quadrupled (Fry, 2014). Not surprisingly, students of color are greatly impacted by student loan debt, particularly Black students. Black students are less likely to possess family wealth and are more likely to acquire more debt (Center for Responsible Lending, 2019). Black students then have a more difficult time obtaining gainful employment to pay off loans (Addo et al., 2016) and are paid the least after graduation (Velez et al., 2019). Other students of color suffer as well. Velez et al. (2019) found that Latinx students are less likely than white students to complete college and take longer to graduate when they do complete college. Furthermore, Latinx individuals were found to earn less than white individuals with similar levels of education, although Black individuals earn the least.

As social work students are exposed to the profession, learners will likely find themselves working with the most vulnerable populations within their field experience. The impact of extreme income inequality may be made salient in classroom discussions through an exploration of the ways in which poverty impacts demographic groups in varied and often unequal ways. This lack of equity may be further applied through the presentation of relevant government policies and programs, and discussion of the individuals and families who tend to rely most consistently on these programs.

For example, instructors may highlight the development of policies and programs addressing poverty in the United States, from the Elizabethan Poor Laws of the 1600s (DiNitto & Johnson, 2016). As noted by the authors, these early laws meant to address poverty assigned value to the worth of the individual utilizing government programs, from the "deserving" to the "undeserving" poor. Although these terms have since fallen out of use in formal policy making, public sentiment towards those who utilize public assistance programs continues to weigh the perceived merit of the individual. Indeed, attitudes towards social welfare policies and programs since the 1600s still often categorize those who rely upon public assistance as "lazy" and undesiring of hard work (Hasenfeld & Rafferty, 1989), despite evidence to the contrary (DeSante, 2013; Tang & Smith-Brandon, 2001). See Appendix 13B for additional economic-related policies and programs, which instructors may choose to explore in their course.

Facilitating Class Exercises and Discussions

An essential element to learning is to practice active learning to gain skills and implement practices (Beidas et al., 2009; Herschell et al., 2010; Rakovshik & McManus, 2010; Sholomskas et al., 2005; Walters et al., 2005), such as case studies, discussion, and writing exercises. It is not sufficient for students to receive passive information through listening to lecture materials and reading alone. It is particularly important when learning about sensitive topics for students to mull over the impact on their personal experiences and opinions as well as both sides to a policy argument. The following two exercises explore ways in which instructors may engage students in active learning when incorporating the Grand Challenge of reducing extreme economic inequality into their social welfare policy course.

Exercise 1

One exercise that may be incorporated into courses with a social justice perspective is a "Privilege Walk," as originally adapted from Peggy McIntosh's work on white privilege and male privilege (1988, 1989). The Privilege Walk is typically conducted by having students stand in a line, side by side, and facing the same direction. The course instructor then reads out a variety of statements indicating some sort of privilege, such as, "I grew up speaking English as my first language" or "I see my race reflected positively in most movies and television shows that I watch." See Appendix 13C for an example of statements separated into categories that relate specifically to economic inequality. Students are then asked to take a step forward or back if the statement read reflects their experiences. It is important to follow this activity with a discussion on the students' perspectives and feelings during the activity as well as the goal and intentions of what the activity represents.

This exercise may be used in a variety of classes and contexts; however, it is important to note that the exercise does pose challenges from a trauma-informed perspective. These challenges include removing choice from students in whether to disclose aspects of themselves, their identities, and/or their lived experiences, as well as potentially further marginalizing already marginalized populations by using their lives as a teaching tool for others. This exercise may be modified and utilized in a more sensitive and trauma-informed way. A further discussion of ways to modify this exercise in a more trauma-informed way for use as a teaching tool in social welfare policy courses may be found in Appendix 13D.

Exercise 2

Another exercise that instructors may explore in incorporating the Grand Challenge of reducing extreme income inequality is through a policy debate. The instructor will introduce this exercise by asking students to prepare an outline of a policy to reduce or eliminate student loan debt as a method to reduce extreme economic inequality or a proposed policy change to decrease wage gaps between women and men. Instructors will direct students to include the parameters around reducing or eliminating student loan debt and the source of funding or the method to reduce wage gaps and fiscal implications. Then, students will argue both for and against their policy, while discussing the pros and cons of a federal or local approach to address the issue and ways this may address diversity and equity. Alternatively, students might argue for and against a predetermined policy provided by the instructor or exchange policies with another classmate and argue against it. If course time allows, the instructor may choose to devote a synchronous course session to this assignment on the date that the assignment is due, through randomly assigning students to groups of proponents and opponents of the policy and engaging in a thoughtful, respectful debate to further collaborative learning.

Managing Difficult Classroom Conversations

Utilizing a trauma-informed approach to setting up the classroom environment minimizes the potential that students or instructors will be re-traumatized as a part of a thoughtful discussion. This approach promotes a safe environment for the instructor as well as the students and sets clear expectations. Instructors are encouraged to discuss with students that it is likely that uncomfortable feelings will emerge when discussing economic inequalities and related issues. The instructor should facilitate a discussion around the discomfort that any discussion about power and privilege will likely evoke, notably, for those who have benefited from privilege.

Instructors are encouraged to acknowledge these emotions in the classroom and invite students to sit with their discomfort rather than avoiding it. Students should be encouraged to practice active listening with their peers and to pause before responding, even if involved in a heated debate, for example, if engaging in the synchronous session debate discussed in Exercise 2. Instructors should also urge students to allow compassion and thoughtfulness to guide their communication and to assume good intentions as well as a willingness to understand one another (Teaching Tolerance, n.d.). The Teaching Tolerance resource also outlines strategies to support instructors in managing strong student emotions. Educators must acknowledge that implicit bias happens both in and outside of the classroom. Implicit bias is most likely to happen when there is limited time, limited knowledge, and increased stress or a heightened emotional state. Instructors can take care to provide adequate time, information, and decrease stress around recognizing and addressing implicit bias.

Evaluation of Learning

As with all learning, evaluating the effectiveness of incorporating the Grand Challenge of reducing extreme economic inequality into the social work curricula is critical in determining students' mastery of the content. An instructor may approach evaluation through several means, including substantive discussion and class participation, quizzes, written and oral assignments, and policy exercises (specifically for Social Work Policy courses).

Class Discussions and Participation

Social work policy courses provide ample opportunity to evaluate student learning within the context of dynamic discussions regarding current and historical policies and legislative agendas. Instructors seeking to incorporate the Grand Challenge of reducing extreme economic inequality can engage students in interactive discussions comparing intended and unintended consequences of social and economic policies, in addition to exploring equality and equity across local, state, and national legislation. Of course, class discussions may expand to discussions of policies across the globe, including how nations outside of the United States do, or do not, address income inequality and what lessons may be derived from such efforts.

When approaching these discussions, instructors may choose a variety of policies impacting income inequality, including the minimum wage and wage gap, unemployment and underemployment, and employment benefits and access to substantive employment in general. Instructors may also choose to explore policies impacting wealth and finances in general, including home ownership, banking, tax credits, and childcare allowances/availability. Instructors may further evaluate students' mastery of a social work perspective when discussing these topics by comparing policies with the core social work values as presented by the NASW (2017). In doing so, instructors may choose to ask students to explore whether and how particular policies align with the NASW core values of service, social justice, dignity and worth of the person, importance of human relationships, integrity, and competence, focusing most intently on the values of dignity and worth of the person and social justice. If a policy does not align with these values, students may be asked to explore how a particular policy may be amended or implemented differently to promote equality in a more substantive way.

Written Assignments and Policy Exercises

Evaluation of student learning within a social work policy course is particularly meaningful through policy analysis. Two such ways to evaluate learning related to the incorporation of the Grand Challenge of reducing extreme income inequality is through assignments asking students to analyze economic policies at either the local, state, and/or national level. These assignments may either include a larger policy analysis brief, where students are asked to take the position of a policy analyst and thoroughly analyze the policy, or a smaller, one-to-two-page exercise asking students to concisely provide a snapshot analysis of a particular economic policy. In each case, students may be asked to analyze if and how a particular economic policy reduces or exacerbates income inequality and provide recommendations for how the policy may be improved.

Conclusion

Power, privilege, and advantages afforded to Americans are becoming increasingly determined by the wealth of one's childhood caregivers. Access to social mobility and opportunity is moving farther and farther out of reach for many. Social work educators are uniquely poised to help students become better equipped to address the challenges associated with poverty and inequality (Uehara et al., 2014). Throughout the curricula, social work educators can work to broaden students' understanding of privilege and poverty, cultural and sociodemographic considerations, and policies and practices that thwart the problems associated with it. In doing so, educators will not only be actively engaging their students in dynamic learning, but they will also be further aligning their course with the CSWE Educational Policy and Accreditation Standards (2022). Reducing extreme economic inequality is an important Grand Challenge and opportunities abound, as discussed in this chapter, for incorporating social justice education and problem-solving to reduce inequality within social work curricula.

Note

1 For example, 23 percent of children were living below the federal poverty level in 1964 as compared with 14.4 percent in 2019 (US Census Bureau, 2019a).

References

Addo, F. R., Houle, J. N., & Simon, D. (2016). Young, Black, and (Still) in the Red: Parental wealth, race, and student loan debt. *Race and Social Problems*, *8*, 64–76. https://doi.org/10.1007/s12552-016-9162-0

Aiyar, S., & Ebeke, C. (2020). Inequality of opportunity, inequality of income and economic growth. *World Development, 136*, 105115. https://doi.org/10.1016/j.worlddev.2020.105115

Ambrose, S., Bridges, M., DiPietro, M., Lovett, M., & Norman, M. (2010). *How learning works: Seven research-based principles for smart teaching.* Jossey-Bass.

Anderson, D. K., & Harris, B. M. (2005). Teaching social welfare policy: A comparison of two pedagogical approaches. *Journal of Social Work Education, 41*(3), 511–526. https://doi.org/10.5175/JSWE.2005.200303120

Bayer, P., & Charles, K. K. (2018). Divergent paths: A new perspective on earnings differences between black and white men since 1940. *The Quarterly Journal of Economics, 133*(3), 1459–1501.

Beidas, R. S., Barmish, A. J., & Kendall, P. C. (2009). Training as usual: Can therapist behavior change after reading a manual and attending a brief workshop on cognitive behavioral therapy for youth anxiety? *The Behavior Therapist, 32*(5), 97–101.

Benefits.gov. (n.d.). Unemployment insurance. *Benefits.gov.* www.benefits.gov/benefit/91

Bronfenbrenner, U. (1979). *The ecology of human development: Experiments by nature and design.* Harvard University Press.

Bronfenbrenner, U. (1986). Ecology of the family as a context for human development: Research perspectives. *Developmental Psychology, 22*, 723–742. https://doi/10.1037/0012-1649.22.6.723

Bureau of Labor Statistics. (2020). Employment & Earnings. U.S. Establishment Survey Data. The Current Employment Statistics (CES).

Buttrick, N. R., & Oishi, S. (2017). The psychological consequences of income inequality. *Social and Personality Psychology Compass, 11*(3), e12304. https://doi/10.1111/spc3.12304

Center for Responsible Lending. (2019, September). *Quicksand: Borrowers of color & the student debt crisis.* www.responsiblelending.org/sites/default/files/nodes/files/research-publication/crl-quicksand-student-debt-crisis-jul2019.pdf

Child Support Enforcement Program, 42 U.S.C. § 651 *et seq.* (1975).

Council of Social Work Education (CSWE). (2022). *2022 Educational policy and accreditation standards (EPAS).* Author. www.cswe.org/accreditation/standards/2022-epas/

Daly, M. C., Duncan, G. J., Kaplan, G. A., & Lynch, J. W. (1998). Macro-to-micro links in the relation between income inequality and mortality. *The Milbank Quarterly*, 76(3), 315–339. doi:10.1111/1468-0009.00094.

DeSante, C. D. (2013). Working twice as hard to get half as far: Race, work ethic, and America's deserving poor. *American Journal of Political Science*, 57(2), 342–356. https://doi.org/10.1111/ajps.12006

DiNitto, D., & Johnson, D. (2016). *Social welfare: Politics and public policy* (8th ed.). Pearson Education, Inc.

Dungan, A. (2020). Individual income tax shares, tax year 2017. *Internal Revenue Service Statistics of Income Bulletin*. www.irs.gov/pub/irs-soi/soi-a-ints-id2003.pdf

Editors of Encyclopaedia Britannica. (2022, March 13). *New deal*. Britannica. www.britannica.com/event/New-Deal

Employment and Training Administration. (n.d.). *Workforce innovation and opportunity act*. U.S. Department of Labor. www.dol.gov/agencies/eta/wioa

Fair Labor Standards Act, 29 U.S.C. § 201 *et seq*. (1938). https://uscode.house.gov/view.xhtml?path=/prelim@title29/chapter8&edition=prelim

Falk, G., Carter, J. A., Nicchitta, I. A., Nyhof, E. C., & Romero, P. D. (2021). *Unemployment rates during the COVID-19 pandemic: In brief*. Congressional Research Service. https://fas.org/sgp/crs/misc/R46554.pdf

Felitti, V. J., Anda, R. F., Nordenberg, D., Williamson, D. F., Spitz, A. M., Edwards, V., Koss, M. P., & Marks, J. S. (1998). Relationship of childhood abuse and household dysfunction to many of the leading causes of death in adults. The adverse childhood experiences (ACE) study. *American Journal of Preventive Medicine*, *14*(4), 245–258. https://doi.org/10.1016/s0749-3797(98)00017-8\

Fry, R. (2014, October 7). *The growth in student debt*. Pew Research Center. www.pewsocialtrends.org/2014/10/07/the-growth-in-student-debt/

Grand Challenges in Social Work. (2021, January 21). *Progress and plans for the grand challenges: An impact report at year 5 of the 10-year initiative*. https://grandchallengesforsocialwork.org/grand-challenges-for-social-work/impact-report/

Kawachi, I., Kennedy, B. P., Lochner, K., & Prothrow-Stith, D. (1997). Social capital, income inequality, and mortality. *American Journal of Public Health*, *87*(9), 1491–1498. doi:10.2105/ajph.87.9.1491

Krueger, A. (2012). *The rise and consequences of inequality*. Presentation made at the Center for American Progress. www.whitehouse.gov/sites/default/files/krueger_cap_ speech_final_remarks.pdf

Hasenfeld, Y., & Rafferty, J. A. (1989). The determinants of public attitudes toward the welfare state. *Social Forces*, *67*(4), 1027–1048.

Herschell, A. D., Kolko, D. J., Baumann, B. L., & Davis, A. C. (2010). The role of therapist training in the implementation of psychosocial treatments: A review and critique with recommendations. *Clinical Psychology Review*, *30*(4), 448–466. doi:10.1016/j.cpr.2010.02.005

Horowitz, J. M., Igielnik, R., & Kochhar, R. (2020, January 9). *Trends in income and wealth inequality*. Pew Research Center. www.pewsocialtrends.org/2020/01/09/trends-in-income-and-wealth-inequality/#fn-27657–13

Internal Revenue Service. (2022, January 28). *EITC awareness day: Important changes mean more people qualify for credit that helps millions of Americans*. www.irs.gov/newsroom/eitc-awareness-day-important-changes-mean-more-people-qualify-for-credit-that-helps-millions-of-americans

Lilly Ledbetter Fair Pay Act, Pub. L. No. 111–2, 123 Stat. 5. (2009). www congress.gov/bill/111th-congress/senate-bill/181

Low-Income Housing, 42 U.S.C. § 1401 *et seq.* (1937). https://uscode.house gov/view.xhtml?path=/prelim@title42/chapter8&edition=prelim

Lynch, J. W., Kaplan, G. A., Pamuk, E. R., Cohen, R. D., Heck, K. E., Balfour J. L., & Yen, I. H. (1998). Income inequality and mortality in metropolitan areas of the United States. *American Journal of Public Health*, *88*(7), 1074–1080. doi:10.2105/ajph.88.7.1074

McIntosh, K., Moss, E., Nunn, R., & Shambaugh, J. (2020, February 27). *Examining the Black-white wealth gap*. The Brookings Institute. www.brookings.edu/blog/up-front/2020/02/27/examining-the-black-white-wealth-gap/

McIntosh, P. (1988). *White privilege and male privilege: A personal account of coming to see correspondences through work in women's studies* (Vol. 189). Wellesley College, Center for Research on Women.

McIntosh, P. (1989, July–August). White privilege: Unpacking the invisible knapsack. *Peace and Freedom Magazine*, 10–12.

National Association of Social Workers. (2017). *Read the code of ethics*. www. socialworkers.org/About/Ethics/Code-of-Ethics/Code-of-Ethics-English

Oishi, S., Kesebir, S., & Diener, E. (2011). Income inequality and happiness. *Psychological Science*, *22*(9), 1095–1100. https://doi.org/10.1177/0956797611417262

Parker, K., Horowitz, J., & Brown, A. (2020, April 21). *About half of lower-income Americans report household job or wage loss due to COVID-19*. Pew Research Center. www.pewsocialtrends.org/2020/04/21/about-half-of-lower-income-americans-report-household-job-or-wage-loss-due-to-covid-19/

Patient Protection and Affordable Care Act, Pub. L. No. 111–148, 124 Stat. 119. (2010). www.govinfo.gov/app/details/STATUTE-124/STATUTE-124-Pg119/summary

Personal Responsibility and Work Opportunity Reconciliation Act of 1996, Pub. L. No. 104–193, 110 Stat. 2105. (1996). www.congress.gov/104/plaws/publ193/PLAW-104publ193.pdf

Piketty, T., & Saez, E. (2003). Income inequality in the United States, 1913–1998. *The Quarterly Journal of Economics*, *118*(1), 1–41. https://doi.org/10.1162/00335530360535135

Popple, P., & Leighninger, L. (1998). *The policy-based profession: An introduction to social welfare policy for social workers*. Allyn & Bacon.

Quadagno, J. (1994). *The color of welfare: How racism undermined the war on poverty*. Oxford University Press.

Rakovshik, S. G., & McManus, F. (2010). Establishing evidence-based training in cognitive behavioral therapy: A review of current empirical findings and theoretical guidance. *Clinical Psychology Review*, *30*, 495–516. doi:10.1016/j.cpr.2010.03.004

Ross, N. A., Wolfson, M. C., Dunn, J. R., Berthelot, J. M., Kaplan, G. A., & Lynch, J. W. (2000). Relation between income inequality and mortality in Canada and in the United States: Cross sectional assessment using census data and vital statistics. *BMJ*, *320*(7239), 898–902. doi:10.1136/bmj.320.7239.898

Seattle Minimum Wage Ordinance, Seattle Ord. 124960, § 45. (2015). https://library.municode.com/wa/seattle/codes/municipal_code?nodeId=TIT14HURI_CH14.19MIWAMICORAEMPEWOSE

Seattle Minimum Wage Ordinance, Seattle Ord. 124960, § 45. (2022). https://library.municode.com/wa/seattle/codes/municipal_code?nodeId=TIT14HURI_CH14.19MIWAMICORAEMPEWOSE

Semega, J., Kollar, M., Creamer, J., & Mohanty, A. (2019). *Income and poverty in the United States: 2018*. United States Census Bureau. census.gov/library/publications/2019/demo/p60–266.html

Shi, L., Macinko, J., Starfield, B., Wulu, J., Regan, J., & Politzer, R. (2003). The relationship between primary care, income inequality, and mortality in US States, 1980–1995. *The Journal of the American Board of Family Practice*, *16*(5), 412–422. doi:10.3122/jabfm.16.5.412

Sholomskas, D. E., Syracuse-Siewert, G., Rounsaville, B. J., Ball, S. A., Nuro, K. F., & Carroll, K. M. (2005). We don't train in vain: A dissemination trial of three strategies of training clinicians in cognitive-behavioral therapy. *Journal of Consulting and Clinical Psychology*, *73*(1), 106. doi:10.1037/0022-006X.73.1.106

Sommet, N., Morselli, D., & Spini, D. (2018). Income inequality affects the psychological health of only the people facing scarcity. *Psychological Science*, *29*(12), 1911–1921. https://doi.org/10.1177/0956797618798620

Substance Abuse and Mental Health Services Administration. (2014). *SAMHSA's concept of trauma and guidance for a trauma-informed approach*. HHS Publication No. (SMA) 14–4884. Substance Abuse and Mental Health Services Administration.

Tang, T. L. P., & Smith-Brandon, V. L. (2001). From welfare to work: The endorsement of the money ethic and the work ethic among welfare recipients, welfare recipients in training programs, and employed past welfare recipients. *Public Personnel Management*, *30*(2), 241–260.

Tax Reduction Act, Pub. L. No. 94–12, 89 Stat. 6. (1975). www.congress.gov/bill/94th-congress/house-bill/2166/text/pl?overview=closed

Teaching Tolerance. (n.d.). *Let's talk: Discussing race, racism and other difficult topics with students*. Southern Poverty Law Center. www.learningforjustice.org/sites/default/files/general/TT%20Difficult%20Conversations%20web.pdf

Uehara, E. S., Barth, R. P., Olson, S., Catalano, R. F., Hawkins, J. D., Kemp, S., Nurius, P. S., Padgett, D. K., & Sherraden, M. (2014). *Identifying and tackling grand challenges for social work* (Grand Challenges for Social Work Initiative, Working Paper No. 3). American Academy of Social Work and Social Welfare.

United States Census Bureau. (2019a). *The history of the official poverty measure*. The United States Census Bureau. www.census.gov/topics/income-poverty/poverty/about/history-of-the-poverty-measure.html

United States Census Bureau. (2019b). *American community survey (ACS)*. United States Census Bureau. www.census.gov/programs-surveys/acs

United States Department of Labor. (2020). *The employment situation – August 2020*. www.bls.gov/news.release/pdf/empsit.pdf

U.S. Centers for Medicare & Medicaid Services. (n.d.). *Affordable care act (ACA)*. www.healthcare.gov/glossary/affordable-care-act/

U.S. Department of Health & Human Services. (2020, November 17). *Temporary assistance for needy families (TANF)*. Office of Family Assistance: An Office of the Administration for Children & Families. www.acf.hhs.gov/ofa/programs/temporary-assistance-needy-families-tanf

Velez, E. D., Lew, T., Thomsen, E., Johnson, K., Wine, J., & Cooney, J. (2019). *Baccalaureate and beyond (B&B:16/17): A first look at the employment and educational experiences of college graduates, 1 year later (NCES 2019–241)*. U.S. Department of Education, National Center for Education Statistics. https://nces.ed.gov/pubsearch/pubsinfo.asp?pubid=2019241

Walsh, D., McCartney, G., Smith, M., & Armour, G. (2019). Relationship between childhood socioeconomic position and adverse childhood experiences (ACEs): A systematic review. *Journal of Epidemiology & Community Health*, *73*, 1087–1093. doi:10.1136/jech-2019-212738

Walters, S. T., Matson, S. A., Baer, J. S., & Ziedonis, D. M. (2005). Effectiveness of workshop training for psychosocial addiction treatments: A systematic review. *Journal of Substance Abuse Treatment*, *29*(4), 283–293. doi:10.1016/j.jsat.2005.08.006

Wolff, E. N. (2015). *Inheriting wealth in America: Future boom or bust?* Oxford University Press.

Wolk, J., Pray, J., Weismiller, T., & Dempsey, D. (1996). Political practica: Educating social work students for policymaking. *Journal of Social Work Education*, *32*, 91–100. doi: https://doi.org/10.1080/10437797.1996.10672287

Appendix 13A

EPAS Addressed in Grand Challenge #12

Reduce Extreme Economic Inequality

Social work higher education requires a deep understanding and thorough awareness of the Educational Policy and Accreditation Standards (EPAS) published by the Council on Social Work Education (CSWE). The 2022 EPAS affords educators the opportunity to align the Grand Challenge of reducing extreme income inequality with CSWE policies and standards. EPAS that are aligned with this Grand Challenge include competencies 1, 2, 3, 5, and 8. The following sections discuss the ways in which these EPAS align with the Grand Challenge.

Competency 1: Demonstrate Ethical and Professional Behavior. emphasizes the importance of reflection, both of the instructor and the student, of one's identities, power, privilege, and biases in an ethical and professional social work practice. This reflection is crucial in using an anti-racist lens, as identified in this competency. Identities, power, privilege, and biases impact ethical decision-making and professional behavior as well as influence supervision, and consultation, which are at the core of this competency.

Competency 2: Advance Human Rights and Social, Racial, Economic, and Environmental Justice. As indicated in this competency, social workers "advocate for human rights of the individual, family, group, organizational, and community system levels; and engage in practices that advance human rights to promote social, racial, economic, and environmental justice" (CSWE, 2022). Engaging students in an effort to comprehensively understand the systemic nature of economic disparities in the United States in order to alleviate extreme income inequality concretely addresses this EPAS as this underpins the entire chapter. Social service solutions to advance economic justice may be incorporated into Social Work Practice courses.

Competency 3: Engage Anti-Racism, Diversity, Equity, and Inclusion in Practice. This competency indicates that social workers

> demonstrate anti-racist and anti-oppressive social work practice at the individual, family, group, organizational, community, research, and policy levels; and demonstrate cultural humility by applying critical reflection, self-awareness, and self-regulation to manage the influence of bias, power, privilege, and values in working with clients and constituencies, acknowledging them as experts of their own lived experiences.
>
> (CSWE, 2022)

This EPAS is particularly relevant when discussing systemic impacts of economic policies and opportunities made available to or withheld from marginalized populations in the United States. For instance, critical analysis of practices such as redlining, as well as utilizing Exercise 1 discussed in the chapter are particularly relevant and meaningful ways to address this EPAS within social work curricula. Further, the chapter encourages reflection of the impact of power and privilege experienced by each student as well as the instructor. The chapter also acknowledges the difficulties in these reflections as well as the discomfort experienced in approaching topics that have significant ties to the impact of racism.

Competency 5: Engage in Policy Practice. According to this competency, social workers

> use social justice, anti-racist, and anti-oppressive lenses to assess how social welfare policies affect the delivery of and access to social services; and apply critical thinking to analyze, formulate, and advocate for policies that advance human rights and social, racial, and economic, and environmental justice.
>
> (CSWE, 2022)

The Grand Challenge of reducing extreme income inequality is particularly well suited for engaging in policy practice. As discussed, social work educators may engage students in policy analysis assignments that encourage students to reflect on whether current or historical policies align with the values and ethics of the National Association of Social Workers (2017). When economic policies are found to limit social justice and promote racism and oppression, social work students can complete policy analysis assignments to advocate for policy changes and/or new policies that promote social justice at the systemic levels.

Competency 8: Intervene With Individuals, Families, Groups, Organizations, and Communities. Social workers "engage with clients and constituencies to critically choose and implement culturally responsive, evidence-informed interventions to achieve client and constituency goals; and incorporate culturally responsive methods to negotiate, mediate, and advocate with and on behalf of clients and constituencies" as indicated by this competency (CSWE, 2022). In addition to the courses discussed, social work field placement courses offer educators the opportunity to incorporate the Grand Challenge of reducing extreme income inequality within the social work curricula. In such a course, students and instructors may process together how socio-economic status impacts access to and delivery of social work services and the ways in which students may intervene with their clients and communities to ensure equal and equitable access to services, when considering economic factors.

Appendix 13B

Examples of Economic Policies and Programs

42 U.S.C. Chapter 8

Title 42 of the United States Code details federal policy governing public health and welfare. Chapter 8 of this title, commonly referred to as Section 8, outlines federal policy related to low-income housing (Low-Income Housing, 1937).

Child Support Legislation

While child support legislation is governed by individual states, federal policy allowing for the allocation of resources to states in the collection of child support can be examined by introducing federal policies such as part D of Title IV of the Social Security Act. The federal Child Support Enforcement Program allows for federal funding to states for the enforcement and collection of child support (Child Support Enforcement Program, 1975).

Earned Income Tax Credit

The Earned Income Tax Credit (EITC) was initially established in 1975 through the Tax Reduction Act (Tax Reduction Act, 1975). Since that time, EITC has become one of the largest antipoverty programs in the United States by providing refundable tax credits to families with low to moderate incomes (Internal Revenue Service, 2022).

Fair Labor Standards Act

The Fair Labor Standards Act created federal policy for minimum wage, overtime pay, child labor standards, and other employee protections (Fair Labor Standards Act, 1938).

Lilly Ledbetter Fair Pay Act

The Lilly Ledbetter Fair Pay Act of 2009 designated discriminatory pay as illegal under federal law and provides protections for workers to recover unlawfully withheld compensation if such practices occur (Lilly Ledbetter Fair Pay Act, 2009).

Minimum Wage Legislation

Minimum wage legislation is enacted at the federal, state, and local levels. Educators may choose to explore efforts to raise the minimum wage at all levels of government and the impact such policies may have on economic inequality. Students may find it particularly meaningful to research the history of minimum wage legislation in their city, while comparing their local government to other areas of the country and/or the world. For example, Seattle, Washington has one of the highest minimum wage laws in the United States, with workers receiving a minimum of $17.27 per hour at the time of this writing (Seattle Minimum Wage Ordinance, 2022).

Patient Protection and Affordable Care Act (PPACA or ACA)

Also known as the Affordable Care Act or, sometimes, "Obamacare," the Patient Protection and Affordable Care Act (2010) is a federal health care reform law with measures aiming to make health insurance more affordable and accessible, expand the Medicaid program, and lower the costs of health care in general (U.S. Centers for Medicare & Medicaid Services, n.d.).

Personal Responsibility and Work Opportunity Reconciliation Act (PRWORA)

The Personal Responsibility and Work Opportunity Reconciliation Act (PRWORA) sought to end welfare as it was previously known through programs such as block grants for Temporary Assistance for Needy Families (TANF) and strengthening the Child Support Enforcement Program. This legislation is rich in content for classroom discussions on intended and unintended consequences of policies and their impact on economic inequality.

Social Security Act and Amendments

The Social Security Act was initially an act for the government to provide aid to older people, then expanded to unemployed individuals and other disadvantaged Americans. However, not everyone benefited from the act in its inception, as certain job categories, such as workers in agricultural labor, domestic service, government employees, and many teachers, nurses, hospital employees, librarians, and social workers were excluded, which disproportionally excluded people of color (Quadagno, 1994).

Supplemental Security Income (SSI)

Supplemental Security Income (SSI) is government aid to adults and children who are US citizens or nationals or lawfully permitted aliens meeting additional requirements with a disability, blindness, or older adults who have income and resources below certain financial limits.

Temporary Assistance for Needy Families (TANF)

States use Temporary Assistance for Needy Families (TANF) to fund monthly cash assistance payments to low-income families with children, as well as a wide range of services. Each state operates their own grant funds. TANF is intended to be temporary and time limited. There are also requirements, such as working a minimum number of hours, to be eligible for TANF (U.S. Department of Health & Human Services, 2020).

The New Deal

The New Deal was a series of programs and projects, including the Social Security Administration, instituted during the Great Depression to stimulate the economy and provide assistance for unemployed people, youth, and older adults as well as reforms in industry, agriculture, finance, waterpower, labor, and housing (Editors of Encyclopedia Britannica, 2022).

Unemployment Insurance

Unemployment insurance provides financial benefits to eligible unemployed workers if they become unemployed through no fault of their own and meet certain eligibility requirements (Benefits.gov, n.d.).

Workers' Compensation

Workers' Compensation provides injured workers with wage replacement benefits, medical treatment, vocational rehabilitation, and other benefits for workers injured on the job (U.S. Department of Labor, n.d.).

Workforce Innovation and Opportunity Act

The Workforce Innovation and Opportunity Act was established in 2014 and uses federal funding to help job seekers, including youth and adults, access employment, education, training, and support services to get employment (Employment and Training Administration, n.d.).

Appendix 13C

Economic Privilege Walk Activity

Ask the group to line up. Read the following statements and ask participants to respond by taking a step forward or backward. This activity highlights aspects of economic privilege. Facilitate a discussion after the activity about the participants' experience.

- If you are employed, take one step forward
- If you were raised in a home that provided you with three meals a day, take one step forward
- If you had two parents/caregivers who were employed, take one step forward
- If you attended a private school or summer camp, take one step forward
- If you own a car or other vehicle, take one step forward
- If you have paid a late fee because of an overdrawn bank account, take one step back
- If you have health insurance, take one step forward
- If you primarily wore hand-me-down clothing as a child, take one step back
- If you have ever had to skip a meal or were hungry because you did not have enough money to buy food, take one step back
- If you didn't have to think about how much money you had when you purchased your last item of clothing, take one step forward
- If you were ever called names because of your economic status, take one step back
- If you were ever ashamed because of your clothes, method of transportation, or home, take one step back
- If you've used coupons to buy food, take one step back

If you or a family member had to take items that did not belong to you/them to eat or drink, take one step back
If you have built up credit, take one step forward
If someone ever coached you on building credit, take one step forward
If you have student loan debt, take one step back
If one or both of your parents is a professional (e.g., doctor, lawyer, etc.), take one step forward
If your family owned a home when you were growing up, take one step forward
If you were ever denied employment because of your race, ethnicity, gender, or sexual orientation, take one step back
If you have ever inherited money or property, take one step forward
If you have more than five dollars in your wallet, take one step forward

Appendix 13D

Trauma-Informed Modifications to the Privilege Walk Activity

One modification to this exercise may be included as a teaching tool in social welfare policy courses, to discuss a variety of social justice topics, including economic disparities. As opposed to conducting the exercise as a walking activity, this exercise may be conducted within the classroom with several decks of cards or, alternatively, with pieces of paper cut to resemble decks of cards to conserve economic resources. Ideally, each student is given a full deck of cards. The course instructor will advise students to keep the deck of cards to the side, as this is not yet their deck, but will be drawing for their deck. As the course instructor reads statements related to privilege, students are advised to draw or return a card from the deck if their life experiences match the statement read. Modifying the exercise in this way allows students to have privacy in their responses to each statement, and whether they choose to draw or return a card. This activity could also be done with each student being assigned a character (perhaps someone famous or a historical figure or fictional characters) and responding to the prompts from the character's point of view.

After the course instructor finishes reading the chosen number of statements, students are asked to count the cards in the deck that they are now holding. The course instructor then provides a metaphor that each person comes to "the table of life" with a deck of cards, although, privilege, power, and difference impacts who is playing with more cards and who is playing with less. A discussion is then held regarding how policies play a role in deciding who gets more cards than others or how the implementation of policies may mitigate the difference so that more individuals are playing with an equal hand.

Students are then invited, as they feel comfortable, to call out the number of cards in their deck. The course instructor will then write the numbers that the students call out on a white board, black board, or flip chart paper as available, taking care not to associate numbers with names. Modifying the exercise in this way allows students agency and choice in whether they would like to disclose the number in their deck, in addition to privacy in that the number is not associated with their name when written on the board or flip chart paper. Using this method may limit the impact, however, as the activity is more anonymized.

The course instructor may then ask students to reflect on the numbers written on the board and their experience with the exercise. When utilizing this activity to discuss issues related to the Grand Challenge of reducing extreme income inequality, the instructor may choose to read statements only related to wealth and poverty, as provided in Appendix 13B. Another variation may be to conduct this activity, while including all categories of privilege, at the beginning of the semester during the first introductory class. The instructor may refer to the exercise at various points throughout the semester when embarking upon a new set of social welfare policies, such as policies related to poverty. The instructor may ask students to reflect on the similarities and disparities between experiences in a room of individuals who have a similar privilege in one area, but may have varied privileges in other areas (such as they are all completing higher education), whether the disparities in circumstances reflect a just society, and how policies related to poverty and public assistance may be altered or created to reduce inequality and expand opportunity for all.

Instructors should also examine how students have benefited from privilege. Ask students to discuss prompts such as: At night, people do not cross the street when they see me approaching; I do not have to worry about whether the color of my skin will influence whether or not I get a loan from a bank; I have someone in my family who can lend me money if I need it; I have physical items from my childhood because I grew up in stable housing. Course instructors may choose to discuss whether students have thought of these as "privileges" before. Importantly, it should be acknowledged that not all cultural groups who are dominant have privilege. For example, course instructors may note that poor white families are often disenfranchised, but that everyone has some privilege that they have benefited from, and that American society affords implicit and explicit bias towards dominant groups in many circumstances.

14 Achieving Equal Opportunity and Justice

Annalisa Enrile, Renée Smith-Maddox and Eugenia L. Weiss

Introduction and Background of the Grand Challenge

Achieving Equal Opportunity and Justice is the Grand Challenge for Social Work that encompasses all 13 of the Grand Challenges (American Academy of Social Work & Social Welfare, n.d.). For example, Eradicating Racism, Building Financial Capability for All, Reducing Extreme Economic Inequality, Promoting Smart Decarceration, Ending Homelessness, and Ensuring the Healthy Development of All Youth are Grand Challenges dependent upon equal opportunity and justice. Equal Opportunity and Justice is the one Grand Challenge that if "achieved" all people would have access to the same basic rights, protections, opportunities, and social benefits. Advocacy and social justice are the cornerstones of the field of social work, distinguishing it from other fields of health and human services (Hoefer, 2016). Thus, it is imperative that students studying social work and social welfare understand how prejudice, bias, and discrimination perpetuate and exacerbate inequities and learn how to integrate social justice principles into their practice.

According to the National Association of Social Work Code of Ethics (NASW, n.d.), social workers have an obligation to be agents of change in their communities and work environments and encourage others to do the same. All of this is true – and yet – social work educators easily miss the mark in adopting ways to teach social justice as a practice. This is not because they are hesitant to teach in this area but rather because equal opportunity and justice are not the easiest concepts to grasp. Indeed, for things that are so central to social work, there is not always consistency and agreement even on definitions. To further advance this challenge, there is a component inherent to teaching, which is the need to interrogate ourselves as practitioners and the necessity of action. These challenges demand action be taken.

DOI: 10.4324/9781003308263-17

Too often, the field has defaulted to reformist models such as one-day strikes, ameliorating aid, or institutional responses that merely uphold and replicate the status quo instead of creating systemic change (Gilligan, 2007). Fighting for a more just world, such as more equitable communities, elimination of health disparities and inclusive work environments requires more transformative, radical models (Wilkinson & D'Angelo, 2019). Models such as the work of the Truth and Reconciliation Commission in South Africa (www.usip.org/publications/1995/12/truth-commission-south-africa) and the Truth, Racial Healing, and Transformation work in higher education funded by the Kellogg Foundation (2016) offer a powerful path toward advancing racial and social justice. Embedded in these initiatives are approaches to racial healing and building equitable communities. The models also emphasize the importance of uprooting conscious and unconscious beliefs in the hierarchy of human value, acknowledging the diverse experiences that people have, and changing collective community narratives to counter perceptions of people of color and various religious and ethnic groups.

This chapter begins by identifying and defining important terms relating to equity and justice work. Then, three conceptual frameworks for developing social justice teaching practices will be presented as a model for curriculum and instruction. Although there are several conceptual models that could be used to explore equal opportunity and justice, such as critical race theory, the chapter will present three that the authors believe are essential to concrete actions: a racial equity framework, transnational feminism, and intersectionality. Current issues around social justice will be presented to provide examples and a context for equal opportunity and justice work. Micro-mezzo-macro perspectives will be presented to exemplify the areas in the curriculum where it can be infused. Finally, curriculum examples and tools will be provided so that educators may put recommendations into practice in their own classrooms.

The Grand Challenge of Achieving Equal Opportunity and Justice has been identified by the American Academy of Social Work and Social Welfare (AASWSW) as one that requires a concerted, multidisciplinary effort and painstaking attention to details. Focusing on marginalized groups in the United States, the AASWSW work group on this Grand Challenge makes several policy recommendations which include: accelerating Latino immigrant integration, expanding the Affordable Care Act (ACA), expanding and strengthening of federal antidiscrimination laws (including the Voting Rights Act) and eliminating zero-tolerance policies in schools (Calvo et al., 2016).

Philosopher Lao Tzo said, "A journey of a thousand miles begins with one step" and so must the understanding of equal opportunity and justice. To teach how to advance this Grand Challenge, we start where you are. This means working together with social work educators, practitioners, and emerging social workers so they can raise their level of self-awareness and see their role in social justice and advocacy efforts.

Next, there must be a shared understanding of concepts and terms. A common vocabulary is essential and for many, this has the potential of being a barrier to justice work. Fear of not knowing proper terminology, the pressure to be politically correct, and the inability to feel open or even safe asking what something means have all been detriments to a shared language around equal opportunity and justice. When discussing definitions, the first thing an instructor needs to do is create a safe and brave space to have discussions on topics such as racial and social injustices, colonialism, systems of oppression and deconstruct the specific role that social work had in perpetuating this legacy. By thoughtfully cultivating these necessary discussions and implementing lessons learned, social work educators can guide emerging social workers to develop a social justice practice that includes reflection, honesty, respect, inclusion, as well as deconstructing stereotypes, dismantling inequalities, and exposing unfair practices. McConnell-Ginet (2020) posits that "words matter" in that words are "politically powerful, both as dominating weapons that help oppress and as effective tools that can resist oppression" (p. 1).

Principles for Doing Social Justice and Advocacy Work

Social justice and advocacy come together when viewed through the principles of diversity, equity, inclusion, equity-mindedness, and social justice. According to the American Association of Colleges and Universities (AAC&U, n.d.), diversity, equity, and inclusion are critical to the mission and institutional life of colleges and universities (www.aacu.org/making-excellence-inclusive). AAC&U defines diversity, equity, and inclusion as follows:

Diversity: Individual differences (e.g., personality, prior knowledge, and life experiences) and group/social differences (e.g., race/ethnicity, class, gender, sexual orientation, country of origin, and ability as well as cultural, political, religious, or other affiliations).

Inclusion: The active, intentional, and ongoing engagement with diversity – in the curriculum, in the co-curriculum, and in communities (intellectual, social, cultural, geographical) with which individuals might connect – in ways that increase awareness, content knowledge, cognitive sophistication, and empathic understanding of the complex ways individuals interact within systems and institutions.

Equity: The creation of opportunities for historically underserved populations to have equal access to and participate in educational programs that are capable of closing the achievement gaps in student success and completion.

Equity-Mindedness: The term "Equity-Mindedness" refers to the perspective or mode of thinking exhibited by practitioners who call attention to patterns of inequity in student outcomes. These practitioners are willing to take personal and institutional responsibility for the success of their students, and critically reassess their own practices. It also requires that practitioners are race-conscious and aware of the social and historical context of exclusionary practices in American Higher Education (Center for Urban Education, University of Southern California).

Social Justice*:* Social justice is an ideal condition in which all members of society have the same rights, protections, opportunities, and social benefits (Finn et al., 2013).

For the purposes of this chapter, and in the name of shared vocabulary, the terms "equity" and "equal opportunity" will be used interchangeably. Similarly, reference to organizational programs of Diversity, Equity, and Inclusion (DEI) will also be interchangeable with Equity, Diversity, and Inclusion (EDI) work.

Situating the Grand Challenge to Achieve Equal Opportunity and Justice Across the Curricula (Human Behavior in the Social Environment [HBSE], Policy and Practice)

In the years since the Grand Challenge to Achieve Equal Opportunity and Justice was identified, there has been growing unrest not just in the academy but also in marginalized communities where social workers serve, where neither equity nor justice has been gained. The danger of considering this Grand Challenge as the auspices of only macro social work is high considering the broad nature of equity and justice. Therefore, it is good to use specific issues, campaigns, and social movements (such as civil rights, human rights, women's rights, and workers' rights) and the positionality of social workers within these areas as examples. For instance, the realm of social movement building might be distinguished by macro practices like community organizing and advocacy but upon closer investigation, the "clinical" skills of motivational interviewing and socio-emotional learning benefit this work. As Grace Lee Boggs (2021) points out, one cannot organize a community without gaining the trust and understanding of its members. Similarly, social workers who might take a service orientation to the community and believe that change happens incrementally through one client or family at a time should understand how this change contributes to greater goals of equity and justice.

Many blame the lack of student preparation and their limited awareness of the power differentials that take place in the policy arena as well as a limited understanding of intervention research and its cultural relevance to marginalized groups (Reisch & Jani, 2012). Often, social work programs fall into a false binary of the micro-macro continuum, when the teaching of equal opportunity and justice is an example of something that must (and can) be infused into all foundational curricula, including human behavior, policy, practice, and research courses. Indeed, even field courses can incorporate this material. For example, at the University of Southern California Suzanne Dworak-Peck School of Social Work, the field department assigns all first-year students the book *Towards Psychologies of Liberation* (Watkins & Shulman, 2008) in order to provide students a basic understanding of concepts of diversity, equity, inclusion, and justice as well as colonization, intergenerational trauma due to systemic oppression and liberation. These seemingly "macro" concepts are thus brought into the internship work of students and may also be discussed in their other foundational courses. For instance, one topic in the text focuses on "collective trauma." In the field and practice courses, this might be a discussion on how to build rapport with communities where racial or political trauma has been experienced. In policy, this may be a discussion on current immigration policies. And, in research, this could be incorporated into participatory action research methods.

One of the biggest mistakes that instructors make is to discuss the issues and "-isms" associated with equal opportunity and justice in a vacuum. To do so makes for shallow understandings and can actually "backfire," such as implicit bias training that is not fully grounded or supported. In these cases, the result is a stronger adherence to one's bias than transformative change (FitzGerald et al., 2019). This highlights the necessity to teach students to understand the root causes of -isms (such as racism, sexism, heterosexism, ableism), inequities, disinformation, and dysfunctional polarizations. To understand the history and impact of these -isms on clients and communities, social work students must understand the root causes of structural oppressions such as colonization and ideologies such as patriarchy and misogyny which are best understood through the intentional use of relevant conceptual frameworks.

Using Conceptual Frameworks to Create a Learning Community

Whether a social work instructor is teaching a human behavior and social environment social work practice, policy, or research course, there are several frameworks that can be used to situate achieving equal opportunity and justice, but it is helpful both for faculty and students to draw upon a framework because it provides specific points of analysis and a direction for discussion. For the purposes of this chapter, three conceptual frameworks are combined to exemplify a model for teaching equal opportunity and justice that includes race equity, transnational feminism, and intersectionality. The core themes of these three conceptual frameworks provide a way for instructors and students to engage not only in the academic discourse and research in social justice education but also offer concrete action and bridge-building options within the field and between different disciplines. Moreover, these specific conceptual frameworks directly explore issues of justice and racism while challenging students to question their own education, perspectives, and role as change agents (McDonald, 2005). These conceptual frameworks also allow for students from marginalized communities to locate their own stories and lived experiences as well as encourage culturally relevant materials that reflect authentic multicultural perspectives (Santamaría, 2014).

The Race Equity Framework (Kellogg Foundation, 2016) pays attention to race and ethnicity while analyzing problems, looking for solutions, and defining success. The framework helps social workers to analyze data and information about race and ethnicity as well as understand disparities and why they exist. A race equity lens allows for examination of societal problems and root causes from structural standpoints, while explicitly naming race when addressing problems and solutions. The framework also sheds light on racial dynamics, social determinants of health, and the intersectional components that contribute to injustices based on race/ethnicity, class, gender, sexual orientation, religion, ability, and age to name a few; and how these, in turn, shape an individual's social and political identities.

A transnational feminist lens, first proposed by Mohanty (2003, 2013) proposes that feminism must not be contained by borders. Rather, global migration, particularly of women's labor, should be understood as a redefinition of nationhood. Additionally, transnational feminism calls out the race-blind perspectives of socialist, radical, and liberal feminism which considered the "woman question" regardless of any nuance of race or ethnicity (Grabe, 2018). Therefore, transnational feminism signifies the importance of a multiplicity of identities within feminist principles of understanding oppression, especially gender inequity through the lens of history and context of power, women's agency, and voice and political allyship and solidarity (Maza, 2019). For example, transnational feminism forces a global perspective that requires social workers to understand their role in the welfare state vis-à-vis populations such as economic migrants to what was considered the "global north" and what types of assumptions were being construed. Students in policy courses would have to further understand immigration policies just as practice courses would have to account for intergenerational trauma as a result of migration (Moosa-Mitha & Ross-Sheriff, 2010).

Intersectionality is the final piece of this conceptual framework that holds all three together. Intersectionality is a framework, an analytical concept, orientation, and a methodological approach that can be used to develop an advocacy practice for social justice. By offering a means for analyzing how systems of power and inequality affect individuals, groups, and communities differently, intersectionality becomes a powerful analytical tool for policy and social change (Crenshaw, 1989). We (the authors) draw upon our experiences and knowledge as social work educators to demonstrate how an intersectional analysis of social identities can contribute to developing an advocacy practice for social justice.

Teaching with a racial equity, feminist, and intersectional framework informs the understanding of how race, class, gender, ethnicity, sexual orientation, ability, and status influence students and educators to develop an advocacy practice for social justice (Hoefer, 2016). This approach has several benefits. First, in social work education, the classroom environment becomes a dialogic space for learning and professional development. Second, the instructor tailors the educational experience to the strengths and needs of the students. Third, the instructor and student increase self-awareness of their social identities, values, and beliefs, as well as their role as change agents.

Teaching Practices

In teaching approaches to Achieve Equal Opportunity and Justice, the following learning objectives are utilized: 1) Identify the systematic denial of opportunity and equal access for marginalized people in our society; 2) Analyze underlying power dynamics (i.e., policies, institutions, and programs) to improve equal opportunity and justice for all; and 3) Discuss the roles of advocacy and activism to close the opportunity gaps. Although these learning objectives could be embedded and applied in any social work course (e.g., HBSE, practice, research, or policy), for illustrative purposes this chapter underscores how social justice and advocacy are central to developing a social justice practice and pedagogy. Additionally, the reader is referred to Appendix 14A to see how the Educational Policy and Accreditation Standards (EPAS) from the Council of Social Work Education (CSWE, 2022) can be applied to this Grand Challenge.

Pedagogical Approach and Engagement

The 5E Instructional Model (Bybee & Landes, 1990) provides a framework for teaching and learning. The model consists of five progressive stages of learning that comprise engaging, exploring, explaining, elaborating, and evaluating. It is an inquiry-based teaching approach adapted for social work education (Smith-Maddox et al., 2020). It allows adult learners to experience common activities, to use and build on prior knowledge and experiences, to construct meaning, and to develop new ideas. Specifically, here's how each of the Es work when creating a learning environment focused on social justice and advocacy:

Engage

The first step in the instructional model is to help students access prior knowledge, generate interest in the topic, and/or provide students with a reason to explore. The instructor starts by acknowledging who is in the room, where students should have an opportunity to share understandings of social and racial justice; make connections between prior knowledge and their understanding of social issues; question the world around them; critique and construct their own opinions and interpretations of social issues; and engage in conversations about how to change a world deeply in need of change.

Explore

For the second step in the model, an instructor provides materials, space, and time so that students may generate their own understandings, in their own words, as they complete a task and/or solve a problem (i.e., social inequities). During this phase, students actively explore a wide array of contextual factors about a social issue through readings, videos, and interviews. From their inquiry process, students determine who is affected by the issue, how they are affected, and what are the main causes of the issue.

Explain

The third step is divided into two parts where the sequence is important. First, students are given an opportunity to formalize and share the understandings generated in the Explore phase. Then in the second part, the instructor uses students' language/descriptions to help structure students' explanations and refine their new conceptual understandings, by directing attention to important elements, clarifying where needed, and providing shared language of terms.

Elaborate

In this fourth step, students are provided with opportunities (i.e., small group discussions with peers with prompts, a dialogue session about real-world situations, lessons learned about the topic, and reflective writing exercises) to apply their understanding of concepts to their practice.

Evaluate

This phase occurs throughout the implementation of the 5E model (not just at the end of a stage) and provides instructors and students with feedback about the learning process and students' progress toward learning goals for their social justice and advocacy practice. This is also a time for reflection on the frameworks and their relevance to the students' social work practice.

Embedding Current Events Into Course Discourse/Materials

The detrimental trend of excluding justice practices within schools of social work and their curriculum is reflected in the world where more and more social problems are being solved outside of social work – where, in fact, social workers are absent from the discussion (Grobman, 2019). A stark example of this was in 2016 and again in 2021, when an unexpected surge of unaccompanied minors from Central America and Mexico crossed into the US. Thousands of children were put into detention centers in rural outposts of Arizona and California as communities refused to take in and accept them (Androff, 2016). On every major news channel, the story was unfolding, and the experts called to the table were policymakers, politicians, lawyers, businesspeople, and public health officials. These were the perspectives that were expected to provide the answers even though 100% of these children would at some point in their journey meet a social worker (Androff, 2016; Porter, 2016). It was sobering to realize that social workers would be expected to implement solutions that they had very little role in designing. In a policy course, policies such as DACA (Deferred Action for Childhood Arrivals) within the context of the history of US immigration, issues of equality, and social justice can be discovered and discussed (Amuedo-Dorantes & Puttitanun, 2017). Conceptual frameworks add further depth and challenge students to understand perspectives from racialized power dynamics of authority, gendered violence at the border crossings, and the intersectionality of, to name a few, avenues of dialogue.

Unfortunately, there are far too many current injustices to use as examples for course materials. One of the most pivotal shifts in social movements happened in the summer of 2020. We witnessed Black lives taken. The murder of George Floyd, a 46-year-old Black man killed by a white police officer who kept his knee on Mr. Floyd's neck for eight minutes and 49 seconds as he lay face-down on the sidewalk handcuffed. Ahmaud Arbery, Breonna Taylor, and many other unarmed Black individuals whose deaths drew public attention and widespread protests for justice from activists. These events reignited the social justice movement through social media. The unnecessary deaths like Floyd's, Arbery's, and Taylor's reveal to us the deeper systemic issue in the way we treat people of color in the United States.

The revealing of how the 1921 Tulsa Race Massacre was covered up for decades tells of a history that was not discussed publicly until researchers started their investigation in the 1970s. On May 31, 1921, a white mob turned Greenwood District of Tulsa, Oklahoma (aka Black Wall Street which was a thriving community with Black entrepreneurial businesses) upside down in one of the worst racial massacres in US history. In a matter of hours, 35 square blocks of the vibrant Black community were turned into smoldering ashes. Countless Black people were killed – estimates ranged from 55 to more than 300 – and 1,000 homes and businesses were looted and set on fire. These traumatic current events shed light on the realities of racial trauma and its residual effects. Despite the challenge to teach antiracist and social justice education material, it's critical to make space for educators and their students to process the destabilizing events and discomforting truths about racism in America where there is no justice, no accountability, and no reparations.

The social and racial injustices and inequities mentioned have sparked a series of collective actions where people engaged in social media activism and advocated for racial and social justice such as:

- **HR7120 – George Floyd Justice in Policing Act** – 116th Congress (2019–2020). This bill addresses a wide range of policies and issues regarding policing practices and law enforcement accountability. It includes measures to increase accountability for law enforcement misconduct, to enhance transparency and data collection, and to eliminate discriminatory policing practices.
- **Black Lives Matter** is an activism organization combating anti-Black racism across the globe. They work collectively with communities to demand the end of police brutality, change policy, amplify the stories of Black people, run for office, and support all Black people.
- **Color of Change** (https://colorofchange.org/) focuses on advancing racial equity nationally.
- Places such as Evanston, Illinois, Bruce's Beach in Manhattan Beach, CA, and Tulsa, Oklahoma are embarking on reparations plans to address the ways in which racial and social injustices have negatively impacted African Americans.

Social work educators have an opportunity to create the conditions for their students to have discussions about racism and colonialism as well as speak out and name acts of racism and hatred for what they are. In addition, they have a responsibility to accurately represent the history and lives of marginalized people. This pedagogical approach also requires us to interrogate ourselves as educators and practitioners to ensure that we are disrupting rather than perpetuating systems of power that are marginalizing. A social justice and advocacy practice requires social workers to demonstrate a commitment to advocacy for social justice which includes persistent self-awareness, constant self-critique, and regular self-examination. To integrate this type of practice into what we do as social workers requires us to understand history, culture, and the distribution of power resulting from racism and colonialism.

Sample Course Structure

Every aspect of the course design must be considered along with the goals of the Grand Challenge to Achieve Equal Opportunity and Justice and how to create an inclusive learning environment. This goes beyond creating a safe place that is the common classroom expectation and into what Arao and Clemens (2013) have dubbed "brave spaces." Brave spaces are where genuine, difficult challenges may be introduced in an atmosphere of sufficient support and affirmation that is nonjudgmental at least and encouraging at best (Cook-Sather, 2016). Safe spaces assume that nothing will harm or cause a feeling of harm for students, but this is an impossible promise when discussing issues of diversity, equity, inclusion, and justice in honest, transparent ways (Simon et al., 2021). Therefore, brave spaces also discussed by Palfrey (2017) are so named because the assumption is that there will be some level of danger, or triggering, and one must prepare for that and enter that space anyway. While an educator cannot always predict what will happen in a brave space, they can prepare for it through course design.

The first is to set up the learning environment – virtual or in-person – as partnerships between faculty and students. This creates a dual responsibility of learning and participation (Zuban Clancy & Ferreira, 2019). A partnership of learning includes activities such as student-led discussions, reflective writing exercises, and experiential learning. A partnership of this type necessitates a level of vulnerability for educators who must relinquish some of their inherent power in the classroom and students who must be willing to be open and flexible in their learning (Siemens, 2014).

Self-reflection is important preparation for facilitating sensitive conversations with our students. As educators, we must process our own feelings and become aware of the ways our own identities and experiences shape the perspective we hold. We must give ourselves and students space to reflect on traumatic and violent events. It is also important for students to not only engage in self-reflection within the class but also outside of class time as a bridge between the classroom environment and their personal experiences. This is best achieved by sharing resources that address the different ways students might connect with material to establish baseline knowledge of the events and dispel misinformation – not just in content but also in form. For example, instead of providing a reading list, which is standard in any course, expand the definition to "resources" in general. This will expand student opportunities to engage not just in the written word (books and articles), but also to listen to podcasts and other recordings, to view movies and short-form videos, and explore websites and organizations.

The final aspect of course design is the activities that will occur during each session. Instructors should recognize how their choices of readings, examples, analogies, videos, and other content may be biased and may reinforce stereotypes. As with the reading list, there will of course be some aspect of lecturing and direction, but as much as possible, this should be kept to a minimum. The main portion of the learning should occur through facilitated discussions and activities that are engaging and participatory. Some examples include experiential exercises such as field trips or site visits, the incorporation of the arts (all formats), role plays, and discussion in small and large groups. Activities that may be considered more "out of the box" may include design challenges such as hackathons and innovation sprints, solution-driving activities and project-based learning.

Example of Course Design

Reflective questions to ask when designing a course to develop advocacy and social justice practice include:

- How have I constructed ways of knowing?
- How do I examine my values, beliefs, and dispositions?
- Is there a diversity of voices in the course materials? Are Black, Indigenous, People of Color (BIPOC) authors and creatives represented in the course materials?
- What are the publishing dates for the course materials? What was occurring in the political, cultural, and activism landscape during that period?

Developing Course Content

Reading from a diverse group of publication outlets that represent progressive and conservative perspectives; listening to podcasts and NPR segments on the topic; viewing videos (such as documentaries, TedTalks, VICE news, and international news (i.e., BBC and Al

Jazeera)); and exploring websites and/or toolkits on issues relating unjust practices, racial equality, discrimination, voter suppression can help instructors and students begin to examine their values, beliefs, and dispositions about these topics.

Course Activities

Course activities are opportunities to engage the students in a variety of ways to address racial and social injustices, deconstruct stereotypes, dismantle inequality, and expose unfair practices. For example, the following activities can be used to emphasize learning about unjust practices, inequities, and why they persist:

- Experiential learning exercises such as guided discussions, small and large group interactions, site visits, use of arts;
- Innovation labs that foster system change and engage a wide range of stakeholders in problem-solving activities;
- Team projects such as project-based assignments, group exercises, and solution-focused activities;
- Role plays focused on situational and contextual experiences such as community organizing, curating brave spaces, and critical conversations;
- Community engagement such as partnerships, collaborations with partner agencies and organizations, and service-learning that focuses on social justice and advancing racial equality;
- Video and social media campaigns.

Example of an Assignment for Policy and Advocacy Course

The Policy Advocacy Campaign, Policy Solution Video, and Team Presentation

This assignment is designed to address a specific policy issue on which to take some action (create, revise, or eliminate) using emerging technologies. Each group will be asked to produce 1) *a policy advocacy campaign* using social media and/or emerging technologies (i.e., information technology, wireless data communication) to influence opinions and the formation of public policy as well as raise awareness of the issue, and directly engage policy influencers (i.e., policymakers, professional organizations, lobbyists, bloggers, online organizers) or mobilize grassroots action and 2) *a three-minute policy solution*

PSA-type video, and 3) a team presentation. The 15–20 minutes presentation requirements are:

- Create a video introducing the policy issue and solution;
- Provide an overview of the social issue and the related policy;
- Identify your target policymaking audience (who are you trying to influence?);
- Identify your target activist audience (who are you mobilizing to act?);
- Provide details on what you are asking your activists to do and exactly how you will get them to do it (how will you pitch the social action agenda to activists? what actions do you want them to take?);
- Create and present a mock-up of a website, text for email messages, #hashtags, blog, tweets and Facebook posts and a video solution;
- Identify your metrics for success (what will you measure? what does success look like?); and
- Include a budget and timeline for launching and implementing the advocacy campaign.

Facilitating Class Discussions and Difficult Conversations

Promoting cross-racial understandings or diversity in any shape or form are the keys to education and changing the world for the greater good. Saad (2020) posits that awareness and exposure to conversations through well-facilitated intergroup dialogue about race and difference can equip people (in this case social workers) to make a positive change toward equity, diversity, and inclusion. Furthermore, privilege is an area that needs to be constantly explored as are our human tendencies toward unconscious biases.

Difficult conversations are best addressed in learning environments that embrace difficult questions, teach active and deep listening skills, and allow room for complexity, paradox, and nuances (Goodman, 2011). Miller and Garran (2017) posit that classroom norms must be established ahead of time about rules for conduct, confidentially, speaking for oneself, appreciating differences, being honest, owning feelings, and the notion that ideas can be challenged without personal attacks. Self-awareness in the instructor is one of the keys to successful management of any strategies to be used in the social work classroom (Bell et al., 2016). Resistance from certain individuals or groups of students (particularly from those of privileged groups) can occur in the classroom (Goodman, 2015) and there are no easy solutions.

Kang and Garran (2018) propose that instructors should engage in faculty development and peer consultations as well as conceptualize microaggressions in the classroom within the context of historical and oppressive structures. A mutual-aid model is presented that encourages awareness, reflection, and skill development for faculty (Kang & Garran, 2018).

Evaluation of Learning

The learning objectives that were presented earlier in the chapter are assessed through written and oral assignments as well as through class participation. Online discussion forums and the use of self-reflective journals are additional ways to capture the students' learning of the material. The students are expected to engage in the classroom activities and provide comments on viewings or readings that have been assigned by the instructor. Additionally, instructors are encouraged to have several small assignments along the quarter/semester rather than two or three large written assignments. The small assignments allow for the development of ideas and opportunities for deeper reflections and faculty feedback. As an example, students can work on a Grand Challenge through a group assignment and be able to apply any of the frameworks presented here to understand the problem area and ways to intervene. Assigning oral presentations is also helpful in promoting student discussions on the selected topics.

Conclusion

This chapter was intended to be a resource for social work educators. However, it is more than that. It is a resource for all of us who are becoming advocates and activists. This resource was developed during a time when incidents of hate and racism remain prevalent throughout the United States. Let us not forget the death of George Floyd, Breonna Taylor, and many others at the hands of law enforcement as well as Ahmaud Arbery and countless others brutally killed by white supremacists. The violent attacks on Asian Americans and Asian American women reproduce an environment that continues to make them vulnerable to harassment, abuse, and murder. Voting rights are under attack nationwide as states pass voter suppression laws. Hurricane Katrina's disastrous effects on New Orleans in 2005, Flint, Michigan's water crisis in 2016, and the Texas water crisis in 2021 revealed examples of environmental injustice and the lack of concern for Black and poor people without access to food, housing, electricity, and access to clean water. Those who survived any of these crises are still haunted by the trauma. The COVID-19 pandemic has exacerbated existing disparities in American society and has resulted in increased hunger, poverty, unemployment, homelessness, and domestic violence. The inequities are typically divided up along class, race, gender, and educational attainment. These incidents give rise to the demands for justice and accountability.

The failed insurrection on January 6, 2021, at the US Capitol was a confirmed act of domestic terrorism by White supremacists. This incident and many more (i.e., anti-Muslim and anti-immigration efforts during the Trump era) confirm how divided we are in the United States. It confirms that our collective action through advocacy and activism is needed more than ever. This means that all schools of social work have a role to play in the healing, antiracism, reconciliation, and restorative justice processes. For schools of social work that have not integrated the knowledge and skills that our graduates need to be advocates for social justice, it is time to redesign the curriculum. The Council of Social Work Education's EPAS (CSWE, 2022) acknowledge the critical importance of advancing human rights and social, economic, and environmental justice. This means that schools of social work have a responsibility to develop and integrate critical analysis of social justice, power, privilege, and oppression in the curriculum. This is an essential component for becoming an advocate. We can no longer wait for another murder to verify that social workers need advanced skills, knowledge, and practices to not only advocate for social justice and equal opportunity but to help us heal from racial trauma.

Social work educators have an obligation to create learning communities that cultivate a problem-solving practice that can be used in various situations and places to address inequalities and opportunity gaps. Social workers have an obligation to engage and promote respectful discussions and critical conversations among social workers and other helping professionals with diverse perspectives. As a profession we have an obligation to create a safe and brave space where a faculty member and a student can say what they believe even if they do not share the dominant political point of view. This should be the expectations in every class in every school of social work. Nothing less can fulfill our field's commitment to the moral imperative of working towards achieving equal opportunity and justice.

References

American Academy of Social Work & Social Welfare. (n.d.). *The grand challenges for social work*. https://grandchallengesforsocialwork.org/

American Association of Colleges and Universities. (n.d.). www.aacu.org/making-excellence-inclusive

Amuedo-Dorantes, C., & Puttitanun, T. (2017). Was DACA responsible for the surge in unaccompanied minors on the southern border? *International Migration*, *55*(6), 12–13.

Androff, D. (2016). The human rights of unaccompanied minors in the USA from central America. *Journal of Human Rights and Social Work*, *1*(2), 71–77.

Arao, B., & Clemens, K. (2013). From safe spaces to brave spaces: A new way to frame dialogue around diversity and social justice. In L. M. Landreman (Ed.), *The art of effective facilitation* (pp. 135–150). Stylus Publishing, LLC.

Bell, L. A., Goodman, D. J., & Varghese, R. (2016). Critical self-knowledge for social justice educators. In M. Adams, L. A. Bell, D. J. Goodman, & K. Y. Joshi (Eds.), *Teaching for diversity and social justice* (3rd ed., pp. 397–418). Routledge.

Boggs, G. (2021). *The next American revolution: Sustainable activism for the twenty-first century*. University of California Press.

Bybee, R., & Landes, N. M. (1990). Science for life and living: An elementary school science program from biological sciences improvement study (BSCS). *The American Biology Teacher*, *52*(2), 92–98.

Calvo, R., Goldbach, J., & Teasley, M. (2016, September). *Policy recommendations for meeting the grand challenge to achieve equal opportunity and justice*. Grand Challenges for Social Work. American Academy of Social & Social Welfare. Policy Brief No. 12

Cook-Sather, A. (2016). Creating brave spaces within and through student-faculty pedagogical partnerships. *Teaching and Learning Together in Higher Education*, *1*(18), 1.

Council of Social Work Education (CSWE). (2022). *2022 Educational policy and accreditation standards*. Author. https://www.cswe.org/getmedia/94471c42-13b8-493b-9041-b30f48533d64/2022-EPAS.pdf

Crenshaw, K. W. (1989). Demarginalizing the intersection of race and sex: A black feminist critique of antidiscrimination doctrine, feminist theory and antiracist politics. *University of Chicago Legal Forum*, *1989*, 138–167.

Finn, J. L., Molloy, J., & Trautman, A. (2013). *Social justice*. Encyclopedia of Social Work (online). National Association of Social Workers Press & Oxford University Press. https://doi.org/10.1093/acrefore/9780199975839.013.364

FitzGerald, C., Martin, A., Berner, D., & Hurst, S. (2019). Interventions designed to reduce implicit prejudices and implicit stereotypes in real world contexts: A systematic review. *BMC Psychology*, *7*(1), 1–12.

Gilligan, P. (2007). Well-motivated reformists or nascent radicals: How do applicants to the degree in social work see social problems, their origins and solutions?. *British Journal of Social Work*, *37*(4), 735–760.

Goodman, D. (2011). *Promoting diversity and social justice: Educating people from privileged groups* (2nd ed.). Routledge.

Goodman, D. (2015). Can you love them enough to help them learn? Reflections of a social justice educator on addressing resistance from White students to anti-racism education. *Understanding and Dismantling Privilege, 5*(1), 62–73.

Grabe, S. (2018). Transnational feminism in psychology: Women's human rights, liberation, and social justice. In *The Oxford handbook of social psychology and social justice* (pp. 193–213). Oxford University Press.

Grobman, L. M. (Ed.). (2019). *Days in the lives of social workers: 62 Professionals tell" real-life" stories from social work practice.* New Social Worker Press.

Hoefer, R. (2016). *Advocacy practice for social justice.* Lyceum Books, Inc.

Kang, H., & Garran, A. M. (2018). Microaggressions in social Work classrooms: Strategies for pedagogical intervention. *Journal of Ethnic & Cultural Diversity in Social Work.* Published online. https://doi.org/10.1080/15313204.2017.1413608

Kellogg Foundation. (2014). *Racial equity resource guide.* Author.

Maza, L. L. (2019). Institutional neglect of women and girls. In K. Zaleski, A. Enrile, E. L. Weiss, & X. Wang (Eds.), *Women's journey to empowerment in the 21st century: A transnational feminist analysis of women's lives in modern times* (pp. 1–4). Oxford University Press.

McConnell-Ginet, S. (2020). *Words matter: Meaning and power.* Cambridge University Press.

McDonald, M. A. (2005). The integration of social justice in teacher education: Dimensions of prospective teachers' opportunities to learn. *Journal of Teacher Education, 56*(5), 418–435.

Miller, J. L., & Garran, A. M. (2017). *Racism in the United States: Implications for the helping professions.* Springer Publishing Company.

Mohanty, C. T. (2003). *Feminism without borders.* Duke University Press.

Mohanty, C. T. (2013). Transnational feminist crossings: On neoliberalism and radical critique. *Signs: Journal of Women in Culture and Society, 38*(4), 967–991.

Moosa-Mitha, M., & Ross-Sheriff, F. (2010). *Transnational social work and lessons learned from transnational feminism.* Affilia: Journal of Women and Social Work. 25(2), 105–109.

National Association of Social Workers (NASW). (n.d.). *Code of ethics.* Author. https://www.socialworkers.org/About/Ethics/Code-of-Ethics/Code-of-Ethics-English

Palfrey, J. (2017). Safe spaces, brave spaces: Diversity and free expression *in education.* The MIT Press.

Porter, K. (2016, Spring). In pursuit of a better and safer life. In *La Linea: The newsletter of the Florence immigration and refugee rights project* (p. 4). https://firrp.org/media/FIRRP_Newsletter_Spring2016_LQ.pdf

Reisch, M., & Jani, J. (2012). The new politics of social work practice: Understanding context to promote social change. *NASW Network*, *21*(13), 1–10.

Saad, L. F. (2020). *Me and white supremacy: Combat racism, change the world and become a good ancestor*. Sourcebooks.

Santamaría, L. J. (2014). Critical change for the greater good: Multicultural perceptions in educational leadership toward social justice and equity. *Educational Administration Quarterly*, *50*(3), 347–391.

Siemens, G. (2014). The vulnerability of learning. *ELEARNSPACE*. www.elearnspace.org/blog/2014/01/13/the-vulnerability-of-learning/

Simon, J. D., Boyd, R., & Subica, A. M. (2021). Refocusing intersectionality in social work education: Creating a brave space to discuss oppression and privilege. *Journal of Social Work Education*, 1–12.

Smith-Maddox, R., Brown, L., Kratz, S., & Newmyer, R. (2020). Developing a policy practice for preventing and ending homeliness. *Journal of Social Work Education*, *56*, S4–S15.

Watkins, M., & Shulman, H. (2008). *Toward psychologies of liberation*. Palgrave Macmillan.

Wilkinson, M. T., & D'Angelo, K. A. (2019). Community-based accompaniment & social work – A complementary approach to social action. *Journal of Community Practice*, 27(2), 151–167.

Zuban, N., Clancy, T. L., & Ferreira, C. (2019). Authentic learning within the brave space created through student-faculty partnerships. *Papers on Postsecondary Learning and Teaching*, *3*, 103–110.

Appendix 14A
EPAS Addressed in Grand Challenge #13

Achieve Equal Opportunity and Justice

Competency 1: Demonstrate Ethical and Professional Behavior. Social workers understand the role ethics play in the practice, research, and policy arenas. To address their professional behavior, social workers are urged to understand the profession's history and mission, along with their roles and responsibilities in social justice and advocacy efforts. Because of the growing unrest not only in marginalized communities where social workers serve but also in higher education, social workers must be reflective practitioners to understand the root causes of structural oppressions such as colonization and ideologies such as patriarchy and misogyny. Social workers are reminded of their ethical imperative to recognize and intervene on behalf of people experiencing social injustices.

Competency 2: Advance Human Rights and Social, Racial Economic, and Environmental Justice. Social workers understand that all human beings, regardless of position in society, should have such fundamental rights as freedom, safety, privacy, adequate housing, health care, and education. Achieving equal opportunity and justice for all requires that social workers take an inclusive approach in their practice and be capable of interacting with people from different racial, gender orientation, religion, ethnic, or socioeconomic backgrounds. Social workers are encouraged to acquire knowledge about human rights, social justice, and advocacy strategies and community organizing approaches worldwide to promote social, racial, economic, and environmental justice.

Competency 3: Engage Antiracism, Diversity, Equity, and Inclusion (ADEI) in Practice. Social workers understand how diversity and differences characterize and shape the human experience and are essential to identity formation. Social workers are urged to recognize that social inequities affect individuals from all backgrounds, regardless of age, socioeconomic status, race, ethnicity, religion, and gender orientation. Social workers are advised to understand and apply relevant conceptual frameworks such intersectionality, racial equity framework, and transnational feminism to help confront the persistent and pervasive power dynamics of structural inequalities and create opportunities for social action.

Competency 4: Engage in Practice-Informed Research and Research-Informed Practice. Social workers understand that their lived experience and evidence-based practices from multidisciplinary sources inform their practice. They also understand the processes for translating research findings into effective practice. To be effective in their work addressing social injustice, social workers must understand and use research to ensure that people have access to equal, fair, and meaningful access to services, social benefits, and the protection of human, economic, social, and cultural rights. It is essential that practice decisions and social change efforts be based on practice-informed research and research-informed practice. Social workers are encouraged to work toward translating research and insights from practice into sustainable approaches for supporting social justice and building equitable communities.

Competency 5: Engage in Policy Practice. Social workers understand the history and current structure and dynamics of social policies and service delivery systems. Social workers are encouraged to recognize the need to advocate for and implement social justice principles in their practice and policy development initiatives. Social justice issues such as racism, prejudice, bias, and discrimination suggest that we must continue to fight for a more just world. The making of equitable communities, elimination of health disparities, and creating inclusive work environments requires more transformative, radical models (Wilkins & D'Angelo, 2019).

References

Council of Social Work Education (CSWE). (2022). *2022 Educational policy and accreditation standards*. Author. www.cswe.org/accreditation/standards/2022-epas/

Wilkinson, M. T., & D'Angelo, K. A. (2019). Community-based accompaniment & social work – A complementary approach to social action. *Journal of Community Practice*, *27*(2), 151–167.

Part Four

The Grand Challenges in the Field

15 Addressing the 13 Grand Challenges for Social Work via Simulation Labs

A New Approach in Undergraduate Education

Amy Ward and Ron Manderscheid

Introduction

The 13 Grand Challenges for Social Work (GCSW) are a call to action for social workers everywhere to improve and eventually eradicate the most complex issues facing society today. They represent a dynamic social agenda, focused on improving individual and family well-being, strengthening the social fabric, and helping create a more just society (Fong, 2018). The GCSW provides the profession with tangible ideas and a call to action that encourages social workers to engage in innovative thinking, utilize evidence-based interventions, and work towards an end to social problems.

The GCSW initiative has the potential to engage social work students in transformational learning that could lead to transformational change within the communities they will ultimately serve. They pose a unique opportunity for social work education to be innovative and infuse the Grand Challenges into the educational experience, aiming to make them relevant to the social work practitioners of tomorrow. The GCSW have the potential to provide students with specific areas of focus, as well as an introduction to the importance of incorporating evidence-based interventions into practice.

Goal of This Project

The goal of this chapter is to provide an overview of the GCSW and offer an approach for infusing the GCSW into undergraduate curricula through simulation labs. This project is multiphasic beginning with an outline of the project, in hopes to accelerate integration of the 13 GCSW into the field. A follow-up study will be conducted to measure project outcomes.

DOI: 10.4324/9781003308263-19

The GCSW may serve as an instrument to ignite interest and excitement for social work students, driving them to create innovations that will help to change the world as we know it. Applying the GCSW in social work simulation labs and embedding these experiences within undergraduate course curricula can provide students with an opportunity to address the GCSW in a hands-on way.

Background

Simulation Labs

Simulation labs have long been employed within various academic disciplines, specifically nursing and other healthcare-related professions. Simulation is a technique rather than a technology that is able to provide realistic environments or practice proxies for the purposes of learning, training, and practice (Gaba, 2004). The use of simulation labs in social work is not a new practice. Schools of social work typically assess students' learning through written examinations, essays, student presentations, or portfolios (Crisp & Lister, 2002). The best measure of students' competence, however, is their ability to effectively perform the core functions of the profession in practice situations (Gambrill, 2001). Simulation labs in social work education have been employed for some time; the literature reveals reports of simulations in the classroom through role plays with classmates (Doelcker, 1987; Kane, 2003; Moss, 2000), scenarios depicted by drama students (Berliner, 1982; Levitov et al., 1999), and use of trained actors as standardized clients (Koprowska, 2003; Mole, 2006; Petracchi, 1999, 2006; Robins and Holmes, 2008). Multiple studies have found the simulation labs utilized at the undergraduate level can improve student outcomes. Rawlings (2008) found previous work experience was correlated with direct practice skills. Baez (2005) indicated that the simulated client experience was associated with increased knowledge of substance use among BSW students. Simulation labs in social work education emerged long before the GCSW were established; however, both innovations have the potential to work well together to improve student outcomes.

The hands-on nature of simulation labs makes this experiential learning opportunity highly compatible with social work education. In 2016, East Central University (ECU), a small public institution in Ada, Oklahoma, began the process of implementing simulation lab experiences into the social work curricula. The goal was to provide students with a realistic scenario that they may face in the field of professional social work. The labs allow students to practice skills obtained in the classroom in a safe forum in which they are allowed to make mistakes and receive helpful feedback. The simulation lab experience consists of two phases and is currently embedded during the practice courses within the social work curricula. The social work practice classes are foundational courses that are based on generalist social work practice; they focus on building knowledge, values, and skills at micro, mezzo, and macro practice areas. At ECU, the Practice I curricula focuses on students working with individuals and groups, and the Practice II content concentrates on communities.

Phase I: Simulated client encounters at the micro and mezzo level, between one social work student and no more than two actors portraying clients.

Phase II: A multidisciplinary simulation lab that incorporates transdisciplinary collaboration between various academic disciplines, including nursing, legal studies, criminal justice, and social work.

Phase I of the simulation lab experience is infused within the Practice I curriculum and is embedded in the application component of the curriculum. This experience is linked with engagement, assessment, intervention, and evaluation, precisely competencies 6, 7, 8, and 9 of the 2022 Council on Social Work Education (CSWE) Educational and Policy Accreditation Standards (EPAS). Specifically, this opportunity is structured to potentially collect explicit and implicit assessment data and help students bring to life the purpose of the CSWE EPAS, as well as give them a hands-on opportunity to address each standard listed earlier in real time. During Phase I of the simulation lab, students are immersed in an atmosphere that closely resembles a client's environment, for example, a client's home. Social work students and an actor who is portraying a client are provided a case vignette, and the social work student is asked to assist the client as a generalist social work practitioner.

Phase II of the simulation lab experience is embedded within the Practice II curriculum. Social work students come together across academic disciplines to engage in a mock multidisciplinary team meeting. Students are divided into interdisciplinary groups consisting of nursing, legal studies, criminal justice, and social work. The groups are then provided real-world case vignettes and have to engage in collaboration, critical thinking, and problem-solving to come up with a solution to the vignette. Students then engage in group discussions regarding their experience and outcome.

Simulation is effective at bringing to life representative clien encounters in a safe, educational setting where no harm can come t participants. It can and has been successfully applied for the teach ing and training of novice learners as a way to introduce concepts o skills, as well as for seasoned providers to provide a safe environmen where deliberate practice, mastery, and upkeep of skills can occu (Sanko, 2017).

Incorporating the 13 GCSW

For the purpose of incorporating the GCSW into simulation lab expe riences, the phases will be re-ordered to reflect the following:

Phase I: An interactive simulation experience in which social work students will be introduced to professionals working in each area of the GCSW. Students will be introduced to each of the 13 GCSW and hear from experts addressing each area. Students then will work together as a team and engage in open discussions. Phase I presents the unique opportunity to partner with other schools of social work that have Master of Social Work or Doctor of Social Work Programs that focus on addressing the GCSW. Students from these programs have the potential to provide expertise on the GCSW to the undergraduate students who are participating in the simulation labs. During Phase I, students will also hear from individuals impacted directly by one or more of the 13 challenges. Phase I is intended to ignite excitement within students as they are introduced to the complex social issues that they will be facing as professional social workers.

Phase II: Students will put into action plans developed to tackle the GCSW and engage in simulated experiences with populations impacted by one or more of the GCSW. This interactive experience permits social work students to engage with simulated clients that are impacted by one or more of the Grand Challenge areas and explore a range of solutions.

An example of Phases I and II applying the challenge of Ending Homelessness could look something like this: social work students receive an introduction to the Grand Challenge of Ending Homelessness. They are exposed to the statistics, current evidence-based interventions, experts in the field, and hear from a person who has experienced living in homelessness. Students then take the information they have obtained and develop action plans to work with homeless individuals. Students can work through these solutions with an actor portraying a client during a simulation lab. Students receive oversight, supervision, and immediate feedback by social work faculty who are present during each phase of the simulation labs.

Not only are the labs an opportunity for students to test their hands-on skills and address the 13 GCSW, but they could also help students to understand and interpret social welfare policy and research concepts that they have been introduced to in the classroom. Phase I of the lab has the potential to help students apply current policy and explore how to improve policy. Phase II of the simulation lab experience may aid in bringing practice concepts to life for undergraduate students in a research framework, such as an understanding of independent and dependent variables. During the simulation lab, students will explore the concept of negative correlation and critically think about potential unintended consequences that occur based upon the implementation of their Grand Challenge solution. The simulation labs have the potential to address the GCSW while reinforcing various social work competencies. These competency standards are vitally important to social work programs. Specifically, integrating the 13 GCSW into the curriculum while utilizing simulation labs will help assess and promote competencies 6 through 9 of the 2022 EPAS.

Considerations

Social work education currently consists of a full curriculum; however, incorporating the 13 GCSW into social work programs can be accomplished by readapting current course work to include these experiences. Programs may also work on expanding internal and external stakeholders to provide increased support. Tools should be developed to assess the impact of incorporating the 13 GSCW into simulation labs. The methodology for querying students about their experience needs to include questions about better learning, empathy, and, more importantly, follow-up with students post-graduation to determine if their experience has influenced their practice. Programs also could create assessment tools that are focused on evaluating skills-based outcomes that could be used to enhance program assessment.

Furthermore, this experience also has the potential to be in-person or virtual. We must begin to incorporate new technology and expand the use of this technology over the next five to ten years to include adaptive and artificial intelligence. Lastly, incorporating the 13 GCSW can be done on an undergraduate or graduate level, and integration of simulation labs should be considered at both levels.

Conclusion

Incorporating the 13 GCSW into simulation labs will engage students, pique their interest, and encourage them to become energized and involved in addressing the GCSW. The labs also have the potential to help social work educators introduce students to the 13 GCSW and continue the momentum of GCSW campaign to eradicate these issues.

Next Steps

Moving forward, social work educators must act quickly to integrate the GCSW into core curricula. Educators have a unique opportunity to teach students about the relevance of the GCSW, and students hold the key to innovation and transformational change, which will help to address the GCSW in our communities.

At ECU, we began to integrate the GCSW into the practice curriculum in Fall 2020. Subsequently we will report these results back to the field after conducting a formal study. Progress in implementing this has been slowed due to COVID-19, however we have started to introduce the GCSW within courses via learning modules and class discussions.

References

Baez, A. (2005). Development of an Objective Structured Clinical Examination (OSCE) for practicing substance abuse intervention competencies: An application in social work education. *Journal of Social Work Practice in the Addictions*, *5*(3), 3–20.

Berliner, A. (1982). Enhancing social work education through the use of drama students as "clients" in role play. *Arete*, 7, 61–67.

Council on Social Work Education. (2022). *Educational policy and accreditation standards for baccalaureate and master's social work programs*. www.cswe.org/getmedia/8d7dade5-2683-4940-9587-5675f6ef5426/2022-EPAS.pdf

Crisp, B. R., & Lister, P. G. (2002). Assessment methods in social work education: A review of the literature. *Social Work Education*, *21*(2), 259–269.

Doelcker, R. E. (1987). Differential use of role-play in social work education. *Arete*, 53–60.

Fong, R. L. (2018). *Grand challenges for social work and society*. Oxford University Press.

Gaba, D. (2004). The future vision of simulation in health care. *Quality and Safety in Health Care*, *13*(Suppl. 1), 12. https://doi.org/10.1136/qhc.13.suppl_1.i2

Gambrill, E. D. (2001). Evaluating the quality of social work education: Options galore. *Journal of Social Work Education*, *37*(3), 418–429.

Kane, M. N. (2003). Teaching direct practice techniques for work with elders with Alzheimer's disease: A simulated group experience. *Educational Gerontology*, *29*(9), 777–794. https://doi.org/10.1080/716100370

Koprowska, J. (2003). The right kind of telling? Locating the teaching of interviewing skills within a systems framework. *British Journal of Social Work*, *33*(3), 291–308.

Levitov, J. F. (1999). Counselor clinic training with client-actors. *Counselor Education and Supervision*, *38*(4), 294–260.

Mole, L. S.-H. (2006). Using a simulated chaotic home environment for preparing nursing and social work students for interdisciplinary care delivery in a Scottish context. *Journal of Interprofessional Care*, *20*(5), 561–563.

Moss, B. (2000). The use of large-group role-play techniques in social work education. *Social Work Education*, *19*(5), 471–483. https://doi.org/10.1080/026154700435995

Petracchi, H. A. (1999). Using professionally trained actors in social work role-play simulations. *Journal of Sociology and Social Welfare*, *26*(4), 61–69.

Petracchi, H. A. (2006). Utilizing actors to simulate clients in social work student role plays: Does this approach have a place in social work education? *Journal Teaching in Social Work*, *26*(1/2), 223–233. https://doi.org/10.1300/J067v26n01_13

Rawlings, M. A. (2008). *Assessing direct practice skill performance in undergraduate social work education using standardized clients and self reported self-efficacy*. Case Western Reserve University.

Robins, D., & Holmes, J. (2008). Aesthetics and credibility in web site design. *Information Processing & Management*, *44*(1), 386–399.

Sanko, J. (2017). Simulation as a teaching technology: A brief history of its use in nursing education. (Report). *Distance Learning*, *14*(1), 21–29.

16 Translating the Grand Challenges in Field Education

Tory Cox, Ruth Supranovich and Suh Chen Hsiao

Introduction and Background of Field Education

Field education, also referred to as field practicum, fieldwork, or internship, is the component of a social work student's education when they apply classroom learning in community settings. Experienced social workers serve as field instructors providing regular guidance and supervision to the student. Typically, the field instructor designs educationally focused learning opportunities to expose students to social work practice with individuals, families, groups and communities, as well as policy and program development and other administrative tasks. Field education faculty play an instrumental role in forging partnerships with community-based organizations that employ social workers and they serve as liaisons between the educational institution and the placement agency. The mutual goal is to prepare students to be proficient in the nine areas of competence identified by the Council on Social Work Education (CSWE) as essential for social work practitioners. In summer 2022, as they do every seven years, CSWE re-envisioned the Educational Policy and Accreditation Standards (EPAS) that included a revised set of competencies emphasizing engagement in anti-racist, diversity, equity, and inclusion practice (CSWE, 2022). These new competencies were released after this text went to press, but the appropriate emphasis on leading anti-racist efforts in practice is reflected in Grand Challenges #9–13 near the end of the first half of this chapter.

Dating back to the 1930s, field education and instruction has been identified as a critical aspect of preparation for the professional social worker (Holden et al., 2011). In 2008, CSWE designated field education as the "signature pedagogy" of social work education and the primary vehicle to socialize students into the profession (Boitel & Fromm, 2014). It is also the critical link between the educational

DOI: 10.4324/9781003308263-20

institution and practitioners of social work in the community, providing a mechanism for social work research to inform practice and for practitioners to inform researchers and academics of the reality of practice "on the ground."

The Grand Challenges in Field Education: Current and Future Possibilities

The 12 Grand Challenges (GCs) were created by researchers and faculty affiliated with the Academy of Social Work and Social Welfare from 2012–2015 when they were launched publicly after intensive review processes. In 2020, a 13th was added: "Eliminate Racism." Field education systems that had been in existence for almost 100 years continued unaffected, challenging the importance of this paradigm for social work practice and research. The question emerged: how to bridge the gap between research and practice, academic and real world, and thinking and implementation to make the GCs usable at the practice level? A method for integration, for implementation, for translation of this effort to meaningful client systems outcomes is needed. The answer? Field education as the delivery mechanism.

The emphasis on GC implementation should be on training students in their social work programs, introducing them to this emerging frame, and then blending this learning through community-based internships to create systems change. Students can provide new thinking and training to agencies, develop thoughts and ideas around innovation and creativity, and establish a foundation they can return to even if employed in traditional social work settings such as with children and families, in mental health agencies, or in health care, which Salsberg et al. (2019) report as the most common social work jobs. Field education as the academic entity that integrates theory, research, and practice can provide experiences through new types of internships that begin to shift social work as a profession toward implementation of the GCs.

Even as institutional hierarchies have limited recognition of the critical role of field education in the curricula (Lyter, 2012), students and community agencies recognize that the field internship contains the most profound learning experiences for future social workers. In this community-based petri dish, the GCs have the best opportunity to influence direct practice and prove their efficacy as a conceptual framework spurring on advancements in social work policy, practice, and research and on behalf of poor, marginalized, and disenfranchised populations.

Grand Challenges Group A: Individual and Family Well-Being

The first four GCs are categorized as "Individual and Family Well-Being." This group includes: 1) Ensure Healthy Development for All Youth; 2) Close the Health Gap; 3) Build Healthy Relationships to End Violence; and 4) Advance Long and Productive Lives. In the following section, each GC is described from a field education lens with an agency placement that fits within its definition. Prospects for future social work internships are also discussed with a focus on the client.

Grand Challenge #1: Ensure Healthy Development for All Youth

Working with children, youth, and families is a popular early career goal for social work students, and thus many schools of social work provide the opportunity for students to specialize in this practice area, including targeted preparation for school social work, public child welfare, and child and adolescent behavioral health. Field internships typically provide students with the opportunity to practice individual, family, and group interventions to address mental health problems or facilitate healing from trauma. Social work interns also play a critical role in providing preventive services through public education campaigns, psychoeducational groups, and serving clients at risk but who may not reach eligibility criteria for reimbursable services.

The COVID-19 pandemic has had a profound impact on the mental health and well-being of children and adolescents in the United States (US) and worldwide (Cowie & Myers, 2021; Masi et al., 2021). Social workers need to respond swiftly and effectively. At a full-service wellness clinic in a large urban school district, social work students are learning to apply Practicewise™ Managing and Adapting Practice (MAP), an evidence informed, web-based tool that assists clinicians in delivering effective, equitable, and inclusive service for youth and families (Chorpita & Daleiden, 2018). Earning partial MAP certification during their social work education, graduates are ready to rapidly respond to the burgeoning mental health needs of youth in one of the largest cities in the US where MAP is a favored service delivery method.

The large number of social work students who want to work with children provides an opportunity to infuse this GC in the many placement agencies where students' complete internships. While examples such as this one demonstrates how to prepare social workers to address this GC, the next step is to frame this work in the context of the GC.

Grand Challenge #2: Close the Health Gap

Recently, opportunities for students to practice in health care settings have expanded and been further encouraged and supported by workforce development initiatives through entities such as the Health Resources and Services Administration (HRSA, n.d.). Many schools of social work across the nation have received HRSA funds to provide stipends intended to entice students to pursue social work careers in interprofessional health care settings to address health disparities and the root causes of health inequities by addressing social, economic, emotional, and mental health factors that influence health outcomes for disadvantaged populations.

Preparing social work students via field education to effectively navigate challenging relationships with other disciplines that have typically wielded the power in health care settings is a critical step to addressing intergenerational disadvantage in the health care system. Studies suggest that the social work perspective is especially important when it comes to meeting desired health outcomes related to prevention, population health, and cost containment (Steketee et al., 2017). Some social work programs are uniquely positioned to find other critical points of contact in the health care system to connect with vulnerable populations. For example, a social work program has forged a relationship with their institution's dental school that serves hard-to-reach populations such as individuals who are undocumented, severely mentally ill, or experiencing homelessness. In this instance, the two schools (dental and social work) received a grant to integrate social work and dental students at their specialty clinics, initially with the intention that social work students would assist with outreach, engagement, and appointment setting. Social work interns quickly identified that their scope of service in this setting included providing psychoeducation, teaching relaxation exercises to reduce anxiety, assessing for needed resources and support, and helping patients access transportation and nutritional support.

Cederbaum and colleagues (2019) suggested that a public health social work approach can provide a "wide lens" for social workers to deliver interventions in multiple environments and at multiple levels. Social work students practicing in interprofessional health care settings are uniquely positioned to widen the lens and help close the health gap.

Grand Challenge #3: Build Healthy Relationships to End Violence

The primary goal of this GC is the prevention and interruption of violence and the promotion of healthy violence-free lives. Social work students engage in this work in many field settings such as schools (e.g. anti-bullying campaigns), primary care settings (e.g. identifying and intervening to disclosures of interpersonal violence), and homeless shelters (e.g. establishing safety). Some agencies have a primary focus on violence prevention and intervention, such as in domestic violence shelters and child protection service agencies. Other health, education, and social service agencies are increasingly training staff to be trauma informed in order to identify and intervene in ways that support and promote healing from trauma and violence. To better support this work, social work education is encouraged to provide trauma-informed educational programming (Sanders, 2021).

The calls for police reform in the wake of the Black Lives Matter protests has provided an opportunity for the social work profession to expand their reach for this GC. Violence prevention can be the focus of student learning activities in placement agencies that partner with law enforcement. A school of social work in a large urban community has worked directly with law enforcement for several years by embedding student social workers in local police departments. The students accompany patrol officers downtown to help homeless individuals find shelter and safety rather than being arrested for vagrancy or trespassing; provide diversion counseling to youth identified as "at risk" for gang violence; and help victims of interpersonal violence and human trafficking secure medical and legal support. Social work faculty provide "professional development" training for the students and the officers, side by side, on topics such as trauma-informed practice and secondary traumatic stress. Initially field faculty provided the student supervision, but seeing the benefits of the social work students in preventing and responding to violence, police departments soon made it a priority to hire a field instructor and later create a formal position for a full-time social worker.

Collaboration between social workers and the police is not a new phenomenon (Patterson & Swan, 2019), and social work field educators have been exploring partnerships with the police and other emergency responders before the recent calls for police reform (Dickinson, 2017). However, these efforts have an opportunity to expand exponentially with President Biden's proposal to provide psychologists and social workers to police departments to help them respond to mental health crises and situations that can be de-escalated with a less punitive intervention (Kaste, 2020).

Grand Challenge #4: Advance Long and Productive Lives

Being engaged in lifelong learning and meaningful activities that contribute to the community promotes health and longevity. Direct practice social workers address this through assessment of employment and work satisfaction as part of a psychosocial assessment and build related goals into case plans. Macro practitioners engage in advocacy within organizations and communities and at the legislative level to secure employment and training opportunities for those in greatest need, and lobby for fair labor practices and employee well-being. Recruiting, training and supervising volunteers is a key activity of most social service organizations both to promote peer support and build community connections as well as to stretch often limited funding to reach the most people. While not necessarily the main focus of social service agencies, leading productive lives is an underlying value and aspiration for most agencies where social work interns are learning the profession.

Transitional age youth (TAY) navigate a critical time in life in terms of education and employment. Not all youth have the option to pursue higher education and even those who do face an uncertain employment future. Attending and graduating college is shown to increase lifetime earning potential (ssa.gov, 2015), but economic downtowns can negate this effect, and changing conditions (e.g. climate change, pandemics) can radically alter a career path with little warning (Irons, 2009; Rinz, 2019). Social work interns often work with TAY as part of their learning experiences, helping them begin the pursuit of a productive life through the building of job skills, identification of early employment opportunities, and enrollment in college courses. For example, social work students at a Youth Opportunity Center in a rural community help identify career aptitudes for young job seekers ages 16–24, teach interview skills and customer service, arrange paid internships and employment in the business community, and connect them to higher education. Social work students also provide individual and group counseling to enhance youth problem-solving skills and promote adaptability and resilience for when they encounter unforeseen challenges. As social work interns are often TAY themselves and facing these same challenges, they are in an ideal position to understand and empathize with this critical life stage.

Social work interns can infuse this GC across many social service sectors – from early childhood to end of life. Intergenerational programs reap benefits for both old and young participants (Jayson, 2018), and social work interns can gain great experience as well as contribute to the community by initiating, developing, and implementing such programs. The increased use of technology by everyone due to the pandemic offers new opportunities for homebound seniors and disabled individuals to not only receive support from others but also support one another. Once again, social work interns can organize mutual aid networks and provide digital literacy skills. Adopting this GC as a lens can inspire creativity in an area so critical to human well-being and yet too often overlooked due to a focus on the immediate problem or crisis facing an individual or community.

Grand Challenges Group B: Stronger Social Fabric

The second set of four GCs are categorized as "Stronger Social Fabric." This group includes: 5) Eradicate Social Isolation; 6) End Homelessness; 7) Create Social Responses to a Changing Environment; and 8) Harness Technology for Social Good. These GCs have been particularly impacted by the COVID-19 global health pandemic as social isolation and technology have been prominent topics in identifying and addressing challenges of connection. The following section examines initiatives that could benefit from social work students' work to strengthen the safety net for clients and communities.

Grand Challenge #5: Eradicate Social Isolation

Social isolation is a health risk factor throughout the life span – a silent killer as dangerous as any health condition. National and global health organizations have underscored the hidden, deadly, and pervasive hazards stemming from feeling alone and abandoned (Holt-Lunstad et al., 2015). Depression and suicide are the ultimate expression of isolation. From 1999 to 2018, suicide rates among females were highest for those aged 45–64 and among males, highest for those aged 75 and over (Center for Disease Control-National Center for Health Statistics, 2020). These statistics speak to the need for social workers to help build more age-friendly communities that strengthen frayed social ties in order to prevent not only suicide, but also elder mistreatment, which have both been exacerbated during the COVID-19 pandemic.

Children and youth are vulnerable to the impact of social isolation as well, as evidenced by data that shows an increase in youth suicides during COVID-19 (Escobar & Yarbrough, 2021). School-based mental health services and health centers located across the nation can help address isolation in youth while offering social work students quality learning opportunities. Placements in adult day health care centers and with organizations advocating for the elderly also help students understand the challenges of social isolation and social work's role in addressing those challenges. Students implement evidence-based assessment and intervention protocols and use a multi-systems approach to assess health issues, including social isolation.

For future placements, social work students could help educate the public, encourage health and human service professionals to address social isolation, and promote effective ways to deepen social connections and community for people of all ages (Lubben et al., 2015). One way to address this challenge is to place social work interns in integrated health and social service systems that deliver seamless, coordinated services to vulnerable populations who are at high risk for social isolation.

Grand Challenge #6: End Homelessness

Homelessness is a complex social issue. Until recently, the role of traumatic stress was not considered nor was the research connecting trauma to a person's health and well-being over time (Felitti et al., 1998) factored into the discussion of homelessness. In Radcliff's 2019 research, 68.1% of respondents who experienced homelessness in childhood reported experiencing four or more adverse childhood experiences (ACEs), while only 16.3% of respondents who reported no homelessness in childhood reported experiencing four or more ACEs. This study supports an approach to ending homelessness that includes trauma services.

While there is significant need for support with homeless populations, social work interns have not historically prioritized these opportunities in selecting field placements. In fact, CSWE statistics from social work programs and graduates do not include a category highlighting work with homeless populations. To increase skill and workforce development, one West Coast university created a homeless initiative using the Housing First model that brought together community leaders, agencies, researchers, field educators, and students to provide social work field placements. The California Department of Social

Services' Project Roomkey (CDSS, 2021) ensured that people experiencing homelessness and exposed to COVID-19 had a safe place to recuperate and properly quarantine outside of a hospital. Social work students working under the local housing authority agency helped these temporary unit residents with crisis intervention and short-term case management to facilitate their path to permanent housing.

Areas to consider for further field education development in this GC include expanding the consortium to involve other local schools of social work, addressing policy development through legislative internships, placing students in street outreach programs to address homelessness needs at the grassroots level, and creating internships with private and public housing agencies to influence funding of social services to address health challenges.

Grand Challenge #7: Create Social Responses to a Changing Environment

Climate change affects global temperature and precipitation patterns, influencing the intensity and frequency of extreme environmental events like wildfires, hurricanes, heat waves, floods, droughts, and storms that have tripled in the last 30 years (Oxfam, 2021). Additionally, the US has experienced several human-made disasters, such as oil spills, water crises, mass shootings, international and national terrorism, and community and family violence (Palinkas, 2015). Social workers are committed to environmental justice, which recognizes that poor, marginalized, and disenfranchised populations are most impacted by environmental issues, including waste dumps, pollution, flood zones, substandard housing, living with crime and violence, and a lack of resources and networks to recover from environmental challenges. Social workers play a critical role in mobilizing local government and community organizations to distribute timely resources to vulnerable communities and promote positive coping. The aim is for social workers to foster collaboration in order to help vulnerable populations who have experienced significant trauma to regain their daily functioning and routine.

Organizations where social work students conduct their field placements include ones that respond to disasters at the local and national level, provide trauma interventions, and distribute needed resources. Students assist with these processes by supporting recovery and casework teams and intervening at emergency shelters. During the COVID-19 pandemic, there were increased social work internships at local public health departments where students were trained to provide brief assessment, crisis intervention, psycho-education information, and timely case management to people seeking support.

Given the large-scale impact of environmental disasters and crises, field education should renew its commitment to environmental justice by enhancing student training in the classroom and the community on reducing disaster risks, assisting displaced populations, seeking community coalitions, building resilience, and promoting environmental justice.

Grand Challenge #8: Harness Technology for Social Good

Although social work has been slow to embrace technology, COVID-19 has forced it to move beyond reticence and hesitation, recognize the increase in access and utility that meets client needs, and invest in online tools that reach more people, are more efficient, and produce similar or better results (Kraus, 2011). Similarly, social work educators reluctant to accept online education before COVID-19 were forced to embrace virtual education. Various technologies offer new opportunities for social work researchers, educators, and practitioners to access data, create timely responsive analysis, and integrate transformative and ethical social work practice that reduces inequalities and improves efficacy and quality of social service delivery. Accordingly, the National Association of Social Workers (NASW) added technology to its seminal Code of Ethics, changing 18 different sections to reflect its influence in social work (Barsky, 2017).

Social work educators have created innovative pedagogy online, including virtual field practicum, evidence-based intervention training, and virtual reality programs that train students in areas such as child safety assessments. Practitioners regularly use electronic health records, online and telephonic counseling, self-guided internet tools, professional social networks like LinkedIn, face-to-face videoconferencing, smartphone apps, e-mail, text messages, and many other tools and programs. Some researchers have also used smartphones to support vulnerable homeless youth populations during COVID-19 while other professionals have utilized virtual shadowing to give students increased access to health care environments.

Field placements for social work students include virtual macro learning opportunities, elderly outreach programs utilizing face-to-face online connections, and telehealth clinical interventions, to name a few. For the future, more virtual internships should be developed, and more students trained in telehealth to both advance career opportunities and meet the needs of clients, especially in rural and medically underserved communities.

Grand Challenges Group C: Just Society

The third and final set of GCs are categorized as "Just Society." This group includes: 9) Eliminate Racism; 10) Promote Smart Decarceration; 11) Build Financial Capability for All; 12) Reduce Extreme Income Inequality; and 13) Achieve Equal Opportunity and Justice. These GCs, with the exception of Eliminate Racism, launched in 2015 when brimming anger at police-sanctioned violence against unarmed African American men erupted in protests in Ferguson, MO. With the murder of George Floyd in 2020, protests were further fueled, and Eliminate Racism was added as a new GC. Calls for defunding police began to enter mainstream consciousness as desperate attempts to end police brutality toward communities of color seized the moment and turned public opinion from apathy to recognition that Black lives matter. The following section examines culture at the societal level, looks at the range of agencies currently utilizing social work interns to effect systems change, and examines future opportunities.

Grand Challenge #9: Eliminate Racism

This ambitious GC seeks to overturn centuries of policies and practices that have embedded racism into societal structures in the US, which presents a challenge: can one change racist systems using processes created and sanctioned within that racialized structure? For example, field education efforts to overturn racism while itself being a product of it can result in programs that prepare students to meet core competencies and get hired instead of teaching them to overturn racist policies or change racist institutions. This inherent conflict between the structure of institutions and the values of social justice and eliminating racism places social work students at the nexus of existing views of professionalism and the mission to advance anti-racist, equity, diversity and inclusion practice as stipulated by the 2022 CSWE EPAS.

As currently constructed, field education opportunities for students exist in organizations that fight against racism within the system through protest, advocacy, legal means, and expository writing. Field education descends from an organizational chart in which institutional leaders seek alliances with entities that benefit from a racist societal structure, which translates into pressure at the placement level – even if indirect – to place student interns in organizations that ultimately align with the current societal structure. Field education can get stuck in routines that seek easier placements instead of more difficult, progressive, social action field placements that might make learning – and leaders – uncomfortable (deVink-Lablanc et al., 2011).

Placements have generally not been developed outside of system-sanctioned efforts in places where protest may mean activities that bring shame to the institution, re-appropriate resources, or intentionally disavow the rules and laws of the settler nation (Tuck & Yang, 2021). Institutions could train students to recognize and advocate for elimination of racist policies, apply the principles of progressive social work, and disrupt their social action field placements (deVink-Lablanc et al., 2011). In this way, students could be vehicles to bring training, activities, and perspectives to organizations that help fight against racism (Poole, 2010). Field education could partner with pro bono legal offices, religious institutions committed to social justice, or community-based economic opportunity agencies (Wiebe, 2010).

Grand Challenge #10: Promote Smart Decarceration

Smart decarceration must upend racist structures arising out of the 13th Amendment, which was billed as an end to slavery but actually endorsed the enslavement of its Black citizens in prisons (Jones, 2016). This amendment cemented the US legacy of hostility and violence toward African Americans, ensured that race and incarceration were inevitably intertwined, and fueled the cradle-to-prison pipeline (Edelman, 2007).

When promoting smart decarceration, field education has focused on either enhancing rehabilitation efforts in jails, juvenile halls, and the prison system or in easing the transition from incarceration into society. Social work internships that address individuals who are incarcerated include those that help end the cycle of victimization, give men and women released from state and federal incarceration the skills and motivation to re-enter society as contributing members, and provide innovative wraparound services that keep people in their communities and out of jails and prisons. Other internships work to end mass incarceration through empowerment, creating support networks, comprehensive re-entry services, and grassroots policy advocacy.

Field education could advance work in this GC by focusing on macro internships that aid in dismantling the cradle-to-prison pipeline with groups like #BlackLivesMatter or as part of efforts to defund the reliance on a police state. Following the GC efforts to restrict incarceration, reduce disparities, remove civic and legal exclusions, and reallocate resources (GCSW, 2021), field educators could place students in agencies committed to stopping employment discrimination through "ban the box" efforts, changing laws that prevent full societal engagement after incarceration, and becoming a stronger presence in the court system in advocacy roles.

Grand Challenge #11: Build Financial Capability for All

Poverty rates have stayed consistently between 11% and 15.2% since 1970, which speaks to the permanency and acceptance of poverty in the US (Chaudry et al., 2016). The US government created programs like the New Deal during the Great Depression and the Employment Opportunity Act in 1964 to help people in poverty improve their socio-economic standing (Chaudry et al., 2016). Other efforts to address poverty have included government-funded welfare programs such as financial benefits, housing programs, nutritional support, health care, and others intended to address basic needs (Chaudry et al., 2016). Referred to as the feminization of poverty, female-headed households have been deemed the "poorest of the poor" due to their experiences in poverty with limited opportunities to emerge out of it (Chant, 2004).

Government and community-based programs are important places for social workers to be employed, and for social work students to have internships. Students have helped innovative programs that go beyond the direct distribution of public assistance to empower families to break the cycle of poverty. Such programs emphasize inclusion of low and moderate-income youth and adults as they expand economic opportunities, build business sense, support community engagement, and otherwise increase community economic involvement. Students have interned at banks, leveraging federal community reinvestment funds to develop relationships that promote savings, college education, and creating long-term goals. At other internships, students have worked for microfinance programs that rejuvenate economies through supporting female expertise and talent in countries where human rights are not widely spread among genders.

Field education programs can focus on internships where students help write policies, participate in legislative advocacy, advocate for child development accounts (GCSW, 2021), and/or contribute to the abolition of policies that disproportionately impact communities of color while seeking financial capability for all. Social work internships in which communities of color are lifted up by economic engagement and community healing through industry could help train future social workers about the power of community-based economic empowerment programs.

Grand Challenge #12: Reduce Extreme Economic Inequality

As this journey through the GCs nears its finale, one could easily feel the futility of temporary approaches that change a policy here, shift a priority there, or otherwise try to reshuffle the existing pieces into a different formation in the hopes of achieving a different outcome. Is it possible to address inequities through these means when wholesale dismantling of the system may be required? Is financial equity possible within a capitalist system that metes out rewards to the top 1% while, historically, a percentage of people continue to live in poverty? And where do social workers belong within these systems?

Programs such as social welfare for all, medical insurance for all, or tax laws that place more revenue into government coffers for redistribution may benefit those most in need, but face very challenging political opposition. Obamacare and the 2020–2021 COVID-19 pandemic stimulus payments that included child benefits are examples of laws that have been passed attempting to reduce extreme inequality. Laws that tax the top 1% and raise the minimum wage could move the US closer to other capitalist countries that have smaller gaps between rich and poor and lower the concomitant social problems that accompany such extreme inequality (Wilkinson & Pickett, 2010).

Social work interns have been placed at agencies that work with pregnant teens, single mothers, or other groups that have been historically under-resourced. These agencies help propel individuals out of poverty through adult education, community business programs, neighborhood initiatives, and legislative advocacy. Internships in political offices have also given students the opportunity to work with elected officials and influence policy-making at that level.

Regarding the future of social work field placements, aligning placement processes with this GC could lead to different field placements outside of traditional social work internships that involve business partnerships and a commitment to community advancement.

Grand Challenge #13: Achieve Equal Opportunity and Justice

This GC on addressing prejudice, injustice, and unfair practices like voter suppression captures current movements that are attempting to reshape the country's justice and law enforcement systems and reflects the revised CSWE EPAS (2022) released in summer 2022 that includes emphases on anti-racism, human rights, and social, racial, and environmental justice. These efforts connect this GC with the previous four in its ties to racism (GC #9), incarceration (GC #10), poverty (GC #11), and economic inequality (GC #12). This GC challenges social workers and field educators to examine if they are truly change agents or have become "unfaithful angels" drifting far from their mission (Specht & Courtney, 1995) or who merely "execute social policy that supports the status quo" (Belcher & Tice, 2013, p. 81).

In students' internships, they are learning how to be professional social workers advancing just causes. The missions of the organizations where they intern are likely consistent with the CSWE core competencies and the NASW Code of Ethics, valuing integrity and social justice in their efforts to meet the needs of clients, while working to meet the new emphasis on anti-racist practice. The connection to the broader GCs could be incorporated more strategically into field placement processes and will be discussed later.

At current social work internships, students help people suffering from domestic violence, elder abuse, human trafficking, sexual assault, and child abuse; advocate for voting rights; endorse fair and equal justice in the criminal court system; provide resources for immigrants and the poor; offer support and connection to those with mental illness; advance opportunities for marginalized populations; expand access to housing; organize communities at the grassroots level; and other practices that seek equal opportunity for all.

For future placements aligned intentionally with this GC, students could address the bias of professionalism standards, develop reverse mentoring programs, commit to community reinvestment, endorse cross-generational learning, create industry mentorships matching successful leaders with impoverished youth, influence changes in law enforcement practices, and undergo other efforts to increase equal opportunity and justice for all. Millennial and Gen Z students are aware of how standards labeled as "professional" can exclude racialized and marginalized individuals and communities and be used as "White favoritism," masking standards as ways to reinforce bias toward those who may wear their hair differently, express their gender identity in non-binary ways, and dress in accordance with cultural beliefs that might conflict with more traditional standards of attire (Gray, 2019, p. 1). How professionalism is defined for current and future generations of MSW students could impact their own experiences with equal opportunity and justice as well as employment choice, lifetime earnings potential, and the development of core social work values. Reverse mentoring is a concept that emphasizes the knowledge base of Millennial and Gen Z students, often in the technology or social media realm, that can benefit Gen X or Baby Boomer leaders (Gadomska-Lila, 2020). Reverse mentoring balances the power dynamics between members of different generations, finds the value that each has to offer, and builds bridges of support for future collaborations (Gadomska-Lila, 2020).

This exploration of the GCs and their connection to field education begs the question for the authors: what would field education look like if the GCs were used to establish organizational internships, place students, and create pipelines of graduates with training and skill to lead efforts focused on achieving the GC goals? The following section presents a conceptual framework developed to guide future field education processes. Additionally, the reader will find in Appendix 16A the Council of Social Work Education's (CSWE, 2022), *2022 Educational Policy and Accreditation Standards (EPAS)* that could be applied to field education.

The Grand Challenges as an Organizing Framework for Field Education

As shown in the first section of this chapter, field education already has a strong presence in the implementation of the GCs as all 13 were represented by at least one example of a field agency. The challenge now is for field educators and administrators to intentionally utilize the GCs in field education processes. Using a conceptual framework, we propose that the GCs could guide field educators in the intentional development of practitioners specific to the GCs and, in the process, create the potential for cross-GC collaborations (GCSW, 2021).

The proposed conceptual framework illustrates how field education could incorporate the GCs into a coherent process for placement either by individual GC or by the grouping of GCs.

As the framework reveals, the GCs can be used to guide field education processes to place students in alignment with the three GC categories or on an individual GC level. The choice depends on the goals of field education, the structure of the social work program, and the relationships that have been formed with community agency partners. If the goal is to show how agencies are aligned independently and collaboratively with each other, perhaps choosing to showcase all 13 categories is the right approach. If the goal is categorizing agencies by group identification, then emphasizing the groupings may be a better

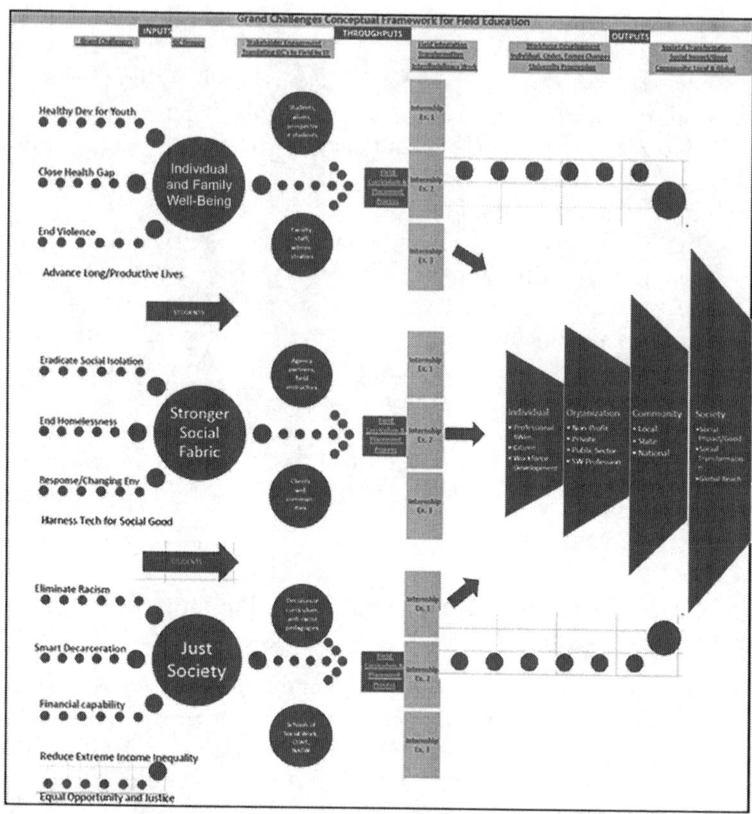

Figure 16.1 Utilizing a Grand Challenges conceptual framework for field education

fit. Either way, field education programs can build on existing collaboratives to create new combinations of career pathways for students while impacting client system progression within each GC or GC cluster. As agencies see this model creating talent pipelines for future hires, their buy-in will increase.

Inputs

Building a GC approach to field education takes field educators to a place where the mission of field education is paramount. The tasks and logistics of translating the GCs to field education will be challenging, but could be liberating. Agencies could be aligned with different affinity groups, creating collaborations that have not existed before. Students could see the development of career pathways that are linked conceptually in innovative ways. And social work programs could build capacity and collaborations to harness the conceptual and practical power of the GCs to frame social work education, practice, policy, and research efforts.

Student interns as inputs in this conceptual framework are a significant presence in the annual delivery of social work services in health care, mental health clinics, children and family agencies, school social work, and substance use treatment facilities (Salsberg et al., 2019). According to the 2019 CSWE Annual Statistics on Social Work Education in the US (2020), there were 68,793 MSW and 56,530 BSW students in social work programs across the nation. Applying the minimum number of hours required of student interns by CSWE, 61.9 million MSW and 22.6 million BSW hours equaling 84.5 million hours of service were delivered by social work students in 2019. When multiplied by a national volunteer dollar valuation of $27.20 per hour, the collective impact of social work interns came to $2.298 billion in 2019. Other inputs include the GCs, their sub-groupings, and other key school and community stakeholders.

Throughputs

The GC framework for field education may impact another challenge currently emerging among students: the right and the fight for paid internships. Using the published and accepted GC framework, schools of social work can collaborate with their marketing and advancement teams to construct donor presentations to foundations and other entities interested in supporting talent pipelines for specific social work careers. These presentations will connect the goals of the foundations with the GCs and introduce ideas for student stipends to fund workforce development efforts. Thus, the GC field framework becomes a marketable visual serving as a hub for multiple offshoots of ideas, coalesced around a central theme: namely, that field education is the delivery vehicle for GC acceptance, expansion, integration, and impact.

As students move through the placement process and digest the field education curriculum, they are also advancing the GC framework in their internships. Consistent with Cederbaum et al.'s (2019) view on utilizing a public health approach to move this work from prevention to intervention, students could form clusters based on the three defining groups. These cohorts of students could develop meaningful projects, or enhance networks, or collaborate on the sharing of job opportunities and other key resources. Programs could co-develop specific macro projects with student, faculty, and field instructor input that serve as a GC capstone for the degree program. These projects could be organized in an extensive database that collects data, analyzes outcomes, and measures the impact of these capstone projects. Programs could also establish expectations that all syllabi integrate the GCs, that all faculty publish at least one article annually on the GCs, and that research faculty pursue grants related to the GCs.

Outputs

The GCs articulate the problems facing society that need to be addressed collectively by the profession in a cohesive and timely manner. The lengthy time taken from basic research to clinical trials to full-scale implementation (www.tcrn.unsw.edu.au/) is not an efficient approach to making the kind of radical and large-scale changes the GCs demand, resembling a slow trickle instead of a gushing flow of information that can facilitate system-wide change. The rigid and outdated hierarchies and silos of academic institutions present additional bottlenecks to the flow as tenure track and research faculty often operate in vastly different academic spheres to the field department faculty and staff, even though they are educating the same students.

Students link faculty lines, staff, and community organizations where grassroots GC implementation can occur. Social work interns can and should be the mechanism to translate the GCs to the real worlds of individuals, families, organizations, and communities whose experience created the need for the GCs in the first place. Students have often been the driving forces behind social change, from protest movements of the 1960s in the US to Tiananmen Square in China to the Arab Spring uprising. Student voice is important as interns can assess agency capacity, identify service gaps (prevention and efficiency), challenge the current system, and innovate solutions for systemic change, especially in the areas of equity, diversity, and inclusion.

Conclusion

Students who choose social work as their career path enter social work programs inspired to "help people" and "change the world." Schools of social work curricula delivered by faculty provide the knowledge and the skills on how to effectively co-construct treatment and give students the opportunity to practice these skills in field placement agencies. If field educators organize practicum processes, structures, and placements more purposefully around the 13 GCs, we may be able to move the needle more meaningfully and impact practice. But until field education is part of the implementation strategy and true translational partners with research enterprises, the GCs will remain a theoretical construct with limited applicability to the experiences of individuals, organizations, communities, and society.

References

Barsky, A. (2017). Ethics alive! The 2017 NASW code of ethics: What's new. *New Social Worker*. www.socialworker.com/feature-articles/ethics-articles/the-2017-nasw-code-of-ethics-whats-new

Belcher, J. R., & Tice, C. (2013). Power and social work: A change in direction. *Journal of Progressive Human Services*, *24*(1), 81–93. https://doi.org/10.1080/10428232.2013.740403

Boitel, C., & Fromm, L. (2014). Defining signature pedagogy in social work education: Learning theory and the learning contract. *Journal of Social Work Education*, *50*(4), 608–622. https://doi.org/10.1080/10437797.2014.947161

California Department of Social Services (CDSS). (2021). *Project room key: Housing and homelessness COVID response*. www.cdss.ca.gov/inforesources/cdss-programs/housing-programs/project-roomkey

Cederbaum, J. A., Ross, A. M., Ruth, B. J., & Keefe, R. H. (2019). Public health social work as a unifying framework for social work's grand challenges. *Social Work*, *64*(1), 9–18. https://doi.org/10.1093/sw/swy045

Center for Disease Control-National Center for Health Statistics. (2020, April). *NCHS data brief No. 362*. www.cdc.gov/nchs/data/databriefs/db362-h.pdf

Chant, S. (2004). Dangerous equations? How female-headed households became the poorest of the poor: Causes, consequences and cautions. *IDS Bulletin*, *35*(4), 19–26. https://doi.org/10.1111/j.1759-5436.2004.tb00151.x

Chaudry, A., Wimer, C., Macartney, S., Frohlich, L., Campbell, C., Swenson, K., Oellerich, D., & Hauan, S. (2016). *Poverty in the United States: 50-year trends and safety net impacts*. Office of the Assistant Secretary for Planning and Evaluation.

Chorpita, B. F., & Daleiden, E. (2018). Coordinated strategic action: Aspiring to wisdom in mental health service systems. *Clinical Psychology: Science and Practice*, *25*, e12264. doi:10.1111/cpsp.12264

Council on Social Work Education (CSWE). (2015). *Educational policy and accreditation standards*. CSWE.

Council on Social Work Education (CSWE). (2020). *2019 Annuals statistics on social work education in the United States*. https://cswe.org/getattachment/

Research-Statistics/2019-Annual-Statistics-on-Social-Work-Education-in-the-United-States-Final-(1).pdf.aspx

Council of Social Work Education (CSWE). (2022). *2022 Educational policy and accreditation standards (EPAS)*. Author. www.cswe.org/accreditation/standards/2022-epas/

Cowie, H., & Myers, C. (2021). The impact of the COVID-19 pandemic on the mental health and well-being of children and young people. *Children & Society*, *35*(1), 62–74. https://doi.org/10.1111/chso.12430

deVink-Lablanc, S., Turner, L., & Carty, B. (2011). Progressive field education: Social justice, human rights, and advocacy. In *Shifting sites of practice: Field education in Canada*. Pearson Education Canada.

Dickinson, R. (2017). Expanding field placement possibilities: Considering public safety/service agencies as placement options. *Field Educator*, *7*(2), 1–10.

Edelman, M. W. (2007). The cradle to prison pipeline: An American health crisis. *Preventing Chronic Disease*, *4*(3), A43.

Escobar, A., & Yarbrough, B. (2021, March 30). *Southern California suicides down during coronavirus pandemic – but not among young people*. www.pe.com/2021/03/30/southern-california-suicides-down-during-coronavirus-pandemic-but-not-among-young-people/

Felitti, V. J., Anda, R. F., Nordenberg, D., Williamson, D. F., Spitz, A. M., Edwards, V., & Marks, J. S. (1998). Relationship of childhood abuse and household dysfunction to many of the leading causes of death in adults: The adverse childhood experiences (ACE) study. *American Journal of Preventive Medicine*, *14*(4), 245–258.

Gadomska-Lila, K. (2020). Effectiveness of reverse mentoring in creating intergenerational Relationships. *Journal of Organizational Change Management*, *33*(7), 1313–1328. https://doi.org/10.1108/JOCM-10-2019-0326

Grand Challenges for Social Work (GCSW). (2021). *Grand challenges impact report, 2021: An impact report at year 5 of the 10-year initiative*. https://view.pagetiger.com/grand-challenges-impact-report-2021

Gray, A. (2019). The bias of 'professionalism' standards. *Stanford Social Innovation Review*. https://doi.org/10.48558/TDWC-4756

Holden, G., Barker, K., Rosenberg, G., Kuppens, S., & Ferrell, L. W. (2011). The signature pedagogy of social work? An investigation of the evidence. *Research on Social Work Practice*, *21*(3), 363–372. https://doi.org/10.1177%2F1049731510392061

Holt-Lunstad, J., Smith, T. B., Baker, M., Harris, T., & Stephenson, D. (2015). Loneliness and social isolation as risk factors for mortality: A meta-analytic review. *Perspectives on Psychological Science*, *10*(2), 227–237.

Human Resources and Services Administration. (n.d.). *School-based health centers*. www.hrsa.gov/our-stories/school-health-centers/index.html

Irons, J. (2009, September 30). Economic scarring: The long-term impacts of the recession. *Economic Policy Institute*. www.epi.org/publication/bp243/

Jayson, S. (2018). *All in together: Creating places with young and old thrive.* Generations United and the Eisner Foundation. http://dl2.pushbulletusercontent.com/Moj5hxfxqtBGfGfXb2O0qeQvIeie9vmi/18-Report-AllInTogether.pdf

Jones, D. E. (2016). The unknown legacy of the 13th amendment. *The Gettysburg Compiler: On the Front Lines of History, 187.* https://cupola.gettysburg.edu/compiler/187

Kaste, M. (2020, November 10). What a Biden administration may do to change policing. *National Public Radio.* www.npr.org/2020/11/10/933548771/what-a-biden-administration-may-do-to-change-policing

Kraus, R. (2011). Online counseling: Does it work? Research findings to date. *Online Counseling*, 55–63.

Lubben, J., Gironda, M., Sabbath, E., Kong, J., & Johnson, C. (2015). *Social isolation presents a grand challenge for social work* (Grand challenges for social work initiative working Paper No. 7). American Academy of Social Work and Social Welfare.

Lyter, S. C. (2012). Potential of field education as signature pedagogy: The field director role, *Journal of Social Work Education*, *48*(1), 179–188. doi:10.5175/JSWE.2012.201000005

Masi, A., Mendoza Diaz, A., Tully, L., Azim, S. I., Woolfenden, S., Efron, D., & Eapen, V. (2021). Impact of the COVID-19 pandemic on the well-being of children with neurodevelopmental disabilities and their parents. *Journal of Pediatrics and Child Health*, *57*(5), 631–636.

Palinkas, L. (2015). Behavioral health and disasters: Looking to the future. *The Journal of Behavioral Health Services & Research*, *42*(1), 86–95. https://doi.org/10.1007/s11414-013-9390-7

Patterson, G. T., & Swan, P. G. (2019). Police social work and social service collaboration strategies one hundred years after Vollmer. *Policing: An International Journal*, *42*(5), pp. 863–886. https://doi.org/10.1108/PIJPSM-06-2019-0097

Poole, J. M. (2010). Progressive until graduation? Helping BSW students hold onto anti-oppressive and critical social work practices. *Critical Social Work*, *11*(2), 2–11.

Rinz, K. (2019, November 19). Did timing matter? Life cycle differences in effects of exposure to the great recession. *Washington Center for Equitable Growth.* https://equitablegrowth.org/working-papers/did-timing-matter-life-cycle-differences-in-effects-of-exposure-to-the-great-recession/

Salsberg, E., Quigley, L., Richwine, C., Sliwa, S., Acquaviva, K., & Wyche, K. (2019). *From social work education to social work practice: Results of the survey of 2018 social work graduates.* George Washington University Health Workforce Institute.

Sanders, J. (2021). Teaching note-Trauma-Informed teaching in social work education. *Journal of Social Work Education*, *57*(1), 197–204. https://doi.org/10.1080/10437797.2019.1661923

Social Security Administration (SSA). (2015, November). *Research, statistics, and policy analysis*. www.ssa.gov/policy/docs/research-summaries/education-earnings.html

Specht, H., & Courtney, M. E. (1995). *Unfaithful angels: How social work has abandoned its mission*. Simon and Schuster.

Steketee, G., Ross, A. M., & Wachman, M. K. (2017). Health outcomes and costs of social work services: A systematic review. *American Journal of Public Health*, *107*(S3), S256–S266.

Tuck, E., & Yang, K. W. (2021). Decolonization is not a metaphor. *Tabula Rasa*, *38*, 61–111. https://doi.org/10.25058/20112742.n38.04

Wiebe, M. (2010). Pushing the boundaries of the social work practicum: Rethinking sites and supervision toward radical practice. *Journal of Progressive Human Services*, *21*(1), 66–82. https://doi.org/10.1080/10428231003782517

Wilkinson, R., & Pickett, K. (2010). *The spirit level. Why equality is better for everyone*. Penguin.

Appendix 16A

Intersection Between Field Education, the 2022 EPAS, and the Grand Challenges

Because field education is where MSW and BSW students are required to demonstrate all nine competencies, this chapter is aligned with all 2022 CSWE EPAS competencies, including the newest one, Competency #3 on Engage Anti-Racism, Diversity, Equity, and Inclusion (ADEI). In *Competency #1 – Demonstrate Ethical and Professional Behavior*, for example, social work students in field education can utilize aspects of GC #8, Harness Technology for Social Good, to improve the quality of their professional practice "using technology ethically and appropriately to achieve practice outcomes" (from Competency #1). Student interns could apply GC #8 to mean appropriate email etiquette by demonstrating "professional . . . electronic communication" (from Competency #1), ethical use of video conferencing to meet with clients, or applying the necessary safeguards when entering and securing electronic notes for client records.

For *Competency #2 – Advance Human Rights and Social, Racial, Economic and Environmental Justice,* student interns are also following GC #7, Create Social Responses to a Changing Environment. When MSW students organize residents in impoverished communities to demand the purifying of contaminated water, work with unhoused individuals suffering severe heat brought about in part by climate change, or provide mental health services to displaced communities after flooding or hurricanes, they are practicing "deep engagement with local communities" battling "climate change and urban development (that) threaten health, undermine coping, and deepen existing social and environmental inequities" (from GC #7). As global warming, urban sprawl, and increasing natural disasters occur, social work students in field education can work collectively to "strengthen individual and collective assets" (GC #7).

Competency #3 – Engage in Anti-Racism, Diversity, Equity, and Inclusion in Practice, emphasizes engaging ADEI and highlighting culturally responsive practice throughout and in the behavioral expectations for all nine competencies. ADEI and culturally responsive practice are aligned with the "Just Society" GCs #9–13. As MSW and BSW interns help organize protests to Eliminate Racism (GC #9), lead support groups for recently released prisoners (Promote Smart Decarceration, GC #10), or hold financial literacy workshops for immigrant communities (Build Financial Capability and Assets for All, GC #11), they are embodying the behavioral expectations of "demonstrating anti-racist and anti-oppressive social work practice" described in Competency #3.

Competency #4 – Engage in Practice-Informed Research and Research-Informed Practice requires social work students to use ethical, culturally informed, anti-racist, and anti-oppressive approaches in conducting research and building knowledge. Understanding the inherent bias in quantitative and qualitative research endeavors, social work interns are positioned to advance the purpose of the social work profession. In the next few decades as these students become professional researchers, practitioners, and policymakers, they will work with all stakeholders to set the priorities for social work research and intervention and engage in a variety of activities that will advance all GCs and ignite social work achievements. GC #1–13 addresses all aspects of societal issues embedded in individuals, families, groups, organizations, and communities. One of the most urgent examples is GC #6 "Ending Homelessness," as housing instability escalates a substantial problem afflicting diverse subpopulations in our country. It is essential for students addressing homelessness to integrate data from Point-In-Time Counts, Homelessness Management Information System, school districts, and other sources such as foster care and health care systems to investigate the interconnected aspects and risk factors of homelessness.

Competency #5 – Engage in Policy Practice emphasizes how social work students use social justice, anti-racist, and anti-oppressive lenses to assess how social welfare policies affect the delivery of and access to social services; and apply critical thinking to analyze, formulate, and advocate for policies that advance human rights and social, racial, economic, and environmental justice. This focus aligns with the "Stronger Social Fabric" GCs (#5–8) to reduce societal challenges and to promote the "Individual and Family Well-Being" GCs

(#1–4). Specifically, GC #5 and #12 call for policy change to address risk factors to eradicate social isolation; decrease risk factors related to economic inequality, unemployment, disability, health disparities, community violence, trauma, disaster, and lack of resources support to individuals and families. GC #7 also spells out the environmental challenges posing profound risks to human well-being, particularly for marginalized communities, as climate change and environmental devastation impede on individual and community health, coping, and existing inequities.

Competency #6 – Engage With Individuals, Families, Groups, Organizations, and Communities asks social workers to apply knowledge of human behavior and person-in-environment through interprofessional conceptual frameworks, to engage with clients and constituencies. Social work students use empathy, reflection, and interpersonal skills to engage in culturally responsive practice with clients and constituencies in field internships. Furthermore, interns successfully engaging with individuals, families, groups, organizations and communities builds the essential foundation to reach the primary goal of GC #13 by achieving equal opportunity and justice. Social work interns can promote equal opportunities to education, health care, basic needs, and resources and will facilitate development of local, state, and federal policies that encourage healthy development across life spans for marginalized populations.

Competencies #7–9 – Assess Individual, Families, Groups Organizations, and Communities; Intervene With Individuals, Families, Groups Organizations, and Communities; Evaluate Practice With Individuals, Families, Groups Organizations, and Communities encompass the nuts and bolts of direct social work practice. Social work students in field routinely apply the process of assessment then intervention then evaluation whether during a one-time interaction or across several sessions or meetings, and whether with an individual or family or with members of a group or stakeholders in an organization or community. The 2022 EPAS shine a light on social workers' mandate to perform these practice elements with diverse constituent groups using culturally responsive approaches.

When assessing (**Competency #7**), students in field are aware of and manage "how bias, power, privilege, and their personal values and experiences may affect their assessment and decision making." Students engaged in GC #3 Build Healthy Relationships to End Violence, for example, may be working in a child protection agency and employ the use of process recordings or reflective learning tools to examine the role of racial bias during a family assessment or how their position of power during an assessment interview may influence the information gathered.

When intervening (**Competency #8**) social work students are directed to select "culturally responsive interventions," which could be demonstrated by a student working on GC #2 (Close the Health Gap) seeking out informal community networks to deliver information and resources to address a critical health issue or acknowledging and supporting a client's desire to seek a spiritual consultation for a medical condition.

Evaluation (**Competency #9**) specifically calls attention to the centrality of applying "anti-racist and anti-oppressive perspectives" when evaluating outcomes. For GC #1 (Ensure Healthy Development for All Youth) and GC #4 (Advance Long and Productive Lives), social work students will need to acknowledge that healthy child development and productive lives may look different for different racial, ethnic, and cultural groups and avoid imposing a dominant framework for expected developmental milestones or life goals. For example, the educational outcome desired by the school or college where a social worker provides social-emotional support to students may not be the central outcome desired by the client. In another example, a social work intern working with a community agency addressing food insecurity may need to challenge an agency outcome of increased distribution of a specific high protein food item if this food is undesirable to a significant portion of the community being served.

In these ways, the nexus between field education, the 2022 EPAS, and the Grand Challenges are illustrated through examples of how social work interns (i.e., practicum students) practice in their field placements. Consistent with the chapter content, evidence of a through-line for social work students from beginning field education to flourishing as a professional practitioner is described in this appendix. The authors experienced increased hope for a future in which the Grand Challenges can guide field education after composing this appendix, and we encourage the readers to as well.

17 An Inclusive Model of Evaluation Capacity Building During the COVID-19 Pandemic

Eugenia L. Weiss, Michael B. Fileta, Sara L. Schwartz and Bryan Jebo

Introduction

This chapter offers a unique perspective into program evaluation in times of COVID-19 and how an after-school program in Los Angeles, California had to shift to meet the needs of the community. One could say that the pandemic is/was a Grand Challenge in its disparate negative effects on vulnerable communities. As with all helping professions, social work has been hard hit by the pandemic. Social workers deliver front-line services such as counseling and case management; mezzo-level programs through schools and clinics; and macro-level services via advocacy to ensure resource availability for society's most vulnerable groups and communities. Social work adheres to an ecological perspective, through which problems are examined with a person-in-environment (PIE) lens (Bronfenbrenner, 1992). This approach enables social workers to engage in multiple levels of practice that consider the multiplicity of social structures, economics, policies, local contexts, and their intersecting impacts (Team & Manderson, 2020). An extension of the person-in-environment perspective is the "program-in-environment" perspective (Mulroy, 2004), which can be useful for examining social programs in the context of the local community and the broader social, political and global forces that consider how social justice (i.e., equity) issues influence all contextual levels, including the organization (Grinnell et al., 2016).

As social workers in human service organizations consider their ability to respond to and understand new challenges and threats to their organization, such as the COVID impacts, the importance of assessing the capacity an organization has to operate and evaluate its programs is critical. The chapter will cover a framework that social workers can utilize in building the organization's ability to

DOI: 10.4324/9781003308263-21

evaluate their programming, particularly when resources and funding are scarce and cannot afford to be able to contract outside or external evaluators. Evaluation capacity building (ECB) is "the intentional work to continuously create and sustain overall organizational processes that make [a] quality evaluation and its uses routine" (Stockdill et al., 2002, p. 14).

The Pandemic as a Disruptor Across All Grand Challenges

The Severe Acute Respiratory Syndrome Coronavirus SARS-CoV-2, COVID-19, is a rapidly spreading coronavirus that originated in Wuhan, China in late 2019 (Brown & Wang, 2020). The virus quickly spread across the world, and at the time of this writing, leading to more than 529 million cases of COVID-19 globally (World Health Organization, n.d.) and over 1,000,000 deaths in the United States (Centers for Disease Control and Prevention [CDC], n.d.). In response to COVID-19, countries across the world executed stay-at-home orders to disrupt the spread of the virus while the scientific community developed best practices for virus containment and worked on vaccine discovery and production. In the United States, between March and May 2020, individuals and territories created and enacted state policies and laws to mitigate the spread of the virus. The first state that enacted stay-at-home orders was California on March 19, 2020, with 41 states following by the end of May (Moreland et al., 2020).

Given that individual states had the authority to respond to COVID-19 in their own way, community-level experiences varied around the country. This case study focuses on an organization located in Los Angeles, California. California's Governor Gavin Newsom enacted the earliest and strictest shelter-in-place order to control the spread of COVID-19. State orders directed residents to remain in their homes unless accessing essential services or walking their dog, during which masks were required and individuals were to maintain a 6-foot distance from people not living in the same household (Hoeven, 2020). Schools, community centers, religious spaces, entertainment venues, parks, and all communal spaces were abruptly closed to the public. As people navigated a previously unknown reality, fear and anxiety contributed to new patterns of behavior that involved panic buying and hoarding to ensure that one's basic needs were going to be met. Loxton et al. (2020) consider this behavior from the perspective of Maslow's Hierarchy of Needs and how the media reinforced these survival behaviors.

While the lives of all California residents were disrupted by the COVID-19 pandemic, already marginalized individuals and families were disproportionately affected (Amadasun, 2020). Team and Manderson (2020) point out the structural vulnerabilities that were illuminated during the early days of the "shelter in place" orders where little attention was given to those with nowhere to shelter, individuals living in temporary or inadequate shelter, or those who already were at risk at home.

During the pandemic, schools and their non-profit partners had to shift the focus and delivery of after-school programming to respond to the immediate needs of their constituents. COVID-19 created new or increased existing family challenges that included financial, food, and housing insecurities associated with sudden job loss. Early data illuminates the detrimental and disparate impacts of COVID-19 on positive youth development, particularly for at-risk youths, such as those with behavioral health needs, children in foster care or at risk for maltreatment, those suffering from chronic medical conditions, and those from minority families and of low socioeconomic status (Wong et al., 2020). The next section will provide the factors that contribute to successful ECB in organizations.

Evaluation Capacity

Efforts to research evaluation capacity can inform social workers on the essential antecedents that lead to strong evaluation practices. Table 17.1 displays key findings from several investigations on evaluation capacity over the last 20 years. Among the most important elements of evaluation capacity is leadership buy-in. The extent to which organizational leadership values and promotes evaluation as a practice can dictate how embedded evaluation is within the organizational structure. An example of this might be a leader utilizing evaluative data during monthly meetings or requiring employees to implement evaluation activities in their day-to-day activities. Two other common elements of evaluation capacity are the provision of ongoing evaluation training and the existence of an evaluation plan. Both elements suggest that an organization cannot simply value evaluation without structurally supporting it. Finally, the literature suggests that the utilization and sharing of evaluation findings is an essential piece that brings all the evaluation activities together. Without the utilization of the insights gained from evaluation activities, the impact of any evaluation exercise cannot be realized. Thus, in order to shift to the changing

Table 17.1 Literature on Key Elements of Evaluation Capacity

Study	*Key Elements of Evaluation Capacity*
Bourgeois and Cousins (2013)	Desire to improve; resources; leadership buy-in; sharing of evaluation findings; skills; ongoing training
Fierro (2012)	Sharing of evaluation findings; motivation for evaluation; leadership buy-in; ongoing training; policies; evaluation structure/plan
Milstein and Cotton (2000)	Ongoing training; motivation for evaluation; evaluation structure/plan; resources
Taylor-Powell and Boyd (2008)	Leadership buy-in; policies; evaluation supporters; resources; evaluation structure/plan; ongoing training
King and Volkov (2005)	Evaluation structure/plan; resources; motivation for evaluation; leadership buy-in
Preskill and Boyle (2008)	Motivation for evaluation; ongoing training; evaluation structure/plan; policies; resources; utilization of findings
Wade and Kallemeyn (2020)	Evaluation champions; leadership buy-in; resources; utilization of findings
Volkov and King (2007)	Evaluation champions; leadership buy-in; ongoing training; desire to improve; utilization of findings

needs of individuals and communities, organizations must take a close and systematic look at their capacity to evaluate their programs.

Inclusive Evaluation Practice to Facilitate Capacity Building

Inclusive approaches to evaluation have evolved over the past several decades to capture shared and differing realities of individuals and communities more accurately within an organizational setting. One important contribution to the field is the recognition of evaluation as an ongoing process that always includes stakeholder engagement. The Centers for Disease Control and Prevention's (CDC) evaluation framework underscores the importance of including the voices, perspectives, and value systems of all stakeholders within the context of a program (see the CDC Framework for Program Evaluation, 1999). Additionally, House and Howe (1999) describe a type of evaluation in which the methods of inquiry focus on fairness, justice, and democracy. They refer to the approach as a *Deliberative Democratic* evaluation. The approach is rooted in the notion that stakeholders across the organization and community would be able to have input to collectively determine the merit and value of the program being evaluated. Greene (2006) also focused on the inclusivity of divergent views where ideas could be more openly expressed throughout the evaluation process. Inviting dialogue across stakeholder groups can provide a voice to members of an organization or community that may not have been structurally included previously. While stakeholder engagement in the evaluation process helps to portray the differing realities, participation alone may not change the deep-rooted organizational structures of exclusion.

Additionally, scholars have written about the importance of including and acknowledging culture and identity throughout the evaluation process. Bledsoe and Graham (2005) highlight the importance of identifying the complexity of the different cultural groups represented in the evaluation. The acknowledgment of the need to respond differently to the various stakeholders represents a type of organizational agility that allows for necessary changes to occur and for those changes to be assessed in terms of their effectiveness and value.

Evaluation Capacity Framework

As an organization takes the important step of understanding its evaluation capacity, the Inclusive Evaluation Capacity Framework (Figure 17.1), adapted from Preskill and Boyle (2008), can be utilized to help guide the process of understanding the evaluation assets and highlight areas for organizational improvement. The framework includes eight components of evaluation capacity. Each component is as valuable as the next, thus, the framework should be viewed as a non-hierarchical list of key ingredients.

Beginning with the top row of Figure 17.1, the framework begins with the following elements: leadership buy-in; inclusivity of stakeholders and methods of inquiry; and evaluation plan and policies. These first components are important structural and top-down (and bottom-up) areas that help to mainstream evaluation activities into the organization's operations. Without intentional structure, evaluation can become an add-on activity that feels like a burden for employees. The second-row highlights: resources for conducting evaluation; ongoing evaluation training; and staff motivation to conduct an evaluation. When referring to resources, this pertains to things such as budget allocations, access to internal and outside experts (as needed), and software. Ongoing evaluation training refers to an organization

Figure 17.1 Inclusive Evaluation Capacity Framework

supporting members of their team to receive training on various aspects of the evaluation processes such as determining the evaluation design, engaging in data collection and analysis, and carrying out the dissemination of findings. Staff motivation to conduct evaluation refers to the sense that staff is motivated to conduct an evaluation. Depending on the culture of the organization, sometimes the staff can feel nervous or overwhelmed by the process. As mentioned, when evaluation is mainstreamed into the organization's culture, staff motivation will likely increase. The final row refers to evaluation actions after data has been collected. Ultimately, even if evaluation activities are routinely conducted within an organization, there must be a carefully crafted utilization and sharing plan. It is not enough to capture the insights from an evaluation, a commitment must be made to act based on the findings that were gleaned from the evaluation process.

The next section of the chapter provides a case study as an example of the shifts in program delivery given the constraints posed by COVID-19 during the height of the pandemic shutdowns in the year 2020. Although this case takes place in the city of Los Angeles, California, it can be used as an exemplar of how community-based organizations around the country were forced to either pivot in times of COVID or had to close their doors and were unable to serve their constituents who needed services. This organization also illustrates the resilience of the staff, leadership, and commitment of community partners and others in supporting the organization's efforts in a time of great challenge.

A Case Study Approach

A case study approach (Yin, 2018) illustrates how an organization serving diverse youths shifted its services and stakeholder relationships during COVID-19 to meet the rapidly changing needs of the most vulnerable youths and families in their community. Consideration of real-world contexts and a community-based participatory evaluation approach (Hacker, 2013) where all stakeholders are considered illuminates the hallmarks of the social work profession and education that are grounded in social justice. The case provides an example of a real-life scenario that serves as a teaching and learning tool for a macro-level social work course. The case study is presented in the next section followed by discussion questions that can be used by instructors in a classroom setting to assist students in applying evaluation capacity concepts through a case example.

Case Study: The Boys & Girls Clubs of the Los Angeles Harbor

In March 2020, schools and businesses, including the Boys & Girls Club of the Los Angeles Harbor (BGCLAH), a non-profit after-school program for youth in Southern California closed their doors due to the COVID-19 pandemic. The youth did not know how they would finish their school year and graduate, parents were worried about how they would keep their jobs to pay rent and feed their families, and everyone was concerned about this new pandemic sweeping across the world.

The mission of The Boys & Girls Clubs of the Los Angeles Harbor (BGCLAH) is *to enable all young people, especially those who need us most, to reach their full potential as productive, caring, and responsible citizens. We achieve this through a commitment to quality programs and services in an environment that is safe, nurturing, and inspiring*. In 1937, the first club site opened in San Pedro to give boys a safe place to be around the bustling Port of Los Angeles. Since then, the BGCLAH has expanded its operations to 20 locations by 2020, serving about 9,000 registered members ages 6 to 18 with an average of 2,400 youth participating in programming daily. Many of these youth come from low-income families in highly impacted areas.

Programming at the BGCLAH includes academics, arts, athletics, character development, and leadership, and a daily snack and supper for all members. In 2020, the BGCLAH's budget was close to $9 million, and they had about 250 staff working across their organization. To ensure the youth who need these services most can receive them, annual membership fees are only $25 per child; an amount that is often waived due to grant funding support or scholarships offered to families with a significant need.

With schools and the BGCLAH closed, parents needed to stay home and watch their children, many of whom were reported to be single mothers and sole providers of the household income. They now had to provide the three meals a day throughout the entire week that youth had been receiving at these other locations. They also had to switch to a virtual learning environment and take on more of the learning responsibilities of their children. This included traversing technological devices and software that many were not familiar with or did not have access to. Children also struggled with this transition to virtual education and the isolation that came with it. One middle school child the BGCLAH worked with during October 2020 had not logged into his classes since the Fall semester began in August 2020 and had over 60 missing assignments. Data shared at the Boys & Girls Clubs of America Virtual Leadership Conference at this same time estimated that most youth across the nation would suffer from a seven-month gap in learning loss, and low-income youth will feel a greater impact equated to that of about 12 months of loss. This all drove the anxiety and stress levels up in local households. Children experienced mental distress from changes in their daily routines, increased stress at home, fewer social interactions with their peers, and a lack of healthy food options or entire meals (Kaiser Family Foundation, 2021).

The BGCLAH started its pandemic support to the communities through food distribution. Waivers in grant requirements that funded their usual meal program made it allowable to provide "Grab n' Go" meals for kids to pick up at the club and eat at home. The BGCLAH was able to start these Grab n' Go distributions one week after they closed their doors due to the pandemic. They started at one club location across the street from a low-income housing community and expanded this to their other grant-funded locations by the second week of the shutdown. This program continued through July 2020 at which time the club gave out about 170,000 meals and snacks. In-person summer programming started in July 2020 and the BGCLAH stopped the daily Grab n' Go program to feed the youth now at the club sites, but the need for food support continued to grow.

A few years before the pandemic, BGCLAH leadership had the notion of feeding families over the weekend who did not have the means to support themselves. In 2015, food insecurity affected 29.2% of Los Angeles County households with incomes less than 300% of the federal poverty level, which is an estimated 561,000 households (Los Angeles County Department of Public Health, 2017). The pandemic forced businesses to close their doors which led to many workers being laid off. According to an economic summary conducted by the U.S. Bureau of Labor Statistics of the Los Angeles area, the unemployment rate increased from 4% in December 2019, which was before the pandemic reached Southern California, to 10.7% in December 2020 (U.S. Bureau of Labor Statistics, 2021). This significantly increased the levels of food insecurity across Los Angeles County and specifically in the areas the BGCLAH served. The CEO and the Board of Directors implemented the "Weekend Wellness" program in July 2020 to help address this growing issue. The program consisted of collecting and storing food from different agency partners and distributing it to families on Friday evenings so they could eat over the weekend. This meant warehouse storage (including refrigeration storage) was now needed along with repurposing youth vans to make food pick-ups, ordering food and vehicles for weekly distribution, and new funding to support this endeavor. Community partners helped to secure some of this at the beginning, but long-term strategies were needed to help sustain this throughout the pandemic and beyond. With these challenges come great opportunities. Funding started coming in from individuals and foundations that mainly supported efforts around food security. Media and external recognition helped highlight the Weekend Wellness program and the efforts of the BGCLAH. Dedicated staff was able to secure more food as the program went on, growing from 300 to 1,200 families receiving food each week by December 2020. In May 2021, the BGCLAH gave out its one-millionth meal to a family of six living in Wilmington, CA. At this same time, the BGCLAH announced that it was extending the Weekend Wellness program through the 2021–2022 fiscal year. Families were so grateful to receive these consistent meals from the club.

The second area that the BGCLAH supported during the pandemic was through case managing youth during their virtual school journey. The club saw that too many children were suffering from isolation and learning loss due to the shift to this new online format when COVID-19 hit. Parents did not have the technology or environment at home to support their children. Many parents also had to work from home while trying to navigate these virtual classes with their younger children, leading to falling behind in both areas and increasing the stress and frustrations at home. Due to this, the club increased its efforts in the Summer of 2020 to ensure that they could safely reopen when the school year started in August. They increased their internet technology at all their club locations to ensure kids could connect to their classes. They rearranged their program spaces to ensure social distancing was in place and shifted to cohort models with a 10:1 student-to-staff ratio. They collaborated with local schoolteachers and administration and started communications for support. They also installed hand sanitizers around their clubs and increased daily cleaning with their staff and janitorial services. All staff were trained on new COVID-19 safety protocols and reopening guidance. The 2,400 youth who used to participate in the club's daily programming dropped to about 450 youth that could receive these services, so decisions were made on who had the biggest needs for this support. These decisions were based on the naturalistic engagement of families through the club's deep community-based relationships with their stakeholders.

The efforts to support the youth in their online classes paid off. The children in the program continued to be present in class and completed their homework and asynchronous classwork that was assigned. They were able to interact with their peers and with adult staff in enrichment programming designed to promote social and emotional well-being as well as safe fitness and recreation activities that most children at home had stopped doing. Parents were able to focus on work without worrying that they may need to leave their children home alone or quit their jobs. Another outcome was that the teachers and administrators from the schools saw the club's support and commitment to keeping their students engaged in class and the partnerships grew stronger leading to more support in the Summer of 2021 around fun literacy and math activities and training for club staff.

The key to making these pivots at the BGCLAH during the pandemic was in quickly identifying the problems, using the resources available, and finding ways of connecting those to possible solutions. All ideas were on the table and the leadership did not stop trying to find ways to be a pivotal resource to the communities they served. Throughout the process, the focus remained on the well-being of the youth in the communities and how those with fewer resources could be allowed to succeed.

In summary, as a result of the pandemic, there was an overall reduction in service capacity from 2,600 youth being served on an average day in 20 regional sites, to 430 youth being served across seven sites. Service priorities changed to addressing food insecurity, social isolation, and overcoming the challenges of the digital divide. For example, the organization provided 1 million meals and at the time of this writing, fed 1,300 families each week. The organization also shifted to online programming to foster socialization among youth and physical fitness, as well as the provision of academic tutoring, and music instruction. Funders demonstrated flexibility to meet the needs of vulnerable clients and the organization created new networks for collaborative partnerships and leveraged existing partnerships with schools and other community-based organizations.

Discussion

In conversation with leadership, we learned that while service priorities changed to meet the essential needs of the community, so did their formal evaluation procedures. Their evaluation protocols took a more informal approach, with even more community engagement and participation. The voices of those constituents (or neighbors) being served and those not served were amplified in terms of how the staff and leadership responded to their constituents' survival needs over business as usual. In "normal" times, evaluation activities and the assessment of capacity for evaluation can look one way, but in times of crisis, it is the voice of the community that matters the most. In the next section, the reader is invited to utilize the case study as a classroom exercise in applying the Evaluation Capacity Framework (Figure 17.1) both in times of crisis and in times of greater "normalcy," whatever the new normal will look like. If it is not the pandemic, it may be another circumstance of crisis. Therefore, the exercise can be modified to fit the situation. Regardless, program evaluation is something that cannot be put on hold until the crisis passes. Rather it needs to be flexible to meet the needs of the community and how the organization can best address the needs.

Class Exercise

Drawing from the case study and incorporating the Evaluation Capacity Framework (Figure 17.1), an instructor might ask students to imagine that they are social workers in a non-profit health or human service organization and are asked to assess the program's capacity to engage in evaluation activities. An instructor could pose the following class discussion questions:

1. Who would be involved in the evaluation activities?
2. What type of evaluation plan could be designed?
3. What type of evaluation policies would be recommended?
4. What resources may be needed to conduct the evaluation?
5. How would staff motivation to engage in evaluation activities be assessed?
6. What type of inclusive data collection methods could be used and for what outcomes?
7. What type of data sharing across the various sites and/or with partner organizations are important?
8. How could the findings from evaluation activities be used to leverage resources or change program implementation given the COVID-19 constraints?
9. How would the leadership's commitment to evaluation be assessed?
10. How would evaluation of knowledge and skills held by organizational staff be assessed?
11. What are other evaluation considerations to keep in mind to support evaluation capacity building in the organization?

In addition to the class exercise, it is important to point out that while this chapter is not specifically tied to any one of the Grand Challenges, the Educational Policy and Accreditation Standards (EPAS) from the Council of Social Work Education (CSWE, 2022) can still be applied as part of teaching a social work macro level course (see Appendix 17A). Program evaluation is necessary for organizations addressing any of the Grand Challenges through service provision towards ensuring effective interventions for diverse populations.

Conclusion

The COVID-19 pandemic introduced new and unique challenges for social service organizations at multiple levels. Shelter-in-place mandates required the physical closure of all non-essential services, including schools and after-school programs. Concurrently, pivots to online school requiring parent supervision and challenges across multiple sectors contributed to new or escalated existing struggles for individuals and families such as food insecurity and social isolation. Service delivery organizations also had to pivot to meet the evolving needs of their stakeholders while also responding to the needs of their employees and the requirements of their funders. A necessary first step in this pivot was to evaluate the emerging needs of the client population and their staff along with an assessment of existing and future funding requirements.

The Program-in-Environment model offers a useful lens for examining mezzo-level, or the social service organization-level experience of COVID-19. It is important to consider organizations independent of each other, as each agency is uniquely situated in its environment. This chapter presents a case study of one organization located in a particular community in Los Angeles, California, the Boys & Girls Club of the Los Angeles Harbor. The BGCLAH serves as an example of how one organization evaluated the emergent needs of its stakeholders and rapidly pivoted services to meet their basic needs. As is detailed earlier, the organization had not been strategically addressing food security at the family level nor had social isolation or the digital divide emerged as needs for their client population before COVID-19. Using the evaluation strategies introduced in this chapter, BGCLAH leaders quickly recognized service gaps and responded appropriately. Program evaluation data suggests that these services benefited the individuals and families served.

The Evaluation Capacity Framework and the case study introduced in this chapter are intended for use in the macro social work classroom. Case studies are a useful tool in higher education and this particular case helps examine the impact of COVID-19 on one large non-profit organization serving a historically marginalized and under-resourced community. Using a Program-in-Environment perspective and the evaluation tools presented, the BGCLAH found a way to thrive during a historic pandemic while also responding to the needs of the community in which the organization is embedded.

References

Amadasun, S. (2020). Social work and COVID-19 pandemic: An action call. *International Social Work*, 1–4. doi:10.1077/0020872820959357

Bledsoe, K. L., & Graham, J. A. (2005). The use of multiple evaluation approaches in program evaluation. *American Journal of Evaluation*, *26*(3), 302–319.

Bourgeois, I., & Cousins, J. B. (2013). Understanding dimensions of organizational evaluation capacity. *American Journal of Evaluation*, *34*(3), 299–319.

Bronfenbrenner, U. (1992). Ecological systems theory. In R. Vasta (Ed.), *Six theories of child development: Revised formulations and current issues* (pp. 187–249). Jessica Kingsley Publishers.

Brown, K., & Wang, R. B. (2020). Politics and science: The case of China and the coronavirus. *Asian Affairs, 11*(11), 247–264. doi:10.1080/03068374.2020.1752567

Centers for Disease Control and Prevention. (1999). Framework for program evaluation in public health. *Morbidity and Mortality Weekly Report, 48*, RR–11. www.cdc.gov/mmwr/PDF/rr/rr4811.pdf

Centers for Disease Control and Prevention. (n.d.). *COVID data tracker as of June 6, 2022*. https://covid.cdc.gov/covid-data-tracker/#datatracker-home

Council of Social Work Education (CSWE). (2022). *2022 Educational policy and accreditation standards (EPAS)*. Author. https://www.cswe.org/getmedia/94471c42-13b8-493b-9041-b30f48533d64/2022-EPAS.pdf

Fierro, L. A. (2012). *Clarifying the connections: Evaluation capacity and intended outcomes* (Doctoral dissertation). The Claremont Graduate University.

Greene, J. C. (2006). Evaluation, democracy, and social change. In *The Sage handbook of evaluation* (pp. 118–140). Sage.

Grinnell, R. M., Gabor, P. A., & Unrau, Y. A. (2016). *Program evaluation for social workers: Foundations of evidence-based programs* (7th ed.). Oxford University Press.

Hacker, K. (2013). *Community-based participatory research*. Sage.

Hoeven, M. (2020, March 20). All Californians ordered to shelter in place. *Cal Matters*. https://calmatters.org/newsletters/whatmatters/2020/03/california-coronavirus-homeless/

House, E., & Howe, K. R. (1999). *Values in evaluation and social research*. Sage Publications.

Kaiser Family Foundation. (2021, February 10). The implications of COVID-19 for mental health and substance abuse. *Kaiser Family Foundation*. www.kff.org/coronavirus-covid-19/issue-brief/the-implications-of-covid-19-for-mental-health-and-substance-use/

King, J. A., & Volkov, B. (2005). A framework for building evaluation capacity based on the experiences of three organizations. *CURA Reporter*, 10–16.

Los Angeles County Department of Public Health. (2017). *Food insecurity in Los Angeles county*. Office of Health Assessment and Epidemiology. http://publichealth.lacounty.gov/ha/docs/2015LACHS/LA_Health_Briefs_2018/FoodInse curity_ REV2018.pdf

Loxon, M., Truskett, R., Scarf, B., Sindone, L., Baldry, G., & Zhao, Y. (2020). Consumer behavior during crises: Preliminary research on how coronavirus has manifested consumer panic buying, herd mentality, changing discretionary spending and the role of media in influencing behavior. *The Journal of Risk and Financial Management, 13*(166). doi:10.3390/jrfm13080166

Milstein, B., & Cotton, D. (2000, November). *Defining concepts for the presidential strand on building evaluation capacity*. Paper presented at the Annual Conference of the American Evaluation Association.

Moreland, A., Herlihy, C., Tynan, M. A., Sunshine, G., McCord, R. F., Hilton, C., Poovey, J., Werner, A. K., Jones, C. D., Fulmer, E. B., Gundlapalli, A. V., Strosnider, H., Potvien, A., Garcia, M. C., Honeycutt, S., & Baldwin, G. (2020, March 1–May 31). CDC public health law program, CDC covid-19 response team mitigation policy analysis unit. Timing of state and territorial covid-19 stay-at-home orders and changes in population movement-United States. *Centers for Disease Control Morbidity and Mortality Weekly Report*, *69*(35), 1198–1203. www.cdc.gov/mmwr/volumes/69/wr/pdfs/mm6935a2-H.pdf

Mulroy, E. A. (2004). Theoretical perspectives on the social environment to guide management and community practice: An organization-in-environ ment approach. *Administration in Social Work*, *28*, 77–96. https://doi.org/10.1300/J147v28n01_06

Preskill, H., & Boyle, S. (2008). A multidisciplinary model of evaluation capacity building. *American Journal of Evaluation*, *29*(4), 443–459.

Stockdill, S. H., Baizerman, M., & Compton, D. W. (2002). Toward a definition of the ECB process: A conversation with the literature. *New Directions for Evaluation*, *93*, 1–6. https://doi.org/10.1002/ev.38

Taylor-Powell, E., & Boyd, H. H. (2008). Evaluation capacity building in complex organizations. *New Directions for Evaluation*, *120*, 55–69.

Team, V., & Manderson, L. (2020). How COVID-19 reveals structures of vulnerability. *Medical Anthropology*, *39*(8), 671–674. doi:10.1080/01459740.2020.1830281

U.S. Bureau of Labor Statistics. (2021, March 3). *Los Angeles area economic summary*. www.bls.gov/regions/west/summary/blssummary_losangeles.pdf

Volkov, B., & King, J. A. (2007). *A checklist for building organizational evaluation capacity*. https://wmich.edu/sites/default/files/attachments/u350/2014/organiziationevalca pacity.pdf

Wade, J., & Kallemeyn, L. (2020). Evaluation capacity building (ECB) interventions and the development of sustainable evaluation practice: An exploratory study. *Evaluation and Program Planning*, *79*, 101777. doi:10.1016/j.evalprogplan.2019.101777

Wong, C. A., Ming, D., Maslow, G., & Gifford, E. J. (2020). Mitigating the impacts of the COVID-19 pandemic response on at-risk children. *Pediatrics*, *146*(1), e20200973. https://doi.org/10.1542/peds.2020-0973

World Health Organization. (n.d.). *WHO Coronavirus (COVID-19) Dashboard for June 6, 2022*. https://covid19.who.int/

Yin, R. K. (2018). *Case study research and applications: Design and methods* (6th ed.). Sage.

Appendix 17A
EPAS Addressed

Competency 4: Engage in Practice-Informed Research and Research-Informed Practice. Social workers use research to inform their practice decision making and articulate how their practice experience informs research and evaluation decisions. Social workers critically evaluate and critique current, empirically sound research to inform decisions pertaining to practice, policy, and programs. As part of building evaluation capacity in organizations to engage in program evaluation efforts, social workers would consider that evaluation efforts would be informed by research and best practices in the field. Program evaluation is a form of applied research. Engaging in evaluation activities would include an appreciation for potential bias in evaluation processes and would utilize and promote inclusive, anti-oppressive and anti-racist evaluation methods and practices.

Competency 9: Evaluate Practice with Individuals, Families, Groups, Organizations, and Communities. Social workers understand that evaluation is an ongoing component of the dynamic and interactive process of social work practice with and on behalf of diverse individuals, families, groups, organizations, and communities. Social workers evaluate processes and outcomes to increase practice, policy, and service delivery effectiveness. This competency is directly associated with the intent of this chapter, which is to promote inclusive evaluation of service delivery in any organization addressing a Grand Challenge. The objective is to assist organizations to build their own capacity for evaluation endeavors. Social workers would also be evaluating their own evaluation practices while supporting organizations.

Epilogue

Mobilizing Social Work Educators in Anti-Racism, Diversity, Equity, and Inclusion (ADEI)

Eugenia L. Weiss

From an editorial perspective and as an educator in the field of social work, education is central to promoting the next generation of social workers tackling the Grand Challenges. The original intent of the Grand Challenges for Social Work was meant as a national initiative based on four guiding principles or pillars on "outlook and action" towards solving social problems, particularly for those vulnerable members of our society that are most often affected (Barth et al., 2019). These pillars include social justice, inclusiveness, diversity, equity, and the recent addition of the *Grand Challenge to Eliminate Racism* (Barth et al., 2022). The Council of Social Work Education's revised Educational Policy and Accreditation Standards (EPAS) also affirms a commitment to anti-racism in social work education (CSWE, 2022). Each of the Grand Challenges described in this book and the various ways to promote the exploration of critical issues (i.e., institutionalized systems of power, privilege, and oppression) in our classrooms and field education experiences all share this common denominator (i.e., the pillars). These pillars form the "guideposts" for action as described by the original members of the Committee on Values and Principles of the Grand Challenges for Social Work by the American Academy of Social Work and Social Welfare. The "Guideposts for Action" as described by this Committee, include the following (Barth et al., 2019, pp. 2–3):

- "Recognizing contexts";
- "Embracing resistance, resilience, and resurgence";
- "Welcoming process";
- "Broadening inclusion";
- "Opening up to all perspectives";
- "Creating opportunities";
- "Engaging purposefully";
- "Evaluating accountability."

DOI: 10.4324/9781003308263-22

However, the pillars of social justice, equity, diversity, inclusion anti-racism, and the associated guideposts that drive prevention, intervention, and policy efforts in addressing the most wicked social problems must all be embraced by us as social work educators and leaders in higher education as well. The American Council on Education and the Pullias Center for Higher Education (Kezar et al., 2022) recently came out with a report on shared equity leadership (SEL), where leaders (including faculty) at all levels of the institution are accountable for reaching their equity strategic goals for systemic equity within their institutions of higher learning. Based on their study findings, the authors recommended that to create equitable environments, it is not just up to a designated Chief Diversity Officer or through a campus or program diversity committee. Instead, a shared responsibility with accountability mechanisms that are multi-level is what they are observing across campuses that are implementing SEL and most likely what is needed to move the needle in diversity, equity, and inclusion and we would argue anti-racism (and all of the systems of oppression) in higher education. The point here is that this is a work in progress for all of us, a Grand Challenge of sorts in the world of social work education; we are not immune from inequity, exclusion, lack of diversity, and the presence of social injustices and racism in the academe but we can be mindful about how we teach about the societal and institutional impacts of racism and oppression and prepare future social work leaders. Anecdotally speaking, not every faculty member is comfortable opening these discussions in their classrooms unless they are teaching a specific class on diversity or oppression (which is often left for the faculty member of color to teach, again a personal observation).

There is an urgency for social work educators to be involved or lead anti-racism, diversity, equity, and inclusion ("ADEI," per CSWE, 2022) programming at their institutions and be held accountable for progress as well as serve as role models for our students by having these conversations inside and outside of the classroom and guide our students towards action. Otherwise, the collective we, as social work educators, cannot speak or teach to ameliorate Grand Challenges in society if we do not address ADEI in our own academic backyards. After all, this (i.e., advocacy and action) is what we do as professional social workers!

References

Barth, R. P., Gehlert, S., Joe, S., Lewis, C. E. Jr., McClain, A., Shanks, T. R., Sherraden, M., Uehara, E., & Walters, K. L. (2019). *Grand challenges for social work: Vision, mission, domain, guiding principles, & guideposts to action*. American Academy of Social Work & Social Welfare. https://grandchallengesforsocialwork.org/wp-content/uploads/2019/09/GCSW-Principles-2-5-19.pdf

Barth, R. P., Messing, J. T., Shanks, T. R., & Williams, J. H. (2022). *Grand challenges for social work and society: Milestones achieved and opportunities ahead* (2nd ed.). Oxford University Press.

Council of Social Work Education. (2022). *2022 Educational policy and accreditation standards (EPAS)*. Author. www.cswe.org/accreditation/standards/2022-epas/

Kezar, A., Holcombe, E., & Vigil, D. (2022). *Shared responsibility means shared accountability: Rethinking accountability with shared equity leadership*. American Council on Education & USC Rossier Pullias Center for Higher Education. https://pullias.usc.edu/blog/tag/shared-equity-leadership/

Index

Note: Page numbers in *italics* indicate figures; page numbers in **bold** indicate tables.

9781032311449